# The Big Book of Belichick

### COMPILED BY ALEX KIRBY

# ALSO BY ALEX KIRBY

Every Play Revealed Volume I – Oregon vs Ohio State

Every Play Revealed Volume II – New England vs Seattle

# TABLE OF CONTENTS

# 1
## TEACHING & FUNDAMENTALS

**Q:** How much do you get back to the fundamentals of things at this point in the season while also working on scheme?

**BB:** That's a great question. It's a fine line. You try to ... There's nothing more important than fundamentals, so no play is good with bad fundamentals.

It's just impossible. That being said, there are a lot of scheme things that come up over the course of the season that teams keep building. We build and our opponents build, and so each week, there's more to get ready for because they're further along. It's a lot different than the first game of the season when you only have so much time to work on stuff.

We've had over 100 practices, and it keeps building and building. So you've got to deal with the scheme issues, and you've got to deal with the fundamentals. So it's trying to find that balance, but they're both critical.

I mean, if you're out-schemed, you're out positioned, then you're in bad shape. And like I said, no play is a good play with bad fundamentals. Just, it won't happen, so that's the balance.

## Q: What is your view of dropped passes from both an offensive and defensive perspective?

**BB:** I don't know. That's a tough question, it's pretty involved. Just like anything else, I think you have guys that have really good hands, really good catch skills and there will be an occasional drop from them and that's usually a concentration thing. Then you have other guys who maybe don't have quite the same hand-eye coordination skill, so catching the ball is a little bit tougher for them. A number of those players that I've coached in the past have had exceptional concentration, so there was kind of technique drops and there is I would say concentration drops. Then sometimes it's related

As you mentioned some degrees of difficulty are harder than others, so it's related to timing and the ball location from the quarterback and so forth. In the end, if the player is not a dependable catcher, I don't think he's going to be involved much in the passing game, but again a lot of those catches are somewhat a function of the degree of difficulty of the ball that is being thrown to them or in some cases the coverage. That's another thing, too, where a player's got really good separation skills, it looks like he's always open and the catches are relatively easier. If a player isn't able to separate then every catch looks like a great catch because there is somebody right there on him.

I would say that there are certain players that without exceptional hands wouldn't be targeted very much because they don't have the ability to create a lot of separation but because of their catching skills they can be productive because they don't need as much separation. I don't know if that answers your question or not, but I'd say there are a lot of components that go into that. And honestly some players are better, just like anything else, like any other skill – golf or whatever – some players are better at some type of catches than others, just like some guys are better off the tee and some are better around the green.

Some players track the deep ball better than others. Some players catch moving routes and routes where the ball radius that they have to catch in is larger than other guys. I'd say not everybody's catching skills are the same on every ball either. Bottom line is you want somebody that's dependable. That's the bottom line – you want to throw to somebody that's dependable.

**Q:** Defensively if a player is open but drops the pass, do you still view that as a completion when you review it on film?

**BB:** There are going to be plays defensively that when you go back and look at – like you said go back and grade the film – when you look at that you're going to get off the hook occasionally on a dropped pass, maybe a quarterback doesn't see a guy who is wide open and isn't covered properly. Maybe it's a penalty of illegal formation or something that calls back a play that you really don't have defended. Those are still concerns. They still need to be fixed.

The next team that you play is going to sit there and say, 'Well if we don't drop the ball or if the quarterback reads it properly or if we don't align in the improper formation, those are good plays for us.' So you're still going to have to stop them. Yeah, the players are accountable. Just because a guy dropped a pass it doesn't mean the defense was played well. That's not necessarily the case. That's why we talk about that after the game – just because the score of the game is what it is, it doesn't mean if you win everything is great or if you lose everything is bad.

There are a lot of things regardless of whether you win or lose that are bad and good that happen in the game that you really have to address so those problems don't continue to occur. Of course at the same time there are a number of plays that will happen defensively where you feel like that's about as good as we can be, but the quarterback makes a great throw and the receiver makes a great catch and it's just a great play. And sometimes that happens, too, where you really want to tell the player, 'You did the job well. You did what you were supposed to do. You were in perfect position and the quarterback got the ball to a place that was a couple inches away from you and they made the play.' There are some of those, too.

**Q:** Do you measure your steps with a player who is learning a new system in terms of not putting him in positions to not succeed whereas maybe earlier in the year you would be able to do that?

**BB:** I think each guy is different. It's really hard to predict how it's going to go with any player. I think you just take it as it comes. You give them the information and then you move them along and see how quickly he adapts to the new assignments, the new techniques, and just the way he's able to handle the assignments that he's given. Again, each player is different so with a player like Barkevious [Mingo], you have a situation where he has a lot of special teams responsibilities, so if we brought in, let's say an offensive lineman, or a defensive lineman, that may not – it depends on the positon and the guy. He may not have that big a responsibility in the kicking game, so it's just really depends on the individual player and how quickly he's able to acclimate himself to the new situation. I don't think there's any set mind frame or you try to go fast, you try to hold back. I think you just kind of take it as it comes.

**Q:** How do you balance having a player use his own instincts on the field versus having him play within the context of the defense?

**BB:** I mean I've coached every player I've ever coached the same way. You have an assignment, you have something you're responsible for and then the instincts come after that. As long as you cover your guy, that's your job. You want to cover him off, you want to cover him on, inside technique, outside technique, back pedal, squat, whatever it is. I mean there's a million different ways to do it. If you have him covered I'm going to be happy about it, you're going to be happy about it, right? So that's the bottom line. Now after that then there is an instinctive part to every play, so I've coached players - that's the way I've coached them my whole career. When I was a special teams coach I had different punters, different kickers. They don't all kick it the same way. They kick it far, they kick it high. I'm happy, they're happy, the team is happy. That's good. If they don't then we've got to try and find a better way to do it. I don't see it any differently now than I saw it when I started coaching. I don't see it really much differently from one positon to another. The techniques are different, the assignments are different but a player's instinct and his style of play - that belongs to each of us. We're all different. But there are certain fundamentals that I think as a coach you are obligated to teach the best way that you know how and work with individual players within that framework.

## Q: At the end of the season, do you sit down with players and ask them to get down to a certain weight?

**BB:** No, look, we do that on a regular basis. So like wherever you want to start, let's say we start the season in April, not every player is here in April, but let's just say it starts in April. Ok, we sit down with that player in April and say, 'OK, here's what we want you to do in the offseason program – weight, conditioning, technique, position, whatever it is, here's what we want you to concentrate on.' We get to the end of that, we say, 'OK, here was your offseason, you did this well, you need to do a better job of this. OK, now we're heading into training camp, here's what we want you to do – this, this, this and that.' We get to the end of training camp, 'OK, you did a good job of this, you still need to work on that, this is better or this still needs to be improved – conditioning, weight, strength, flexibility, etc.' We get to somewhere in the midpoint of the season and we sit down and have the same conversation. 'Look, this is what we told you at the beginning of the year, you've done a great job with this, you still need to do better at this, this, this and that, here's what you need to do – strength, flexibility, conditioning, weight, etc.' Injuries may play a part of some of those discussions. We get to the end of the year, somewhere close to the end of the year, 'Alright we have X number of weeks to go, here's what we need from you the last three weeks, four weeks, whatever it is, here's what you need to concentrate on. You did a great job of this, that and the other thing, but now we're into a different, here's what you need to do.' So we do it on a regular basis. We're not going to sit around here and waste a whole year and then say, 'OK, let's have a meeting and like alright we think you ought to do this.' We're not going to have a meeting every day, but there are certainly different points in the year were you can ... And we do it for the entire team, too. It's each individual player, it's each coach, each position, each unit, offense, defense, special teams, running game, passing game, kickoff return, punt coverage, whatever it is, that we evaluate those at various points and, 'OK how are we doing? Alright we're alright on this, we're not so good on this, we need to make this change – whatever.' We're our own R-and-D team. We can't hire some consultant to come in here like a company can do and, 'Alright let's take a look at this and you guys do a study on that and tell us this, tell us that.' Who's going to do that?

## Q: Do you taper practices to make sure you're at full strength at the end of the season?

**BB:** Well, there could be. It depends on the situation and it depends on the player, absolutely. You have some players that need more, some players that need less. And again, I think that's not just each player, it's the team. Even some guys that maybe are OK at where they're at, they need to work with their teammates. We can't just put 11 guys out there that have never worked together. In the end, we try to do what's best for the team, whatever that is. If it's work more, if it's work less, if it's taper down, if it's however we set the practice schedule. We can't do everything. We try to pick out the things that are most important, that have the most impact and do what we think is best. And sometimes doing what's best for one guy isn't what's best for another guy, but I don't know how else you can run a team. It's not like we've got a tennis team with nine guys playing their own singles match. We've got to work together.

## Q: How does the fatigue, conditioning and health of players impact how the coaches structure practices?

**BB:** That's a great question, and part of that answer is it's not the same for everybody. Where one guy is or sometimes even a group is ... Sometimes you have another group that's in the exact opposite place. One group maybe needs a little more recovery. Another group maybe needs a little more work. I'd say we go through that throughout the year. It happens in training camp sometimes because of numbers and experience levels and so forth, but bottom line is you try to do what you feel like is best for the team.

You have to take individuals into consideration, but you have to take the team into consideration, too. We just can't structure everything for one or two guys and be negligent of the other 61, including practice squad players. We try to balance that the best we can. It's not always the same for everybody. Sometimes guys who need more work we try to get them more work, but we have to try to get the team ready and that encompasses all those things. I don't feel like there is any right or wrong answer.

I've been on teams and with coaches that ... Well when I was younger, a lot of times, my job several years was to write up the practice schedule. So when we would meet and go through the schedule, then I'd write it up, put in what everyone is doing and hand copies of that to all the coaches. We have coaches on our staff now that do that, and I can remember I could have written the practice schedule for December, a Wednesday in December, in July easily and there wouldn't be one thing that was different. A lot of times it's, "Alright what did we do last Thursday,' and it was the exact same thing. And that's not the way we do it. And I'm not saying it was wrong to do it that way, but there were some times, certain programs

I've been in, coaches, it's just their routine and you do the same thing every Wednesday, every Thursday, every Friday, every Saturday, so you always know where you are. We would do blitz pickup and the other team hadn't blitzed in two years or vice versa. So, we kind of do it differently. We kind of talk each day about what the team needs, we have a basic structure of this is what we do, but we change that depending on what we feel like our needs are, and that is definitely a big part of it is the health and I'd say the overall readiness of the team. And that's very subjective, obviously, but we do the best we can in consultation with the training staff, the strength and conditioning staff, position coaches, a lot of times they have a good tempo of where their individual group or particular players are and sometimes that affects the rest of the preparation.

**Q: Tom Brady took blame for a couple of the plays, especially the deep balls to Randy Moss. How much of his development is him missing last season and do you expect him to have been on track by now when it comes to timing?**

**BB:** I think in the skill positions you are always working on timing. You are doing that all the time; every year, every quarterback, every receiver, everybody's doing it. The routes always change a little bit. The coverages change. The team you're playing - their personnel changes, you play against different guys week to week, so there's always a little bit of a timing adjustment on a game-to-game basis. So it's an ongoing process. It's everybody. It's the receivers, tight ends, backs, the quarterback.

It's no different in the passing game on offense than it is on defense. It's protecting to throw the ball and hit whatever the receivers are, whatever the passing combination you have, whether you're running - then, it involves the backs, tight ends and receivers - that combination displaces the defense enough so the quarterback has a place to throw, and the receivers are open, and the protection is there for him to get it off. That is the offensive coordination of the passing game. It's the compliment of the defensive coordination. We need to do a better job on that all the way around - that's everybody. That's all 11 guys out there on the field. It's not one man in the passing game [and] it's not one man in pass defense; it's all 11. And it's coaching, too. We've got to do a better job of that as well, the design and the overall execution. So if it's not getting done well, then that's also a function that we're not coaching it well enough.

# Defensive Backs

**Q:** When a cornerback is covering a receiver like A.J. Green yesterday or Antonio Brown this week, do you try to stress that the reception likely will be made and not to panic or react when that happens? And just how important is it to have a short memory at that position?

**BB:** Well I think that's a little bit of a part of the position. There are great skill players in this league - great quarterbacks, great receivers - with a lot of receiving skill, different types of skills. There are times when defensive players, it could be any position really, you have great coverage on a receiver, the defender is doing everything that you taught him to do, everything that he really can do, and sometimes the opponent, quarterback or receiver makes a great play. The ball is placed perfectly or makes a great catch.

There's not much more that you could have done. It's just great execution on their part. I wouldn't say that that's normally the case but there are certainly plenty of those. So when that happens, maybe there's a little correction you can make, something that the defender could do a little bit better. But overall, he did a lot of things right. Ninety-five percent of the time, that would be an incomplete pass or maybe better for us, but on that one particular throw, catch, the way the route was run or whatever it is, he just can't quite make it. I don't think those are plays you want to forget as a defender. Those are plays you want to do again.

Again, every throw is not perfect, every catch isn't perfect, every route isn't perfect but sometimes they're just a little bit better than the best you can do. That's professional football. That's the great skill we have in this league. Sometimes that happens and you've got to give them credit. The throw that [Andy] Dalton made to [A.J.] Green in front of our bench on that flag route, the coverage was about as good as it could really be. It was a great throw. [A.J.] Green is a tall receiver with length and long arms and [Andy] Dalton put the ball where only he could get it and he got it. So there's going to be some plays like that when you're talking about that kind of skill and athleticism at those positions.

It could be a star receiver or it could be somebody who doesn't have the same kind of resume. But look, everybody in this league is very talented or they wouldn't be in this league. So when that happens you've just got to move on and like I said, if you've done everything right then you try to do it all right the next time and maybe their execution isn't quite to the same level that it was on the play that they just hit on you.

### Q: Does a good nickelback have to be good in traffic?

**BB:** Yeah, definitely has to be able to deal with more people. That's the difference between playing safety and corner. Again, you're closer, there's a lot more people in the middle of the field, a lot more people that can get to you, a lot more things that can happen. The nickel corner is similar to the safety in that he's dealing with a lot of those elements in the middle part of the field. He's more of a coverage player than sometimes the safeties are in that position where they can be more zone players.

It's a little bit different but there are certainly some similarities having to deal with more bodies. Again, your help is closer, you have more route combinations, you have more people that can get into your area, or in man coverage, the receiver you're covering has more route options going inside and outside from the middle of the field than a perimeter receiver does. There are definitely a lot of differences there.

### Q: How critical has Josh Boyer been in developing this current set of cornerbacks, considering the personnel changes?

**BB:** There's no question Josh has done a really good job with that group, and as you mentioned, there is certainly ... Look any time you coach a unit, there is a dynamic in who you're coaching and your coaching style is somewhat altered or affected by who is in that room. When I was the defensive coordinator with the Giants and coached the secondary, Everson Walls had been in the league for whatever it was – 10 years, 50-some career interceptions. There were certain things he did that as a coach you didn't want to change because he had so much success doing it that way and maybe he wouldn't be comfortable doing it another way, but that wouldn't work for a younger player.

You wouldn't want to coach a player the way Everson played, but the way Everson played was very productive for Everson so you kind of find the balance in there. [Darrelle] Revis would be another example of that. Not every player can play like Revis, but Revis played very good the way he plays, so you're kind of coaching Malcolm one way and you're coaching Revis another way. And a guy like [Brandon] Browner is different from Revis, different from Malcolm, but he also was a productive player.

Again, whereas this year we're looking at a lot different makeup on that group – younger players who can be instructed more in the basic fundamental way to play that haven't been in other systems, that don't have other habits, that don't have other things to change that you can build it a little bit more from the ground up rather than from the top down. And again it's not a good or a bad. It's just different.

But Josh has done a good job of that, including [Justin] Coleman, [Rashaan] Melvin, Leonard [Johnson] – the guys that have come in here, the way that the whole group has evolved, even [Patrick] Chung who has played really a lot of if you will corner for us and played it well, so it's been a different dynamic, but again he's spent a lot of time with those guys, not just on the X's and O's but also off the field – preparation, the communication with the group, all the things that go in there.

I'd say Logan [Ryan] has a done a great job of – he's not a coach, but in terms of taking leadership of that unit, in terms of their preparation, their communication, their on the field adjustments, helping guys like Leonard, Malcolm, working with the safeties. Logan has been a big part of the development of that whole unit as well. But again the growth of Malcolm from somewhere in the middle of last year to probably somewhere in the middle of this year was pretty steep.

**Q: You have a lot of respect for Greg Schiano in terms of his football acumen.**

**BB:** Definitely.

**Q:** Is there something with the way he coaches defensive backs that you particular like? When I say that, I'm referring to Devin McCourty, Logan Ryan and Duron Harmon and now Leonard, who he coached.

**BB:** I haven't really thought about that. Look I think Coach Schiano is a great defensive coach and he's really coached all the positions – line, linebacker, DBs. He's had a lot of extensive work with defensive backs and I think he does a great job with them, but I'd say the overall way that he presents his program, the way he runs his program, runs his defense, teaches and so forth, that that's all a great part of preparing players either in a similar way that we do it or when he was in college prepared them to come into our program with some changes but minimal maybe compared to other teams. We've had other players – Justin Francis, [Steve] Beauharnais, guys like that and others – guys that aren't DBs. But he certainly does a good job with that group.

Obviously he likes players who are disciplined and well prepared and have good communication skills and good awareness, and I'd say all the players that we talked about fit in that category – Devin, Duron, Logan. I haven't spent a lot of time with Leonard but those guys, like we talked about before, they know what the three-technique is doing – basically – but they know what the three-technique is doing which there are a lot of secondary players that I don't know if they really know what a three-technique is. But these guys have a good understanding of the overall defense and the concepts and why one thing impacts another and that's a good thing. I'm not saying it's mandatory but it definitely helps.

**Q: It looked like the Giants tried to run a couple rub routes on their final drive. How do your cornerbacks work in tandem to defend those routes? Is it coordinated pre-play or is it based on something they see as the play unfolds?**

**BB:** Right, any time you're in man-to-man coverage and there is multiple people involved – two-on-two, three-on-three or sometimes you can be three-on two or four-on-three, whatever it happens to be – yeah, I think the communication is the key thing there. There are a lot of different ways you can play it. The most important thing is that you clearly know how you're playing it and everybody is playing it the same way. If one guy is playing it one way and the other guy is playing it another way, then you're dead. Yeah, so on two-on-two's, we can combo those and switch them.

Sometimes the rule changes a little bit about when we switch or when we don't depending on the type of route that they run. Yeah, that was the case. I think on the first play, which was a second-down play, we also got some pressure on that play with I want to say it was Akiem Hicks and maybe Rob [Ninkovich] coming off the edge there. I don't know if it would have got to [Eli] Manning because he kind of grabbed it and threw it but there wasn't a lot of time for him to sort out the pattern, whereas on the second one it was kind of a rollout play and then that extended a little bit longer all the way to the sideline and finally whoever it was – Rob or Malcolm [Butler] or somebody – came up there and kind of forced him to …

He just went down and took the sack and kept the clock running. But the first play he really never got outside at all. It was just pressure and Logan [Ryan] took the outside route to [Dwayne] Harris and then Malcolm kind of fell off it and the combination of the pressure and the coverage, there just wasn't much there.

**Q: If a guy is playing man-to-man defense, is it possible for him to have good coverage even if he doesn't look back for the ball or is it just luck?**

**BB:** There are certain situations where we're coached not to look back for the ball. There are other situations where we are coached to look for the ball. So it depends on a lot of things. It depends on your relationship with the receiver, where you are, what part of the route you're in, what part you're talking about, because once you get down the field you're not really in a double move situation. You start looking back for the ball in the eight-to-10-yard range, and if the ball is not thrown there is another part of the route that may exist.

I wouldn't say it's luck. I think it could be. Sometimes a guy just happens to put his hand in the right place and it hits the ball, but I think a good defensive back that plays the ball properly with his back to the ball can definitely affect the catch and legally affect it and put his hands in the right place based on reading the receiver, his hands, his eyes, his overall mannerism on the catch, which the receiver is trying to disguise that, too. Guys like Randy Moss who were great at it, not raising his hands to catch the ball until the ball is almost past him. You couldn't do that against him, but the other receivers, when they move their hands to catch the ball, defensively if you match their hands, then that's where the ball is going to be. I think there is a lot of technique involved there, but I'd say more technique and more concentration and finish to the play than luck, but it might be a little bit of that, too.

**Q:** Malcolm Butler talked yesterday about how if you put your hands in the wrong place on DeSean Jackson, he can blow right by you. How much of a lesson was that in joint practices last year?

**BB:** I'm sure it was good. They have a lot of good receivers and they have different skills, but that's the way it is with our players. You wouldn't defend [Julian] Edelman the same way you'd defend [Brandon] LaFell, the same way you'd defend [Rob] Gronkowski. Each guy is different and you're different, each of us is different, so how one defensive back matches up against a different receiver, it's all a little bit different and you have to figure out what works best for you against different styles of receivers. That's the great thing about practicing against another team is you get to work against your eight, nine, 10 receivers, however many guys you have in camp, plus the tight ends, and then go to another team and you get to work against another dozen guys and you'll see something from them that's different from the guys you're seeing on your practice field. That part of it, you can't really put a price on that because it's experience that you wouldn't otherwise have gotten.

And you're on a practice field so there is a level of trial and error, experimentation, whatever you want to call it, that you're probably a little more willing to do than when you're in game situations. That's how you get better is you practice the technique, it doesn't work, you practice it again. Maybe you end up not using it in a game because you don't have confidence in it or maybe you start to develop some confidence in it and you're able to refine it in practice and it becomes a tool for you in the game. I think all that is important.

**Q:** With so many athletes like Devin McCourty and Darrelle Revis relying on sports performance centers when they're doing offseason work, how much freedom do they have when it comes to technique? How consistent is what they've learned? Does that make sense?

**BB:** Yeah, well it does make sense, and it's a good question and an interesting point. I mean look, first of all, we're not allowed to work with the players, so let's start with that. So from the end of the season to the middle, end of April, we can't work with the players. We can't do anything with them. We can't tell them anything. We can't instruct them, so that's the way we wanted this CBA created. That's what was agreed on. So, that's what it is. There's no coaching, there's no guiding or getting players to do whatever it is you want them to do in the offseason, whether it's their personal conduct, whether it's football related, whether it's anything. There's zero of that from the team, and then all of the sudden they show up here in April, and all of the sudden it's like, well there's some problems. I mean, that shouldn't really come as a big surprise. But I take it as a positive that the players take that time from the end of the season whenever that is until the start of the offseason program – let's call it late April, mid to late April – that they take it upon themselves to work on something that will help their game, help them be a better player. They can't get it from us or any other team. So where are they going to get it from? They've got to go get it from somebody else, so I think that's a positive that they do that and they proactively try to seek instruction, training, physical conditioning, whatever you want to call it, some component of all of those, to become a better player. I think that's a big trend in the league. I mean there are a lot of players who do that – certainly not all of them, but it's a high percentage. I don't even know what the percentage is, but I'd say it's a significant percentage certainly on our team and other players that I'm familiar with. But that's their only choice because the teams aren't allowed to do anything, so that's the way we set this up. Is that the best way to develop professional football players? I don't know. That's what was decided on, so that's what we do. But is that really the best way to develop a guy in the NFL – go train somewhere else, come back, and then figure out what the team wants you to do? I don't know. It wasn't my job to do that. My job is to coach the team, but the amount of time we have to coach the team is restricted. So, what happens in that other time is totally out of our control.

**Q: How important is it to for the secondary to be able to tackle and support the run, and how has your group done in that regard? Is that something that you can notice coming right out of the college ranks, or is it a skill you can practice and improve?**

**BB:** For me, I learned a long time ago – my dad told me this and Coach [Bill] Parcells told me this – that the most important thing on defense is to get 11 guys out there that can tackle. I mean look, defensively, your job is to get the guy with the ball on the ground. In the end, that's your job. All the other stuff is great, but if you can't do that, then what do you really have? Now, that's not to minimize coverage skills. There is certainly a place for that, don't get me wrong. But in the end, somebody has got to get the guy on the ground. I think that is a critical component for me, for us, for any player on the defensive side of the ball, regardless of what position they play, but particularly in the secondary, where you're right, you can be higher on coverage skills, but if you're willing to give up poor tackling for coverage skills, eventually there is going to be a problem there. You might be able to live with it, but eventually it's going to be a problem. I put a high priority on it. We put a high priority on it in the organization. On our defense, we practice it every single day. I don't think there has been a day we haven't worked on tackling this year or any other year. It's the most fundamental, important thing for a defensive player to do well. That and defeat blocks. Everybody is going to get blocked at some point, so defeating blocks and tackling, those are the two most critical fundamentals that any defensive player needs. So, yeah, there is not really much that goes above tackling for me.

**Q:** Can you teach that?

**BB:** Tackling? Every day.

**Q:** Does a guy either have it or not?

**BB:** No. Well, it's like anything else. You're never going to make me fast. But we can all improve. Whatever the skills are, they are, but you can certainly improve technique, you can improve leverage, you can improve the fundamentals of tackling, just like you can improve the fundamentals of running. I mean, look, those are the most fundamental skills in the game, so to not work on those on a daily basis, to not work on them and try to improve them continually I think would be a mistake. I think it'd be irresponsible of me as a coach to not teach blocking, tackling, running on a daily basis.

**Q:** Who is the best tackler you've ever coached?

**BB:** They come in different shapes and sizes, but not many guys got away from [Lawrence] Taylor, I'll say that. But probably one of the biggest tackles that I've ever been a part of was by a guy who had a reputation of not being a great tackler and that was Everson Walls. But he brought down Thurman Thomas in the open field to keep it from getting closer in Super Bowl XXV. That was a huge, huge play that if you would have said Everson Walls tackled Thurman Thomas, I don't know which one of those you would have bet on. It depends on maybe who you were pulling for. But that was a great tackle. We've always had good tacklers. Terry Kinard was a great tackler. Devin McCourty is an outstanding tackler. [Patrick] Chung is one of the best tacklers that I've had at safety. Look, everybody is going to miss, just like every receiver is going to drop a pass, just like every quarterback is going to throw an interception, just like every running back at some point is going to drop the ball. But the guys that don't miss many tackles, you want them on your team. And it shows up in the kicking game, too. The kicking game is the same as the defense – you've still got to get the guy with the ball.

**Q:** Malcolm Butler seems to get his hands on a lot of passes in coverage. Is there a special trait a cornerback needs for those kind of ball skills?

**BB:** I think it's a combination of physical skills, speed, quickness, instincts, just awareness or instincts - however you want to call it - and then there are ball skills. They're all important. Being able to run fast or move quickly in a short area is certainly paramount to getting to the ball. Sometimes instinctively you can kind of get a jump on the play just because of the combination of the route or the way the quarterback is looking or the way the receiver maybe is giving away the route, the way he runs it you're able to anticipate it. But then there is the final part of it, which is of course the ball skills and playing the ball. There are a lot of times when defenders are close to the receiver, they're close to the ball, and the receiver ends up with it, and they either misjudge it or aren't able to get to the reception area with their hand in order to break it up. They reach for it and miss it or whatever. That's a key component, too. Being close to the receiver is good, but being able to have the ball skills, the timing to reach and touch the ball at the right time in order to break it up is important.

And obviously the final thing, the fifth thing would be hands in terms of intercepting the ball. It's almost another skill. Breaking up passes is one thing; actually intercepting them is another. Some players might have good ball skills but they don't have good hands. Some players might have good hands but not necessarily have great ball skills. Of course the great ones have speed, quickness, anticipation and awareness, ball skills and hands. At each level, the more of those the better. Some guys get by on one or two or maybe three of them; some guys don't. The good ones have more, and the ones that are not as good have less. And then, I think depending on what kind of coverage you're playing, some of those things are more important than others. That's just in term of pass defense. I'm not talking about tackling now, which that is another issue. Man coverage, zone coverage, press man, off man, so there is a variety of skills involved depending on the techniques and the coverages that you're playing, which is why you have a lot of different players that have different skills that can still be productive. It depends on what scheme they're in and how their skills fit that scheme. That's a component of it, too. Sometimes it's challenging when a player doesn't have all the skills, which there are not a whole lot of them that have that at an elite level, and you watch a player do one thing and you're trying to project his skills to a different scheme, to a different way of playing. Until you actually see him do it, sometimes it's hard to be accurate on that.

**Q:** Is a defensive back on the outside virtually helpless on an underthrown ball when a receiver stops short and starts running back? What's he supposed to do?

**BB:** Turn and look for the ball.

**Q:** If you're running top speed and stop.

**BB:** Well, the receiver you're covering slows down, right?

**Q:** If he slows down.

**BB:** Why is he slowing down?

**Q:** For the ball.

**BB:** Turn and look for the ball.

**Q:** If you're running stride for stride with someone right on them.

**BB:** When the guy slows down –

**Q:** What if there is no slow down?

**BB:** Then he's not coming back for the ball. Then it's a back-shoulder throw and you're going to try to match his hands and put your hands where his hands are on the back shoulder. But if you're chasing a guy and then all the sudden you catch up to him as he slows down, then why is he slowing down? That means the ball is about to be caught, that means you turn around and look for it. If you turn around and look for it and contact the receiver, then it's not a foul. If you keep running into him and you contact the receiver, then it's a foul.

**Q:** Even when the head turns, you're still sometimes going to see that flag. It's a difficult spot on those underthrown balls.

**BB:** It's a technique thing. If you play the technique properly then you're OK. If you don't play it properly, then it's going to be a foul. Back-shoulder throws, that ball comes in a lot tighter. The receiver, he doesn't come back through the defender. He usually comes back behind the defender. The ball is behind him so the defender has to try to quickly turn and match where the receiver's hands are and try to get his hand in there. Assuming he's looking at the receiver, which is usually the case. It's usually when the quarterback throws it. If you're chasing a guy down the field and the guy slows down, why is he slowing down? You're not that much faster than the other guy. Really, you have to see that space close and close quickly and then turn around and react to it.

## Q: Your defense has also been good against those deep passes. Why do you think that might be?

**BB:** We've certainly put a lot of time and work into it. It could definitely be better but it hasn't been anywhere close to the issue it was last year. So, thank God. I mean obviously the players are doing a good job. But we've spent a lot of time on it and we've spent a lot of time on the deep part of the field because it's so critical. Hopefully we can continue to play fairly well back there because it's just so important. When it all happens in one play – there's nothing else you can do. There's no chance of stopping in the red area. It takes a lot of other people out of the game too. There's nothing a nose guard can do about a go-pattern. There's nothing the inside linebacker – those plays are so far beyond them that it kind of takes them out of the game. When you're giving those up, that's below the line.

Our below the line comments from last week – we just can't play like that. Those guys have worked hard. Our safeties have good range back there, our corners have played the ball pretty well. We haven't had a lot of pass interference calls. Even the ones we've had, like the one in the Baltimore game – it's a tough call. There are some that are just obvious, they're flagrant. Then there are other ones that you're like, 'That's a tough call.' They had one too, so that's kind of the way it goes. I think overall our decision-making and playing the ball in the secondary has been obviously a lot better than it was last year. Not that that would take a lot, but it has been better.

## Q: What are the differences between playing slot corner and playing on the outside?

**BB:** I think when you play inside, you're really playing to a degree, a linebacker or a safety position. Even in man-to-man coverage, it's different because the receiver has more options and the [slot] corner, if there is help, is closer to help than the [outside] corner is, if there's some kind of inside help. If there's no help, then the inside corner has more space to defend, across the ball or back outside as well as vertically compared to a corner who is more isolated in the area he has to defend.

Once you get into combination of zone coverages, then that player's responsibility is either that of a safety or linebacker depending on the coverage and what exactly you're playing. That brings in a whole different awareness and conceptually playing as a linebacker or a safety as opposed to playing as a corner, if that makes any sense. All positions are difficult but I think it's a difficult position to play because of the amount of things that happen and how fast they happen: tight ends and backs coming in or outside receivers coming into your zone or things like that.

Whereas, as a corner you're defending more space but there are less moving parts out there. There's less guys that can get into your area. It's usually just one or maybe two guys, whereas when you're inside in the slot, there could be four guys easily that could get in there and once they get into tight splits and things like that, trying to sort all that out, I'd just say it's a different game. It's not playing safety but it's not playing corner. It's a little bit of a hybrid spot. There's certainly a lot of awareness, a lot of things that those players have to see that are unique. It's not a linebacker, it's not a corner, it's a nickel position.

**Q:** Is a guy that plays both well an exception or should guys at this level be expected to play both well?

**BB:** No, I think it's like anything else. Some guys you can move them from the left side to the right side, from inside to outside, from 'X' to 'Z' and you wouldn't even know it, you couldn't even remember where they are. Other guys, you move them from left corner to right corner and it's like teaching them a different language. It's like English and Chinese. Or from right outside linebacker to left outside linebacker or left tackle to right tackle or left guard to right guard. I've seen players that you try to move them and it's just, they're not comfortable doing it, they don't perform well and then you put them in that spot. Then there are other guys that you can move them around, inside to outside linebacker or left end to right end or 'X' to 'Z' and it's seamless, apparently, it seems seamless. I'm sure it's not to them but that's the impression that you get. I think each player is different, each situation is different.

I don't know that you ever really know the answer to that until you actually work with the player in your system and put him through that situation and see how he responds to it. I've coached a lot of players and I wouldn't want to sit here and say, 'Well, this is the way it is or isn't.' I've had them on the punt team: you move a guy from one side of the center to the other side of the center, it's the same protection, everything is the same but it's not the same. Then the next guy you move and you can't even remember which side he was on because they both look the same.

## Q: Technique-wise, what's the best way for a defensive back to defend when the quarterback throws it up into the end zone, kind of like a jump ball?

**BB:** That could be a 45-minute meeting, but it depends on the situation and what the coverage is, whether you're in man coverage, zone coverage and the different passes you have to defend depending on how close you are to the sidelines and how far away you are and all those kind of things. The bottom line is in the red area and in the end zone, there're a lot of tight throws and less space to throw in and it's hard to get interceptions because usually the quarterback doesn't throw the ball right to the defender; he throws it where he can't get it and so a lot of times you're trying to break up the pass more than you're really trying to intercept it - on fade patterns, back shoulder passes and things like that.

Playing defensive back is a position that really goes for a long time relative to other positions. You're playing technique and playing technique on the release and the route then the finish of the route and ball in the air and throw and all that. So it's not like offensive and defensive lineman that line up this far away from each other. It's a much more extended thing, so there is a lot of technique involved in a defensive back's play, from the snap until the ball arrives at the receiver.

**Q:** When a defensive back can't get himself turned around, does he just watch the guy's eyes and use that to judge when the ball is going to come or where does that reaction come from?

**BB:** If the defensive back can't see the quarterback then he has to watch the receiver and play the ball based on what the receiver's catching motion is.

# Linebackers

**Q:** What is it about Barkevious Mingo or really any player that allows them to attack the line of scrimmage so quickly? Is it a matter of timing the snap properly or is it more attributed to their physical skills?

**BB:** Well, it can be both. It could be pressure and timing or it could be a quick read and reaction. Obviously, the only way you can penetrate the line of scrimmage is if somebody on the line doesn't block us. Sometimes that happens because it's a mistake, sometimes it happens because we get through there before they can really get a clean hit on us, kind of like what happened on Jamie [Collins]' play where the ball ended up going backwards for a seven or eight-yard loss on what ended up being a lateral play. But you know, sometimes you run into a protection where one of the linemen has that player picked up and he's not able to penetrate. There are some of both. Certainly it's a good situation where we can go through the line and into the backfield because they're blocking other people, but depending on what the play is and how they have it blocked that's not always the case.

**Q:** Do most of your reserve linebackers have positional versatility with all three spots? Do you coach them that way or are they plug-and-play with one specific spot?

**BB:** It depends on the player, yeah. That's a good question. That's one of the things that we go through in training camp. As we build through the season, as some players have kind of [have] one specific responsibility and sometimes we have other players that have more than one. Some of that depends on the player, his skills, his experience, what else he has relative to the kicking game as an example, roles in sub defense or other situational defenses. Sometimes that changes over the course of the season, from week to week. That's one of the things that we do every week really, is we come in with the game plan for the Jets, as an example, and then,

'OK, this player is responsible for this. This player is responsible for that. This player is responsible for not just this position but you're also backing u this position and maybe another position.'

In our different personnel groupings, whether it's on special teams or on defense, we have goal line and sub groups and regular groups and short-yardage groups and same thing on offense, we have short-yardage and goal line and multiple receiver groups and multiple tight end groups and two-back groups so somebody has to double or maybe even triple up and then there are other guys that don't. They just kind of have more one spot or they're just backing up one spot.

It varies. It depends on the player, depends on the situation but somewhere along the line you have to account for that. No question about it, you have to find a way to do that. Sometimes you just say, 'Look, if we lose one of these players, that would knock us out of this personnel group and this is what our alternative would be.' Sometimes you just feel like you can't back a player up for whatever reason, you just shift out of that and go to something else that you feel is better. That's another alternative to sometimes having too many, if you have a lot of personnel groups, having too many variables. You just say, 'OK, if something happens then we drop it and a play the game in these other groupings that we practiced.

### Q: What is it that allows Jerod Mayo to kind of wade through blockers and see the backfield the way he does?

**BB:** I think that's kind of just the reverse of being a running back: as a linebacker, you take your keys and you sort of see all those bodies in front of you and basically I think what you look for is some space, because that's what the runner is looking for. You don't want to end up where you already have people; you want to end up where there is space and that's where the backs are looking to go. It's not where the bodies are, but where they aren't. It's sort of the same thing.

Defensively, you're sort of reading the same thing that the running back is reading. Once the initial blocks and the initial contact kind of takes place and then starts to sort itself out or separate a little bit, then the defender is looking for kind of the same thing the running back is looking for from the other side of the line of scrimmage. Jerod has terrific instincts. He had those in college and I think that's one of the impressive things about watching him at Tennessee - just the way he was able to sort plays out, find the ball, get over trash, get past guys that are around his feet or in the pile in the way and get past that to make the tackle. Of course he's a strong tackler.

I've talked, I've coached it a long time, coaching Harry [Carson] and Pepper [Johnson] and Carl [Banks] and those guys [and] in Cleveland, Mike Johnson, Clay Matthews, Marvin Jones, Mo Lewis. The more you talk to them, the more it's hard for them to explain it. 'What did you see on this play?' 'Well, I just saw it.' 'Why did you go there?' 'I just...it was there and I just felt it was the right thing to do.' There's just so much happening in front of you that it's really hard to say, 'It was this. It was that.'

But just put the whole picture together and they see something and that's why they go there. It's probably the same thing the back sees on the other side of the ball. 'What exactly did you read?' 'I saw this, but in the end I saw a space to run and that's where I went.' That's where the linebacker went to meet him.

**Q:** Based on instinct like you just talked about, does that make middle linebacker a harder position to coach since the guys that are really good just kind of see it?

**BB:** I don't think it makes it hard to coach, but I think some players are more instinctive than others. They have more of a knack for it, and that includes the safeties, too. The safeties are really looking at the same thing: play actions and running plays and plays that are designed to go one way but are counters and cutback plays that go to the other side that the offense tries to make them look like it's one thing but it's actually something else or they try to make it look like a run and it's a run, or pass plays like draws that turn out to be runs.

Again, it's the same thing for safeties and for linebackers of trying to recognize that, sort it out, and figure out what it is. again, it's the same kind of thing coaching the secondary, coaching the safeties. Going back to Charlie West and Billy Thompson and guys like that, when you talk to them and say, 'How did you know that was a play action?' 'I don't know. It just didn't feel like a run.' And sometimes they read those by the tempo of the line, like how hard they are actually coming off the ball against the defensive line. They can just get a feel of what's a running play and what looks like a running play. Even though it's the exact same blocking, it's just not the same tempo.

It just doesn't feel like a run to them and they're out of there. It goes the other way too, but it's really fun when you get around guys who can sort that out as a play action pass and they're 15 yards downfield and never even take a false step. And then it's the same running play and they're five yards across the line of scrimmage in the backfield.

It's just kind of knowing, like all positions - receivers, tight ends, defense - there are times when you've just got to make decisions on the field and some players just instinctively almost always seem to do the right thing - the Troy Browns, the Kevin Faulks, the Wes Welkers, the guys like that. They know when to stop, when to keep going, when to slow down, when to speed up, when to come back. You just have to kind of figure out what the right thing is and do what they expect...what that quarterback expects them to do. It's hard to really put a finger on that, but you know it when you see it.

**Q: We often talk about a quarterback's growth in a system in his first few years. Can you make the same comparison for a linebacker, like Jerod Mayo who comes in and plays a lot and grows?**

**BB:** Yeah, I think a lot of times rookies come in and they're talented, they're big, they're fast, they can run and chase the ball, but a lot of times I would say they're just kind of running around out there. As they gain more experience and more understanding of the total defense and where their teammates are and how things fit on different runs, they usually play with a little more patience, maybe a little more recognition in terms of play-action passes and misdirection plays like that. Although, Jerod is very good and has been very good at those, but I think certainly you get better at them through time and understanding the different matchups: which guys really try to knock you off the ball, which guys really try to come and fit up with you and use their athleticism to mirror you, which guys are holders, which guys are cut blockers in addition to the actual 'Xs' and 'Os' of the scheme, but how the individual guys play. Same thing with tackling backs.

We see a lot of different types of backs: which guys you can really load up on, which guys have a lot of wiggle, which guys are faster than you, not faster than you. So, I think all those things play into it. It's kind of a like a quarterback; the linebacker has to make multiple, multiple decisions on every play. Not only what his assignment is and what the play is, but all the way along the line, different angles, how to take on blocks, how to tackle, the leverage to play with, the angle to run to and so forth, the technique. So many different things happen in a split second during the course of the play, just like it is for a quarterback.

The more of those things that you can do right, slow down, get the most important things, not get distracted by all the stuff that's happening, but just really zero in on a target. I think a good quarterback or a good linebacker, a good safety, even though you have a lot of bodies moving out there, it slows down for them and they can really see it. Then there are other guys that it's a lot of guys moving and they don't see anything. It's like being at a busy intersection, just cars going everywhere. The guys that can really sort it out, they see the game at a slower pace and can really sort out and decipher all that movement, which is hard. But experience certainly helps that, yes.

**Q:** How difficult is it to find the Will linebacker and related to that do you feel like Adalius Thomas and Tully Banta-Cain are

## interchangeable at the Will and Sam?

**BB:** I think for most teams, the outside linebacker in a 3-4 defense is probably if not the most important quality, one of the two most important qualities he needs is to be able to rush the passer. Just schematically it's hard to get great pass rush on a 3-4 from your three interior people. They just don't have enough leverage - based on where they are lined up - to really attack the pocket. They are in front of the blockers, they're not on the edge. A lot of times, they are the contained rusher so they are kind of working from the inside out instead from the outside in.

It's just schematically those players are not in a great position in that defense to rush the passer, whereas the outside linebackers are. So that's a big part of that. That's a big part of that job, unless you're playing a 3-4 where those guys have a lot of coverage responsibilities. If that is the case, then I'd just say you better find your pass rush from somebody else because [with] most teams it's the [James] Harrison's, it's the Joey Porter's, the Jason Taylor's, guys like that that are the Lawrence Taylor's of the world.

Those [Shawne] Merriman's and all the guys you think of as outside linebackers that are really probably college defensive ends or 4-3 defensive ends, if you're playing a 4-3 defense. That's a big part of it. To me, it doesn't matter if you play strong side or weak side, if you can rush the passer, then you can play in a 3-4 defense. Now you have to decide, 'OK, how much coverage responsibility do you want to give those players?' And some do more than others, and some are better than others and sometimes that versatility offsets their pass rush. So if you've got it, yeah.

But an outside linebacker to kind of do everything, then there is a lot of value to that. If you have a guy who's a really good pass rusher, then there's a lot of value to that, so you just find that balance of those different skills that an outside linebacker has. Again, when you have a 3-4 team, most of the time those 3-4 linebackers are your defensive ends in sub and that's true of almost every team. To look at a team like Miami with [Joey] Porter, Jason Taylor, [Matt] Roth,

[Cameron] Wake and [Charlie] Anderson, those guys all play outside linebacker, they all rush off the edge. That's kind of what that position entails. I don't know if I answered your question or not, but I would say Tully and Adalius and Pierre Woods and Rob Ninkovich, all those guys to a certain degree are interchangeable.

And you kind of have to be because if you just motion to the tight end or flip them like all teams do or use two tight ends and one back, which we see almost every week, then both guys are playing the Sam, both guys are playing the Will - however you want to look at it. You've got to be pretty interchangeable. And if they're not then you can expect to see a team make you change them. They will make the Sam the Will and they will make the Will the Sam formationally as much as they can because they see that your players are pretty imbalanced there - one guy does one thing and the other guy does the other thing. Well, let's reverse it for them and make them try to work to get their guy to do the thing they want him to do.

# Defensive Line

**Q:** When a guy moves from the outside to the inside, what are the adjustments they need to make? I know you're supposed to play with good leverage all the time, but is playing with good leverage the most important adjustment you have to make when moving inside?

**BB:** Yeah, I think you put it well. You always want to play with good leverage, no matter where you are, but the players out at the end of the line – the tackles and the defensive ends are generally longer and maybe have a little tendency to play higher. A lot of times you have players that are a little bit shorter in there in the interior positions, although there are some six-foot-four guards, too, so I wouldn't characterize them all that way. But generally speaking, [there's] a little less length inside than outside. I think the biggest difference, though, is just how fast everything happens inside and how quickly they have to react, whichever side of the ball they're on. I don't know what the percentage is, but it's got to be pretty high – 85 percent, 90 percent of the time, the offensive tackle blocks the defensive end, in a four-man line anyway.

If you did that on every play offensively, you'd probably get most of them right. Inside, it's a little bit different. Centers and guards block combinations of linebackers and defensive linemen, depending on how the plays unfold and if there is movement inside, which usually there is a little more movement inside than there is outside. For a defensive tackle, you have the potential down-block, double team blocks from both sides – both the tackle and guard, center and guard, or if you're on the nose, from either guard with the center.

So, it's a lot of more of a question of where they're coming from, whereas for a defensive end, the number of times he gets down-blocked by a tight end, it happens, but the frequency is a lot lower. How quickly those guys are on you and how they can come from different spots, it's a much higher variety and it happens pretty quickly. I'd say that's the big adjustment in there.

**Q:** What are some things a rookie defensive end has to learn to make the jump, whether that's year one to year two or year two to year three?

**BB:** I think most all rookies make their biggest jump from year one to year two, that's not always true at the quarterback position, although I'd say it probably usually is if the guy is playing. I just think it's everything. Any rookie that comes into the National Football League, instead of being the best guy on his team and probably the best guy on the field or one of the best guys on the field in college is now just another guy. They're not the biggest, they're not the strongest, they're not the fastest, they're not the most experienced. They're pretty much back at the bottom of the totem pole for most part, certainly in terms of experience and technique and lot of times in physical skills too. These guys just train harder, they're older, their bodies are more mature, especially in the interior line positions. You see that a lot, offense and defensive linemen. There's physical development, there's a lot of technique, there's a lot of room for growth for all those guys. You learn by doing it and you learn by training hard and building your body up. I think that's something that all those guys, no matter what position they play, they almost all need to do that or they certainly can improve on it.

# Offensive Line

**Q:** Do you recall a player that has played well at tackle, guard and center? How rare is that?

**BB:** I'd say it's rare, but I think there are probably a lot of players that can do it – you just don't ask them to do it. Like [Logan] Mankins obviously played guard for us, we always had him as a tackle, but we never needed him because our tackles were very durable. I'm sure he could've played center. So, there is one, just to pick a name. We had that at Cleveland with Steve Everitt – guys that could have played multiple positions, but you have them at the primary positon, or maybe it's one of two positions and you're not really looking to move those guys around.

Hopefully you have enough players, enough depth that you're not juggling that. [Cameron] Erving was a good example last year, kid out of Florida State, played a lot at left tackle and midway through the season they moved him to center. I think those are probably the two hardest positons to play on the offensive line, so it'd hard to imagine that he couldn't play guard given the fact that he played left tackle and center, but I think there are other players that had they been asked to do that, they probably could have done it, but there are not many teams that would take a starting left tackle and move him into center. It's not a move that's commonly made. But there are probably more guys that can do that than have done it, but you don't see many that do it, I agree.

**Q:** Last week when Marcus Cannon went down, did you give equal thought to using a tight end or using a guard? What goes into that thought process?

**BB:** I'd say it starts during the week. It starts on Tuesday when we look at potentially what are the players that are going to be available, who's going to be active for the game. Sometimes we have a pretty good idea who that's going to be and sometimes we don't. Whatever the case is, we take that information and work it from there, so if we know who's going to be active, then we practice those backup moves, whatever they are. So, whoever the backup right tackle is practices that. Whoever the backup right guard is, center and so forth, whether that's another player who's already on the line, which when you only have seven players, that could definitely be part of it, sometimes you go into the game with your five guys and the other two, they are the plug-in guys and nobody else moves.

But sometimes that's not the case. If you go into a game where you're not sure who the active players are going to be because you have game time decisions looming, then you practice those contingencies. If this player is at the game, here's how we're going to do it. If this player is not at the game then that's how we're going to do it. It's the same thing at every positon. Honestly, I think it would be pretty irresponsible if we got a player hurt and then we had a meeting on the sideline like, "What are we going to do?" Now is the time to talk about that, not in the middle of a game. Now, when you start losing multiple players at a position, if you lose two players at any position, on any team – that's an issue. I mean, two of anything with anybody, pick any team in the league, I doubt that wouldn't be an issue.

Once you start getting into that area, then you've got to think about kind of what's our emergency move? How do we get through this? Maybe it's not so much who would play there, but what you could actually do with that person there, how you would manage the game, what you would call if you got to that point. Third quarterback, third tight end, third right tackle, third defensive end, third safety – third anything – if you're going that far down the line, it would be an issue. It would be an issue.

I'm not saying you couldn't handle it, but it would be an issue. Some more than others, but I would say everything … You don't go into the game thinking about losing two guys at the same position. When that happens, that's a difficult situation. And particularly in the kicking game because now you're talking about that's 66 players on special teams – kickoff, kickoff return, punt, punt return, field goal, field goal rush – that's 66 players. That means you have to have 66 backups. I mean, you've got to have it. So, this guy is out on this team, who is going in for him? You've got to have somebody. It might be the same guy for five positons, but you've got to have somebody.

OK, now you lose two guys at the same spot, again two anything – two safeties, two corners, two linebackers, two whatever they are – and they're going to be playing the same players in the kicking game. You're not going to have your middle linebacker as your gunner, so if you lose two gunners, you lose two gunners. If you lose two interior punt protectors, you're losing two interior guys on the punt return, you're losing two frontline blockers on the kickoff return, you're losing two interior, so the multiples in the kicking game, I can tell you from experience having been a special teams coach, you're really talking about making some adjustments.

Like I said, it's hard enough to lose one because you're looking at 66 plus 66. You start dropping down below that, then the opportunity to even give that guy reps at that position when you get 11 guys on the field, whoever that guy is, just getting him out there is one thing, him having reps at what he's doing is probably that would be a dream I would think that most likely didn't happen during the week.

So, those are tough. Lose two long snappers, lose two punters, lose two anything – that's pretty challenging. But special teams, people don't realize how difficult it is to just manage the roster in the kicking game because there are a lot of guys you can just eliminate from special teams. You don't seen any offensive linemen on the kickoff team, you don't see any defensive linemen on the kickoff team, you don't see any quarterbacks, other than the kicker and the punter, so you can take probably 15 to 20 players and just eliminate them from a lot of those teams. So now you're working with a much shorter list.

And what that total number is, is one thing, but realistically what that number is, is it's another ball game. So you start talk about how many players you actually have and then you're looking at 66 spots minus the field goal team, you start looking at 66 spots and then who backs those 66 spots up and then who's behind them.

**Q:** If you start seeing Brady running out on the kickoff coverage team, you know you're in trouble.

**BB:** But I'm telling you though, when you're a special teams coach and you lose that first guy, like alright so this player is out, now we make our move on the punt team, on the punt return team, on the kickoff team, on the kickoff return team, maybe the field goal rush team or wing on field goal, whatever it is, OK. Now, if something happens to him, who's the backup on the next play? And again you don't know when that's going to happen, so you could be sitting there on third down and there's the guy out there and now he hobbles off the field on third down and now you're out there on punt return or punt team or they score and now you're in a kicking situation.

So, forget about all the X's and O's, forget about all the situational things that come up in the kicking game, the one-play-type situation things, all the other things, personnel management on special teams is a huge part of the responsibility of that position. I know that's a lot more than you wanted to know about this. We could make that long answer even longer if you really want to. Joe [Judge], Scott [O'Brien], those guys, and Joe as Scott's assistant or Bubba [Ray Ventrone] as Joe's assistant, those guys, you've got very little time to work fast and a lot of times you're trying to make those substitutions and a guy might already be on the field. Somebody is out, alright what are we going to do, and you look out there and that guy's out there playing defense or he's out there playing offense or he's with the coaches about to go in or out in those situations, and kind of getting all that straight.

**Q: What goes into the relationship between center and quarterback, especially a quarterback as experienced as Tom Brady and a center as inexperienced as David Andrews?**

**BB:** I think it's just them being on the same page, snap count,

THE BIG BOOK OF BELICHICK

defensive identification, things like that, which in this league can be challenging. Then when you throw crowd noise into it or fast tempo, just making sure that both the line and the quarterback see it the same way. It's not necessarily a right or a wrong there. It's just making sure we're on the same page. We could do it sometimes either way where one way has a certain advantage, another way has a different advantage, but just making sure that we all have that. Changing up the snap count, using different timing on the count so the defense can't jump the snaps, particularly on the road – again, it's being on the same page. Of course, Tom has been in a lot of those situations. David is very quick to pick it up. He's played center a long time, so I don't think there is a lot maybe that's new for him. It's just, again, all of us getting on the same page.

**Q: What kind of characteristics do you look for from a player that is moving from guard to center?**

**BB:** There are a lot of similarities between those two positions, with obviously the big difference being the ball, and that is a big difference. They're both interior positions. Sometimes there's a center bubble, sometimes there's a guard bubble, sometimes the center is covered, sometimes the guard is covered. Whichever one you play, it's similar and you're working with that other player. There are a lot of combination blocks between the center and the guard, so again there is a lot of carryover there. The ball is a big difference and the exchange and the cadence and all that. So, I'd say physically the characteristics are similar. Technique-wise and assignment-wise, there is a little bit of a difference, and then the whole guard issue is left guard to right guard, which we've talked about. For some players, that's easy, and for other players, it's not so easy. And then of course center to guard is the same kind of thing. Some players see those positons as side by side and it's pretty seamless. With other players, there's a big difference for them and they have difficulty making that switch from one spot to the other, regardless of which way it goes.

But physically, there are a lot of similar characteristics. Now again, it depends on what type of offense you're running. There are some offenses, particularly I'd say the zone schemes, where there are a lot of similarities between guard and tackle, where you're not pulling guards, you're zone blocking, so you don't have a lot of necessarily lateral movement by those guards or pulling or screens or plays where they're getting out and running, and it's more of a zone-blocking scheme or pass-protection scheme. We have probably a little more multiple assignments for those positions than maybe some teams do. Again, I'd say looking at the zone teams, there is sometimes more carryover between guard and tackle than there is center and guard, but for us, we're probably a little more center-guard, finding our guard-tackle combos less frequent or maybe less likely in our system.

**Q: For a college center coming to the NFL, in your experience, is there one thing that is the biggest adjustment for that position?**

**BB:** I'd say probably the biggest adjustment for any player from college to NFL is the passing game. So, whatever part of the passing game that player is involved in, that's probably the biggest adjustment. For a center, pass protection, the number of protections relative to probably what he ran in college, the number of different defensive looks and fronts and potential adjustments would all be multiplied, probably exponentially. I'm not saying the running game is the same but it's more the same than the passing game – the type of players that they're blocking and the schemes that they're facing and the amount of variables in an offensive system plus the amount of systems in a defensive system, that adds up in a hurry.

If you're only doing one or two things, even if they do five things, it's 10. If you're doing 10 things and they're doing 10 things, now it's 100 but it's really a lot more than that. It adds up pretty quickly. I think that's – the center has to control some of that. He has to make decisions, calls, to some degree, adjustments, and there's a lot of gray area. Is the linebacker up in the line? Is he not in the line? Did he start in the line and move out? Did he start back and move up? What is the line of demarcation in some adjustments or designations? That's a lot of experience and recognition and communication so it's hard.

**Q: From the outside it looks like Matt Light is having a pretty solid year against solid pass rushers. When you go into a game and he see he's handling a pass rusher for the first few series and you had planned on giving him help, how do you adjust the game plan?**

**BB:** I think the concept of giving help, if you will, is circumstantial. Who are you helping him with? Is it a back? Well, that back has a blitz pickup assignment. So if his assignment blitzes, he can't help anybody. He has to block the guy he's supposed to block. Or the tight end or if you're trying to slide your line to a certain - you have three guys to block two.

Let's say they're in a four-man line so you have a center, guard and tackle to block a tackle and an end. If they bring a guy or if they line up in an alignment where those three guys have three guys to block then nobody is helping anybody. You have to block them. What you can do is you can create a presence, in other words, you can line your tight end up to one side or the other if you want to block him, you could block him and then if the guy he's supposed to block drops into coverage then he could help on somebody. Again, you can't guarantee that you're going to help because he has an assignment.

You only have 11 guys on offense, one of them is the quarterback so you only have 10, I'm talking about the passing game, so you're already outnumbered. If you're outnumbered by another guy, these two guys are going to block this one, now you've got nine guys and I'm just telling you, you run out of guys. The concept of helping really only applies to if that player doesn't get occupied by his protection assignment.

When you say, 'Well we're going into the game, we're not going to do this, we're not going to do that.' You might not be able to do it anyway. You might think you're going to give this guy all the help in the world but if they, and again, that's some of what they do. They know, 'Okay, here's how we're going to keep you from getting an extra guy over there. We're going to line up in a certain front or blitz a certain linebacker or bring a guy and drop somebody.'

They're playing that game too. That's kind of what you get into but you can put a body there - you could put a tight end there, you could put a back who releases there who if he runs up the field and his protection doesn't come, he could chip him on the way out. I'm not saying you can't have a way to help but you can't guarantee that help.

Also, if you talk to any tackles in the league, I'm sure most all of them would tell you that in a lot of cases, they would rather not have help because they just can't count on exactly how that back, what he's going to do, when he's going to do it. If he doesn't do it because his guy threatens to blitz but he backs out or whatever it is and now you're counting on that help because you can't see what's behind you, you're counting on that help and then the guy either is late or he's not quite where you think he's going to be or the rusher spins back inside to get away from it.

A lot of times, I don't want to say it causes more problems than it solves, but there's an element of that, there really is. If you talk to tackles about that sometimes, I'm sure and I've coached them and I've coached good ones and I've had plenty of times I've heard them say, 'Coach, let me just block the guy. I know he's good, but let me just block the guy because I can't, I'm not sure about -'

Again, if you don't line the back up over there where he's in position to help him, if you try to line him up behind the quarterback and then go over there and help him, it's a higher degree of difficulty too. Like I said, I think all that sounds good and there is some element of merit to it but it's not quite as easy as, 'Okay well this guy is going to help that guy and that will take care of it.' There is a lot more to it than that. Long answer to a short question.

## Q: How important is it to have someone with the ability to play both guard and tackle?

**BB:** That's a good question and it's definitely an interesting question when you look at your offensive line. When you go through the draft, you go through free agency, you look at the players in the league, there are a lot of guys who are tackles, there are a lot of guys who are guards, there are a lot of guys who are centers and that's the only position they play. Then you have some players who can play center and guard and then you have some players who can play guard and tackle and probably, I don't want to say they can't play center, but that would be the least of the three. Trying to find the versatility of that player, it changes the makeup of your roster, too, particularly when you take seven linemen to a game.

If you have a guard-tackle, swing player then you could potentially go to the game with five inside players - your three starters, another inside player and then a guard-tackle swing guy as opposed to having just a three position swing guy inside and then trying to find a swing tackle, if you will. Just trying to figure all that out but somewhere along the offensive line you have to have some position flexibility because you can't - nobody takes ten offensive linemen to the game, you'd have a backup center, backup left tackle, backup right guard, you just can't do it. You have to find some versatility in there somewhere. A center-guard combination - there are a lot of players that do that.

We had [George] Bussey - he was a guard-tackle swing player as an example. And then we've had certainly plenty of guard-center swing guys so it's just a question of finding the right mix. It doesn't rule anything out, but it just changes it, it just changes it a little bit. We've had more inside swing guys than we've had guard-tackle swing guys, but there are plenty of them in the league. Maybe Marcus is that, but I'm not sure.

## Q: Some of your former offensive linemen have said that you required them to wear knee braces when they were with the team. Was there something that happened in your coaching

career that made you decide that was the best decision?

**BB:** The braces that the players where now are a little different than the braces that I think we first started wearing back in the 80's when I was with the Giants and then at Cleveland, and they were kind of like a steel hinge that was usually taped or wrapped to the side of the knee as opposed to those bigger, DonJoy braces that most guys wear now.

So, I can remember on multiple occasions seeing the brace like literally bend in half or not maybe in half but bent significantly, so that it had taken a blow and the brace bent and the player maybe had a minor injury or a low MCL sprain or something like that. And the braces were strong. Had they not taken that blow and protected the player, you have to imagine the injuries would be a lot worse. I think that was a pretty vivid image that I had, and we did that with the players as well, too.

When that happened, in a meeting I'd just hold the brace up and say, "Well it's fortunate that so-and-so was wearing this protective brace. It looks like he might miss a week or two or maybe he isn't going to miss any time at all but I think we can all picture a more severe injury if he didn't have this protective equipment on." So, that type of thing. The braces now, just the way they're constructed they're really not conducive to that type of a visual example, but you still see plays on film where guys get hit in a way that it looks like it's going to be a pretty bad injury and then it isn't as bad as it looks and I'm sure part of that is the protective equipment.

**Q:** Have you ever had a player come to you and say that they don't want to wear a brace because it's affecting them negatively?

**BB:** Sure, yeah, I've had a lot of conversations with a lot of players over 41 years on various subjects, including that – yeah, sure.

# Receivers

**Q:** You've had a lot of success with slot receivers over the years - what makes a good slot receiver?

**BB:** It's a little bit of a different game in there, different than the perimeter, obviously a lot of different coverages. You have guys outside, guys inside, guys behind you, so a lot of different things can happen to that receiver, and of course it all depends on what the offense is doing, what type of route that player is running. There are different teams that do different things with that type of athlete, so therefore, there are different physical makeups of guys that are in there. For a slot receiver, part of his job is a function of what the team asks him to do, but they have to deal with more coverage, options, variations; there's a lot more blitzing with the player on the slot than it is with the perimeter players, obviously, because they don't have a spot to go. There are a lot of adjustments there and you just have to deal with more people. It's a little bit of a different game in there and it's a little bit of a different game defensively, too. You have help closer to you in various spots, depending on what the coverage is and what you do out on the perimeter - whatever help you have on the perimeter is usually some distance away, other than a couple of specific coverages, but if you take those out, the majority of the time, that help is further away than what it is inside. There are just some different elements of the game.

**Q:** How do you talk to the receivers about beating press coverage?

**BB:** It's a long answer, but some of the things you need to think about are: who's the receiver and who's the defender? And they're not all the same. Different players would use different techniques. They have different body types, different skill sets and so forth on your team that you're trying to release and you're up against different players on the other side of the ball. Some guys are longer, some guys are faster, some guys are stronger, some guys want to jam you, some guys really don't; they just want to get in position off the line of scrimmage. It's more of a struggle for position than it is trying to physically knock the guy down or something like that. So, I think all those things come into play, and then of course what route are we talking about?

There's a difference between running a deep vertical route or running an intermediate route or running some type of crossing route or something like that. I don't think press coverage is that big of an advantage because you're not trying to go through the defender, you're trying to get on one side or the other and trying to create leverage. What's the receiver's split? Where is his help? Is it half help? Is it middle of the field help? It's a long, much longer discussion than, 'Oh, it's press coverage.' It's all the other things involved, too. That's something that we talk a lot about and the quarterbacks also need to be aware of that.

But it can change the timing of the route. Then it gets into the whole timing element, so a 16-yard route on air and a 16[-yard] route against competitive press coverage, it's not the same timing. It's just not. You either hold the ball longer or that 16[-yard] route becomes a 12-yard route. It becomes a timing issue. It depends on the jam, too. Sometimes guys get up there and they aren't able to jam their receivers or they miss them. There are a lot of variables there and they all come in to play. That's where timing and execution is so critical.

## Q: Is it more difficult for receivers who primarily play on the outside to move inside or vice versa?

**BB:** That's a good question. It's an interesting question and it's certainly one that that whole conversation is one that we spend a lot of time talking about as a scouting staff, in terms of evaluating players and scouting players. Let me say this, first of all, I think it depends on obviously what the players are asked to do. Not every outside receiver plays like every other outside receiver, just like every inside receiver doesn't play like every other inside receivers. There are some things that some inside receivers do that are similar but also there are some that are very different from what other guys do. So I'd say, again, it depends what you're looking for. If you're looking for an inside receiver to do things that are similar to what outside receivers do, then I'd say that transition is probably not that big of a deal. If those routes and the type of passing game that's done on the inside part of the field is quite a bit different from the outside part of the field, then you're probably looking at mostly different type of guys. Obviously some players are good enough to play anywhere.

Then there are other guys that probably fall into more of one role or the other. But forgetting about all that for the moment, I would say that the game inside in the slot is different from the perimeter because of the number of people that are involved. You're not just looking at – a lot of times outside, you're pretty much dealing with one guy. It's the wide receivers and the corner. You have to have an awareness of the safety, whether he's over the top or rotated in the middle or into a seam area. That's pretty much about it, for the most part. When you're inside, you have a corner outside, you have a slot defender, you have a safety, you have a linebacker so there are at least four guys that you really, I would say, pretty much have to deal with one of them or two of them one way or another. That creates a lot more variables than playing on the perimeter.

I'm not saying it's harder [or] easier, it's just different. The same thing is true on defense covering that position. You have the proximity of the next inside player, the next outside player and some type of player in the deep part of the field, unless it's an all-out blitz. That changes the relationship a lot from what it is when you're playing on the perimeter as a corner. You just don't have that – you have the sideline but you don't have the number of players. So in terms of like, what does this player do? What does that player do? I think it starts with, like anything else, just like if you were hiring someone for a job – what's the job description? What do you want that player to do? Once you prioritize what you want that player to do, then you try to fit the player into that job description. Some of the things they have to do are the whole intelligence of recognizing different coverages and different relationships. How much do you want a vertical speed guy that can go in there and get through the middle of the defense? How important is blocking in the running game because it's going to be a factor when you're in there that close. How important is quickness and creating separation on five to seven-yard type routes on third down. What's your priority? Then you want to get a player that fits those priorities.

**Q:** Do you feel like Julian Edelman and Danny Amendola have been able to find success both inside and outside this year?

**BB:** Sure, yeah. But I think a lot of times you see, sometimes even our outside receivers in more of an inside position, where they'll stack or come together. So which guy is the inside guy, which guy isn't? There's some of that too. Yeah, I think they have both been successful there. They both have the versatility there. I would say our team uses multiple inside receivers, whether it's the inside receiver or whether it's an outside guy that also can work somewhere into the middle of the field. I would say not all teams do that.

**Q: Eric Decker plays in the slot, but he seems like a taller, longer player than some of the smaller, quicker guys we've seen play that position. How does that help him?**

**BB:** I think it's just different, but I think those are the two you've identified, those are kind of the two categories you see. [Marques] Colston from New Orleans, [Mohamed] Sanu from Cincinnati – those guys are bigger, longer guys that have a different skill set than the Troy Browns or [Danny] Amendolas or whoever. You get the guy that is in the offense, or you fit your offense to that guy, however you want to look at it, to what those skills are. But you see both of those. Some weeks you see the bigger slot guys, maybe more vertical players, bigger, stronger guys, better blockers, and other weeks you see guys that are fast, quick, work well in those short areas, kind of returner-type player, like [Jeremy] Kerley is for them. So they've used both of them in there. They're very different and they challenge you differently defensively, both with the matchup and the things that they do and the skills that they have. But again, that's kind of the way it is every week. Each player has his own characteristics and they're not all the same. We have to deal with blocking tight ends, we deal with fast receiving tight ends, we deal with skillful receiving tight ends, we deal with big receivers, small receivers, quick receivers, fast receivers, possession receivers that are physical. It's the NFL. Everybody you've got in there has got skills. They're not all the same, but they have skills you have to deal with or they wouldn't be playing in this league.

# Running Backs

## Q: What is the biggest challenge for a running back in pass protection?

**BB:** I'd say the number one challenge, the first challenge is to get the right guy based on the call, the identification of the defensive personnel and then post-snap what happens if they cross, if two guys cover the same gap. If they all go straight ahead, that's fairly straight forward, but when more than one comes or when they come in different locations or they're up in the line and they drop out or they start in one place in the line and then come somewhere else, just getting it right – that's challenge number one. And then of course challenge number two is physically getting the player blocked. There are a lot of different aspects to that. Certainly cut blocking is something that a lot of backs do on blitz pickups, but not something that we would practice even though we might do it in the game. There's a game aspect to it and then there's also a practice aspect to it, but the fundamentals of pass protection are still what they are – getting your body in between the man you're blocking and the quarterback and protecting the inside part of the pocket and handling the power rush and then being able to adjust to some type of rush that's not a power rush – some kind of edge rush or spin move or whatever it is. So, it's under all those components. But number one is getting the right guy and then number two is being able to physically keep him away from the quarterback long enough to execute the play.

**Q:** How difficult is that to work on during this time of the year?

**BB:** Now is a good time to work on it. Now is the best time to work on it. Now is honestly – I wouldn't say the only time – but it's definitely the best time to work on it. [We] can't really do it in the spring. We can do assignments in the spring, but there is no physical contact and during the season there are limited physical contact opportunities, so this is the time to do it. Just like everything else, this is the time to build any fundamentals that involve contact, whether it's punt protection, pass protection, defeating blockers, tackling.

Whatever involves contact, you've got your training camp practices and then minimal number of practices during the season to work on those set of skills.

**Q: I think that was something we noticed from both Stevan Ridley and Shane Vereen in some of their big runs. It seems like that's sort of an interesting quality in that it's not just eyesight. What allows a running back to have good vision? Stevan talked yesterday about being patient and setting up blocks.**

**BB:** It's a good question. It's kind of probably a hard thing to put into words and define. But I think patience, a key to it is knowing when you have time to set blocks up and use the blocking scheme ahead of you to pull defenders one way or the other and cut off them and when you don't and you just have to hit it and get through there because there's just not enough time. That's an instinctive thing that backs I'm sure learn through experience and some have better than others. When you have that ability to have a little bit of space and you have the patience to set up those blocks and force a defender to declare one way to set the block for whoever it is – lineman, guard, center, tackle, whoever it is – and then be able to cut off, that's really ideal. Sometimes you just don't have that luxury as a back. You have guys closing in on you and you just have to get through there and run with good pad level and get what you can. But patience is a key to that when used at the right time.

We all hate to see the backs that run in there and have patience and then don't gain any yards. You want them to get the ball into the line of scrimmage and go. So, there's a fine line between when you have time to do that and when you don't. I thought that the run that Shane had on the third-and-[16] play, last week where he set the block for [Dan] Connolly, he would have gained the three or four yards there. The linebacker, I think it was [Emmanuel] Lamur was there coming over the top and he started outside to take the linebacker outside, set the block for Dan and then cut up inside and ended up going for the first down. Those are yards you kind of have to give to the running back for making that run happen. He didn't break a tackle, but the way he set the block gave him an extra 10, 12 yards, whatever it was. Vision is part of that, patience is part of that.

Having an understanding of how to draw the defender to the blocker and then cut off it is all part of it. I don't know where one starts and the other one ends. They all merge together, but there are elements in that in terms of running and I'd say using your blockers. Some backs sometimes tend to run away from them which sometimes that works, too. But sometimes you see guys run, they have a blocker, but they run past them and the defender makes a tackle. If they had waited a little bit and set it up, but they have to decide whether they have time to do that or sometimes they think they can beat the guy without the block.

**Q: Running back is generally thought of as a position that has a quicker acclimation process than others. Has Shane Vereen been able to jump back in there and is that that general thought true of him?**

**BB:** That position is quicker than others?

**Q:** Yes, it would seem that it's easier for a rookie running back than say a rookie offensive tackle.

**BB:** I don't agree with that. I'm sure that there are other people that have other opinions, which is great. I'm sure I'm wrong about a lot of things but I wouldn't agree with that. Talk about blitz pickup, all the different fronts you can have, all the different blitz assignments, with various protections and all the combination blitzes that we see these days. I think running back is a very mentally challenging position to learn. All the different run reads, the fronts that teams run, the way they stem to them, the stunts when the ball is snapped, things that happen after the ball is snapped, reading coverages, recognizing man, zone, combination man and zones, guys that are blitzing, guys that are faking that they're blitzing but they're really in coverage, guys that start off in coverage and then turn around and blitz. I think the running back's job is very difficult. And that's not saying that everybody else on the field doesn't have a tough job too. But I think they're involved in every play to a high degree, just like linebackers are, just like safeties are, just like all the people in the middle of the field are. You can't hide that position, whatever play you call, they're pretty involved in. I think that there's a lot they have to do I think it's a very challenging position for any player, of any experience level, first, tenth, fifth [year].

**Q:** Does the University of California system prepare Shane Vereen better than other colleges because they run a pro style system?

**BB:** I don't know. I haven't been in the Cal system, so I'm not familiar with it. I mean, I've watched it, but I don't know the teachings of it and all that so I couldn't really answer that question.

## Q: What are some of the things James White had to do in order to take his game as a runner to the next level?

**BB:** Well, I think any runner needs to develop a timing with the line and the blocking pattern. You get to the hole too fast and you kind of don't have the chance to really see the blocking pattern develop. You get there too slow and it closes. Setting up blocks, knowing which way you're going to cut but trying to keep the defender in the gap that he's in as long as possible before you cut to the gap that's really vulnerable. If you go there too soon then they just adjust and fall off and make the play. What we refer to as pressing the line of scrimmage, pressing the blocks, keeping the defenders in the gaps they're in. He's had several good runs on that.

Again, second level decision making for a back is important. Once you're through the line of scrimmage then working off of the receiver blocks and the leverage that they have on the defenders, trying to maximize the space and the potential yardage there. I mean just all of those things, experience, and again, he was a good runner in college.

It's not that he like hasn't done it but I think just more experience doing it, more experience of running our plays with our blockers against the timing of the play and so forth has gotten progressively better.

# 2
# COACHING PHILOSOPHY

**Q:** Can you describe Matt Patricia's coaching style and in particular how he relates to his players?

**BB:** Good, yeah, good. Matt's really smart. He's had a lot of different experiences. He's coached in college, he's coached on the offensive side of the ball, coached on the defensive side of the ball, has been in this situation, this program for a long time so he has a pretty good understanding historically of things like the Vrabels and the Bruschis and the Troy Browns and all things like that that can have some relationship to sometimes current situations. He's really smart. This guy could probably build a plane and fly it – like this guy is smart-smart. He's got great recall and a really high IQ level in terms of just processing a lot of information. He's the kind of guy that he's got 10 projects going at once and then you're like, 'Hey Matt can you do this and do that – oh yeah, no problem.' He's got 12 going at once. Some of us can only handle barely one thing at a time. He's the type of guy that can keep a lot of balls in the air. But again, he's a blue-collar guy, certainly wasn't born with a silver spoon like most players, so they're just working for everything, working his way up through, I think he has an appreciation for that and I think he relates well to other guys who are doing the same thing.

**Q:** Do you guide him because of your defensive background?

**BB:** Matt and I have worked together for a long time so he's definitely a huge asset to me in a number of areas – again both historically, like, 'Hey this is what we did in this situation, think about that or should we do that again or the timing of it and so forth.' And again over a period of years, Josh is the same way, over a period of years, things that you did five, 10 years ago, I'm not saying they come up every day, but it might be, 'Hey remember when we did this against so-and-so back in '07 or '05 or whatever?' It's kind of the same thing here. For somebody that just got here last year or somebody that's been here for a year or two, there's no way that that's coming up – here's what we did in this situation back when we had this player. So there is some value to that. I'm not saying it happens every day, but guys like that – Brian Daboll, Matt Patricia, Josh McDaniels, guys that have been here for a really long time – they have some of those perspectives that are really good, so it's very helpful.

**Q:** They understand your thinking?

**BB:** Yeah, and again they can take a situation that happened, whenever it happened, and maybe it applies to something we're doing now and it's a good idea. If it was a good idea then, it might a good idea now, but maybe you're not really thinking about it or I'm not thinking about it. And again, a big part of the whole staff is just working together – offense working with the defense and particularly the defense working with the special teams because most of the players in the kicking game are defensive players so working their roles together and who's active and who's doing what and how to make it all work together as efficiently as possible, it's not the easiest thing to do in the world, I can tell you from experience. So I wouldn't say that's as much of a thing on offense. Again there are usually only a handful of offensive players in the kicking game. The majority of players are on defense, but that affects your defensive game plan and the roles that those guys play and the way that plays off each other. Again, there's a lot of staff chemistry things or staff relationship things that work like that that are maybe not as obvious, but they're really important and when they don't work well eventually it causes you problems and you're not efficient or just don't get the most out of what you have.

## Q: Do you have a go-to list of how you want to approach game-day coaching?

**BB:** I definitely believe in a process. I don't know that that's the same in every single game. Well, I'd say it's not the same in every single game. It depends on who you're playing and kind of what they do or what you anticipate them doing as to how you want to approach it. It's a great question. It's a very interesting point of discussion. I think there are a lot of things to look at throughout that, but it's all critical in the communication and coordination of processing the information that you get during the game, I'd say it's not easy to do. I'm not saying it's impossible, but it's not easy to do because it comes from a lot of different sources and you definitely want to prioritize it. I'd say those are some of the components of it.

Number one, getting the most important things handled – whatever they are. It could be what you're doing, it could be what they're doing, it could be the weather conditions – whatever the most important things are making sure that you start at the top. And also you don't have all day. You don't even know how long you have. If you're on defense the offense could be out there for a seven-minute drive, they could be out there for a 30-second drive, so you've got to prioritize what you're doing so that you get to the most important things first, so if you're running out of time, you haven't used your time inefficiently. So that's number one.

Number two, there's the, what we're doing versus what they're doing. A lot of times just making sure that you're right is more important than identifying what they're doing. Sometimes identifying what they're doing, until you get that cleared up then you're kind of spinning your wheels in the sand and you're not making any progress because you don't really understand exactly what the issues are. In the game situation that changes all that. You have the information from players, which is they're in the heat of the battle. You have information from the press box, who can get as much of an overview as you can get. You have sideline information. So sometimes that's the same, sometimes information – you don't see it quite the same way.

The way one coach sees it, the way the press box sees it, the way the sideline sees it, the way a player on the field sees it, it's not quite all the same way. So you've kind of got to sort all that out. And then there is the balance of fixing what is in the rearview mirror and looking ahead. So like, OK we've got to take care of these problems, here's what happened, but at the same time, you're spending all your time on that, some of that is not even relevant because the next time you go out there, OK what are we going to do? We've corrected those problems, maybe we're going to make a different call or maybe we're going to be in a different situation, how do we handle that? So there is the balancing of new information versus analysis of previous information.

There are a lot of components to that, and I think a good coach, the decision making that they make within all that is what makes him a good coach. What information is important, where do we start, how do we get the most information across in the least amount of time and making sure that we get the information to the right people? Some coverage adjustment, the guard doesn't care about. He doesn't care about what coverage they're running. The receiver doesn't care if the nose is shaded or not shaded. But I'd say that's a very interesting part of game day from a coaching standpoint and one that's important, it's critical, and there are a lot of components to it.

**Q: How important is it not to get caught up in the emotion of the game when trying to make game day decisions?**

**BB:** Again, that's part of it. I think playing emotionless is not good, so there is a balance between I think when you're alert, when you're emotional, when you have a lot of energy that you're on a higher alert, but there's a point where that can go over the edge and be detrimental where its more about that than it is about the execution of your job. So there is a fine line there between poise, composure, decision making and energy and emotion and enthusiasm. And they're all good and they're all important, but there is a balance there. There's got to be a balance in there somewhere. But in terms of decision making I think you've got to try to make decisions based on what's right, not where your heart is, but what's best for the football team. But in terms of talking about or conveying that to your team or to a particular unit, that's discretionary and judgmental.

**Q:** Is a rule of thumb that celebrating and congratulating a teammate on a great play is the way to go, as opposed to trying to get in the head of somebody else on the other team?

**BB:** Yeah, first of all you never want to ... We don't coach penalties. So, we don't want penalties, we don't coach them, so judgment to do the right thing, whatever it is, tackle a guy, be physical, celebrate – it's all got to be within the rules. That's number one. Like, we're not trying to go beyond any rule ever. But yeah, just in general, I mean, look, these guys work hard, they work hard every day, they work hard all week, they prepare for the game, yeah, if you go out and make a good play you should be excited about it. If anyone else works hard at something and it comes out well, hey, we feel good. We should feel good. And when you do it together as a group, you feel good with your group. The guy who scored feels good for the guys who blocked for him. The guys who blocked for him feel good for the guy who scored and vice versa. You throw a pass, you catch it, somebody had to block, somebody had to run the route, somebody had to throw it, somebody else took the coverage to help somebody else get open or whatever, you intercept a pass, you had a good pass rush, other guys were covered. So there is a lot of team excitement on those plays.

You see it on the sidelines. A guy on the field makes a play, you see the bench explode. That emotion comes out with hard work and success naturally. I don't think it's something that you want to restrain. At the same time, there is another play. I mean unless there is a touchdown or a drive-ending play or turnover, but a lot of times there is another play, so one good play, that's fine, but if the next play is a bad play then that offsets it. But again there is a balance there in all that. But I don't think it's good when a team goes out and we make a good play and nobody cares. I don't think that's particularly … It's not anything that I'm proud of any more than if we make a bad play and we don't care. If we make a bad play we want to get it right. If we make a good play we should feel good about it.

## Q: How does this team fill the void when captains are injured? Does leadership come more from the whole team rather than a few captains?

**BB:** I think the latter. You really identified it there. Everybody on the team has leadership. You don't have to be a captain to be a leader. You don't have to be a 10-year veteran or anything else. Rookies give us leadership. Veterans give us leadership. Captains represent the team in various ways, but in the end, I think every player that's a participant on the team provides leadership. If they have a good attitude and they work hard and they put the team first, then that's really what leadership is all about. We have a lot of guys who have played quite a bit of football for us, and they all have a role in that.

It's not just the captains, but even whether it be last year with Jerod [Mayo] or this year when Wendy [Ryan Wendell] wasn't playing, before he was actually on the field and then even for yesterday, we still get a lot of good leadership from those guys. Even if they're not playing, they still do what they can do and that's helpful. I think it's a combination of all those things.

I think leadership is really something that comes from your whole team, not just one or two guys. Not saying that one or two guys can't have some influence, but I think it really can be a whole team thing as opposed to just counting on one or two guys to do that. That's kind of where we've been for a while. I don't see this year as being too much different than the past.

**Q:** Last year, Malcolm Butler told us he went to the coaching staff and said he wanted a chance at DeSean Jackson during the joint practices. Do you like it when a player does that?

**BB:** You take it with a grain of salt. It depends. Some guys want them, some guys really don't want them, but they want to kind of say they want them. I've seen it go a lot of different directions.

**Q:** Have you seen it go different ways?

**BB:** Oh yeah, you definitely have the guy who comes in here and says, "Can I get on No. 68 this week, I mean I could kill him, let me get over there on him." There is that side of it, too. Or, "Let me cover so and so, I can really get all over this guy." Yeah, alright. How about taking the best guy? What about that? But we have a pretty competitive group.

I think on this team there are a lot of those situations, especially in training camp and when you're going against each other, guys kind of get to the front of the line or get where they're matched up against another really good player, whatever it is, and they have a little bit of a competition going there, and certainly that carries over to our opponents. I would think our guys like to go up against who they think are our best players or go up against the other team's best player and try to ... But again sometimes that's part of the game plan, sometimes it isn't and that's just something we kind of have to sort out.

I don't think that's a bad thing to want to take on their best guy, but I would say we've got a lot of guys like that. I wouldn't put Malcolm as the only guy in that category. I definitely wouldn't characterize it that way at all. But I've definitely seen the other side of that, too. "Even though I play over here at this position, if you put me over there somewhere else against the guy on the other side of the line, I think I can have a big day against him." Or, "Normally I would be covering this guy, but if you put me over here on this other guy who's not very good, I think I can cover him." I've seen that, too.

**Q:** How do you try to incorporate new guys to your system while also maximizing and utilizing their skills initially before they get a grasp for the scheme?

**BB:** That's a good question. I think what you really try to do there … I mean first of all, every coach tries to do that. I don't think any coach says, "OK, here are this player's skills, let me ask him to do something completely different." I don't think that's really what you try to do. I think there's kind of two ways you can go about it. One, you can have a system that is pretty flexible and you take the skills of the players that you have available and put them in the situation that fits them and your system is flexible enough to do that. Or maybe you have a less flexible system, a system that has fewer variables, and you find players to do very specific things in that system. Here's what we need this position to do and so you find somebody who can do those things. Here's a different position, this is what the requirements are for that. We find somebody to do that.

I mean obviously the better player the better, but you do it in a realistic way so that you feel like you can find whatever it is. So there's a blocking tight end or a receiving tight end, or a blocking fullback or a receiving fullback, or an inside runner or an outside runner, or whatever the offensive system is – and the same thing is really truly on defense – and try to find a player who will fulfill that role. I would just say in Chan's case, it appears to me that he has pretty good breadth to the system. They are able to use a lot of different players – players who play the same position, like a guy like Marshall or a guy like Kerley, whose skills are different but they have a role and they have a productive role in the offense. Or Ivory or [Bilal] Powell or guys like that.

They are able to use them in different packages or use them in situation plays that really make it hard for you to defend those players because of the things that they are being asked to in those aspects of the offense. So both ways can work. It is just a question of adapting the personnel to your system or adapting your system maybe to the personnel, and there's a little bit of that in everything, but I think that the needle can move a little further one way or another depending on what kind of philosophy you want to favor, if that makes any sense.

**Q: Do you measure your steps with a player who is learning a new system in terms of not putting him in positions to not succeed whereas maybe earlier in the year you would be able to do that?**

**BB:** I think each guy is different. It's really hard to predict how it's going to go with any player. I think you just take it as it comes. You give them the information and then you move them along and see how quickly he adapts to the new assignments, the new techniques, and just the way he's able to handle the assignments that he's given. Again, each player is different so with a player like Barkevious [Mingo], you have a situation where he has a lot of special teams responsibilities, so if we brought in, let's say an offensive lineman, or a defensive lineman, that may not – it depends on the positon and the guy.

He may not have that big a responsibility in the kicking game, so it's just really depends on the individual player and how quickly he's able to acclimate himself to the new situation. I don't think there's any set mind frame or you try to go fast, you try to hold back. I think you just kind of take it as it comes.

**Q: How do you balance having a player use his own instincts on the field versus having him play within the context of the defense?**

**BB:** I mean I've coached every player I've ever coached the same way. You have an assignment, you have something you're responsible for and then the instincts come after that. As long as you cover your guy, that's your job. You want to cover him off, you want to cover him on, inside technique, outside technique, back pedal, squat, whatever it is. I mean there's a million different ways to do it. If you have him covered I'm going to be happy about it, you're going to be happy about it, right? So that's the bottom line. Now after that then there is an instinctive part to every play, so I've coached players - that's the way I've coached them my whole career.

When I was a special teams coach I had different punters, different kickers. They don't all kick it the same way. They kick it far, they kick it high. I'm happy, they're happy, the team is happy. That's good. If they don't then we've got to try and find a better way to do it. I don't see it any differently now than I saw it when I started coaching. I don't see it really much differently from one positon to another. The techniques are different, the assignments are different but a player's instinct and his style of play - that belongs to each of us. We're all different. But there are certain fundamentals that I think as a coach you are obligated to teach the best way that you know how and work with individual players within that framework.

## Q: Is it a coaching challenge to sometime find opportunities to get guys involved?

**BB:** Yeah, it really is. That's a great point that you brought up there and it's one that we constantly talk about and try to maximize and it's not easy. For me, it went back to kind of my days as the defensive coordinator for the New York Giants. We had a lot of depth at linebacker. Honestly, there were times when we could have played six linebackers, and there were even some passing situations where we did, where we took the defensive line out of the game and put all of the linebackers on the field. But it's hard to do things like that over an extended period of time.

Say you have a scheme, and you've worked on that scheme all week, all year, and then to do something that is pretty far off of that, it's okay as a changeup I guess, but then it takes away what you've been working on and what you've been trying to construct. It's hard to feature that. I know I give you guys a hard time every week. You look at the production sheet, carries, receptions, targets, whatever, and there are going to be guys on the top of that and there are going to be guys that have fewer and you always ask what happens to them, what happened to them in this game. Sometimes that is a function of the game, the game plan, or just the way the game played out. But if they're on our team and we put them out on the field, it's because we want them out there, we think they can be productive, they've earned that opportunity, and sometimes they got more opportunities than others and sometimes after a period maybe of lesser activity or fewer opportunities, then those opportunities come and they do well with them, and then it looks different than what it really is, like all of sudden there was some really big improvement and it really is just a question of opportunity.

Some of those opportunities you can control as a coach, but a lot of them you can't. When the ball snaps, we don't know what's going to happen, especially on defensive side of the ball. We don't know where it's going to go or what they are going to do, we just have to react to it. It definitely is a challenge. You want to have guys involved and you want to have them have roles, but each game sometimes the scheme overrides an individual player and you have to be in a particular scheme for a percentage of the time that takes certain players out of play, but you feel like that's what you need to do to be competitive.

So, it's definitely a challenge. It's a good problem to have. You're certainly better off having more players, where it's hard to utilize all of them rather than having a few players and it all falls on one guy's shoulders, kind of like when I got here with Troy Brown and 15 passes a game were going to him. I mean, he's a good player, but in part because there weren't a lot of other options. It's better to be in the other position where you have more options and you use the ones that you feel are best for your team, and that's probably something that's helped our team though the years win games is the depth that we've had at positions and how many different players we've had come through in one way or another, whether it be the skill positions or not at the skill positions to help the team win when they were called on.

That's part of having a good team. It is definitely a challenge, but you have to, particularly on the defensive side of the ball, you have to stop what they do, and some players on your roster may be better suited to stop certain things than others, as opposed to having the same guys out there for every single play. People my age, your age, that's kind of the way we grew up watching the game. I know when I watched pro football and when I first came into the league, it was basically the same 11 guys out there. It didn't matter if you had the ball on their one-yard line or if you had the ball with five seconds to go in the game, there were two receivers, two backs and a tight end, and the defense was in 4-3. And then it was such a revolutionary step to add a third receiver or put in a nickel back, even though the nickel back really wasn't a nickel back – all he was was a linebacker that was a smaller or more athletic guy.

So, you're used to seeing the same people out there. So, that production is more consistent and comparable than what we have now where, so frequently in the league, us and everybody else, at the end of the play, two or three guys run onto the field, and two or three guys run off the field. It's just a different way of getting used to that. I'm not saying it's a bad thing or a good thing, it's just different.

**Q:** Do you draw a distinction between emotion in football and intensity in football? How important is the latter in not allowing the former to get the best of you? Penalties and mental mistakes seemed to provide some key plays in the first week.

**BB:** That's a good question. I don't know – there's a lot of gray there. I'm not sure where one stops and the other one starts, but in the end, we all have to find a way to block out all the noise and go out there and execute and do our jobs, whatever they happen to be. Emotion is definitely a part of football – a good part of it – so I don't think as a team you ever want to lose that.

Usually high emotion and high energy leads to better execution, so I think that's a good thing, but at the same time there is a line you can cross where you end up, as you said, getting a penalty or overreacting to something and being vulnerable to something else – a reverse or a pass or whatever it is that then sets you back. It's a fine line there. It's a balance. But in the end you've got to be able to do your job, you've got to be able to do it well in order to win in this league. There are so many good teams and players and coaches. That's really the key is being able to go out there and execute it under pressure on a consistent basis.

**Q:** I guess that was the point I was trying to get at was how not let emotions prevent you from doing your job.

**BB:** I think emotion is part of it. It's a good thing. I don't think it's a bad thing. You want that emotion, but like you said, you don't want it to cross the line. You don't want it to negatively affect what you're doing. But high energy and positive emotion can go a long way. There is a balance there.

### Q: We talk a lot about players having good instincts or playing with good feel. Do coaches ever make decisions based off of instinct or feel?

**BB:** Yeah, absolutely. That's hard to quantify really, but it's something that you feel. I've called plays for a significant part of my career and there are times where you just get a feeling that maybe it goes against the tendency or there's something that you just can kind of instinctively feel like is going to happen and you do something to try to take advantage of it, or the right time to call a double pass, or the right time to run a blitz. Or you just anticipate what they're going to do.

You just anticipate what the other play caller is going to do and you happen to guess right. Look, we all guess wrong plenty of times, too. I'm not saying that. But yeah, there's definitely some of that where you just kind of get a feel for the way the game is going or a particular situation as it unfolds and you make that call just based on what you feel at that time - not what was the tendency, what did they do in this situation in a bunch of other games. You just feel like at this point in time, here's where you're going to put your chips and you think they're going to blitz you and you call a play that's a good blitz-beater play, or you think they're going to whatever - fake it and pull out of it and not going to do it. You've got to be able to handle whatever they do, but yeah, there's definitely an element to that. And [it's] the same thing in the kicking game, too.

I think that Josh [McDaniels] and Matt [Patricia] do a great job of that. They call a majority of the plays, and they do a great job of anticipating what could happen in certain situations. You have to be ready for two, three, four different things - whatever it happens to be - but then every once in a while you just get that feeling that this is the time, this is when we want to do it, and they're right quite a bit.

**Q: I know how much respect you have for Aaron Rodgers. As a teaching tool for your young players, is that something you work on in terms of mental toughness?**

**BB:** I think it's a great opportunity for our team defensively. They were out there for a quite a bit. It would probably be the equivalent of close to a half of a regular game – it was 30-some plays. Certainly with a quarterback the caliber of Aaron, any mistake that you make is a problem. He was able to take advantage of some of our coverage that maybe wasn't as tight as it needed to be in certain situations. There were times we didn't do a good job in our overall coordination of the pass rush, and he escaped the pocket relatively easily. That's really just more of a communication and discipline of our pass rush against that type of a quarterback. We needed to do a better job than we did.

He exposed some things and those are good learning situations for us. That same type of thing could come up and the quarterback [could] not take advantage of it, so you get a little bit of a misconception that everything was OK on a play when really it wasn't. We'll get to see that again this week with Drew Brees and practicing against Brees.

However much he plays, I don't know, but at least on the practice field I'm sure it will be a similar thing that if we show our coverage early, if we don't do a good job on the pre-snap, if our coverage isn't tighter, competitive enough, if the pass rush isn't balanced and gives them an opportunity to extend the play, then that will cause us trouble. This was a great opportunity for us to play against one of the top, if not the top quarterback that we would play against and that'll be true again this week with Brees and it'll be true the following week with [Cam] Newton, who brings a different element to the game, but another [quarterback] at a very high level.

And then finally with [Eli] Manning, however much he plays in that game. But again, those are four different, but very high quality players at that position, which will get our defense and particularly our pass defense as much of a challenge other than scheme-wise – I know we're not getting over-schemed in these games – but in terms of the quality of the player and the execution, I don't think we're going to run into four guys much better than these four.

**Q: How do you balance a player getting accustomed to a new system against keeping a practice moving and having productive reps?**

**BB:** It's kind of what we talked about yesterday – you see what the player can do. You put him in there based on the things you think he can do – if he can do those then you give him more, if he can't then sometimes you have to go back and spend a little bit of time to build the foundation and get it right before you move ahead. We're kind of going through the same thing with Ryan [Groy] today. You just kind of take it day by day. We meet with the players, the coaches get some feedback and get kind of a feeling for how they're picking things up – what they are comfortable with, what things they maybe have questions on or don't seem to have as a good of a grasp on.

They substitute them or call plays based on what we feel they are able to handle and what's going on on the other side of the ball – how complex that is or what the degree of difficulty is there. You're right – we don't want somebody in there that doesn't know what to do and then that fouls up practice, but at the same time you want to try to evaluate them on what they do know how to do and see how that looks and then move forward at as fast a pace as you can go at, but it has to be one that the player can keep up with. Each situation is different – you just have to read each one independently.

**Q:** Are you ever surprised by a player's ability to pick things up that quickly?

**BB:** Yeah, all the time – to varying degrees. Some guys, if you haven't been with them – until you've really been with them you don't know exactly what they can do and how they process, how they can adapt to your system. Some guys can move very quickly, other guys move at a different pace. Sometimes guys are kind of in a little bit of a fog and then all of a sudden it just sort of comes together, and sometimes it doesn't, so it's hard to tell until you've really spent enough time with a player to know exactly what you have. Some guys, when they learn stuff they have it – they won't make a mistake on that, but you throw something new or have to make a quick adjustment in a practice or in a game, then sometimes that's hard for some people to deal with.

Other people, they just get it, roll with it, understand it and move on, but until you've gone through that experience it's hard to know. That's part of what training camp and these preseason games and all that's for, is to try and get a feeling for what your team can do, what it can't do, with certain individuals, how they handle things. We put them in different situations, and a lot of times they don't get it right the first time, but if we keep working at it and build on it, then sometimes it changes, sometimes it doesn't.

**Q: But as you're preparing the team for the whole season, how do you also stay sensitive to wearing out the veterans who have had less recovery team because of how late you played into last season?**

**BB:** Yeah, that's really been a big challenge for us over the last 15 years. It's a good problem to have. Obviously, you want to play long into the season, but it definitely shortens the time period for the players to recover and be ready for the next year, particularly the ones who have more significant injuries – surgeries, depending on what the surgery is – but some type of ligament repair-type surgeries, sometimes those things take a little bit longer. Our timeframe there is a lot of times a month to six weeks less than where some other teams are, and then that affects us on this end of it, particularly in the training camp period.

Usually most of those players are ready by September, generally speaking – this is a general question, we're not talking about any player in particular – but the end of July start versus the early September start, that kind of six week gap there is a lot of times the difference between players being ready in September versus ready in August. The problem is in September they may not be in the full training period that a player who is healthy is coming into training camp.

So, it's definitely something that we've had to deal with through the years and particularly a year like this, where a lot of players after the length of the season and what happened at the end of the season with some postseason activities and parades and this and that, sometimes it gets pushed another week, 10 days, two weeks back, which just comes up here on the other end. So, timing and the ability to get some of those things taken care of at the end of the season isn't always optimal for us relative to some other teams in the league. It's definitely a challenge.

Fortunately or unfortunately – however you want to look at it – we've had a lot of experience with it, and we've learned to work in that timeframe and trying to bring players back at the right pace for each individual player depending on what his situation is to try to have them ready and prepared physically, mentally and from a competitive standpoint in terms of reps and on-the-field experience, so we're not just throwing a guy in there cold. We talk a lot about having to manage that situation.

It's a bad problem, but it's actually a good problem to have. But, [it's] an excellent question and something that I think is a very big part of how we have to look at I'd say the first four to 10 weeks of the season – training camp, early part of September into October – there are a lot of situations that kind of fall under that umbrella somewhere along the line. And obviously this year, we have whatever it is – nine players on PUP – and we're into the second week of August. So, we still have a number of guys we're dealing with, and some guys are practicing who have been fully cleared to practice, but they're not 100 percent yet.

**Q:** When you guys are determining how much you use a player over the course of the season, do you think at all about how the player might feel at the end of December or is it all just about winning the game in that moment? How do you balance that?

**BB:** It's a balance. I think it is a balance, yeah. No, we definitely think about it and talk about it. Sometimes talk about it with a player, about what the kind of plan is. Sometimes you're able to stick to the plan that you want to have. Sometimes you have to adjust it. Sometimes you may feel like you have made the right decision and need to adjust it one way or the other, more or less depending on how it goes, depending on how your team is and depending on what the challenges are week to week. Certainly every week is not the same.

So no matter what the plan is it changes every week based on the team that you play and the circumstances surrounding that individual game – where we are, where they are and so forth. I think that's always something that's in transition or something you have to evaluate on a weekly, at least a weekly basis. But we look at it. I think we try to be aware of it. But it's hard to always get it perfectly the way you want it. Sometimes you're closer than others. Sometimes you look at the end of the season and say, 'This was about right,' or sometimes you say, 'Well, we were hoping for this, but didn't quite work out that way for whatever the reasons were.'

**Q:** What's the balance you have to strike as a coaching staff between acquiring a new player like Ayers and trying to make adjustments in what you're doing when you lose players to injury?

**BB:** That's the NFL. That's the way it is every week usually somewhere along the line, some positions, some situation. That's something you deal with weekly. Look at every team we've played – they've had something. Look at us – we've had something to deal with every week. I'd say that's the National Football League.

**Q:** You said that's the way the NFL is. When injuries happen, do you feel like it aggravates you when your guys get injured or is it more, 'Geez, we can't get a break?'

**BB:** I think you just do the best you can with whatever the situation is. That's the way it is every day. We deal with that in training camp. You don't ever have every player out there in training camp either. You still have to try to have productive practices. Get the players who are out there practicing to have the most productive day that they can have, whatever that consists of. It's week to week. Like I said, it's the National Football League. We're not talking about some breaking story here, are we? It's been like that for 40 years for me. You hate to see it happen. You hate to be without any player, there's no question about that. But every week there's something like that that you have to deal with. I can't think of too many where it wasn't like that.

**Q:** When you go into a game where you know the weather could be a big factor and could be a factor in terms of sapping energy and fatigue, do you acknowledge this with the players going in or do you not want to put it in their minds. If you do or have done some things, what did you try to concentrate on in July and August to get these guys ready for South Florida?

**BB:** First of all, the game has been on the schedule for quite a while so it's no secret that we're opening in Miami in September. Every player has been aware of that for months. We've had some hot days here at the beginning of the season. I think you can get a hot day pretty much anywhere. It really comes back to the conditioning of your team. Whether it's hot or not, it's the same for both teams and the player's conditioning level and his ability to perform at a high level is going to be reflected later in the game based on his physical conditioning.

I think you always want your team to be in good physical condition regardless of where the game is and certainly in the early part of the season or I would say in any dome game at any time of year. Those are obvious situations that are going to be challenging. They're the same for both teams. We played down there opening night a couple years ago [2011], it was a night game but it was still a hot, humid night. I think that we've been down there every year. We know what it is. I think it will just come down to what kind of condition the team is in. that comes from the practices, the preseason games and the conditions that we've worked in. I think this week is a good week for the guys to at least get used to it. I would say, look, it's always hard to play down there.

They have a good football team. That's the number one thing. It was hard to play them up here too. Personally, I would rather play in a warm climate at the beginning of the year than at the end of the year because at least we've been practicing in it. Likewise, when the teams come from the south in December and play up here, it's probably a lot harder than coming up here and playing in October. In the end, we're playing the Dolphins. I don't think this game is going to be decided on the heat or the weather. Just like I don't think the ones at the end of the year are decided by the cold. It's a little bit of a factor in the game but we're playing a good football team. If we play well, we'll be competitive and we'll have a chance. If we don't play well, it won't make a difference what the conditions are, we'll be in a lot of trouble. That's where most of the emphasis is going to be this week, and where it should be.

## Q: How can you tell if a player can be motivated or will respond to your coaching?

**BB:** When we evaluate players, it's a long, thorough process we go through. Obviously it's very inexact. We've been right on players, we're been wrong on players, just like every other team, every other coach, and every other personnel person has. So we do the best we can. It's a long process that involves visiting the school, interviewing with the player, talk with the people who have had the most involvement with him, like his coaches, college coaches, high school coaches, even beyond that. Other people that have had associations with him, former teammates, so forth and so on.

It's a mosaic composed of a lot of different pieces and you try to fit them all together and put some type of evaluation on the player. You do that for all the players. Each one is different. Each one is unique. But at the same time you have to have some type of system that accounts for what you feel the player's value is to your football team. That's what it's all about.

**Q:** A lot of times when you win, people will say 'Coach Belichick made the move that won this game for this team.' In this case, do you feel like you were outcoached and they were better prepared? When is the last time you've ever felt like that?

**BB:** Well, first of all, teams win games. Individuals don't win them – teams win them. Look, I feel after every game, I go back and look at the game and I feel like there are things I could have done better, whether it was on the preparation, adjustment end, decision-making end, all those things. When you compete in a game and have 160, 170, 180, 190 plays, however many plays are in the game and you look at the preparation on those things, there are always things you look at and you can do better.

There's never been a game that I've felt like everything went perfectly. There are always things that you feel like you can do better. I feel that way today, I felt that way last Sunday after the Indianapolis game, I felt that way after the Buffalo game. I felt like that after every game that I've ever coached in the National Football League. I can't imagine it would be any different.

**Q:** When you were flying back, how much did you dwell on the things you could have done better? Did you ever feel hamstrung by injuries while making adjustments?

**BB:** Look, in every game – as a coach and a player – I think you try to make the best decisions you can. Whatever the results are, they are. But I think at the time you make those decisions, as a coach you're doing what you think is best, as a player you're doing what you think is best. It doesn't always work out. When you look back on it, you can say, 'Well, should I have done that?' Well, maybe not, but at the time you did it, you did it with the intent to do the best thing or the right thing.

If you feel like you make a mistake on that after you analyzed it – which again, nobody makes more mistakes around here than I do, I'll be the first to admit that – that you look back on them and you say, 'OK, what could I have done differently? What will I do the next time?' and you put that in the bank. Hopefully [when] that situation comes around the next time, you'll feel better about the decision you make. There are a lot of decisions that could go either way. Sometimes you bat them back and forth and say, 'Hey, I think I'll do the same thing again,' but at least in your mind you've gone through the process and you've done that.

We've done that. That's one of the things we did in the bye week prior to the Indianapolis game. We went through a ton of situations and talked about what we would do, what our strategy way, what kind of call we'd make, what coaching points we'd give the players, what would be our best option in those situations regardless of who the opponent was or maybe against a specific opponent that was a team that a team that liked to pressure in those situations or liked to cover or whatever their tendencies were offensively, just in generic terms. That's something that as a coaching staff we try to stay on top of and I personally try to stay on top of all the way through the year. But there are always things you can do better.

**Q: When you evaluate potential changes to your scheme, do you have to establish that scheme first before you identify players to fit that scheme or is it fluid?**

**BB:** Well, yeah, I think it's fluid. They all go together. Again, we've talked about some of those things all through the year. It's not

## message it's not acceptable but you also don't want to hurt the team?

**BB:** I'd say absolutely. I think that's the perfect way to put it actually. That's the balance they're trying to strike. I think that's true probably every day of the football season, let's put it that way. Every day of the football season, including OTAs, including training camp. Everybody has to understand that there's a below the line level. When it's below the line, we can't live with it. It hurts the team. Now, we're all going to make mistakes and nobody makes more of them than I do. I understand that mistakes are part of the game. I've been in it long enough to know there's no perfect player, no perfect game or practice.

If you go out there and compete against high level competition, that they're going to make some plays too. But there's a below the line and we just can't live with that and expect to win. That's the bottom line. Things are going to happen that are below the line that we have to correct but we have to stay above the line. It's as simple as that. That line is drawn at every position with various criteria that apply to those players at those positions. It's not scientific, there's no textbook on it, on how to handle each situation. Those are decisions you have to make on a daily basis and ultimately on a weekly basis and ultimately on your decisions to keep or not keep certain players. Things like that come into play. How each decision gets made, that's a whole other discussion. That's a critical part, I think, of coaching in any sport, particularly football but any sport.

**Q:** Is it a huge challenge for a coach to set that line? I remember Jimmy Johnson saying, 'If Troy Aikman walks into the meeting late, I'm not cutting him.'

**BB:** I think what Jimmy is referring to, and I certainly would agree with that, is that there are different levels and players earn different levels of status, if you will, on the team. I mean, everybody on the team has the same status to a certain degree but we all know it's not quite the same for everybody. That being said, I think that there's a certain way to deal with different players on the team. But as far as below the line, or above the line, I don't think there's really too much doubt about that. Whatever the position is, if you're playing defensive back, you can't have the ball thrown over your head for an 80-yard touchdown. It's not acceptable. I don't care if the guy is a Hall of Fame player or if he's a rookie free agent in his first practice. We can't play like that. We can't throw a pass into a team meeting where there's four defenders there and try to jam the ball in there and get it picked off when they have four guys standing there. It's unacceptable. We can't win doing that. I don't care who the quarterback is. It doesn't make any difference. We can't jump offside and false start and be in first-and-15s and first-and-fives and let them convert third downs and third-and-fours because we jump offside. You can't play like that. It doesn't matter who the player is, it's still below the line.

We just can't play like that and expect to win with those kind of mistakes. Now, is that going to happen? Yeah, it's going to happen, sure. I understand that. But if it happens too often, we can't play like that. And there's going to be a new coach up here too if it happens too often. I know that too. The things that cause you to lose, you have to eliminate. Before you can win, you can't lose. When you do things as a coach or as a player that cause you to lose, then you won't be in this job long.

**Q:** How does a guy get above that line?

**BB:** By performing. You go out there and perform. You don't drop below the line. Take Ozzie Newsome. There's a good example right there. When Ozzie was a rookie, he played 13 years, when he was rookie, he fumbled, lost the ball, team lost the game. Never fumbled again the rest of his career. Never fumbled again the rest of his career – 600 and 700 [662 receptions] passes, however many passes it was, however many times he touched the ball the rest of his career, never fumbled again. Why is Ozzie Newsome in the Hall of Fame? That's why. That kind of commitment, that kind of performance.

It was important enough to him. Fumbled once, didn't fumble again the rest of his entire career. Now think about that. Want to know how a guy gets in the Hall of Fame? That's one reason. Lawrence Taylor. How many sacks did he have? How many times was he offside? Go back and look how many times he was offside. It wasn't very many. There's a guy that hit the quarterback, made as many plays defensively as any player in football, certainly any player I've ever coached but any player in football – I'd put him up against anybody in terms of big plays, hitting the quarterback, tackles beyond the line of scrimmage. I don't care what the stats are, a lot of plays that he made, that somebody else made, but he was an impact, dynamic, as disruptive a player defensively as there's probably ever been in the National Football League. How many times was he offside? Was he offside? Yeah, but he was a pretty disruptive player without doing that. I think those are examples of what I'm talking about – for all of us.

We all make mistakes, even the great ones, but they don't repeat them, they don't make very many of them, they correct it, it's important enough to them to move on and get it right. That's how you do it. You get it right.

## Q: Are there specific things you can track regarding how well your offense is playing, like completion percentage or is it just an overall eye test?

**BB:** Well, it starts with points. That's what they go out there for, is to score points. Unless sit's the end of the game where you're trying to run out the clock, all the other possessions we're going out there to score points. If we score points, then that's probably a good thing on the drive. If we don't get in the end zone, then what's the reason we didn't get in the end zone? If we don't score points, then why didn't we score points? Was it plays that created long-yardage? Was it our inability to convert on third down? Was it missed assignments? Whatever it is, we break it down from there. Scoring points is about being consistent.

You **have** to be able to string good plays together. When you have a bad play in a drive, usually hat puts you in long-yardage and that knocks you out of the drive. You could have six, seven, eight good plays but a sack, a penalty, a negative run, whatever, now you're in second-and-long, you're in third-and-long and you're giving the ball up. I'd say it's eliminating negative plays, that's a big part of it. Making sure you that you're moving the ball closer to the goal line when you snap it, that's objective number one.

Well, objective number one is not to lose it, objective number two is to move it closer to the goal line. Number three is to stay on the field and move the field into scoring position and put points on the board, so all the things that lead into that. I would say that's kind of how we look at it. All those other statistics have some relevance, I'm not saying that, but in the end, it's points. That's the same thing on defense. If you're not giving up points, then you're probably winning. If you're giving up points, you can have whatever other stats you want and I doubt you're going to get the results you want. This game is about scoring.

## Q: With so many new pieces at the skill positions, do you consider simplifying things with your scheme?

**BB:** I think you always, in everything that you do, you go in with an idea of how you want to try to do it. You start on a certain course and then as you go along, you always end up making some type of modifications in some form or fashion based on the athlete's skills, the way the group fits together and what your success or lack of it might be as you start to do the things that you do. Some things sometimes work out a little better than you think, sometimes not as good, sometimes about the same. That goes for each individual player and it goes for the entire group as to how they end up working together as well.

It's an ongoing process; we'll deal with it day by day. As we see that the course needs to be altered a little bit, then we'll do it. If I knew how it was going to turn out...we're doing it in a way that I think will be right but I know we're going to have to make adjustments. That's the way it always is. If we knew exactly what that was, we'd start there but sometimes it takes a little time or trial and error to get there and I think that's where we're at.

**Q:** Have there been cases in the past when you had a new group –

**BB:** We have that every year.

**Q:** Has there been a case in the past where simplifying it was better?

**BB:** I don't think that necessarily has anything to do with experience but it could. But yeah, there are times where you take things and water it down a little bit. There are other times where you expand more than where you think you're going to be or faster than you think you're going to be able to. You never know exactly. You have an idea of it, but you never know exactly how it's going to go. Sometimes it goes in stages, sometimes it starts slow and then picks up speed.

Sometimes it starts at a level and then kind of fizzles out. That's part of what training camp is for, is to put a lot of training camp practice days out there together, get a lot of snaps, get a lot of reps, have a volume of evaluation and then be able to, from that volume, figure out what the best course is. That's, until you go through it all, I don't think you can really make the same type of intelligent decision that you can just trying to guesstimate how it's going to happen. There are too many variables.

**Q: How do you manage the line between looking back on yesterday and finding what you need to get better on but not getting too caught up in one game because there is another one coming around the corner just six days away?**

**BB:** That's the way it is every week. We take the same approach every week. We look at the good things, try to build on those, correct mistakes, see our errors – coaching errors, playing errors, communication errors, whatever it happens to be – and try to address those and correct them and move forward. Then start to prepare for the new team that we face on the schedule, take into account what things would carry over and apply them to the next game, which there are always some that will and some things are probably more unique or specific to the team that we played and may not have as much application to the new team for whatever reason and then the new challenges that come with a new team and try to bridge those together.

It's really a continuous cycle there. Some of the situations that we talk about every week will eventually resurface at some point, it may not be the following week, [but] at some point along the line, those certain situations will show themselves again somehow. So hopefully we can learn from them, put them in the bank and when it comes up again, be able to refer back to it. On a weekly basis, it's a combination of rolling the old into the new and continuing to build our overall awareness.

Of course, our execution of whatever it is that we're doing in that situation, to build the higher level of execution, whatever the play happens to be because in the end that's what it always comes down to, is how well you can do whatever it is you happen to have called. It's really the same every week. It's that balance. Whenever you lose though, those plays and those situations probably hang with you just a little bit longer than when you win but it's still the same process.

**Q: We have seen you guys take a couple shot plays with Brandon Lloyd the first two games. I am sure you guys practice that all the time in practice. Are those the types of plays that you can practice it all the time with reps but are those the plays that are going to be different during the game because of adrenaline and all that?**

**BB:** I think, really just about every play is different in the game. You try to simulate it in practice but it's just different in the game. I think the big thing for the quarterback and the receivers is just to be able to take advantage of those opportunities. You call plenty of them, I won't say every play but there are an awful lot of plays have guys running deep – post patterns, flag patterns, go-routes, whatever it is – you don't throw them on every play but they're there on every play depending on what the coverage is and what the matchup is. If the quarterback sees it and the receiver runs a good route then that's a good option.

If the coverage takes that part of it away or they roll into that or whatever it is, then the quarterback reads the rest of his progressions. Sometimes you can play the percentages and think that, 'OK, there's a pretty good chance that we're going to get this pattern on this coverage' or if you run that pattern on this coverage, sooner or later you're going to get the coverage you're look for and you're going to take a shot at it. But there's also plenty of times that we go out in practice and run plays and then we get in the game and we see something and it takes us to that and maybe we've practiced it and maybe we haven't. When you think about it, say you run 100 plays during the week in practice – 35, 35 and 30 or whatever it is – and then you have goal-line plays and you have a lot of other plays that are situational plays in there and then you think of all the different coverages a defense can play – on third down, on second down, on first down, in the red area.

I understand they're only out there 60 plays too, but you've seen on film, you've seen on film, you've seen them play six, seven different sub coverages, a couple different blitzes, six, seven regular coverages, three, four, five blitzes on that. You go into the game with whatever number plays you have; the variables are just exponential. It's just so difficult to really match up something unless you really have a real strong tendency that they're going to do this when you give them a certain look or certain situation. I'd say that's maybe 10 percent of the time. It's not a high probability. You go out there and run your plays.

You can't run them against all 10 different coverages that you could get in that situation; you run them against the ones you think are most likely or maybe what their tendency is or maybe what you think they'll do to you. But a lot of times it doesn't turn out that way and you have to adjust to it. I'd say that's kind of the challenging part, like your question about practice and all that, as opposed to college where you have the scout team go out there, you have the freshmen and you run maybe 60 plays in practice, 70 plays in practice. Well, we're running half that. The amount of execution you get is different. That's why training camp is important, building that base, building that consistency when you're going out there day after day and running 60, 70 plays in practice, against your defense so the number is higher, you're not running them, splitting them in half, you're getting plays on both sides of the ball that those reps are really important to build technique and consistency and timing, understanding the plays and all that. It's definitely different in the game, there's no question.

**Q:** You mentioned a lot of moving parts. Is there a fine line between giving a guy who is joining your roster right before the first game too much and overwhelming him?

**BB:** That's definitely a concern. I think you want to err on the side of not overloading him because then that could not work out well. You probably would limit his role to what you feel confident that he can do and then build into something else the following week or whenever you think the player is ready.

I think that's definitely and concern and it's something that you have to manage. At the same time, I think it's more important to get your roster set now in the best possible way you can get it, whatever that is, going forward over a 16-game regular season schedule then to be short-sighted about one game and then cost yourself or your team the opportunity to have a stronger roster through the remaining 15 games. Everybody wants to win the first game but it's a long season and there are a lot of games after this one.

There are considerations this week, there are considerations for next week, there are considerations for the entire 16-game season. There's some balance that you're always trying to find there. Where is that sweet spot? I don't know. Sometimes you're not as good now as you are later; sometimes you're better now than you are later. I think you want to try to give yourself an opportunity to develop and improve and grow as a team and don't put a roadblock in front of it that this is the high water mark and everything is downhill after that. I don't think you want to position your team like that, at least I don't, I don't like that.

## Q: Have you had any talk of going to an iPad playbook? I know several teams have done it.

**BB:** There's so much technology out there, you could go to whatever you want. I'm sure we have enough technological equipment in here to put the whole team on the moon.

**Q:** So you like sticking with the binders?

**BB:** In the end, it comes down to - you're at all the games - it comes down to blocking and tackling and running and throwing and catching and kicking and solid fundamentals and all that. You could put the iPad on the super-duper wizard computer and whatever you want. You could throw all that crap on there and I'm sure it would come out great. I'm sure you could get some statistical analysis that would provide 28 theses for MIT. In the end, you have to go out there and play football. Personally, I wouldn't lose too much sight of that.

Same thing in baseball. Tony [La Russa] and I, we've have talked about that a lot too. You have to throw the ball, you have to hit it, you have to catch it, you have to field it, you have to run the bases. You could go out there and talk about some guy's batting average when the count is 2-1 at night. I mean, sooner or later, you have to go out there and play. I think you have to keep sight of that. As you know, I'm not the most technological person in this organization. I rely on some other people to try to help, like you said, streamline things or find a way where we can do things a little bit more efficiently. I understand that the people coming into the organization, that's what they were brought up on and that's not what I was brought up on, so I understand there's a difference there. I think there's a marriage but at the same time, I don't think that's the highest priority.

**Q:** Sterling Moore mentioned that when he got here, he was told to learn all three positions - I guess boundary, nickel and safety. Is that something you tell all young defensive backs when they get here or was it something specific to him?

**BB:** No. When you bring a player onto your team, especially during the season, you just don't want to leave it up to him as to what he should learn and what he shouldn't learn. You sit down and you specifically tell him, 'Look, this is what I want you to do. This is what you're responsible for. This is what I expect you to get in a certain period of time,' whatever that framework is. 'Here's what you're going to do. By the end of the week, I expect you'll be able to do this.' Or 'After the bye, we expect you to be able to do this,' whatever it is. It depends on the player, yeah absolutely.

One player might come in - Brian Waters. 'I want you to learn right guard and I want you to be ready to go for the Miami game. Don't worry about center. Don't worry about left guard. Don't worry about tight end. Don't worry about field goal rush.' We didn't talk about any of that. We just talked about get ready for one position for the Miami game. Bring in another player and say, 'This is what we want you to do.' It would depend on that player, it would depend on the situation that your team is in at that point, and then you would probably modify it as you go along. You'd say, 'Okay, we told you to concentrate, work on these areas, but now this week we want you to concentrate on this.'

That's actually pretty common from week-to-week too. A lot of weeks we talk to certain players about, 'This week, we really need you to work on this. This week, we really need you to concentrate in this area. This is going to be a big role for you in the game.' Or 'You're backing up so-and-so in this and this is a key thing for us. Here's something you really have to work on.' We try to do that on a regular basis, too. It's not just a onetime thing. That's with all the players, not just the new players. It could be with Kevin Faulk or Patrick Chung or whoever it is.

**Q:** Is there something physically in Sterling Moore that made you think he could go back and forth between corner and safety? You don't see too many guys do that.

**BB:** I think he has good size for a corner, probably a little undersized for a safety, so he's a little bit of a tweener there in terms of size. He played corner in college [and] he had a lot of production as a corner in college. He's also played the inside position, what we call the star position or the nickel back as you call it. We felt like, just from his overall experience, ball skills, [and] kind of the way he played, we thought that he might have some ability to play safety along the lines of, as an example, like Eugene Wilson, who we moved from corner to safety who ended up playing the majority of his career at safety in the National Football League.

There are certain players that, based on their physical skills [and] their mentality, are potential corner to safety moves. Then there are plenty of players that aren't. It would depend on the particular player. I think in Sterling's case, he's got a number of different skills that he's got some things going for him at safety, he has some things going for him at star, he's got some things going for him at corner on the perimeter. How does all that play out when you get a new player? You try him at all three spots a little bit and see how it goes.

**Q: Can you talk about carrying a third quarterback? In terms of your roster, for someone like Ryan Mallett, how do you keep him involved and prepared?**

**BB:** All of our quarterbacks pretty much go through the same game preparation in terms of meetings, film [and] game plan. They all take a certain number of reps in our walk through. The player who goes first gets the most and the player who goes second gets the second most and the third guy gets the least. And then we split those reps up also with when the offense is working for the defense and so they get their practice opportunities there and after practice they stay after and work with different receivers, tight ends, backs, whatever it is in that aspect of the passing game, timing, routes and so forth. There're plenty of throwing opportunities for all three quarterbacks.

There're only so many opportunities to actually take a snap from center in a team setting, but I think that all three guys should be able to learn, just like any other position, something about their play when the other person is doing it and they're there watching it: looking at the reads, looking at the checks or the pre-snap reads, the decision with the ball and so forth. I think that's how you develop as a player. Whether you're in there or not, you still gain that experience if you're paying attention and listening to what's going on, no matter which place you are on the depth chart.

**Q: When guys come here for the first time do you want them to watch the film from last year to see how everything was, or when they come here is it just focusing on moving forward?**

**BB:** Well anytime we install a play, put in a kickoff return, running play, blitz or something, we usually show examples of that so that the new players sort of understand how that works and that they have the general concept of the play. I think the best way to learn is to understand what all 11 people are doing. If you just try to memorize your assignment on every play then ultimately if you don't know what's going on around you, you end up making decisions that impact the players around you, and if you really had an understanding of what the whole concept was, it's probably less likely that that would happen.

So, we try to teach the concept of the play. We show the play usually in multiple examples because of different things that can happen on the play, and it refreshes the veteran players who have done the play or maybe were even in the play when it was run before. But it also serves as a visual illustration to new players as opposed to X's and O's in a diagram - 'Here's actually the play against whatever its being shown against, and this is how it works or this is one of the problems we'll have to adjust to with it and this is how we will handle it or whatever'.

Those are what we call training tapes that are shown in conjunction with the installation of our plays - that's part of the teaching tools. You show it on paper, you show examples of it on film, you go out on the field and spatially walk through the plays in the relationships and so forth. You go out there and practice it in individual drills: one on one, seven on seven, nine on seven - whatever the drills are, and then ultimately you bring it together in a team drill, and that's kind of the teaching progression no matter how you're - whatever you're doing. So, that's part of it. Do we look at last year or some other year? I mean, we've shown films from '03, '04, 2000. There are plays, there are situations that came up then that maybe haven't come up since, but they're still good teaching plays.

**Q:** Going back to the event here today, were you ever fortunate enough to play in a high school championship game?

**BB:** No, nope. Our games, the seasons ended when the season ended - there were no playoffs. You played for your league title and all that but there were no playoffs in football, kind of like the old college system, sort of.

**Q:** Can you imagine how these kids are feeling playing out there on the Gillette Stadium field?

**BB:** Oh, yeah, absolutely. I was at the Rivers-Pingree game here a couple of weeks ago for the private schools, and it was awesome. It was a great environment. I'm sure it was a big thrill for, like I said, everybody involved. It was an awesome experience. I know people at both schools and talked to a lot of them and they were very appreciative of the Krafts for letting them use the facility for that game and how much it meant to everybody involved. It was a huge game anyway, but sure, to be able to play here, it makes it even [more] special for them.

We all know that, really, the backbone of our game is high school football. Without high school football, you don't have college football and you don't have professional football. I'll just say that, through the years, of all the kids that we talk to in the draft, in Indianapolis, visits and all that, whenever you ask a kid who had the most influence on them as a person and in his life, it's usually one of two people: it's either some family member - a parent or some other family member - or his high school coach. It's usually one of those two. I know how important high school coaches are to the development of young student athletes at that point in their life and how it really formulates a lot of your life lessons that you need to learn. You learn them on the football field. You get down, you learn how to get up. You learn how to compete. You learn how to mentally deal with things that aren't the most pleasant: losses or injuries or whatever setbacks you have. You learn how to deal with those things at that age and those are all things that we have to deal with later on in life.

It's a great environment to participate as a team and have that camaraderie and chemistry as a group of people all trying to accomplish the same goal. It's a great venue for young kids that want to grow up and become men. It's part of the steps that some of us have been fortunate to take. But the only playoff games that I've really participated in were in college, in lacrosse, which, again, there is just something about being in a playoff game - it is just different than a regular-season game.

Of course I've had the opportunity here, but not as a player. As a player, you definitely remember those games. You remember the shots that you missed. I was talking about it with Paul Rabil about it a couple of weeks ago after the Indianapolis game. We were out there on the field playing catch and one of the things he talked about was the last shot he took as a college lacrosse player in the Syracuse game. How he shot it low, and they saved it, and maybe he should have taken a different shot. Those are things... You remember those games; they're special.

**Q:** What makes Dante such an effective coach?

**BB:** He's got a lot of experience. Dante does a good job with details, a lot of fine coaching points, fundamentals. He really teaches the guys how to block from step one and how to handle all the different schemes that we have and also that we have to see from other teams. Players work hard [and] they work together. The offensive line is really a combination of the coach and all the players and the quarterback seeing the same thing at the same time. That's not easy to do, but that's what it takes. You can't really operate independently on the offensive line.

You have to know what the guy beside you is doing and all five of you have to block the five players that you're accountable for, whatever the play is: run or pass. All the different looks and all the different things that can happen out there, all five of those guys have to see it the same way. And sometimes that works with the backs and certain protections or the tight ends, but certainly those five have to be on the same page and Dante does a good job preparing them and getting them to that point, whether it be [in] meetings, walk throughs, practice film or so forth.

### Q: Can you contrast the difference in preparing between the defensive systems of Pittsburgh and Indianapolis?

**BB:** Well, I think both teams, defensively, have a system that they believe in and they follow that system. I think they both have a lot of variables within the system that they can use to keep you off balance. I don't see a lot of, from either team, 10 new defenses every week. That's not really what they do. They take their playbook and they use the things that they feel like are best against that particular opponent and if something happens during the game that they need to adjust to, they make some adjustments.

It's a different scheme, but I think the overall philosophy is actually pretty similar. It's just one's a three-four team, the other is a four-three team, one's a zone-blitz team, the other is more of a combination of zones, zone-blitz and man-to-man. Not that the Steelers don't play man, they do play some, but the Colts play a different type of man-to-man. Both teams create a lot of turnovers. I think the philosophies are similar, but I think the schemes and the techniques are drastically different.

### Q: Speaking of taking ideas from other coaches, when you first

### decided that you wanted to pursue coaching, did you ever find yourself looking at other guys and taking ideas?

**BB:** Sure. I grew up in a coaching family and I had a great opportunity as a kid to see... you know, Navy had some very good football teams in the early 60s and some not so good [teams] after that, but there were a lot of great coaches that came through there. In addition to that, my dad ran a football camp in the summer for three weeks, the Chesapeake Football Camp, and he invited other coaches - not just the Navy coaches, but coaches at Maryland, Penn State, Pittsburgh, Virginia, in that area - to come to the camp.

So I not only knew a lot of the Navy coaches or got to observe them or watch them in practices and meetings and so forth in my dad's football camp, [but it] was a great opportunity to see a lot of coaches coach. Everybody had their own different style and you look at some coaches and you see strengths or weaknesses or different methods of doing the same thing - sometimes equally as effective, but totally different - as opposed to just being locked into one coach.

I guess I was fortunate - well, it was interesting, because when I was in high school, we had a real good high school program with Coach [Al] Laramore, who was a legendary Maryland coach and Hall of Fame coach and all that, and we had four plays. Literally, we had four plays - that's it. We had the same punt return. We had the same kickoff return. I mean, there were two defenses: split-six and gap-six. So I mean, you could put in the whole thing in, I'd say, 10 minutes - literally, 10 minutes.

And then, when I went to [Phillips] Andover, we had really a great team there; we were 8-0 and New England Champions and all that. We had a bunch of plays and the quarterback called his own plays, and there was structure, but it was a totally different structure, which was the way it was with [Coach Ted] Marchibroda in Baltimore. Bert Jones was a young quarterback and Bert called his own plays. Today, I think that would be pretty much unheard of. It would be the most critical situation in the game, it would be third-and-two, and there would be a timeout, Bert would come over to the sideline and I'd stand over there with Ted, Bert, and Whitey Dovell, the line coach, and kind of listen in on the conversation and Ted would say, 'Well, we got 36-bob, we got 24-hunch, we got a pass-136 y-flag and we got the boot.' And it was just, 'Whatever you feel good about Bert,' and he'd go back out on the field and everybody was looking at him like, 'Alright, well, what are we going to call?' 'Well, I don't know, whatever Bert calls - that's what'll be.'

So there are a lot of different ways to do it, that's the bottom line. I think you learn something ... I've learned something from every player I've coached; I think I've learned something from every coach that I've had an opportunity to observe or coach with and I'm sure that's true in reverse.

**Q:** Who do you look at now to exchange ideas with? Are there any younger coaches?

**BB:** You talk to a lot of people. It depends on what kind of information you're looking for. If it's another team or someone that's familiar with that team or a player and they're familiar with that player, that's one thing. And if they're not, or it's something that - I won't say they can't help you with - but they're not as familiar with as somebody else, then, [it's] just like you. Who do you ask the questions to? Somebody to give you the answers you're looking for. So, it's kind of the same thing - it depends on what you're after.

**Q:** Are you still refining practice schedules and techniques and drills?

**BB:** You do that all the time. Absolutely, we do it all the time. That's one of the great things about going out in spring, going to talk to Coach [Nick] Saban or Coach [Urban] Meyer, wherever the travels take you to - Will Muschamp at Texas, you can just go right down the line - Al [Groh] when he was at Virginia - whatever it happens to be, and see how they do things; see how they break up practice.

Like before the Atlanta [preseason game], going over to Georgia Tech with Coach [Paul] Johnson and just actually watching a practice. I mean, how many practices do I get to watch, other than my own? Maybe one, two a year - that'd be a lot. It is just interesting to watch somebody else run their practice, how they set up the drills, how they break it down time-wise, [and] different things like that. So, that's good. A lot of times you talk to people about that and say, 'Hey, how do you handle this? How do you handle that?' And they tell you, but a lot of times you don't actually get to see it, so I think there's a lot of value in that. So it is interesting, but I think it's an ongoing process.

You are always looking for better ways to do things and [figure out] how you can best teach and instruct your players and team most efficiently, and we are always striving to improve that. We talk about it every year. I mean, we talk about it multiple times during the year, too. We talk about it every year - what's our meeting time? How do we break that up? What's our practice time? How do we break that up? What's our walk-through time? When do we watch film? How do we do that? How can we do it better? Should we do it more together? Should we do it in different groups? Should we change the structure of the groups? How much should players watch by themselves? How much should they watch with the coach? How much should they, you know, all those different kinds of things. And maybe it's not the same for the receivers as it is for the linebackers or whatever. But that's a continuous self-evaluation that you do as a team to try and find the best way to do things.

**Q: What is it about Scott O'Brien's approach to special teams that allows him to get the most out of his guys, especially with his history, the success of the second year in leading the special teams group?**

**BB:** Well my relationship with Scott goes back a long way, back to '91; it's almost been 20 years. I have a tremendous amount of respect for him as a football coach, period, but very good in the special teams area as well. I think he does a great job of coaching football players in whatever the capacity is. I think anytime that you're with a group of players for a year you just have a better understanding of their strengths, their weaknesses, and how different combinations work together and just what can work good with that particular group of players. There are always new players involved that there are some key guys to work around.

I think he's [done] a real good job of putting guys in spots going back early into training camp, letting them work together, letting them progress, and grow and teach them the things that they need to do, their keys and techniques and so forth at those spots. And then we have production in preseason in our different phases of the kicking game, and we continue to have it. We've also had some breakdowns, but I think it's always easier the second year to have a little better feel for individuals and their aptitude and capacity and their skill set. He does a very good job of not only evaluating our opponents, but more importantly, evaluating the players that are on this team and putting them in good positions and getting the most out of them. The players work hard to make that happen. It's a good situation.

**Q:** With installing so many plays in training camp, do you ever have to worry about the players' ability to retain it all?

**BB:** Absolutely. That's all we worry about. That's what training camp - that's what coaching is in training camp, is trying to give the players the right amount of information. You don't want to not move ahead, but at the same time, you don't want to move ahead too quickly, where you then have to go back and do it over again.

It's kind of like building a house. You cut some corners, and then you don't have the walls put up properly and then the sheet rock doesn't go on right and then you have to go back and fix it up and everything. That's not the way to do it. You want to get it in right, but at the same time, we're on a time schedule, too; we don't have forever. We have a preseason game in two weeks and we open the season against Cincinnati, so we have a schedule where we have to have everything ready by [then], to some degree. You try to manage those two things, but you don't want to move at a pace that's... and at the same time, everybody on your team isn't at the same place. You have some players who are much more experienced and are further ahead than others, so you try to find that balance and that's really what coaching is. Sometimes some groups can move faster than others on your team and so as a head coach and as a coordinator, you have to talk about those things and try to figure out what the best thing is for the team. And that might not be the best thing for each individual player, but again, that's what football is. It's a team sport and we all have to give up some individual preferences when we sign up for the team. That's part of it, too.

### Q: How much of your evaluation process involves getting away and not thinking about football?

**BB:** I think it's good to go from a clean slate. Again, and I've been through this so many times, but you sit here today and what do you remember? You remember yesterday's game. You remember the Houston game. You remember the Jacksonville game. But you kind of forget - and it's not as fresh in your mind - some of the earlier games in the season and the first half of the season or the first 10 games of the season. [I'm] not saying we don't remember anything from those games, but you certainly don't remember the details of them like you do the last couple. And I'm not minimizing the last couple games, certainly the Baltimore game is an important game in our evaluation process because there was so much at stake and clearly it was the best effort from both teams, there was nothing else to play for but that game.

But, on the other hand, you can look at an entire body of work and see something that was relatively good over a longer period of time and then something that wasn't good over a shorter period of time. And I don't know if the best thing is always to say, 'Well let's get rid of that because it wasn't good yesterday' when over a longer period it was probably one of the more productive things you did or what you feel like was a strength of your team. That's a balance.

I don't know what the answer to that question is, but I think that's why I would say it takes a little time to sort of back off and then come back and recalibrate and look at the shorter term, look at the longer picture. Sometimes you make comparisons to other years just as a relative basis, your overall production in a certain area over the last couple years. Why it was at one place at one time and another place another time? What were the factors that went into that? And so forth. But do I think it's good to step back a little bit and just let the dust settle? Absolutely, I think that's important. [It's] not always possible. Sometimes situations come up that you have to address that are timely and you've just got to deal with them.

## Q: Given the fact that there are a lot of young guys on your team, how much do you think you can expand what they are doing?

**BB:** I think each week there's something that's a little bit new in preparing for the opponent that's a little bit different from last week, or a little bit different than something we've done. [We're] not trying to reinvent the defensive system - I'm not saying that - but you add a call or you add an adjustment or you do something to take care of a problem that they're giving you, whether they're giving you a lot of it, or maybe they're not giving you that much of it, but just when it comes up, here's how you want to handle it. Those accumulate through the year and for young players that's part of the process. It's not just learning the stuff at training camp, but learning the adjustments and the additions throughout the year. Some of those you might come back to you when that situation from earlier in the season presents itself again.

You might come back to that, so that kind of experience is good for them. So do we keep doing more? Yeah, we do, because we have to defend more. To be honest with you, we have to defend more from the offense. You look at any team in the league right now after seven, eight, nine games [and] they're doing more than they were doing in week two, and we're doing more than we were doing. The multiples add up.

**Q:** Is it an issue, too, of prioritizing and saying, 'This is what you have to know'?

**BB:** Yeah. That's always an issue. You always want to prioritize what's important, because by the end of the week we're sitting here on Friday or Saturday and every player has been told 1,000 things: 'Do this,' 'Do that,' 'When this happens, do this,' 'When that happens, do that,' 'If they do this, you're going to check to that,' ' this guy,' ' that guy.' He's got 1,000 things in his mind and I think it's important to boil it back down to, 'OK, those are all techniques and they're all adjustments and they're things we need to do, but what do we need to do to win this game? Let's make sure we've got first things first.' Because somewhere between those 1,000 things, there's one and then there's 1,000. There's got to be some kind of priority, so I think every time you come to the end of the week, you want to bring it back to what are the most important things to do as a team and at each position, whether it's tight ends, 'Here are the three most important things for you to do this week.' For the corners, 'Here are the three most important things for you.' That type of thing, so that you don't lose sight of the big picture and so you don't take a chance on players not knowing what the most important things are and making those decision themselves. You remind them that this is how the game is played. This is what your role is. This is what your job is. First things first.

**Q:** When does that final distillation happen?

**BB:** Today and tomorrow. Friday is certainly a coming together time and Saturday a lot of times is just a further coming together or further solidifying. Maybe we put some things on the back burner. 'We've got this if we need it.' 'We've got that if we need it.' 'If this situation comes up, this is how we're going to handle it, but this is where we're going to go with. Here's how we're going to play the game.' Now if we have to adjust it, we adjust it. Because again, when you go through all of that in the beginning of the week, the players don't really know - and sometimes the coaches don't know for sure either - exactly how it's going to unfold.

Again, I think to just identify and get everybody on the same page - 'Ok here's how we're going to start, so let's don't get confused with this other stuff. If we need it, we'll come to it, but that's not what we're going to lead with.' So then the players can really zero in on, 'Ok, these calls, these adjustments...if this is called and that happens, here's what we're going to do. There's another play were that might happen, but that play is 40 plays down the road. That's not what we're thinking about right away.'

**(on what the day before a Super Bowl is typically like and if he likes to use any sort of motivational tactics like a speaker or a video)**

"Well, again, I think each game's different, each team's different, each situation's different. So whatever we feel is best for that particular game and situation is what we'll try to do. It could be any of the above or none. Just depending on the circumstances and situations and timing and maybe what we feel like is the most beneficial. The day before the game is kind of as much as we can make it a normal day before the game.

We've done that for the entire season and I don't think that this game would be the time to all of a sudden come up with some new, creative, innovative schedule. We're all creatures of habit, we have a routine, we know where – I think coaches, players all know where we need to be Saturday morning in our preparations, Saturday afternoon in our preparations, Saturday night in our preparation, Sunday morning in our preparation. So we always try to take the time of the game and work backwards so that in the days leading up to the game, our pattern is as consistent as it can possibly be on the road, at home, wherever the game is.

Obviously there's differences, there's changes, but we try to make them as consistent as possible so that our players, our team, our staff can get a routine and we can be as productive as we can and not be worried or thinking about, 'Is it this? Is it that?' We know where we should be and we hopefully try to be there."

**Q: I know there is no right or wrong to this stuff, but in regard to**

**hitting in camp, how does a coach know when to take his foot off the pedal and is there a point where you feel like it's a risk to have guys out there in pads hitting?**

**BB:** I think as a coach you do what you feel is best for your football team in every area, whether that's practicing in pads, conditioning, not conditioning, meeting longer or meeting shorter. Whatever it is, you do what's best for your team and there's a balance on that. I think you try to practice in the right way to minimize risk and minimize potential for injuries, but inevitably they're about to happen even if you take all the precautions in the world. I don't think we can just sit around and talk about it all year, here's what we're going to do and sit down, hold hands, chant and talk about what we're going to do.

Somewhere along the line, you got to get out there and perform it on the field and somewhere along the line you've got to perform it in practice to have a chance to perform it in a game situation. It's pretty unlikely that if you can't do it on a practice field that all of a sudden, magically everything will crystallize and you'll have a lot of perfect plays run in game situations. I just don't think that's realistic. You know, get out there and run them in practice. I think it's hard to expect those kind of results to happen in games. With that being said though, a wall of diminishing returns and there's a point where you've got to balance with what you're doing and who you're doing it against.

Sometimes less can be more, so I don't think there's any good right or wrong answer. I don't think there's any specific criteria. I think as a coach you have a feel for your team and your staff has a feel for their individual groups of players, which that's important to me, too, how they feel about their specific player or groups and that's not always in balance. Sometimes one group is under a little more stress than another based on numbers or the practice schedule or what you're asking them to do. You try to balance all those things and do what's best for the team.

**Q:** Yesterday Dont'a Hightower talked about Patrick Graham and his cerebral approach as a coach. What is it about Patrick's personality and approach that helps develop players?

**BB:** Pat's a very hardworking guy. He's had different responsibilities on our staff: the line and linebackers and other responsibilities as it relates to situation presentations or part of the scouting report, that kind of thing. He's pretty well versed in the game and a really smart guy. [He] can comprehend and process a lot of information. Again, [he] has a lot of experience at multiple positions, so [he] can tie it all together, knows what other guys are doing [and] how it all fits together. He works hard. He's bright, he's on top of things and he's a very demanding coach.

**Q:** Is that more than coincidence that he would have experience at multiple positions? When you hire a coach, do you want him to have experience at multiple positions?

**BB:** Not necessarily, but I don't think it's ever a bad thing, but not necessarily. Some guys coach the same position for a length of time. Other guys are shuffled around: been on offense to defense. Matt [Patricia] was on offense, now he's on defense. Josh and Brian Daboll were both on defense and on offense. Josh Boyer came in, was on defense and has pretty much been on the same side of the ball, same kind of location. Brian Flores was in scouting and has worked in the kicking game and defense. I don't there's any locked-in formula.

**Q:** Can you think of any coaches who have advanced very quickly as an assistant on one side of the ball and then maybe got to a coordinator position or they were say a linebackers coach for 10 years and then transitioned to the other side of the ball successfully?

**BB:** [Raises hand] First year, I was on defense and special teams at Baltimore, coached the tight ends and special teams in Detroit, coached the receivers and special teams in Detroit – Floyd [Reese] was the special teams coach, but I helped in those areas. [I] went back to the defense in Denver and worked with special teams. [I was] special teams coach at the Giants, [then] coached the outside linebackers, [became] defensive coordinator. Josh [McDaniels] was in the scouting department, broke down film on defense, replaced [Brian] Daboll as the film breakdown guy then shifted over coached the quarterbacks the last year Charlie [Weis] was here in '04 – helped Charlie with the quarterbacks I should say.

[Josh] took over the quarterbacks in '05, became the coordinator. That's not very many years – five years, six years, whatever it is. Yeah, I'm sure there's – I don't know everybody's professional line of progression, but I think there's plenty of them in our organization. Matt [Patricia] came in, broke down film on offense, helped Dante [Scarnecchia] with the offensive line, shifted to defense, he's worked with all three units; coordinator. So, yeah.

**Q:** How much can you see or judge from a coach or someone potentially getting into the NFL about their ability to break down film and see things?

**BB:** It definitely helps. It's a big part of it. Certainly the on the field interaction with the players – teaching, motivation, on the field coaching – that's a big part of it too. Game management, game decisions, adjustments, seeing things during games, it's all important. It's a different skill, a different tool. The better you can be at any of them or all of them, the more value you create for yourself and for your team. I think it's something that as a young coach, you're always trying to improve on. Even as an experienced coach, you're always trying to improve on that too. So, yeah, it's one of many tools – an important one.

### Q: Do the nerves play into the excitement level?

**BB:** I think there's an anxiousness whenever you play. You always have that unknown of going up against a new opponent. Who knows how the game will go – what they'll do, how things will match up, what adjustments you'll have to make and how the game will unfold. There will be different beaks or situations in the game that will make each game unique. That makes it exciting. There's no way to predict how all that's going to happen, you just take it as it comes. You never know how it's going to go.

You're always, there's always certain elements that [are] a guessing game or playing percentages, however you want to call it. This is what we're going to do, what we think we're going to get. This is how we think it's going to work out. It never quite goes that way. As a coach, you want to try to put your team in the best position you can so they can be competitive. As players, it's the same thing.

It's like when you talk to the Navy SEALs and those guys about when they go on a mission, how they talk about, 'Alright, so we get there and we practiced going over a six-foot wall and the wall is 30-feet high.' Well, that's the way it is in the NFL. You practice for whatever – you think you're going to swim across a 200-yard lake and the lake is 800 yards across. You have to get across it. You get in an NFL game and think you're going to get this and then you get that. Or you think they're going to play this guy and they play some other guy. You face new challenges. That's part of gamesmanship and part of the competition. You figure out which team can do it better than the other one.

There's always that unknown in the game, but things happen that you just can't predict or you can't prepare for because they're working on things; we don't know what they're doing. They'll come up with something that will cause us to make an adjustment. I'm sure we'll do the same thing to them somewhere along the line. Everybody has to figure it out and make the best of it. That's what makes this a great game.

**Q:** What about the butterflies in the stomach?

**BB:** I think you have that anxiety going into the game and when the ball is kicked off then you're just in game mode. All the things you think about of what could happen and what you want to call, what you want to do, what situations might come up, once that opening kickoff happens then you're playing the game or coaching the game, whatever you're doing, whatever your role is. In my case, I'm coaching and I'm trying to do the right thing for the team in each situation that comes up and try to anticipate things a play or two ahead of time.

What we want to do or what situation decisions we have to make, that type of thing. Once it starts – but the leading up process, yeah sure, there are definitely butterflies in your stomach. But I get that in preseason games, regular season games. It's different than practice because I can control everything that happens in practice. As a coach, you know what plays you're going to run or even if you don't, there's more control in practice. When you play a game, a preseason game, a postseason game, whatever it is, there's the element of unknown – that's the competition. Sure, each of those is a little bit different.

**Q: How valuable is Dante Scarnecchia? We were talking about some of the changes on the offensive line - how important is he?**

**BB:** He's awesome. Dante's a great coach, on every level. He's real good with 'Xs' and 'Os'. He does a great job with the veteran players. He's brought along and developed so many of our young players, rookie players, draft choices, free agents; taken guys off the practice squad and built them into starters or contributors on the line. He's invaluable.

I think not only myself, but a lot of other people on the staff as well, other coaching staff members, rely on him for advice or ask him questions, take advantage of his experience. He's had not only experience on the offensive line but he's coached special teams, he's coached defense. He's really got a great breadth in his coaching career and experience level as well as great proficiency in the offensive line and how well he's done with that group since I've been here and before that. He does a tremendous job.

**Q:** Does the fact that he coached so many different positions help him now that he's focused on the offensive line? Does coaching on the other side of the ball help him coach on offense?

**BB:** I'm sure it has, yeah, I'm sure it has. If you're coaching one position, if you've coached the one on the other side of the ball then you have an appreciation for what that group is thinking, what they're seeing, what their keys are in a certain defense or how they change in a different defense, how their responsibilities change. It helps you attack them better, no question.

Again, the whole special teams thing just gives you a total appreciation for the game. Guys don't just have offensive and defensive assignments to go back and study at night - they have special teams responsibilities. I think an experienced coach that has done that, you know how things can pile up on players and how one thing can run into something else. I know when I first came into the league you kind of lose sight of that. This is the position you're coaching and you want them to do better but there are a lot of other things that they have to do. If you haven't, like I said, coached on the other side of the ball, sometimes the things that you're telling them as a young coach may be with less accuracy or maybe less confidence because you're not sure exactly what that guy is being told or you just haven't been around long enough, there's just a different level of confidence.

Having coached that really makes a difference. I know when I was coaching the tight ends at Detroit and we had Charlie Sanders and David Hill, I remember several meetings that we were in when they would ask questions about, 'What if this happens? What if that happens?' which I hadn't really thought about that happening. Like, 'Here's your assignment, here's what you do,' but then 'OK, if there's [something] a little unusual, what would we do in this situation?' I wasn't really sure and Charlie would usually say, 'We would do this if that happened, right?' because that's the way they'd done it before. Usually that was right but not always.

Then when I coached the linebackers at the Giants, I can remember relating back to my experience of coaching the tight ends with the Lions of how a tight end thinks, how a head-up technique or an outside technique or the change of a stance or jamming a tight end, not jamming a tight end, how that affected all the tight end things. I could talk with a lot more confidence to an outside linebacker about 'Hey, here's what the tight end is going to do' or 'If you do this, here's what he wants to do or where he wants you to be' or whatever it was on a specific play a lot differently than I could a few years before when I was coaching the other position. Yeah, I think there's great value in that.

**Q: Do you measure your steps with a player who is learning a new system in terms of not putting him in positions to not succeed whereas maybe earlier in the year you would be able to do that?**

**BB:** I think each guy is different. It's really hard to predict how it's going to go with any player. I think you just take it as it comes. You give them the information and then you move them along and see how quickly he adapts to the new assignments, the new techniques, and just the way he's able to handle the assignments that he's given. Again, each player is different so with a player like Barkevious [Mingo], you have a situation where he has a lot of special teams responsibilities, so if we brought in, let's say an offensive lineman, or a defensive lineman, that may not – it depends on the positon and the guy. He may not have that big a responsibility in the kicking game, so it's just really depends on the individual player and how quickly he's able to acclimate himself to the new situation. I don't think there's any set mind frame or you try to go fast, you try to hold back. I think you just kind of take it as it comes.

**Q: How do you balance having a player use his own instincts on the field versus having him play within the context of the defense?**

**BB:** I mean I've coached every player I've ever coached the same way. You have an assignment, you have something you're responsible for and then the instincts come after that. As long as you cover your guy, that's your job. You want to cover him off, you want to cover him on, inside technique, outside technique, back pedal, squat, whatever it is. I mean there's a million different ways to do it. If you have him covered I'm going to be happy about it, you're going to be happy about it, right? So that's the bottom line.

Now after that then there is an instinctive part to every play, so

I've coached players - that's the way I've coached them my whole career. When I was a special teams coach I had different punters, different kickers. They don't all kick it the same way. They kick it far, they kick it high. I'm happy, they're happy, the team is happy. That's good. If they don't then we've got to try and find a better way to do it. I don't see it any differently now than I saw it when I started coaching.

I don't see it really much differently from one positon to another. The techniques are different, the assignments are different but a player's instinct and his style of play - that belongs to each of us. We're all different. But there are certain fundamentals that I think as a coach you are obligated to teach the best way that you know how and work with individual players within that framework.

## Q: At the end of the season, do you sit down with players and ask them to get down to a certain weight?

**BB:** No, look, we do that on a regular basis. So like wherever you want to start, let's say we start the season in April, not every player is here in April, but let's just say it starts in April. Ok, we sit down with that player in April and say, 'OK, here's what we want you to do in the offseason program – weight, conditioning, technique, position, whatever it is, here's what we want you to concentrate on.' We get to the end of that, we say, 'OK, here was your offseason, you did this well, you need to do a better job of this. OK, now we're heading into training camp, here's what we want you to do – this, this, this and that.' We get to the end of training camp, 'OK, you did a good job of this, you still need to work on that, this is better or this still needs to be improved – conditioning, weight, strength, flexibility, etc.'

We get to somewhere in the midpoint of the season and we sit down and have the same conversation. 'Look, this is what we told you at the beginning of the year, you've done a great job with this, you still need to do better at this, this, this and that, here's what you need to do – strength, flexibility, conditioning, weight, etc.' Injuries may play a part of some of those discussions. We get to the end of the year, somewhere close to the end of the year, 'Alright we have X number of weeks to go, here's what we need from you the last three weeks, four weeks, whatever it is, here's what you need to concentrate on. You did a great job of this, that and the other thing, but now we're into a different, here's what you need to do.'

So we do it on a regular basis. We're not going to sit around here and waste a whole year and then say, 'OK, let's have a meeting and like alright we think you ought to do this.' We're not going to have a meeting every day, but there are certainly different points in the year were you can … And we do it for the entire team, too. It's each individual player, it's each coach, each position, each unit, offense, defense, special teams, running game, passing game, kickoff return, punt coverage, whatever it is, that we evaluate those at various points and, 'OK how are we doing? Alright we're alright on this, we're not so good on this, we need to make this change – whatever.' We're our own R-and-D team. We can't hire some consultant to come in here like a company can do and, 'Alright let's take a look at this and you guys do a study on that and tell us this, tell us that.' Who's going to do that?

## Q: Do you taper practices to make sure you're at full strength at the end of the season?

**BB:** Well, there could be. It depends on the situation and it depends on the player, absolutely. You have some players that need more, some players that need less. And again, I think that's not just each player, it's the team. Even some guys that maybe are OK at where they're at, they need to work with their teammates. We can't just put 11 guys out there that have never worked together. In the end, we try to do what's best for the team, whatever that is. If it's work more, if it's work less, if it's taper down, if it's however we set the practice schedule. We can't do everything. We try to pick out the things that are most important, that have the most impact and do what we think is best. And sometimes doing what's best for one guy isn't what's best for another guy, but I don't know how else you can run a team. It's not like we've got a tennis team with nine guys playing their own singles match. We've got to work together.

## Q: How does where the fatigue, conditioning and health of players impact how the coaches structure practices?

**BB:** That's a great question, and part of that answer is it's not the same for everybody. Where one guy is or sometimes even a group is … Sometimes you have another group that's in the exact opposite place. One group maybe needs a little more recovery. Another group maybe needs a little more work. I'd say we go through that throughout the year. It happens in training camp sometimes because of numbers and experience levels and so forth, but bottom line is you try to do what you feel like is best for the team. You have to take individuals into consideration, but you have to take the team into consideration, too. We just can't structure everything for one or two guys and be negligent of the other 61, including practice squad players. We try to balance that the best we can. It's not always the same for everybody.

Sometimes guys who need more work we try to get them more work, but we have to try to get the team ready and that encompasses all those things. I don't feel like there is any right or wrong answer. I've been on teams and with coaches that … Well when I was younger, a lot of times, my job several years was to write up the practice schedule. So when we would meet and go through the schedule, then I'd write it up, put in what everyone is doing and hand copies of that to all the coaches. We have coaches on our staff now that do that, and I can remember I could have written the practice schedule for December, a Wednesday in December, in July easily and there wouldn't be one thing that was different.

A lot of times it's, "Alright what did we do last Thursday,' and it was the exact same thing. And that's not the way we do it. And I'm not saying it was wrong to do it that way, but there were some times, certain programs I've been in, coaches, it's just their routine and you do the same thing every Wednesday, every Thursday, every Friday, every Saturday, so you always know where you are. We would do blitz pickup and the other team hadn't blitzed in two years or vice versa. So, we kind of do it differently.

We kind of talk each day about what the team needs, we have a basic structure of this is what we do, but we change that depending on what we feel like our needs are, and that is definitely a big part of it is the health and I'd say the overall readiness of the team. And that's very subjective, obviously, but we do the best we can in consultation with the training staff, the strength and conditioning staff, position coaches, a lot of times they have a good tempo of where their individual group or particular players are and sometimes that affects the rest of the preparation.

**Q:** Tom Brady took blame for a couple of the plays, especially the deep balls to Randy Moss. How much of his development is him missing last season and do you expect him to have been on track by now when it comes to timing?

**BB:** I think in the skill positions you are always working on timing. You are doing that all the time; every year, every quarterback, every receiver, everybody's doing it. The routes always change a little bit. The coverages change. The team you're playing - their personnel changes, you play against different guys week to week, so there's always a little bit of a timing adjustment on a game-to-game basis. So it's an ongoing process. It's everybody. It's the receivers, tight ends, backs, the quarterback. It's no different in the passing game on offense than it is on defense.

It's protecting to throw the ball and hit whatever the receivers are, whatever the passing combination you have, whether you're running - then, it involves the backs, tight ends and receivers - that combination displaces the defense enough so the quarterback has a place to throw, and the receivers are open, and the protection is there for him to get it off. That is the offensive coordination of the passing game. It's the compliment of the defensive coordination. We need to do a better job on that all the way around - that's everybody.

That's all 11 guys out there on the field. It's not one man in the passing game [and] it's not one man in pass defense; it's all 11. And it's coaching, too. We've got to do a better job of that as well, the design and the overall execution. So if it's not getting done well, then that's also a function that we're not coaching it well enough.

# 3
# HISTORY

**Q:** Are there any similarities between Chuck Noll and Paul Brown and what kind of respect do you have for Chuck Noll?

**BB:** Yeah, you know, [I have] tremendous respect for Chuck Noll and certainly through the whole Paul Brown connection and all. I talked to Chuck on a number of occasions and I had a relationship with him. They didn't have much turnover in their staff and so a lot of the coaches on their staff stayed there for a long period of time. A couple of them I knew pretty well through my dad [Steve Belichick] or other connections. Dan Radakovich was there for a long time. Rollie Dotsch was there for a long time and I coached with Rollie at Detroit and so, you know, I would ask a lot of questions about the Pittsburgh System.

Bud Carson was another very influential coach there with the whole cover-2. He kind of brought the whole cover-2 scheme to the Steelers in the way they played it and the way they read it and that was obviously a great defense, but the techniques and all the reads they used in that defense under Coach Noll were I'd say pretty innovative. And so I learned a lot about that through Coach [Jerry] Glanville who worked with Coach Carson at Georgia Tech so I felt like I had a lot of connections to Pittsburgh but obviously never worked in Pittsburgh, never worked directly in that system, but through some of those other coaches I learned as much about it as I could. Of course when I went to Cleveland Coach Noll was there. It was his last year.

Actually it was his last game when we played them in '91 and then Coach [Bill] Cowher took over after that. [I have] great respect for Coach Noll. He was a very intelligent guy. He had a great way of mixing football with life. Football's important, football was - not trying to make it insignificant - but he had a lot of other interests and he was very diverse. [He] had a lot of diverse interests as well, a very food fundamental coach. The trapping scheme that they ran on offense was very innovative. Coach [Tom] Landry had some of that in Dallas but certainly not to the extent that Pittsburgh had it. When I was with the Giants we always played the Steelers in preseason every year - the Rooney/Mara family relationship.

We always played them and so that was always a great preseason game for us because you could really kind of measure your team even though it was a preseason game. It was usually the third game. Usually the starters played into the third quarter and it was a very competitive game that kind of gave you a good sense of where your team was going up against a physical, well coached, tough football team, especially when it was on the road in Pittsburgh when you have to deal with being on the road and the fans and so forth. I've learned from competing against the Steelers going back to Coach Noll and then Coach Cowher. I've learned a lot because they've been so consistent.

They've stayed very much the same; three coaches in the last - I don't know, whatever - 40 years or however long it's been, a long time. Because of their consistency I've learned a lot from studying that organization and I think Coach Noll was just - did a tremendous job. He had great stability, very good fundamental coach. He believed in what he believed in and they got good at it and they always had tough, physical, hard-nosed, smart football players. The receivers blocked, the offensive line was tough, defensively they always tackled well. They played good fundamentals. They were just very well coached and all of the people that I've talked to that have coached on his staff, they've affirmed that with their recollections of it.

So I never worked with Noll and I never worked with Landry but in 1977 when I was with the Lions Ed Hughes was our offensive coordinator and he had been with Landry for - I don't know - 20 years or 15 years, whatever it was. So he kind of brought the Dallas system and we ran that in 1977 in Detroit and so I learned a lot about the Cowboys system because, again, nobody left the Cowboys. There wasn't much turnover on that staff so I learned about the Steelers from Coach Dotsch and Coach Radakovich, Jerry through Bud Carson and so forth, and then the Dallas system through Coach Hughes from Landry. They were very impactful. I would say learning, part of the learning tree in the early part of my career. Even though I wasn't with those coaches, I felt like I learned a lot about their programs and what they did through people that were very closely in that program.

**Q:** You broke into the league right around the time that the Steelers were starting their dynasty there with a handful of Super Bowls.

**BB:** Yeah, so on that note - in '75 with the Colts, we started out 1-4 and we won the last nine games to go 10-4 and win the division. It was a tremendous turnaround. Then we went to Pittsburgh for the playoffs, and they had a great team. We really had a chance in that game. I think it was like, 17-13, I think it was in the fourth quarter. We drive down, we're on the like five or six-yard line, whatever it was, and they intercepted, ran it back for a touchdown. So instead of going ahead, now we're down by two scores and we end up getting beat.

For my first year in the league, the point being for my first year in the league, just seeing how good they were, I mean, they were so good on defense. Every guy was better than the next guy. From [Joe] Greene to [Jack] Lambert, that whole front four, and then the secondary, and offensively - and then at the Giants going against them every year, I mean literally we played them every year in preseason, plus a couple random games here and there in the regular season. They were very - when you're a young coach and you're looking at, ok - who does things in a way that you admire or respect or want to emulate, or what can you take from a good program to help you as a coach, or if you ever get a chance, what would you do that they do? They were one of those teams. Not to cut you off on a question, but yeah, from the first year, the Steelers had a very strong impact from the outside on my philosophy as a coach.

**Q:** What was it like trying to game plan for those guys on any given week?

**BB:** Yeah, I was on the defensive side of the ball, so with [Lynn] Swann, [John] Stallworth, [Franco] Harris, [Rocky] Bleir, [Terry] Bradshaw, it was, [Mike] Webster, I mean you could go right down the line, one Hall of Fame guy after another, one All-Pro guy after another. It was a very, very solid team. But again, I would say from going against them in '75 to going against them in the '80s or even into '91 when I was in Cleveland, not a lot changed.

They had a very consistent philosophy of what they did. They drafted players into it. Of course that was all before free agency so they kept their players; they built them up in the system. They had a very good training program. That was another thing that was impressive about the Steelers and Coach [Chuck] Noll was in terms of the offseason program and player development and how strong, physically their players were. That was uncommon at that point in time, I would say. I went to the Colts [and] we didn't even have a weight room. We didn't have a weight coach, either, but there was no weight room. There was a little universal gym that had four or five stations and that was it. You could have put the weight room in a corner. That was it. But that wasn't like that in Pittsburgh, and then when I went to Detroit, we had a much - it was a legitimate weight room, it was a legitimate weight program; probably similar to what the Steelers had, but kind of trying to keep up with that.

Floyd Reese was the strength coach, so then I saw the difference between no weight program and a weight training offseason conditioning program. But that was all, of course, predated by what the Steelers were doing. Again, there were a lot of things like that that they did that were definitely on the forefront that they did a great job of developing.

Younger players, bringing them up through the system, guys that might not play for years one, two, three, whatever it was, but then they get in there and then they're pretty good. So they developed players and they had a very, very well-balanced team. That was another thing about them, too. It didn't matter if it was offense, defense, special teams; they were just good at everything. It wasn't like, 'Well, they're pretty good here but we can take advantage of them there.' There wasn't really much of that.

**Q: Some of your players took photos in front of the Jim Brown statue after yesterday's win. What are some of the things that today's players can connect to Jim brown and his legacy and career?**

**BB:** Well, I think honestly any person, football player or otherwise, can learn a lot from Jim Brown and what he represents and what he stands for. But particularly as it relates to our football team, Jim Brown's in my opinion the greatest player that ever played. I've had an opportunity to have known him Jim for over 20 years now. I met him when I was the coach at the Browns and just had so much more respect and appreciation for him knowing him well as a person and as a friend, even just as an observer from a distance, but I think he's meant so much to this game.

He's paved the way for all of us; players and coaches. [He's] part of many people who have made professional football, the game of football, the great game that it is. I just felt like it was an opportunity for us as a team after the game to recognize and pay a tribute to Jim and all that he stands for, both in and out of football. But in particular, what he has meant to the game of football and how much he has done for us, for the game, which means for all of us. That statue was recently put there. It's kind of remarkable that it hadn't happened sooner, but regardless, I'm not sure how many of our players really understand or appreciate what he meant to the game and what he has meant to the game through his continued involvement not only with football, but with young football players, be they Browns players or just other youth that he interacts with primarily on the West coast but as we know he's been involved in projects through his Amer-I-Can program throughout the country, which I've been very fortunate to witness and be a small part of.

That's why we did it and I'm glad they appreciated it and hopefully that's something that's part of their football career [and] will be one small memory [as] just the recognition of a great player and a great person and somebody who has really made the game better for all of us. Honestly, I wish Paul Brown's statue would've been right there with it because then we could have knocked out two birds with one stone. Paul Brown's name is up there.

Obviously, that's who the franchise is named for and his name is up there on the stadium as part of the players that are recognized on that ring of honor there in the stadium. It's a little special quirk for me when you think of Paul Brown, and you think of Jim Brown, and the Cleveland Browns who were named for Paul Brown and being in that stadium, not because I was the coach there, but because of what Paul Brown and Jim Brown did for professional football in that city. It's a special place in my heart.

**Q: How much did your upbringing around the Navy football program prepare you to deal with the uncertainty and unexpected circumstances that can surround football?**

**BB:** Probably quite a bit. As you know, growing up and when the team you know the most about is the Navy team, you know those kids have to deal with a lot. Like all colleges, there's no redshirting so they graduate in four years and there's a lot of turnover pretty quickly. Just watching some of the coaches there - Coach [Wayne] Hardin, Coach [George] Welsh, people like that, Coach [Rick] Forzano - had to adapt to different things that happened to the team as just part of the normal course of events and how they handled them.

I watched my Dad in some of those situations, being observant, not really being part of any decision or anything, but just listening to them talk about how they made decisions or what their options were and then how to pick the best one, things like that. That was great, a lot of great learning experiences there. I still remember in '64 when [Roger] Staubach was coming off of the Heisman year and hurt his Achilles early in the year and Coach Hardin had to manage that, managing the practices and so forth because of what Staubach wasn't able to do for many of the games, in preparation for the games, each game in the '64 season, just things like that. I'm sure I learned a lot there, probably more than I can even remember.

**Q:** Did it help you as a younger coach coming up the ranks as a part of a smaller staff where you were able to fulfill more roles and wear several hats in terms of responsibilities on the staff?

**BB:** Well, it certainly helped me. I'm not sure if I can speak for a lot of other coaches because I don't know what their individual experiences were, but yeah it certainly helped me. I was very fortunate in my first job with Coach [Ted] Marchibroda that the staff they had was small and he had come from a large staff with George Allen in Washington. So honestly, I got to do the work that the Redskins probably had nine other assistants doing so it gave me a lot of experience. I got paid what I deserved. It wasn't about that. But the experience was great and then being able to work in the kicking game, work on special teams at Baltimore, Detroit, Denver and then the Giants.

Being able to work on offense at Detroit, being able to work on defense at Baltimore, and Denver and the Giants really gave me exposure to every - literally every player on the team - especially as the special teams coach. Other than the quarterbacks - maybe a couple of situational plays with them - but basically other than the quarterbacks, you're working with every position group and pretty much every player on the roster, so I don't think anything prepared me for being a head coach as well as being a special teams coach did. But, and also I'd say the other thing about a special teams coach, it forces you to learn a lot about strategy and how the kicking game effects situational football. Not that you don't know that offensively or defensively, but when you're the special teams coach I'd say you understand a little more about the - and sometimes you learn the hard way - a little bit about the strategy and the situational play that's involved there.

So, the fact that those staffs were small, the fact that I was able to have those different experiences with those different organizations unquestionably was a big benefit, especially that early in my career to have that. Bruce [Arians] is a head coach. He coached under some of the great coaches like Bear Bryant, Jackie Sherrill, Bill Cowher and so forth. So, he has got a long list of mentors. He has had head coaching experience at the college level, at the professional level, position coach, quarterback coach, coordinator. Mike [Zimmer] had a lot of experience, too.

His father is a high school coach; things like that. Pete [Carroll], obviously the same thing; coordinator, positon coach, head coach, college head coach, pro head coach a couple of times, third time in Seattle. So, yeah, I mean it all adds up. Sometimes getting kicked around a little bit early in your career; there are sometimes some benefits to what you learn and experience and then later on at some point maybe it helps you or helps to bring things together a little bit.

### Q: Can you recall your favorite Kevin Faulk moment?

**BB:** There are a lot of them. They were talking about them today. The two - point play against Carolina was a huge play; it was the only time he scored all year. Kevin didn't have a lot of touchdowns, he wasn't a big scorer. He was big on third - down conversions and a returner, more of a situational player. The touchdown against the Jets during the playoff game when they were in an all - out blitz; it was another smart play. We were able to get him out and it was about a

10, 12 - yard touchdown, something like that. One play I remember for sure is the kickoff return he had against us when I was coaching in New York in 1999, his rookie year. He ran it back to about the five - yard line. It was about a 95 - yard return or something, so I remember him on both sides.

So many of his plays were just, third - and - six and he got seven, third - and - four and he got five, third - and - three and he got four. He just had a great knack [for making plays], like Troy [Brown] did. [He was] a very instinctive player; had a great knack for playing the game. He always seemed to do the right thing, even if it wasn't a play made, maybe there was no more than what he could get, he got what he could get. He did the right thing, he made the right play. Maybe he was supposed to go out on a pass, he saw somebody come free on a rush, left his pattern to protect so we could get the play off. I mean, whatever it was, that's what made him great is all the little things, the kind of unsung plays.

They weren't little plays, they were big plays, but they weren't necessarily all 90 - yarders. They were just those plays that kept drives going. That third - and - 11 against the Colts in the AFC Championship game in 2004, we were on our own 10 - yard line or something, backed up, and we get out of there on third - and - 10 with an 11 - yard conversion and Corey [Dillon] ended up scoring on that drive and it kind of iced the game, plays like that. The Denver game out in Denver, the Monday night game, catches the screen after he took the safety, got the ball back, catches the screen pass, goes down and puts us in position where we hit [David] Givens on the touchdown, but it got us into field goal range, so if we [had to] make the kick, it would have put the game in overtime.

They just go on and on, and you know what, those plays were the same thing in practice, too. It wasn't just the games. We ran those plays in practice and he converted most of them there too. When he said he looked up to Troy Brown and tried to emulate Troy Brown, he did a pretty good job of it. Those two guys were, between them, receiver and running back, both returned kicks. They were both tough, great team players, clutch players, really good hands, caught everything, great decision - makers, great teammates. You're lucky to have one, we had two. I feel blessed. Certainly, they were great additions to the team. Kevin, 13 years – that's a long time for a running back – and he was durable. He was durable.

## Q: What are your thoughts on the passing of Ted Marchibroda?

**BB:** Yeah, appreciate [the question]. It's with a real heavy heart that I stand here. I probably wouldn't be here if it wasn't for Ted Marchibroda. He gave me a great opportunity. I learned so much from him - a lot of X's and O's, but it really wasn't the X's and O's. It was a lot more about just being a football coach, being a professional coach - preparation, work ethic, dependability, what goes into having a good football team. Every time I heard about the Kansas City Chiefs - which they had a tremendous this year I'm not taking anything away from them - they start off 1-5 and then won 11 straight or whatever.

That was us in 1975. That was my first year in the NFL and we were 1-4 and won our next nine straight, whatever it was, and then lost to Pittsburgh in probably a game similar to this - driving down to take the lead and gave up an interception that was run back 95 yards for a touchdown, so the game kind of got away from us. But it was the same kind of team. It was a young team that got off to a slow start, but we gained our confidence, and that taught me a great lesson in football of just keep working, keep fighting, just one day at a time. Don't worry about the record at the end of the year. Just have a good day, have another good day, win this week and then move on to next week. That's what we did in 1975. Ted gave that team great leadership.

They were like 2-14 the year before we got there or something like that - 2-12 - however many games there were. They were terrible. But he gave the team great confidence, great leadership. Ted is one of the most positive people I've ever been around. He was always confident, even when it was fourth-and-17, he was always sure we were going to make the play or do what we need to do. He was such a great person for me.

I lived with Ted. We stayed in the same hotel, drove him to work every day, drove him home every day. We had our staff meetings in the car. We ate breakfast together. He was such a mentor, and I just can't say enough about Ted. I know everybody that's coached and worked with him probably has the same exact feelings. They'll all tell you the same story because that's what Ted was. My sympathies to Ted's family and his two kids, his grandchildren. He's got a great family. He's a great father and great grandfather. It's a sad day - just a sad day.

### Q: How different was Dick LeBeau's zone blitz when he came out with it?

**BB:** I'd say he definitely popularized it. When I was at the Giants, we ran some of that, but it was nowhere near to the degree that he ran it. We would just bring an extra guy at times based on formation or tendency or particular key, that kind of thing where we just add another guy in and still play zone behind it. When you have a 3-4 defense, the teams that ran the West Coast offense, they only had one protector on the strong side, so they get three guys out to the strong side and they would only have one blocker, so they would have to throw hot if you brought two guys over there.

But the zone blitz really killed that because there was a guy standing there to the guy that you were throwing hot to. I think once kind of everybody saw – and again the West Coast offense was pretty I'd say more prevalent and it didn't have as many variations as it has now both in the running game and the passing game. Back in the early to mid-90's with San Francisco and Mike Holmgren and all those guys, the zone blitz was a very effective way to play that offense because of the amount of three out strong, only one protector on the strong side, that if you brought two, they didn't have it. I think it really became popular there, and then that evolved into bringing two up the middle and two off the weak side and doing it out of sub and everything else. Dick was really the one who made it an entire package.

I would say at the Giants when we used it, it was more of either a very small situational call like short yardage or tight formations or that kind of thing or it was again something kind of specific. He made it just as a general defensive principle and developed it in a way that was very comprehensive on a number of levels –from a coverage standpoint, from attacking the pocket standpoint and also from a run defense perspective. Dick was really the guy that put that whole package together. Again I think there were maybe some random satellite elements of it here and there, and again I had some experience with that at the Giants, what we did, but nowhere near to the degree that he did it and popularized it.

**Q: Has the sub-type, receiving back always been a big part of your system? Can you identify a time when it became a big part of your offense and other offenses around the league?**

**BB:** I'd say it kind of started in the 80's as I remember it. In the early 80's and 70's, usually the same 11 guys were on the field for every play, and then you got a little bit to the third receiver, but the tight ends were pretty good and those guys were good receivers – they weren't really guys you were looking to take off the field. So you played the same 11 guys on offense, you played the same 11 guys on defense. There was a little bit of nickel defense in the late 70's where teams would put in a defensive back for a linebacker, but it was the same thing. It was just kind of a one-for-one substitution.

Then I think you saw teams like Washington when [Joe] Gibbs was there have the big back, whether it was George Rogers or [John] Riggins or whoever it was, and then they had [Joe] Washington or Kelvin Bryant or that type of player as their sub back, and it would be a true one-for-one situation. We did that at the Giants, had a lot of success with [Dave] Meggett, Tony Galbreath, guys like that. That was into the late 80's and the 90's and then a lot of teams started doing it where they found that third-down back first of all was less of a load for one guy to be out there for every single play, and then secondly the skills of that player, ability to separate and have quickness and make plays with his hands in the passing game as opposed to just the ball carriers, sometimes you could have both instead of just trying to find one guy to do everything, which is harder ...

There are always going to be some backs in the league that can do that, but I think it was a little easier to find two guys rather than find one who can do everything or find two – one to do it and one guy to back him up. It was a way of splitting the load. So I'd say that's kind of evolved, evolved trough the mid-80s and by probably a decade later it's the way a lot of teams were going. When you had guys like Tony Dorsett and Billy Sims and Thurman Thomas and guys like that, you didn't need to sub anybody. You put them in there, do whatever you want with them – throw it to them, run 20 times a game. They were all really good at that. But the specialization gives in particular with Washington and the guys that went on from his system like Dan Henning and guys like that. They adopted that same type of philosophy.

**Q:** Who is the best one that you've coached?

**BB:** We've been lucky. We've had a lot of good players at that position. Certainly Meggett was ... And again it depends on what the guy's role was. The thing about Meggett was he gave you all those plays in the kicking game – kickoff returns and punt returns, as well as third downs – so he was a very impactful player in terms of the number of times that he would catch the ball. Kevin [Faulk] probably caught more passes than Meggett did, but he didn't have the same production in the return game. Probably had more production as a running back, actually carrying the ball. But going back to Tony Galbreath, he did a great job for us at the Giants.

**Q:** Eric Metcalf?

**BB:** He was a little different. He ended up being a receiver in Atlanta. He was a little different. I mean, he was, but he wasn't. He was a little different style of player there. Those guys, they all kind of have a similar skill set but then what their role is as it relates to the kicking game. Metcalf was a great returner – seven, eight career touchdowns – whatever it was. So probably more impact in the kicking game than in some cases on offense. But those players are explosive.

**Q: We've been honoring this year the 1990 Super Bowl Champions that you were a part of. When you think back to that team, what comes to mind?**

**BB:** Well I mean there were a lot of great things about that team, but for me it was really about the defensive players that I was most closely associated with. And that's not taking anything away from Phil [Simms] and the job that Jeff [Hostetler] did and all the other great players and great plays that came from that season on offense and special teams. But the group that I was with defensively was really a special group. They worked well together and we got a lot of leadership in the secondary from Everson Walls – I mean, the tackle he made on [Thurman] Thomas in the Super Bowl was a huge play. But [Carl] Banks and Pepper [Johnson] and L.T. [Lawrence Taylor] and our front, we had a lot of good days defensively that year and particularly in the postseason. I was proud to coach that group and we had a good coaching staff, guys I really enjoyed coaching with, and the players, it was good chemistry. It was an amazing year.

**Q:** Your game plan from that Super Bowl went to the Hall of Fame and has gotten a lot of credit over the years. Do you feel your game plan got too much credit or the right amount of credit? How do you feel about that?

**BB:** I think games are won by players. Players are the ones that go out there and make plays, so it's always about the players. As a coach you try to put the players in a position where they have a chance to compete, but players are the ones that make the plays, absolutely. We have a lot of great players and they're the ones that made the plays, and that's why we won. You can put anything you want down on a piece of paper, but you've got to have players go out and make them and we had it.

**Q: In the 1950's and 1960's, Tom Landry came up with the shift on the offensive line. What was the point of that back then?**

**BB:** Basically what they did was they gave each player, tight end, well actually every player, they had different spots, so it could be like eight, nine, 10 spots they could line up in, and when they double shifted, which they usually did, then the player had to line up within two spots of where he was going to end up. So, the first time he could shift from A to B and then B to C, where he was going to end up, or from C to B back to C or wherever. And so when the line went up and went down, that was just another distraction and I'd say temporary loss of some vision for the defense to recognize where the back was.

I'd say back when Coach Landry put it in, most all plays were two-back sets, so it was basically three formations – red, brown and blue, strong backs, weak backs and split backs. Then eventually we got into the I-formation in the 70's, so that was kind of the fourth position, and every once in a while, you'd have a guy up on the wing in a one-back set, but that wasn't that common. But the tendencies from those formations – I, strong backs, weak backs and split backs, on every team were I would say pretty strong in those days, depending on who the players were and the scheme, but they were still pretty strong. Strong backs, there was a lot of running strong side, weak backs, a lot of running to the weak side, split backs, a lot of running to the strong side, a lot of passing. So, there were a lot of strong tendencies.

I think Coach Landry's idea probably was to keep those tendencies from being recognized until as late as possible by the defense and force the defense to communicate, like, 'We're doing this on brown, we're doing this on blue, we're doing this on red,' so we're this to that, this to that and the ball is snapped, so you don't really have time to get into your adjustments if you have any or even your final recognition, where good players that were prepared – here's what they do out of brown, here's what they do out of blue, here's what they do out of red – but it's red to brown to blue, and boom. But that line up and down was a little bit of a distraction – not distraction, but it just blocked the vision a little bit of the linebackers from recognizing exactly where everybody was until they went back down.

They go on some quick counts, so it would force you to declare if you were going to do anything because they might snap it with everybody in a two-point stance, but most of the time they were up and down, and it gave the quarterback a little bit more time to watch the defense and see where they were going to go. When Ed Hughes came to Detroit – Ed Hughes was the running backs coach for Coach Landry a number of years down there – when he came to Detroit in 1977 when I was there and I coached the receivers that year, so I learned that offense.

That was kind of the offense that we installed that year and ran, so it was pretty interesting. It was only one year, but it was pretty interesting to learn the Dallas offensive system because very few people left Dallas. That staff stayed together. There wasn't a lot of movement out of there, so it was pretty interesting to learn the way that it was written, the way it was presented, the coaching points, how different plays fit off each other.

**Q:** How come you don't see it anymore?

**BB:** There are a lot of things you don't see anymore. First of all, it was a pretty complex scheme, so if you weren't well versed in it, that's not the kind of thing you just pick up and say, 'Oh gee that looks good – why don't we start running some of that?' I think you've got to really know it and know all of the nuances to it and understand how it all fits together because it was protections, it was routes, it was the volume of offense because they were together for so long.

It was kind of like Paul Brown's offense that he developed that then eventually [Bill] Walsh built on, but after not years, but decades, a couple decades really of running the same thing, you build up a lot of volume, but there is a reason for everything and each play has a complement and if you're not really in that system, I think it'd be hard to start it up somewhere else. You'd probably start up what you've been familiar with and what you know rather than jump into something that's as intricate as that. Same thing with the flex defense – unless somebody left there, like when Coach [Gene] Stallings left, but you didn't really see anybody else doing that because I don't know if anybody really understood it or maybe they didn't believe in it or whatever. But they didn't know it well enough to coach it and install it like Dallas did.

**Q:** It's much more of a gimmick in your eyes, though?

**BB:** I don't think any of their things were gimmicks. I think there was a lot of thought into all of them. There was a reason for everything. The hard thing for us in Detroit that year in '77 was trying to get to the point where the Dallas offense was after 15 years or whatever it was in one year. It was impossible. You have to pick out a few things, try to get good at those, build on those. But the Dallas offense after years and years and years and years of coaching it, drafting players into it, developing it, doing all of the things they did with it and then you try to run it, you're a long way from being where they are on a lot of levels.

Even if you have good talent, it's still the system was pretty involved. It was a great learning experience for me. I learned a ton. It was something that prior to, I had never been involved with obviously and since then haven't. I'm not saying I understand it but at least I've coached it. I understand some of the principles of it, whether we actually run those plays or not. But the principles that were involved, what they tried to do was very, very educational. I was taking a graduate course in that, which along the same lines, in addition to, but I also learned a lot about the flex defense. Even though we didn't run it, the fact that Ed had come from Dallas, kind of had the Dallas system, we were able to talk about it.

He understood what they were doing. That was also very educational. I was fortunate my first few years in the league. I worked for a lot of different coaches, worked with a lot of different assistant coaches, worked in different systems, worked in different cities, a lot of different players, different organizations, so I got a lot of exposure – a lot more than I wanted – but I got a lot of exposure in a short amount of time to a lot of football. In the end that's not a bad thing. Wasn't that great at the time, but in the end it turned out to be beneficial.

## Q: Does Hank Stram's moving pocket have any application now? Are there any trends like that?

**BB:** I think there's always an element of not putting the quarterback in exactly the same spot for the defense to rush to on every single play. Sometimes it's, depending on who your quarterback is and what your style offense is, it's, I'd say, easier to do than others. Again, it's a pretty general question so it's got a pretty general answer. It would depend on specifically what your style of play was and who you're talking about and all that.

I think that the fundamental part of the passing game is just a very – where the quarterback is, the type of protection that you're using, the timing of the passing game – quick, intermediate, longer – again, just to keep the defense off balance so they're not always facing the same type of pass. Therefore when you do that the route depths vary, the combination of receivers – you can change those receiver routes and combinations that force adjustments by the defense. But in doing that there's a tradeoff in the protections or in the location of the quarterback and so forth. I think all that is part of it somewhere along the line. You just don't want to do the same thing every time.

## Q: Do you still associate the Vikings and Bud Grant very closely?

**BB:** Yeah, sure. When I was at Detroit, Bud was the coach there. They probably played as basic a defense as anybody had every played – two coverages – but they had a great front four and some very instinctive players on defense. They played the same thing, pretty much the same defensively, pretty much the same thing all the time.

But again, they had really good recognition and anticipation. They knew how to, because they were always in the same thing, they knew what to look for and how to react to it.

They were very good and they had a great pass rush so their defensive backs played aggressively and they would jump routes and get interceptions. [Paul] Krause had 50-some interception but a lot of that was due to the pass rush and how little time the quarterback had to hold onto the ball. he'd recognize routes and anticipate them and jump on them. They had some really good linebackers there – [Matt] Blair and [Wally] Hilgenburg, those guys. You knew they were mentally and physically tough. You were definitely going to get that from them. That was a trademark of [Bud] and those teams.

**Q:** Ozzie has talked about your influence when you were both in Cleveland. Was there something about him that stuck out that you knew he'd be a great personnel evaluator?

**BB:** Yeah, no question. My first year in Cleveland was Ozzie's first year not playing. He had retired after the '90 season and we sat down, it's one the first things I did when I took the job. We sat down, talked to Ozzie about his future. He wanted to have a future in the organization, he wasn't sure if it was in coaching or scouting or some other aspect of public relations or player development or whatever it was. He did a number of different things for me there.

He coached, he was in the scouting department – similar kind of maybe to what Nick [Caserio] has done here, kind of going a little bit back and forth. I think in the end probably all those experiences benefitted him because he got an appreciation of the scouting end, the player end of it – of course he had been a player so he had great familiarity of what it was like to be a player in the NFL – but scouting players, developing players, being a coach, creating game plans, making personnel decisions from a coach, as opposed to as a scout, and all those things.

He did a great job for me and I learned an awful lot from him, again because of his experience as a player and how his playing career

– he was a wide receiver in college and then he became a tight end so there was a lot of development and progression of his career. Like every player, had a great career, peaked and at the end was at a different point in his career and how that whole transition worked for him.

He taught me an awful lot about that and just the whole passing game, receiving, being a receiver, playing for different quarterbacks, playing in different offensive systems as he did and so forth. He was a great resource for me. He taught me an awful lot and he's been very complimentary about his comments of what he learned from me but I think I probably learned more from him than he learned from me.

He's a very astute, sometimes quiet kind of guy, but the wheels are always turning, he's taking a lot in. when he speaks, you listen because you respect him and you know that he's just not saying things to hear himself talk.

He's saying them because he's given it a lot of thought and he has a very important observation or opinion to share. He's had a great career. I can't think of many people that did what he did as a player and then in his current position and all the other things along the way – as a scout, as an assistant coach and so forth. He's a pretty special person, special football person too.

**Q:** How's your relationship with John Harbaugh?

**BB:** It would be a lot better if we didn't have to play each other every year. I have a lot of respect for John. John's another guy that kind of started like I did – started as a special teams coach. As he and I have talked about, I think that's a great way to learn the game of football. You learn situation football, you learn the kicking game, you learn how field position and all those things relate to the other aspects of the game. If you're an offensive coach, you know defense. If you're a defensive coach, you know offense.

You have to learn those things as part of knowing what's going on on the other side of the ball. The kicking game is kind of its own entity. John, obviously again had a great background – football family. He grew up with it, as I did. He's really paid his dues. He's been a good coach in this league, whether it was on special teams or defense or obviously as a head coach. I have a lot of respect for John. I'd love to have a closer relationship with John if we weren't in the same competition.

It's kind of similar to, I'd say different but similar to my relationship with Bill Cowher. Before I got to Cleveland when Bill was at Kansas City with Marty [Schottenheimer], we spent a lot of time together, we talked, we visited each other, shared ideas. We were both young coaches anxious to learn and feed off the other guy and get some ideas and techniques and things like that. It was great. Then I'm the head coach at Cleveland, he's the head coach at Pittsburgh and we play each other twice a year. I love Bill, but you're playing him twice a year, you're trying to do everything you can to find a way to beat him.

As that situation changed, and then ultimately now with not having to compete against him in the league, it's a lot easier to have a relationship that isn't based on the direct competition that you're in. Different, but there are some similarities there.

**Q:** Sort of similar when Nick Saban went to Miami.

**BB:** Exactly. Oh, yeah. Yeah.

**Q:** Did you just call him up and say, 'What are you doing – in the division?'

**BB:** Two Croatians in the same division. Yeah, it's crazy. Yeah, I mean Nick, I've had as close a relationship with Nick professionally and personally through the years, even before when he was at Ohio State, when he was at Navy, when he was at Michigan State and then obviously the four years in Cleveland and Michigan State again and LSU and then at Miami – that was hard, for both of us because we had a great personal relationship but we're trying to win, trying to beat each other.

I love that he's at Alabama and he's not in our division. He's not shutting us out like he did the last time we played him down there in Miami. But it's so much better that way on a personal level.

**Q:** You're one win away from passing Chuck Noll. You got a chance to coach against him in his final season. What is your level of respect for his body of work and what it was like to go against up?

**BB:** I have tremendous respect for Coach Noll. Yeah, he was one of the great coaches when I came into the league in '75 and for the next 15 years. I had the opportunity to coach with several coaches who were at Pittsburgh with Coach Noll. Some of the things that I learned from them, or about him through them, whatever you want to call it, and of course competing against him. When we were at the Giants, we played them every year in preseason. It seemed like every year, maybe we might have missed one but it seemed like we usually played him in preseason so we played him on a regular basis. Of course in Cleveland, they were in the division, as you mentioned, that first year that he was there.

I have tremendous respect for Coach Noll and his whole program there. They were an excellent team and they were a good, sound team, a team that you always, as a coach outside of Pittsburgh, always tried to look at what they were doing and learn from it: their fundamentals, their technique, their scheme, which wasn't overly complicated but it was very sound. When Nick [Saban] came to Cleveland, who coached with George Perles at Michigan State when they ran the Pittsburgh defense, the 4-3 defense, Nick brought a lot of those ideas and concepts to Cleveland. Nick and I kind of merged there with some of the things that we had done in New York, some of the things that he had done as the defensive coordinator under Perles at Michigan State, which was the Steelers defense and so forth. So that was another great opportunity for me to really gain knowledge of that system without actually being there.

When I was in Detroit, Rollie Dotsch was there, who was at Pittsburgh for a number of years. I think that their program, what they did there schematically and all was very, very good. Coach Noll and his approach to the game, his consistency, his level demeanor and the consistency that they had, I thought was always exemplary, right at the top of coaches that I tried to learn from and take things from them. I don't know how much was him or Bud Carson or Perles or where one stopped and the other started, but the whole combination of what they did there at the Steelers I thought was pretty impressive.

Going against him every year, as a defensive coach against their offense, when I was with the Giants through all those years in the '80s was also always a good, it was a great experience because they were so well balanced, they threw the ball down the field, they ran the ball, they had a good balanced attacked. I think I learned a lot from the outside, looking at that program that Coach Noll ran. Bill [Cowher] really kind of had somewhat of a continuation of that, even though they changed defensively to his blitz-zone package but a lot of the things that they did fundamentally there, especially on the offensive side of the ball, with Dick Hoak there in the running game and all that, it was a couple decades of stuff really that was a carryover from Coach Noll and the consistency that they had all the way up into this century, the 2000s.

I don't know when Dick retired, but when Coach [Ron] Erhardt was there, there was still a lot of carryover from some of the things that Coach Noll established. But as far as the other part of it goes, I'd say my focus is really on this game and whatever win it is or isn't, it's not really that important right now. Whatever wins we have had [are] because players have played well. I'm not out there throwing any passes or making any tackles.

## Q: Did you have any odd jobs before you got into football?

**BB:** Yeah, high school, college, I had plenty of them. I was fortunate that I was able to work at my dad's football camps, which was two-to-three weeks over the summer. That was really, it was a great experience for me. It was a summer job that was a week off from my other summer jobs, whether that was waiting or working for Mayflower Moving or whatever it happened to be. It was good because I had an opportunity to work with a lot of college coaches, other guys who eventually became pro coaches. A couple coaches like Ralph Hawkins and George Boutselis that I actually worked with my first year at the Colts worked in my dad's camps; Whitey Dovell also. There were three of them on that staff. That was a great opportunity for me too, to work in those camps. It was a lot of good coaches, working with kids in high school, junior high school, not that I was like a full-fledged coach or anything, but just the experience of being around it, seeing a lot of the things, hearing coaches talk, exchange ideas, seeing different coaches coach different techniques at the same position. It was a great experience too. That was another – it wasn't a high paying summer job but it was a good job; glad I had it.

**Q:** Did you know at that point that you wanted to go in that direction?

**BB:** I'm not sure. I was playing lacrosse and that was probably my better sport. But I loved football and then when the opportunity came up to go with Coach [Lou] Holtz down to N.C. State, in the spring of '75, that was something I felt would marry well with continuing my education, trying to get a Master's and coach with him. When that didn't work out – Lou was the first coach that hired me and the first coach that fired me, as I like to remind him of – then it fortunately worked out [with] Coach [Ted] Marchibroda at the Colts.

I didn't really have anything; I didn't really have anywhere to go at that point because the N.C. State thing fell through. I was totally open and fortunately that was able to work out with Ted and as I said, some of the other coaches that were on that staff, like George [Boutselis], like Whitey [Dovell]. They were able to recommend me, Jerry Falls who my dad coached and who was Ted Marchibroda's son's coach in high school, so all those connections kind of helped me get started. Plus, I think the price was right.

**Q:** How much did you play yourself and what were your limitations?

**BB:** Pretty much everything: size, speed, athletic ability.

**Q:** Did you play much?

**BB:** I played in high school and college, yeah.

**Q:** What position?

**BB:** Center, tight end, linebacker; snapped, poorly.

**Q: Can you share your thoughts on what you remember from what Bill Parcells did in New England? From competing against him and his career in general, as he goes into the Hall of Fame.**

**BB:** Career in general: he coached four different franchises and was with five different franchises. Pretty much every one he came into was not doing well when he got there. Either they were the bottom or close to it. He made them all pretty competitive in a very short amount of time, on several occasions, the first year. Two Super Bowls in New York, and that franchise really wasn't...hadn't done a lot in awhile.

Great coach, great evaluator, does a great job with his team, whatever capacity it was – when he was the coordinator under Coach [Ray] Perkins, head coach or his other administrative duties at Miami most recently. A lot of respect for Bill, learned a lot from him, glad I had the opportunity to work with him and work for him. Certainly well deserved. Patriots was definitely an example of a team that was pretty much rock bottom when he got here; rejuvenated the franchise. We competed against him in Cleveland but again he made the Patriots very competitive in a short amount of time. Putting them into a strong position, '96 we won the AFC, we had a good, young football team that came up just a little bit short against Green Bay.

I think he certainly deserves the lion's share of putting that team together and the whole program together during that period of time. We can go on and on but I think all the accolades for Bill are well deserved and I personally value his friendship and have a lot of respect for him as a person and as a football coach slash football person. It's not just coaching; it's beyond that with him.

**Q: Have you ever seen an example of a playoff game where a team that was doing one thing during the regular season switched**

**completely what they were doing for a playoff game? Is that dangerous for any team to do?**

**BB:** I'm not saying this is right or wrong. You asked a historical question so I can give you a historical answer. I can tell you that in 1990, when I was with the Giants, we played Chicago in the first playoff game. We played a 4-3 defense. They had a certain style of play that we felt was more conducive to that. The next week we played San Francisco, we played a 3-4 defense and that was predicated on what we thought would be best to play the 49ers that week. Then the following week we played Buffalo and we played a 2-4 nickel, 3-3 nickel, whatever you want to call it, depending on what part of the game you were in.

I'd say that was a different style of defense. Is that trying to be creative? I don't know. It's trying to win the game. It's trying to do what you felt like you had to do to match up against those particular teams – Chicago, San Francisco and Buffalo in that particular year that were very, very different. Playing Chicago wasn't like playing San Francisco and playing San Francisco wasn't like playing Buffalo. There were just different matchups, different style offenses, different personnel groups on the field. I think at this time of the season you do what you need to do to win one game.

You don't worry about your system, you don't worry about playing time or how many guys do this or this guy does that. You worry about what you need to do to win the game – that's what we're here for. You put the best you have out there to do the best you can against whatever it is you're facing – offensively, defensively whatever it is – and you try to make that work. Sometimes that means it's the same thing, sometimes it's doing what you've been doing, sometimes it might be doing something differently.

I'm not saying that's the right way to do it, I'm just saying that's what happened in that particular year. Had we played somebody other than Chicago, San Francisco or Buffalo, I'm sure you'd be looking at a bunch of different chapters in a book but we didn't, that's the way it was. I don't know, I don't know if it's the right thing or the wrong thing to do but that's what we did.

**Q:** You've talked about you guys being a game plan offense. Where was the idea of being a game plan offense born from for you? In terms of it being the right way to do it, compared to a team like the Steelers when Bill Cowher was there, that this what they do and you have to stop it?

**BB:** I don't know, I guess I've always had that philosophy. You try to do what you think works best against that particular opponent certainly within the framework of what you're comfortable doing, whether that's offense, defense or special teams, it's all the same. [Former Head Coach] Wayne Hardin at Navy maybe, if you want to go back a ways; Detroit, the Giants. I don't know.

**Q:** Would you agree with the thought that it's an ambitious thing to try to do because you have to be able to execute in all areas, as opposed to majoring in one thing?

**BB:** I'll just give you this example. When I was in high school at Annapolis, I played for Al Laramore, who was Maryland Coach of the Year, a Hall of Fame high school coach in Delaware and all that. So, he's a pretty good coach. We won a lot of games, we won a ton of games and we ran four plays. We ran four plays: 22 Power, 24 Quick Trap, 28 Counter and Sprint Right and that was it. When we ran them to the other side, we just flipped formation. The whole line flipped and the play went the other way: 22 Power, 24 Quick Trap, 28 Counter and Sprint Left.

That was the offense, that was the entire offense and we won a lot of games. Then the next year when I went to Andover and played for Coach [Steve] Sorota there, who again was a great player, great coach, played with [Vince] Lombardi at Fordham and was one of the most renowned coaches I'd say ever in New England prep school football or maybe high school football period for that matter. The quarterback called his own plays. They didn't send them in; they didn't tell him what to call. They got in the huddle and he may have asked for a suggestion from me or Ernie [Adams] or somebody, but he called whatever he wanted to call and that was the offense. So, that was about as opposite as you could get it from one year to the next year. We won just as many games. It was totally different, but both were very successful.

So what's the right way to do it? What's the wrong way to do it? I don't know. Whatever works, whatever you believe in. But then it all has to line up that way.

I got to Baltimore with Coach [Ted] Marchibroda, Bert Jones. Bert called all the plays. I want to say it was his second year in the league. He called all the plays. Call timeout, come over to the sideline, fourth-and-one, Burt would say, 'What do you want me to call?' Ted would say, 'We have 24 Hunch, we have 36 Bob, we have Play Pass 37 Y Flag, whatever you feel good about.' 'Alright.' Other players and coaches would come up and say, 'What are we going to run?' 'I don't know, it depends what Burt calls.' There are other teams, Coach [Ray] Perkins, Coach [Bill] Parcells, those guys, called every play. Not that we wouldn't audible to a play or something but he called every play.

So, what's right and what's wrong? I don't know. It can all work. If you do it right and you have the other things – if you do it one way, you have to have other things that are in place to do that. There's a reason for doing it. There are also some drawbacks to doing it that way. When that happens, you have to have some way to counter it. That's the same way on defense.

When I was with the Broncos and Joe Collier, there were game plans where we had 60 different fronts – fronts. It's hard to imagine 60 different fronts in a 3-4 defense really, but that what it was. It was 60 different alignments, which would include a linebacker that was blitzing so any one of the four linebackers were blitzing so that was part of it. I got to the Giants when Bill [Parcells] came in, we put in a 3-4 there.

We played one front with one adjustment. We reduced the end on the weak side from a four-technique to a three-technique and that's it. Then I'd say 95 percent of the snaps that we played from '81 to '90 that weren't nickel snaps; over 90 percent of them had to be either base or reduced front, maybe 95 percent. It might have been higher than that. Two good defenses: the Orange Crush, the Broncos defense, that was a great defense. The Giants defense, that was a great defense. The same 3-4, two totally different philosophies. So what's the right way to do it? Both work.

**Q:** Are you a combination of all the people you've played for or coached with?

**BB:** Again, it's hard to say. I think my first five years in the league, it was a different head coach every year with a lot of different assistant coaches in that group, from Baltimore to Detroit to a new coaching staff in Detroit, to Denver, to the Giants, to actually a couple years later a new coaching staff with the Giants when Bill [Parcells] came in and all that.

My first few years in the league, different head coaches, different coordinators, different assistant coaches. It was a lot of good things from a lot of them. I wouldn't say I was overly influenced by one person or another person. There were some people I would say I was influenced to the point of: 'If I ever coached that position or if I'm ever in charge of this, I'm never going to do it that way.' There's some of that, too. There are also plenty of things that I did learn. It was a little bit like that at Navy.

There were different coaches that went through there. Coach [Wayne] Hardin, Coach [Lee] Corso, even after I'd grown up and left there, like Coach [Nick] Saban and people like that that were there, Coach [Paul] Johnson when he came in and ran all the option stuff. Just being around those people and all, you learn different things, different ways of doing it, different ideas.

I was probably influenced a little bit by everybody. I couldn't really – besides my dad, that was a constant – but there were so many other coaches involved that I had the opportunity to observe or spend time with or be in meetings or on the field with and that kind of thing, football camps. My dad ran a football camp every summer, so there were another dozen coaches there, some of whom were Navy but plenty of other ones were from other colleges and other associations that he had. I've worked with and observed a lot of coaches. I don't know. It's kind of a menagerie.

**Q: You mentioned Buddy Ryan earlier. How come we don't see more 46 defense? I'm not talking about for a full season – not everybody is the '85 Bears, but in a one-game situation. Is it because of the quarterbacks and the shotgun?**

**BB:** A lot of the success that Buddy had with the 46 defense came in the '80s when there was a lot of two-back offense. It was one of the things that probably drove the two-back offense out. If you remember back in the '80s when Buddy was in Philadelphia, he had a lot of trouble with the Redskins and their one-back offense, a lot of trouble. There were a lot of mismatches of Art Monk and Gary Clark on the middle linebacker and stuff like that. I think the 46 was really originally built for two-back offenses, whether it be the red, brown, blue and the flat-back type offenses and eventually even the I-formation.

I think it still has a lot of good application; a lot of teams use it in goal-line situations. They either use a version of it like a 5-3 or cover the guards and the center and however you want to quite fit the rest of it, but that principle you see a lot in goal-line, short yardage situations. You see it and some teams have it as part of their two-back defensive package. As it has gone to one-back and it's gotten more spread out, if you're playing that, it kind of forces you defensively to be in a one-linebacker set.

You lose that second linebacker and depending on where the back lines up and what coverage you're playing, then there's some issues with that. If you're in a one linebacker defense and you move the back over and the linebacker moves over then you're kind of out-leveraged to the back side.

If you don't move him over, then you're kind of out-leveraged when the back releases and that kind of thing. There are some issues there that, I'm not saying you can't do it, but you have to work them out. In a two-back set, I'd say it was probably a lot cleaner and it always gave you an extra blitzer that was hard for the offense. Even if they seven-man protected on play-action, there was always an eighth guy there somewhere. You didn't have to bring all eight; if you just brought the right one and they didn't have him or somebody would have to have two guys and that creates some problems.

I think that's what Buddy really, where the genius of that was; he had by formation a different combination and group of blitzes so depending on what formation you were in, then he ran a blitz that would attack that formation and then when you changed formations, then he would change blitzes. Now, plus the fact [he] had Dan Hampton, Richard Dent, Mike Singletary, [Otis] Wilson, [Wilbur] Marshall, that was a pretty good group there. You could have probably played a lot of things and that defense would have looked pretty good, especially when they put Hampton on the nose. That was pretty unblockable.

## Q: What are some of your memories from your first season down there with the Colts?

**BB:** It was a little different, a little different. We went to camp July 5. The first game was September 21, I think. So, six preseason games, three scrimmages against the Redskins. It was a whole two and a half months of training camp basically before we even played a game. It was a long, long preseason. Squads were small so, I snapped a lot to help the timing for the offense, passing, 7-on-7 and one-on-one drills, things like that. It was great experience with Coach [Ted] Marchibroda and [Defensive Coordinator] Maxie Baughan and the rest of the defensive staff, George Boutselis, the special teams coach.

I learned an awful lot, I didn't know anything. I was just thrown into an environment where I think there were only seven coaches on the staff – three on offense, three on defense and one on special teams. I was like the eighth guy, I didn't know anything but at least I was a warm body. I got thrown a lot of responsibility and opportunity to do things that had there been a bigger staff, I would have never gotten to do. That was a great opportunity for me.

We started out 1-4, playing in front of 20,000 people there at Memorial Stadium. Then we started winning and Bert Jones had a tremendous year, we had a real good defense. The front four there of [Fred] Cook, [Joe] Ehrmann, Mike Barnes and John Dutton, they had like 50 something sacks that year or whatever it was. We won our last nine games. We went from 1-4 to 10-4. We went from playing in front of 20,000 to whatever that holds, 60 some. So, that was pretty exciting. We lost to Pittsburgh in the playoff game; they eventually won the Super Bowl. Started training camp off at Goucher College and we were there until the first of September.

Then we went from Goucher College to McDonogh School and practiced out in the pasture there. It was crazy. We were there for a couple weeks then finally the Orioles finished up. They were in the World Series that year I think, so we didn't even get to Memorial Stadium until around the first of October. Of course, at that point, the whole infield was still down. They re-sodded that so we only practiced on half the field so we had about 40 yards to practice on. That wore out pretty quickly so then we would go across the street to Eastern High School and practice. The whole team walks out of Memorial Stadium, hits the 'Walk' button, goes across 33rd Street and walks over to Eastern High School, which had two blades of grass, dirt, glass, rocks.

It was inner city football practice field, about what you'd expect; filming from a step ladder. But it worked. Team gained a lot of confidence, started slow, gained a lot of confidence and came together. That was really a good football team. Bert Jones was a great quarterback and he continued to be until he hurt his shoulder. There's no telling how good that guy would have been. If he'd had a full career, he could have been up there with anybody I've been around certainly. I learned a lot. I didn't put a lot of money in the bank but in terms of experience I did, not actual cash. That was a fun year.

## (on how much of his football philosophy and what he feels about the game came from his father, Steve)

"How much of it? I'd say quite a bit. Growing up with it, it was my life as a kid from when I first remember; four, five, six years old through the rest of my life. He had a huge impact on my childhood, my love for the game and my involvement in the game as a coach, even though I played poorly. It was still a good experience to play, but coaching, really, has always been the love. I think a lot of little things he did in terms of work ethic and teamwork. Being around the Naval Academy, of course, that is a very unique atmosphere, particularly as it relates to football, but the teamwork that comes with that, and the commitment that those players and teams have, I saw at a young age. The Joe Bellinos, the Roger Staubachs, the Tom Lynchs, the Pat Donnellys, it's hard to really measure exactly what percentage of impact it was, other to say it was significant. It's huge.

I still maintain a close contact with those players today. It's something that has stayed with me through my life, even though I wasn't really a part of those teams. I've been adopted by some of them, and that is a special feeling. I'd also say that my high school coach, Al Laramore, who is a hall-of-fame coach in the state of Maryland, had a similar attitude and a different style for sure. Coach won championships in three sports: football, basketball and lacrosse. He had a lot of the same attitudes toward playing and teamwork.

I grew up that way, and that shaped me to a large degree, as has all my coaching experiences and certainly those 10 years with (Bill) Parcells in New York, as well as New England and New York again. He was a huge influence as well. He reinforced a lot of things as well."

## Q: Who is the best special teamer you've ever coached against or coached?

**BB:** There have been a lot. Obviously there are a lot of good players. Certainly Larry Izzo did a great job for us here as a player and special teams captain, leader. He was a great tone setter. I would definitely put him up there at the top of that list of the players that I've coached. We had a lot of good players at Cleveland. We've had a lot of them here, going all the way back to Detroit and Leonard

Thompson, Baltimore. I can think of guys that you really had to game plan for. Obviously a lot of guys that have been in the Pro Bowl the last few years - the [Brendon] Ayanbadejos of the world. You have to double them on your return units; you just can't leave guys like that running free down the field, with 20 yards of space to dodge a blocker and make a tackle.

You have to take care of guys like that. The Giants have a lot of good ones - [Greg] Jones has done a really good job for them. They've had a lot of production out of their young linebackers: [Jacquian] Williams has done a good job and his role has increased defensively but he's covered extremely well. They've gotten plays out of their receivers on the coverage units. You see them every week.

## Q: You have a long history with Tom Coughlin. Can you talk about how that relationship has evolved over the years?

**BB:** Tom came to the Giants staff when I was already there and I was coaching the secondary and Tom was coaching the receivers. That was a really a good situation for me. As a defensive backfield coach and a defensive coordinator, but as a secondary coach, you work a lot with the receiver coach - one-on-ones, seven-on-seven drills and also you talk to each other about 'We're playing this technique - what do you see, what can we do better or how would you attack it?' Tom and I had a good relationship and a good give-and-take on that.

He would tell me things with our defensive backs - how they were trying to beat them, what they saw from this guy, how they would attack another defensive player with the same route, how they would run it differently on a different player. And the same thing: 'This is what I see from your receivers, this is how we're trying to play this guy, he really makes it easy for us on this route by doing this or doing that.' So it was good; it was constructive and it was good.

Then of course after the '90 season, Tom came here and I went to Cleveland, so we haven't been together since then but we've had, whether he was there or in Jacksonville or in New York or I was in

Cleveland or I was in wherever I was before coming back here, we've always maintained a good friendship. He and his wife and his family have been friends for quite a few years. I coached the linebackers with the Giants for most of the time that I was there and then the last couple of years I moved over to the secondary, so it was good for me - because I had less experience in the secondary at that point - to be able to work with Tom and get a perspective on our passing game from the offensive side of the ball, so that was good.

### Q: What do you remember from that meeting with Al Davis? What did you take away from that?

**BB:** I thought it was good. It was good. It was good experience for me. I went out there after the '98 season. We had a good couple days of conversation. I told him when I got out there – it really seemed like a waste of time because I felt pretty certain that he wouldn't hire a defensive coach, because he hasn't since Eddie Erdelatz in [1960]. It's a parade of offensive coaches out there. He's really a defensive coordinator and has been. You know, it was good because we talked a lot about football and he's very, very knowledgeable about the game, personnel, schemes, adjustments and so forth.

He was asking a lot of questions about what we did defensively. You kind of don't want to give too much information there because you know, he's running the defense. He wasn't really too interested in talking about offensive football – a little bit. He's a great mind. It was unlike any other interview I've ever had with an owner because he was so in-depth, his interview was so in-depth really about football, about 'Xs' and 'Os' and strategy and use of personnel and acquisition of – all the things really that a coach would talk about, that's really what he talked about.

That made it pretty unique. But he hired a good coach, [Jon] Gruden. Which is again, in all honesty, the way that I expected it to go because that's been all the Oakland coaches from Art Shell to Mike White, Joe Bugel, [Mike] Shanahan, you know right down the line, Lane Kiffin, they're all offensive coaches. They have their own way of doing things which is interesting but certainly well thought-out and well planned. I'm not saying that in a negative way at all, they just have their own of doing it – they've had a lot of success. It was a great experience for me to have those couple days of conversations with him and also some other members of his organization relative, again, to the overall way of doing things.

**Q:** You're obviously someone who has taken things from other great coaches and coordinators in the past. What mark did Al Davis leave on you defensively when you look back at his Raiders teams from the '60s and '70s?

**BB:** Well, you look at the same thing today, there's not a lot of difference. Like I said, he's really run the defense and to a large extent the kicking game out there for the '60s, '70s, 80's, 90's – 40 years, maybe more than that, I don't know. But he's, again they have their style of play, they have their way of doing things.

As much as you can say this is a copycat league and things like that, you can't really say that about them because they've done the same thing now for decades defensively and to a certain extent, offensively. Through the course of my career, I've had the opportunity, just as luck would have it really, that some people that I was very close to in coaching were in that organization. In talking football, I feel like I know a lot about what they do, how they do it, again through third parties now, not directly, but through third parties.

It makes a lot of sense. They definitely have a plan. I think I understand basically what they're trying to do and how they're trying to do it. I think it's consistent and I've taken a lot from that. The personnel side of it, the way they look at certain things in the game and what their priorities are. I definitely have tried to look at those and incorporate some of them into what we do. We do things a little bit differently than they do, but that's okay. You just want it to be consistent and you want it to finish at the end game – where you want to be. That's what everybody is trying to do. It's well thought-out. I don't think it's a trial-and-error system. It's a proven system, they believe in it and they're going to follow it.

**Q: I saw a high school team is using 11-man blitzes and is having success with it. What is the most you've sent or you've seen in the NFL?**

**BB:** When I was with Detroit, in 1976, we did a lot of it. We called it the 'Sticky Sam Blitz.' Probably ran it, had to be 50 or 60 times. It was a lot.

**Q:** Did it work?

**BB:** Yeah it was good defensive team. Jimmy Carr was the defensive coordinator. Jerry Glanville, he blitzes a lot and blitzed a lot when he was a defensive coordinator and head coach in the NFL. A lot of maximum pressure there.

**Q:** Does anyone do that today and what's the highest you've seen?

**BB:** You see Rob [Ryan] and Rex [Ryan], they give you a decent amount of maximum pressure. I mean maximum being, when you bring more than six, then somebody has to have coverage too. So you can bring seven or eight, but somebody has to peel and take those receivers - the fifth receiver, fourth and fifth receiver, if they get out. In the end, you can only bring six and cover their five. If you bring more than that, really, somebody is going to have to come off the blitz, if they release.

If they stay in, then you can add in the blitz and it can be as many as - if they keep them in, you can just keep adding one more. Six becomes seven, seven becomes eight, eight becomes nine. Again, right now, we're focused on getting ready for San Diego. I couldn't really give you a breakdown on defense.

I don't know what everybody else in the league is doing. That's not really their [San Diego] thing. Their thing is they play a lot of man, man free coverage, free safety and cover up the receivers and rush four, rush five, make you block them.

**Q:** As a former defensive coach yourself, what is it like watching Dick LeBeau go into the Hall of Fame?

**BB:** I think it's awesome. Yeah, I think it's awesome. Dick is such a football guy. I've never had the opportunity to coach with him, but I know Dick. I've spent some time with him and he's just an outstanding person - just a great individual. I don't think anybody that I know that's ever known or spent any time with Dick could say a bad thing about him. I mean, he's just such a quality person, tremendous coach [and] great player. He did a great job as a coordinator and had a lot of success as a head coach and [he] is just, really, a football guy.

I think for all of us that really appreciate football in its purest form, [he's] a guy that I think we're all happy to see get recognized. I think there are a lot of other assistant coaches along the lines of Dick LeBeau that could easily be included among the other great people in the National Football League. The Hall of Fame has its list of contributors or whatever in there, but I would certainly say there are a lot of assistant coaches and people like that - even some other people that have contributed, not even necessarily in the coaching aspect [but] trainers - a couple people like that that have been lifers in the National Football League that, really, depending on what the criteria is, could certainly be expanded for consideration. But I think it's awesome.

I think it's awesome. I can't think of anybody that's any more deserving than Dick, although I can think of a lot of people that you could put into that category certainly for consideration, relative to the recognition that goes with that, with the Hall of Fame and with those kinds of positions, the people that have contributed a lot to the NFL.

**Q:** You mentioned a couple of years ago that you had a lot of respect for Holmgren for leaving Seattle and keeping the west coast offense alive. Can you talk about the challenges that you face defensively?

**BB:** I think that when you look at all the west coast coaches, all the guys that came from [Bill] Walsh's tree, which are [Jon] Gruden and [Brian] Billick, and Andy Reid, you can just go right down the line - there's been a lot of them, - that he's modified it to a) his team or b) things that he, in particular, wanted to do that were a little bit different from the way that [Walsh] ran it in San Francisco, but I would say that Mike probably stayed closer to it than a lot of other coaches did.

That was the way it was in Seattle and there's a lot of elements of that here in Cleveland. Like every offense and every defense, you have ways to handle problems. You go through enough games, enough years, you pretty much see a lot of what you have to face and you have some way of dealing with it. As time goes forward, you either stay with those or you modify them and change them based on either your personnel, or, for some reason, you think you have a way that works better than the one you're currently using. That happens in a lot of cases. It looks like, in Mike's case, he is less inclined to do that and more inclined to stay with things that he's done through the years.

## Q: What are your thoughts on Jimmy Johnson going on [the TV show] Survivor?

**BB:** Well, that's quite a contrast from the environment that I usually see him in. The times that I've seen Jimmy most recently [were] either in this [football] environment or on a boat fishing or relaxing on a nice day down in the Keys, having a good time. I hear it's pretty rough on Survivor [and] everybody takes some mosquito bites. Jimmy is great guy. We've had a great relationship.

I have so much respect for what he's done. At the time he did it, he really kind of was one of the first guys to do things the way he did it and build a team from scratch with the responsibility he had and all of that. But seeing him out in that environment, I give him a lot of credit. My hat is off to him. I don't think I could handle that.

**Q:** You mentioned your relationship with him and how you've met with him a number of times and he's kind of enlightened you on things. Do you as a coach in the fraternity of coaches have kind of the same thing with Sean Payton?

**BB:** It's different, but yeah I think there are some similarities there. It's so much easier with somebody like Sean who is not in our division. We don't play him very much. It's a lot easier to talk and exchange ideas and all that than it is with somebody like when Bill [Cowher] was at Pittsburgh and we're trying to hammer each other once, twice every year and playoff games and everything else. It's hard to do it in that situation.

Sean and I have both worked for Bill [Parcells] and in a way we have similar backgrounds in a structural sense. He has more of an offensive background; mine is more of a defensive background. That being said, we've worked for the same head coach and a similar environment and we've been able to talk. We really got to know each other at the Pro Bowl after the '06 season and again, that was another pretty relaxing environment, going fishing and just hanging out and talking about all different things: organization, staff, players, away trips, you name it. Just the variety of stuff that comes up… 'Hey, what do you think about this? What do you think about that?' Sean is a sharp guy. He's got a lot of great ideas.

He's innovative. He's creative. He certainly has a strong philosophy, but I wouldn't say he's so set in his ways that he wouldn't change anything. He's experimented with some different things and it's good to exchange ideas like that. But Jimmy has really been helpful to me personally, just being able to talk with somebody who has sat in pretty much the same situations that you've been in. 'What did you think about? How did you make this decision? When you had to consider A, B, C, how did you sort that out? What was your thought process? Why did you do what you did?'

We actually had a number of interactions between the two of us while I was in Cleveland and he was in Dallas and also in Miami [when] he was there. Just talking about different things. Why did you do this? Why did you do that? That's been very helpful, too, and he's really given me some great advice and guidance. [Patriots Strength & Conditioning Coach] Mike Woicik worked for Jimmy in Dallas and so even though, obviously, I wasn't there, I think I have - from Mike's perspective, at least - a pretty good understanding of some of the things they did. And we actually incorporated some things into our program here when I took the job that were really Dallas things kind of through Mike Woicik, as an example. Jimmy has been - and again, it's a lot easier now that he's not in Miami. I mean, he is, but he isn't. He's not with the Dolphins. So we can talk about things. It's not competitive; it's just as friends.

**Q: You've certainly seen a lot of training camps. In your mind, has it changed much since when you came into the league?**

**BB:** Compared to when I came into the league, there is no training camp. It's very short. The number of two-a-day practices that most teams have [is less]. When I came into the league in 1975, we started camp July 5 and our first regular season game was September 21, so it was two and a half months of training camp, three scrimmages against the Redskins and I don't know how many two-a-days – it had to be 30. It was forever; it was two and a half months. It was all of July, all of August and half of September of training camp, preseason games. It was like a full season and then a regular season. So has training camp changed? They [the players] have no idea.

Q: Is this good or bad? That sounds so incredibly excessive –

**BB:** I'd say two things: one, in those days, you didn't have the offseason program that we have now. At the Colts, our weight room consisted of an open room with a universal gym in the middle of it. That was the weight room. That was the weight program. There were no OTAs. There was none of that. So you take the spring and add it on the fall. And we were in camp a long time.

A lot of teams like the Vikings and Bud Grant and those guys, they didn't come to camp July 5, believe me. I think that you need time to get a football team ready, to get a football player ready. I think it's hard to just walk out there and start playing at a high, competitive level in our sport without putting players at risk. And we'll see, at the beginning of training camp all teams will start to have – the injury list will pile up and that will gradually decrease by the end of training camp and then when the regular season starts, those injuries will reoccur. Some guys will be out for the year, some guys will be out for a length of time and then as the season goes on, the guys that are out for the season will start to come back. That's the way it usually goes and I would expect it to go this year.

I think we are probably in a good spot right now. This is probably about right – you get two weeks before the first preseason game and then play four preseason games. It gives you a chance to evaluate the younger players in about half of those snaps, and it gives you a chance to use your veteran players who are competing for playing time or who are your better players. It gives you a chance to give them about half the snaps in practice or in games to get ready. Could it be a week longer, a week shorter or whatever? I think generally speaking, this is a pretty good pace to get a team ready for a regular season game. I don't think we need the time we had in 75 – let's put it that way. Nine preseason games - because those three scrimmages against the Redskins were about 120 plays per scrimmage – so it was a long camp.

**Q:** Would I be mistaken to say you went through one of these mid-season coaching changes early in your career in Detroit?

**BB:**Yeah, '76.

**Q:** Do you remember some of the challenges that go into that and how tough that can be on a team, because obviously Buffalo is going through that now?

**BB:**Well, I mean, I think each team and each situation is different so it really would be hard to lump them all into one pot and say, 'Well, this is what it was.' That particular time for us in Detroit, I think we were 1-3, 1-4, whatever it was, and we were playing New England and they had just come off three huge wins - Oakland, Pittsburgh, and somebody else - won by like 2 or 3 points. And we just decided to do something a little bit different and a little new, and went into a formation with Charlie Sanders and David Hill - two tight ends and one back - which is something that now is common, but back then really wasn't. And we had a pretty good day with that and won pretty handily at home, and then the rest of the year was a little bit of an up and down year. That was certainly the high water mark, was that particular game against the Patriots during the week of that change.

I think when a new coach comes in, you can't change everything. You already have a training camp and a certain number of regular season games already under your belt. Your team's already at a certain point in those areas. Can you go in and modify some things and change them, or maybe try to change an attitude or approach or something if you feel like that's what it needs, then I think you try to address that. How easy that is to change or modify would depend on the situation. I have a lot of respect for Dick Jauron. I think Dick is an excellent coach. I've known him a long time; in fact, he was on that Detroit team back in '76.

I think Dick does a good job. His teams are well-prepared. We have a lot of respect. We've competed against them a lot. I mean, they played as well as anybody other than New Orleans in the first game. [If] they don't fumble that kickoff, maybe that's probably a different game. I have a lot of respect for Dick, but I have a lot of respect for Perry too. What exactly their differences are, what Perry has emphasized that Dick didn't or changes he's made or whatever, I think that's really a question you'd have to ask them. But they were over halfway through the season when they made the change, so it's not like they put in a whole bunch of new plays and all that.

**Q: There was a story about Dan Henning when you and he were together at the Jets. I think you said each week he'd bring in five new plays or new things that he wanted to put in. What kind of creativity did you see from him offensively when you were coaching with him, and does all of the stuff they're doing now not**

surprise you because you saw where he was willing to go with that?

**BB:** Yeah, when Dan was with the Jets, when we were together there with Bill [Parcells] there in the late '90s, of course we worked against him in training camp, and then you saw their plays and all during scout team periods. They'd run them against us and then we'd run our defenses against the other team's stuff, but you would see their plays and I thought they were very creative. Bill - I mean Dan - well, Bill too, but Charlie [Weis] and Dan [and] Todd Haley was part of that, Bill Muir, all those guys, so it was ... You did, you saw a lot of different things.

And a lot of the plays that you see there now are plays that we ran at New York. Honestly, some of them are plays that we still have that Charlie - when we came in 2000 - were the same plays that we ran there. [They were] some of the same plays that we saw in Carolina back in '04, so there is definitely a lot of carryover. But it's a very multiple - I don't want to say 'complex' is the word - but it's simple within it, but from an outside look it's complex because of the formationing and the personnel grouping and all of that. When you get right down to it, it's not a zillion plays; it's a core group of plays that get dressed up and disguised differently.

And of course, that all stems back to Joe Gibbs and Dan Henning when they were with the Redskins in the '80s. I mean, Joe Gibbs and Dan Henning, they had two running plays. They had the Counter and they had the Counter Trey - I mean the zone play and they ran the Counter Trey and that was it. They had two plays and won whatever it was, two Super Bowls. But you could never get ready for the play, you had to get ready for the formations, the shifting, all of the different ways that they broke up.

They probably had 20 passes, 25 passes. It wasn't a lot of plays. But one play you've got [Art] Monk in this position, the next time Monk's somewhere else, the next time Monk's somewhere else. One time it's three tight ends. One time it's four receivers. One time it's two tight ends. So that was hard. It was a core group of plays with a gillion formation and differ looks. It's more than that now, but it has those elements to it.

## Q: What's your favorite gadget play you've run?

**BB:** Favorite gadget play that we've run? I'd have to say it'd be something that worked.

**Q:** The Tom Brady down the sidelines against Miami in 2001?

**BB:** Yeah, that was one of the days where everything kind of worked, even throwing it to Brady and Patrick Pass in the flat there for a touchdown. The double pass against Pittsburgh a couple years ago. The ones that work, you remember those. The ones that don't work you try to forget them pretty quick.

**Q:** What's the worst gadget play you've seen run on any level?

**BB:** Well, one of the worst ones I'd say that I ever ran was in '79 against the Rams, when I was the special teams coach on the Giants. We had run five or six fake punts that year, and hit all of them and so we went out to play L.A. in the Coliseum and we didn't have a real good team. [Dave] Jennings was our best ... It was [Phil] Simms' rookie year and Jennings was one of our best players, All-Pro punter.

I mean, he was great, and he could throw. He was a very athletic guy, so we had several fake punts that we hit. And unfortunately we were punting a lot, so that gave us more opportunities than we needed. We went out to the Rams and Brian Kelley was a fullback, so we snapped the ball to Kelley and he ran a sweep. And kind of once he was about to get tackled, he stopped, turned, and lateraled it back to Jennings on the other side of the field.

The play didn't work very well. It wasn't very well executed and then when Jennings caught the ball, he thought he had a chance to get the first down, but he really didn't. But he thought he did, so he ran for the sticks there on the sideline and then about three guys hit him about four yards short of the first down, knocked him out of bounds. I mean, he got knocked over by the cheerleaders. His helmet was on sideways, he's looking out through the ear hole. The ball is out there on the track somewhere and [Head Coach Ray] Perkins looks over at me with that look of 'what are we doing? This is our best player,' and he looked like he got run over by two Mack trucks. So we go all the way over to the other side of the field and get him off the track and put him back together again. He got killed and then Ray said - which I would have done the same thing [but] I wouldn't have done it as nicely as he did - he said, 'Look, we're not running any more fakes like that again. Just forget that.' He didn't quite put it that way, but you get the idea. So that was one that didn't work that luckily Dave and I can still smile about. I mean, to be honest with you, it wasn't a lot different - the play was different - but the result wasn't a lot different than what we ran with Brian Moorman on the fake in the Pro Bowl.

Sean Taylor hit him and I mean, that was ... I mean, Brian could have taken less of a hit on that. Jennings caught the ball coming from the other side of the field and didn't really have ... Brian was running. At least he had a little chance to, but Sean Taylor hit him. That was a massive hit. It was right in front of our bench. I thought it was ... Oh, my God.

**Q:** Did you get any calls from Bobby April about the Brian Moorman hit?

**BB:** I'm telling you because he ran that one against us in '02 or '03 - it was like the longest run of the year. He gained 38 yards or something. We couldn't come close to catching him. We had a force guy out there; he just out ran him and the whole rest of the team. And then you get out to the Pro Bowl and say, 'Well, this guy's fast. I don't know how much they're playing for a fake punt over there,' but he wasn't as fast as Sean Taylor was, I'll tell you that.

**Q:** He popped up pretty good from that.

**BB:** He did. He did. I mean, he took it. I mean, Brian's a heck of an athlete, he really is, but I mean, he got killed. But he did, he bounced up and I was happy to see that because you hate to see a guy [get hurt] on that kind of play. That wasn't the idea. And in all honesty, on special teams out there in the Pro Bowl, there's hardly any contact. I mean, that's almost flag football, really. So it kind of surprised me that ... But he got lit up though. That was a big hit.

## Q: You mentioned the no-huddle. Do you remember when you first saw a team did go to that?

**BB:** Well, when Sam Wyche was in Cincinnati, they ran all those 'Sugar Huddles' with Boomer [Esiason] and those weren't at the pace of the no-huddle. I think the no-huddle now with Buffalo is similar to the 'K-Gun' back with [Jim] Kelly when he ran it and [Alex] Van Pelt, obviously, that it was the speed of the game. It was how fast they came to the line, how quickly the ball got snapped with sometimes as much as 20 seconds left on the 40 second clock. So it was a much faster pace than - for example - the Cincinnati no huddle. The big difference here is speed and communication. Again, it's the teams that huddle at the line and don't really get back in there. You usually have time to get your communication and do what you want to do, but when they're going that fast, you've got to be ready to match the speed of the game that they're playing at. So that's challenging.

## Q: When did the long snapper become such a specialized position?

**BB:** I would say at about the time I came into the league in the 70s, middle to late 70s. A lot of teams, when I first came into the league, I'd say there were a couple long snappers in the league and most teams had a position player that snapped, either a center, linebacker, tight end. Then, in the 70s and the early 80s, that transitioned to having a snapper, a kicker and a punter. In a lot of cases, you had punters and kickers who were also position players still in the 70s.

Then you got the specialists, like [Pete] Gogolak and guys like that, who came in and they were just full-time players. In the early 70s and even into the middle 70s, there were still teams that had punters, kickers and snappers that were position players. Even if you look at the Pro Bowl voting, I'm not sure exactly when that changed,

I'd say 10-15 years ago. It hasn't been that long where the rule was you had to select a player who was a position player to be your long snapper. Like when you send in your ballot, you had to include somebody that was a snapper so that each team would have one or they picked one.

At some point - I can't remember exactly when it was - they went to just strictly selecting a long snapper because, in all honesty, those players didn't snap anymore. It kind of got phased out, like the Lou Groza's and the Gino Cappelletti's and the George Blanda's, who were great kickers and also position players [who] went the way of specialists. A big part of that also was the expansion of the roster. The bigger the rosters, then the more specialization you have. So when you were looking at 39-, 40-, 42-, 43-man rosters, you have to combine some of those things, whereas now you get to the specialization with higher numbers. There's a certain movement out there amongst different teams and coaches and media and so forth about expanding the rosters and saying: 'Well, we have more players and are already paying a certain number of guys. So why not let them all play?'

I think the downside to that is the more players you have, then the more specialization you have. So now you have a kickoff guy, a field goal guy, a snapper, a punt return guy, a kickoff return guy, you've got a blocking tight end and goal-line, you've got a receiving tight end and third-down and - defensively - you need all the people to match those. Before you know, you've got a plus-50 punt return guy. Then you got a guy on the long field to return punts when you don't have a lot of ball-handling situations.

Yeah, you could take the roster to 70 and find a spot for everybody for that one situation, kind of like in college; you have a field goal snapper, a punt snapper, you've got 20 guys to do 20 different things. I'm not sure if that's good for the game. But obviously it's a longer discussion here. I don't mean to get carried away on a simple question. I just love to help you guys out and give you some information. Now, you can rip me on it for answering a long answer.

**Q:** [On Coach Belichick's relationship with Jimmy Johnson]

**BB:** Well, my relationship with Jimmy [Johnson] goes back to when I was the Head Coach at Cleveland and he was in Dallas. I was in the AFC; he was in the NFC. So we weren't in direct competition. It could have been more direct, let's put it that way - not that we weren't in competition - but it could have been more direct. We were able to work out some trades and help each other out in some different situations during that time.

Then, after he left Miami, he was a guy that when I was in Florida, [I] connected with and we spent some time together and he's really been helpful. He's done this job; he's been a head coach. He's been in a lot of big games. He's coached a lot of good players. He's been in a lot of situations that NFL coaches, like myself, face from time to time. I asked him a lot of questions. He was very open with his responses and advice and how he handled situations and things like that. So I enjoyed talking with him and going fishing with him, relaxing on his boat, all those kind of things. It's kind of a good trade off, I guess: go down to Florida, hang out with Jimmy, catch some fish, relax, get a lot of good advice. I don't know what he got out of it, but it was good for me.

**Q:** Can you comment on the passing of Jim Johnson and what he meant in terms of football?

**BB:** I think Jim's probably as good a defensive coordinator as I've seen in the league in the time I've been in it. I spoke with Jim quite frequently. We exchanged a lot of ideas and I have great respect for his philosophy, his schemes and the way he attacks offenses [and] his ability to utilize personnel. I think he's got a real good football mind. Tried to work with him several times and that never quite worked out, but I've always ... I first knew him when he was at Notre Dame. I've had great respect for him. He's a good friend and a real good football coach - tough guy to compete against. Certainly, on behalf of the team and organization, our condolences go out to the Eagles and

Jim's family. He's one of the best.

**Q: You were out here 10 years ago interviewing with Al Davis. What were your impressions of that meeting and of the Raiders organization back then?**

**BB:** It was a pretty interesting interview to be talking X's and O's with an owner. Al's had six decades in the NFL, so he has as much history and knowledge about the game, what he wants and what's going on in the game during that time as anybody. We talked a lot about strategic football, X's and O's, as well as overall organizational stuff, and personnel and philosophy. It was great to sit down and talk with him. We shared some views and conversations on different aspects of technical football. It wasn't a big social interview. It was much more detailed and specific to football.

**Q:** It was more chatting X's and O's than actually interviewing for a job?

**BB:** Well, no, we talked about a lot of organizational things: putting a staff together, putting a team together, different ways of doing things, how to organize it and how to build an organization. He shared what his views were with me and I gave him what some of my thoughts were at that time.

**Q: Talking about Buffalo's special teams – Steve Tasker is the first guy that I remember as really standing out as being a special teams specialist. As important as that role has always been in the game, when did that idea of a guy who really made his niche in special teams begin?**

**BB:** I'd say probably George Allen when Dick Vermeil was special teams coach going back to the Redskins days. I think George, if I'm not mistaken, I don't want to speak out of turn here, but I want to say George was the first coach to employ strictly a special teams coach.

When I came into the league I would say a few teams, maybe a quarter of the teams if I had to guess, had a true special teams coach and the rest of them it was broken up, kind of like it is now with a lot of college teams because they're limited in their staff size. You'd have maybe the defensive coaches would have the coverage teams like punt and kickoff and the offensive coaches would have the return teams like punt return and kickoff return, field goal, where more of the offensive guys were on, that type of thing. Or maybe it would be one coach on the staff would have running backs and special teams or whatever.

I came right during that transition period. I wasn't at the beginning of it, but I was still before everybody had a special teams coach and also before every team had a snapper, a holder and a kicker. There were times where there were some teams there that had guys that played other positions and snapped and even in a couple cases where you had guys that kicked or punted that also played another position. Less of that, but there weren't very many pure long snappers in the early to mid-70s. There were a few but not [many] – that was kind of the whole evolution of the coach, the specialists, soccer style kickers. That was a kind of transitional period there. So, I'd say Allen had a couple guys like that that were just really special teams players, impact type guys.

When I was at Baltimore my first year, I think we had Howard Stevens who was a little 5-5 running back, was the returner. I think the Patriots might have had Mack Herron then, who was another kind of returner only. That was the same thing, too. Not every team had a specialized returner. A lot of teams had position players that also returned. But there was, again, a little bit of trend toward using a roster spot for a guy that just returned kicks. Those roster spots were pretty special back then because you had fewer players.

To dedicate one to a snapper or a returner – you could really, back in those days, you could really save a spot if you added a guy that could do both like we had at Baltimore with the snapper situation. [Ken] Mendenhall did PATs and I'm trying to remember who did field goals [Toni Linhart]. There were a lot of guys, the [Bob] Kuechenbergs and guys like that that were good players that also snapped so that was an extra roster spot there if you had a position player that could also double up for you. But those days are long gone. We've seen the end of that, quite a few years now. But I would take it back to Allen.

# 4
# PREPARATION & GAME PLANNING

**Q:** Will you watch the Seahawks on television tomorrow night, or is it more beneficial to just wait for the All-22 to come out?

**BB:** It will definitely be more beneficial to see the coaches' copy on it, but this is kind of a unique situation. We're pretty far ahead on Seattle. We've had a chance to work on them all week. We've done all their games up through the Saints game, so there's no more to do, and there won't be any more to do until Monday night. I think Monday night will be a good opportunity to kind of take a look at the game against Buffalo with a little bit of a blank slate.

Buffalo is a team that we know well from just having played against them and being a division team, so I think when we see what Seattle is doing, we'll be able to figure out why they're doing what they're doing against Buffalo, what they perceive as an area to attack or what type of game plan to utilize. I think it will be interesting to watch it in reverse – to watch Buffalo, a team that we know well, attack Seattle. We're a different team than Buffalo, but still, there are certain things that carry over so we'll be able to watch how they attack Seattle and kind of do it on a timely basis as opposed to going back and looking at it after the fact.

We'll sort of watch it unfold and picture plays or situations, plays and calls that we've talked about making in certain situations, and then when those situations come up, see how it would hypothetically match up against Seattle, as a I said, on kind of a timely basis, rather than when the game's over and you already know what happened. This is a little bit of a different chance to do it. As I said, I think that makes it a little bit interesting, so yes, we'll watch the game.

**Q:** How much self-scouting do you and your staff do in determining whether a player has a 'tell', or some kind of pre-snap indicator that gives away what they might be doing on a play?

**BB:** Right. Well, I think that's important. One of the best places to start is with your teammates. So we work against each other each day and what a good teammate will do, a defensive player will tell an offensive player 'Hey, I can tell when you're pulling. I can see your depth,' or 'I can see whatever it is,' or vice versa. An offensive player would tell a defensive player 'I can tell when you're blitzing,' or 'We see a man coverage stance or a zone coverage stance.

In zone your feet are here. When you're in man it's a little bit different. Your hand's a little bit different,' or whatever it is. I think a lot of it starts on the practice field or our coaches who work against each other, the receiver coach with the DB's [defensive backs] or DB's with the receivers or whatever it is. We'll do that.

**Q:** Is there big value to having that cleaned up before going into a game?

**BB:** Look, I think if one of our players can pick it up you've got to assume that one of their players watching film can pick it up. If it's a stance or a mannerism or whatever it is, something, and I know that the quarterbacks and Josh [McDaniels] do that with the secondary or Matt [Patricia] and the defensive coaches will do that with the offensive coaches especially in training camp but even sometimes in the scout team stuff.

We talk about what the quarterback saw. How did he know this was going to happen or somebody tipped it off or defensively how did the defense know that this was going to happen? Well because they're not threatened by something else. We haven't run this kind of complimentary play to it and that's why it's being overplayed by a guy in practice or that kind of thing. So we definitely try to watch ourselves but I think on the practice field or on practice film, however you want to call it, that there's a good give-and-take there between the staff and the players to try and help each other. I mean look, if we know what the play is that doesn't really help us, right? I mean what's it going to be the next time we don't know what the play is so we're better of telling you 'Hey, you're tipping off the play,' because realistically that's the way it's going to be most of the time. We're not going to know what the play is.

**Q: I believe you started the process in 2001 of meeting with the quarterbacks on Tuesday's to go over the game plan. Do you still take part in that process and how does that meeting time help them prepare for the upcoming game?**

**BB:** Well, yeah I meet with the quarterbacks at least a couple of times per week. I'd just put it this way - I think as the head coach it's important to have a relationship with, particularly in our offense, with the guy that the offense is kind of running through. So, we talk about a number of things in those meetings. We talk about our opponent's defense, we talk about how we want to attack our opponent and we talk about numerous other things that come up weekly or from time to time regarding a whole variety of subjects that I think relate to that position.

That position - how it relates to our team and how we want the position played. Josh [McDaniels] and the offensive staff do a great job of coaching all the positions, of putting together the offense, of coaching the quarterbacks and preparing them I'm sure as well as any quarterbacks in the league are prepared. So, that's not really what it's about. I'd say it's more about the head coach maintaining a relationship with the quarterback and how the game is going to go so that we know and I know when we call a play or when we get into a certain situation and were trying to do something that the quarterback and the head coach and everybody else involved on that side of the ball - that we're all on the same page in terms of what we're trying to do, how we're trying to do it and if we have options what those options are and how they would be processed. So I think that's just to me part of my job as the coach in coaching the team.

But I certainly would not represent it as coaching a position or coaching the offense. That's Josh and the offensive coaches. I mean they do a great job of what they do. That's not really, although there's maybe some overlap, that's not really what my involvement with the quarterbacks is about.

**Q: With the Bills' offensive and defensive coordinators both being former players, I'm curious if you ever take into account the way they played the game as oppose to the way they coach it?**

**BB:** I'd say it depends on who the person is and what the system - I mean I think we know where a lot of the decisions on defense with Buffalo are coming from. And I'm sure there's certainly a team effort and a group effort and group ideas and so forth, but I think we also know where some of these are coming from and so to me its whoever the decision maker is. It could be the player. I mean look it could be the player; a team like certain offenses in the league that really run through the quarterback.

In the end it's the quarterback that's making a lot of decisions on the play, whether it's the play that's called, or the change of the play or a modification of the play on the line. In some cases it's the coach. In some cases it's the head coach, the coordinator, the quarterback coach or positon coach, whatever it is. In some cases it's the player and there are a lot of defenses where the middle linebacker or the safety, whoever that guy is, controls the defense kind of like a quarterback does. And in the end the game kind of goes through him, especially in certain situations.

I know as a defensive coach where I've put the game to those guys because of the confidence that I have in them and their ability to see things on the field a lot later and that are a lot more accurately than you could see them on the sideline when you're calling the defense based on down and distance and what players they have in the game. You don't know what formation they're in, you don't know how big their splits ae. Now once a team comes out there and gets in a certain look then that's more information.

There are times, a lot of times, where we give our players a lot of responsibility to run the defense at that point or run the offense at that point once they see how the defense is deployed. Again, it just depends on who the decision maker is. I don't think there's any right or wrong to it. It's just figuring out who it is and trying to really compete against that person.

**Q: How long does it take for you to be able to identify what it is a team wants to do from week to week and you can rule certain things out, as opposed to the early season when there is an element of surprise?**

**BB:** I don't know that you can ever rule them out but I'd say the term 'midseason form' is pretty accurate. What a team has done by that point, I mean it's pretty much who they are. They've seen a lot of different matchups, however they've evolved, they've evolved. There might be a few things that are a little bit off, a little bit out of the fairway, but they're pretty close or there's a reason for why they were a little off the mainline.

But you know, you just need to get enough looks - five, six, seven games; whatever it is - to see that. It doesn't mean somebody couldn't throw in a new wrinkle. I think that's always part of football, but you know there's only so many of those you can get ready in practice in a normal week so you still have to be able to go out there and execute it. I don't think it ever goes away but there's a certain point where every team pretty much shows they're out there trying to win every week, they're not evaluating players, they show their hand, and you tell everybody what kind of team you are.

**Q: What is the process in determining your matchups between**

your cornerbacks and opposing receivers? Is it a week-to-week process or do certain guys have skills that work better against certain receivers?

**BB:** The best way to determine it, I guess, is experience. I think that's one of the things that when you practice against a team like New Orleans and Chicago that you get exposure to different receivers. I'm not saying who's better or who's not better. It's not even about that but it's another seven or eight guys that we get to cover in addition to the seven or eight guys that we're covering on our team, and another seven or eight guys the next week when Chicago came in here, so just the exposure of playing bigger guys, quicker guys, faster guys, different type route runners, how they stem and set up their routes, how they use their hands downfield, whatever it is.

So, it's just sooner or later over the course of the season you're going to get all of that to some degree and the more you can practice against it and understand what they're trying to do, what's best for you, how we individually - how you play a guy, how I play a guy - we both have to cover them but maybe we do it differently because our skillsets are a little bit different. It's just working through that whole process. I think it's really a lot of - I don't want to say trial and error - but experience of doing it against different type guys.

And there are some players that they have a specific skillset but they also have may have a very specific route-tree, that they run if you look at the whole route tree 80 percent of their routes are a certain type of route; vertical routes, or lateral-breaking routes, whatever it happens to be, and then as it relates to that individual player then the techniques on him are a little more specific to what he actually - forget about what he can do - but what did they actually ask him to do?

That becomes now a little bit of an overriding part of the criteria. If they want the guy to go deep, even though he could do other things, but that's mainly what he does then you've got to work more on defending that.

**Q:** How do you prepare for a player like Chris Conley, who didn't have a lot of action in the regular season?

**BB:** You go back to where you go back to. Sometimes if they pick a player up from another team, you look at him. You look at whatever you can look at, whatever that is - preseason, maybe it's with another team, could possibly be in college, depending on what the guy's situation is. But again, that's a common thing every week. There are always players on the roster, particularly at this time of year, that maybe haven't played a lot during the regular season but they're one play away from playing. It could be a quarterback. It could be anybody. It could be a pass rusher or receiver or corner - anybody.

So you have to be ready for those guys, and we prepare for everybody on the active roster. We don't know who they're going to play. They may put a guy in for certain plays and we need to know what his skills are and how we want to defend him or attack him as the case might be. It's really a common thing every week. It's just a different subset of players, but we always have to be ready for those guys, including the practice squad.

There have been many weeks where guys have popped up from the practice squad the day before the game or it could be the day of the game if it's a Monday night game, but it could be one of those late things and you don't want to be spend a lot of time on a player five minutes before a game, so look here are the guys on the practice squad, here are the potential guys that could come up based on an injury situation or a position on your opponent that you think this guy might factor into. I don't want to say it's common, but it's certainly not uncommon.

**Q:** How much extra works typically comes from preparing for an opponent that doesn't know or is choosing not to say who is going to play quarterback?

**BB:** We prepare for all guys on the active roster. We just don't prepare for one guy. It wouldn't make any difference. Last week, [Tony] Romo was out, so we didn't have to prepare for Romo, but it was [Brandon] Weeden, it was [Matt] Cassel, [Kellen] Moore - we don't know what they're going to do. And after the first play of the game, anything can happen. Whoever you think is in there could be somebody else anyways. It's the same thing with [Blake] Bortles or [Ben] Roethlisberger or any of those guys. Roethlisberger is there to start a game, can't finish the game and he's not there the next week. That's the NFL. It's like that at every positon.

We know who the players are, we know who the backups are we think based on what we know, what we've seen, what we anticipate to happen. Who would be the next perimeter corner, who would be the next inside corner, who would be the next safety, who would be the next dime guy? Maybe they wouldn't use dime; maybe they'd use nickel. Who would be the next nickel guy? Whatever it is, we have to be ready for that. It's one play away from happening.

We always prepare for all the players that are on the active roster. Then we come to the game and before the game we cross off the seven guys who are inactive. So, OK, this week they only have two tight ends active or they only have, whatever, five linebackers. Or here are the guys who are inactive - whether they're injured or whether they're inactive for other reasons, whatever it happens to be - then before the game, that hour, well the meeting we have before the game after the inactive list has come out and we can cross some guys off, and maybe that gives us an indication, a little bit more information of maybe what type of game it might be.

If a team has got maybe it looks like extra DBs active for our game and maybe less defensive linemen, maybe that's an indication it's going to be more of a nickel game. Or vice versa, a team keeps extra tight ends and running backs and fewer receivers, maybe it's an indication they're going to try to play bigger, that type of thing. But until that point, we work with everybody.

With all due respect, I know a lot of people live and die on the injury report, but I don't really care what's on the injury report. Look,

I don't know how these guys are going to be, either. We can put down whatever we want. But they're humans - some get better, some stay the same, some don't get better. There is no way to know for sure, and there are a lot of times it comes down to game-time decisions. I'm saying that about our team, and I'm with them and I'm talking to our doctors and trainers every day, but other teams, they're going through the same thing, too.

Just because a guy is on the injury report, and whatever he's listed as, that doesn't really mean anything. Guys that aren't well can make quick recoveries. Guys that are well can not turn the corner. So, we're ready for those guys, too. Honestly, I don't even care what's on the injury report. I really don't even look at it. Unless the guy is definitely out, then OK. If he's not, then to me, we've got to be ready for him.

**Q:** How often do you alter your game plan after the inactives are announced?

**BB:** I guess it would depend on what's on that list, but I'd say probably not too much. Look, you know a lot more after two series into the game than you will after looking at that inactive list. Obviously if there was a player that was a critical player for you in your game plan that wasn't going to play, then maybe that would alter something a little bit. You're going to double a receiver, and the receiver is inactive for the game, then OK, we're not going to double him. That knocks that call out.

Do you replace that with a different call or do you go the next guy, or do you just say, OK were not going to double anybody. Here's what we're going to do. But I'd say those situations are not that frequent. If you had that situation going into the game, like OK this guy has got a bad hamstring, not sure whether he'd be ready to go or not, then we're going to sit there and say, alright if the guy plays then here's what we're going to do.

If he doesn't play or maybe he doesn't play all the time because we know he's dealing with something, maybe he's in on some plays and out on some plays, then we wouldn't game plan him when he's not on the field. There really aren't too many of those situations where out of the blue somebody that you think is going to play that's a very significant part of the game plan totally catches you by surprise. But if that were to happen - say a guy got suspended or he had a family member die or whatever, came down with some bug or something the day before the game - it's no different than if he got hurt on the second play of the game. You make that added adjustment.

**Q: When you go to a stadium you've never played at before, what do you do pregame to prepare?**

**BB:** I'd say each player's position is a little bit different, but from my standpoint, it's just a familiarity of the 40-second clock, the scoreboard, the location of where things are on the field, like the communication system. We had a game – I want to say it was the New Orleans game – where instead of being located right between the benches, it was all the way down to one side. So, just to kind of remind yourself of those things so when it comes up during a game, you save a few seconds or you're more comfortable looking at the right plays, going to the right plays, doing the right thing.

**Q:** Is that the type of thing that you'll give yourself a little extra time on Sunday to familiarize yourself with?

**BB:** You do it all the time, check the wind, check the sun conditions, the lights, whatever is applicable to that game, and then the players the same thing, whether it's footing, again the 40-second clock, especially the 40-second clock location because that varies from stadium to stadium. Whatever the conditions are, a lot of times the wind is different at the middle of the field than it is in the end zone or the corners of the field or that kind of thing. So, the players do that. Sometimes the surfaces are a little bit different depending on the specifics of the field and the time of year that you play there. But it's all part of the regular routine, just to check it out even if you've been there before, even if you've played there 100 times just to re-familiarize yourself with it because you haven't been there in probably at least a year. But in this case it's new. We went through it last year when we played Minnesota. That was a new venue, too. It comes up from time to time.

**Q: How much harder is it to prepare for an opponent you rarely see?**

**BB:** Well it's a lot harder. You have to spend more time doing it. There is no real shortcut for it, you've just got to look at the film, study the scouting report, go back and not just look at the past few games, but go back and look at teams that are maybe more similar to you in style or scheme and see how the coordinators, Coach [Rod] Marinelli or Coach [Jason] Garrett or Coach [Scott] Linehan attack your type of scheme. You go to a division team, if it's been a carryover with coaches and players, you can go back to where you were and add in some new things since the last time you played them and you have some pretty good background and you can see, is it the same or what kind of modifications have they made during that time.

With a new team sometimes it's hard to get a handle of what was a specific thing they did for a particular game versus that's what they would do, they have done that multiple times in similar situations. It's hard to get a feel for that sometimes. We have done a lot of work on that in the offseason as well. Coach Garrett has been there and Coach Marinelli and Coach Linehan have had long careers in the National Football League, so it's not like we haven't faced them or are unfamiliar with their schemes. But as it relates to the Cowboys players, most of those guys our team hasn't played against.

**Q: When you're dealing with a less familiar team, what do you tell your players differently?**

**BB:** Got to get to know them. We've got to get to know them. We've got to spend more time studying them, each individual player understanding how they use them, what their skills are and understanding the scheme and how they fit within that scheme. I mean, look, there are some tests you study for where you kind of know the information and you review it – maybe division teams. There are other tests you study for where you don't know the information and you've got to study a lot harder, you have to work harder, put more into it, do more research, spend more time, and this definitely would fall into that category. Now part of that is our job as coaches to help them understand that this defense relative to the Seattle defense, this offense relative to the Oakland offense last year, the kicking game relative to the New Orleans kicking game when Mike [Mallory] was in New Orleans – things like that – how the players are used, what the players skills are.

But again, each of us individually, player and coach, has to prepare ourselves. I can't do somebody else's job, they can't do my job. We all have to put that same time and effort and concentration into it and that's what this team has to do. Now the team we're playing, they have the same issue we do. We haven't played them since 2012 and they haven't played us since 2012, so the competition on Sunday really starts during the week in terms of which team can practice, prepare better than the other team over that period of time. None of us will know the answer to that question until we get to Sunday. But the competition is going. We're competing with them. They're practicing today, we're practicing today. Competitively, we need to get more out of it today than our opponents do. That's the way it is every week.

**Q: How does it complicate matters when preparing for a team like Jacksonville that you don't play as often? Do you take a sneak peek in the offseason to get a better look at their personnel?**

**BB:** Yeah absolutely. We spent, even before the draft, but particularly after the draft, in that period from April till mid-June, one of the things that we do as a staff is we look very hard at our new opponents and also our early-season opponents just to make sure that we see what's relevant from last year and then when we see this year's film, is it the same, is it different. Maybe some things are the same, but they're using players differently or they've added a different component to their scheme somehow, that type of thing.

Yeah, absolutely, we spent a lot of time on Jacksonville. I've seen probably well over half their season from last year, from 2014. Now they're changing offensive coordinators, so that's obviously effected it some, but we've put a lot of time in trying get to know the players on the team from last year, what changes they've made this year, how they're using those players the same or differently. Obviously if it's the same, then that's a pretty good indication that you know what is and this is what it's going to be. There is definitely a big component in that, making sure that we are fully prepared for what our opponents have done and what they are capable of doing and if they are trending one way or another, that we are trying to keep up with that trend and not react to something that's maybe no longer a big part of what they are doing.

**Q: When you don't have much tape on an offense like the Bills, is it hard to determine how you want to defend them and what you want to take away because you don't know what they will prioritize?**

**BB:** I think that's a pretty common situation to be honest with you. You go into every game, and you have to over-prepare because as you said they can only run so many plays - let's call it 70 plays. But you have three, four, five, six - sometimes way more than that - games that you're looking at, so now you're looking at a neighborhood of three to four hundred plays.

Some of that they repeat and you try to get a tendency and you try to get a basic read on it, but each game is different. Teams that game plan a lot, like Buffalo does on both sides of the ball, you go in with a general plan, a general idea, you certainly know what their personnel is and how you want to defend certain individual players, but then as the game unfolds, then you can generally start to see this is how they're going to try to attack us.

And then at that point you have to make sometimes some in-game adjustments or maybe some things that you had prepared for, that you've gotten different things ready for doesn't look like they're going to come up, so you kind of put those off to the side and focus on the things that either they're hurting you with or the things that it looks to you like the way they're going to try to play the game. It starts wider and then it generally funnels in as the game starts to unfold. Fifteen, 20 plays into the game you should have a pretty good idea of this is what they're going to try to do. I'm not saying it doesn't move a little bit from there, but you certainly know a lot more after 15 plays into the game than you knew going into the game. So, I'd say that's a pretty common theme every week.

**Q: How difficult is it to lose a day of preparation and how much easier is it, if any, to prepare for a team in the division you know well?**

**BB:** Well, I think there's always advantages to playing teams that you're more familiar with. Of course, the more you know, the more you know, the more you know and you have to prepare for. We're looking at literally 15 regular season games from Buffalo plus we did a ton of work on them for the opener from the preseason and even going back offensively to Syracuse and going back defensively to the Jets defense.

We have way more information than we would be able to use in this game or they would be able to use in this game. We're looking at a couple thousand plays and there's going to be 60 to 70 on each side of the ball. It's an advantage and it's a curse. The opener is the same thing. You look at so much for the opener and you go into the opener and again, it's whittled down to whatever the game plan is for that game. But your preparation has extended well beyond that. We have a lot of information. We'll have to try to put our chips on certain numbers and play the percentages and know that there's also other things that they can do and they have done that we can't ignore but we can't prepare for everything. We just have to wait and see how the game plays out.

If something becomes more of a featured thing, then we'll obviously have to adjust to it. I'd say for the most part, when you get to this point in the season, there aren't too many things that are going to come up that you haven't dealt with already during the year. I'd be surprised if they could throw a lot out there that we would say, 'Oh my God, we've never seen that before.' But I'm not saying it's easy. It's not like, 'OK, we'll handle this the same way we handled it with some other team or some other situation.' Same thing offensively, the thing that I'd say is a little bit different about them is just their tempo. Like Baltimore was a no-huddle team but they weren't a fast no-huddle team. Buffalo is much more of a fast no-huddle team, similar to what we saw in training camp against Philadelphia. But again, we've seen that before.

Obviously we played them once earlier but that's a little bit of a challenge and that's not the easiest thing to simulate in practice because sometimes when you're running their plays, it's hard for your offense who is running their plays to do it at the tempo that they do it at. That's not the easiest thing to simulate. So our communication, our ability to get plays called, get them in, get them communicated, get them run properly, that will be a challenge for us. We'll work on it the best we can in practice but I'm sure it will be faster in the game than what we'll be able to do in practice. But I would say those are some of the things we have to be able to deal with.

**Q:** When you're trying to decide where to put down the chips, does self-scouting help?

**BB:** Yeah, sure, if there's something we've had a problem with and it's something that they do, then that's easy. Why would they not do it? They have it, we've been hurt with it. I think the real question is, you've been hurt with something and they don't do it, you're saying, 'OK, do you think they would put this in? Because it's not something they would normally do.' You could be defending a ghost because they haven't done it, but on the other hand if you've been hurt with it, it's hard to ignore it and say, 'Well, why would they not try to do the same that somebody else was successful with?' So, that self-scouting certainly plays a role into that.

On the other hand, I don't think any team at this point in the year is going to have been working on everything they've worked on all the way through the year and just junk it. They're going to do what they do and what they're familiar with. We have to be able to stop that but certainly anything that we've been hurt with that we know is a core part of what they do, I'm sure we're going to get that. It's just a question of what they want to add on to that. A lot of times, it will be complementary play. They're running the stretch play, running the stretch play and now's the time for the reverse, which maybe hasn't been shown a lot, things like that.

We have to be ready for complementary plays to go with it: the boots, the reverses, the misdirection plays, the double moves, the things like that that will come off a lot of their core plays. They've shown some of those anyway but I think that's definitely a part of it too. The more you do something, whatever it is in your offense, you run outs, you runs outs, you have to start thinking sooner or later somebody is going to jump this, it's time to get the out-and-up.

**Q:** When you prepare for a coach or coordinator who is with a new team but you've seen before, do you spend a lot of time looking at the back log for tendencies or do you mostly look at new personnel?

**BB:** Yeah, I think any time a coordinator changes, you go back to your notes for that coordinator, with the team that he was at and what he did there. Sure, no question. That travels with the guy. Now, again, sometimes that stays the same. Sometimes it gets modified a little bit. Sometimes it changes. Depending on who the head coach is – you just have to look at it. Sometimes it matches up pretty cleanly, sometimes part of it matches up, like maybe it's the third-down package but their base defense is different or vice versa. You see certain elements of it.

Maybe the pressures are the same but the zone coverages are a little bit different or whatever it happens to be. But yeah, absolutely that always – the same thing in the kicking game, offense, defense. I think you definitely want to track those guys. That's part of what you do in the offseason. You look at your opponents on the schedule. You look at coordinators who have changed or maybe a particular person that's been added to the staff. Maybe it's not even a coordinator but like a new offensive line coach, something like that, that that guy might have his protection system or he might have his running game, certain schemes or that type of thing. You see that scheme element has been added and then as you go through the year and you look at it, you say, 'OK, how much of an influence is this?' Yeah, we know they have that but they're not using it or they're using it a lot. It looks like this guy is running his protections and maybe the coordinator is running his pass patterns or whatever it is.

**Q:** When you're playing a team you haven't seen in four years, with new coaches and coordinators and a new quarterback, you can't really use your old film so much. How do you look at film to pick apart how they do specific things?

**BB:** I think it all starts in the offseason. When you have a team like this or like we had with Atlanta and New Orleans earlier in the year, you look at them and you go through the 2012 season and you see what they makeup of the team is, what they're trying to do, what their basic makeup is, what they're successful at, what they have trouble with. Then as you look at this season, you kind of compile it a little bit with last year. if it's the same, then it's the same. If it's different, then what are the differences and why have they gone the way they've gone? Is it because of personnel? Is it because they've changed their philosophy? What is it?

I think that's the way you try to get a handle of a team. when you have a new team like we started with this year, with the Jets, with a new coordinator, we knew Marty [Mornhinweg] but he was new there and Buffalo with again, a new staff there with Doug [Marrone] coming from Syracuse and so forth, you don't really have much to go on. You're looking at maybe the coordinator with a different team and different personnel, you're kind of penciling in a game plan but there are a lot of unknowns.

But I think if you look at a team like Carolina, with I know [Mike] Shula is a new coordinator but he was there and obviously there was going to be a carryover from what Rob [Chudzinski] did and Rivera was there. You have a lot better idea from year to year. I would say we took our notes from 2012, put them with what we had this year and I would say there a lot of things that are the same. The things that are different, we've noted those and said, 'OK, it looks like they've made a little bit of a shift here. It's a little bit different from what we saw in the offseason but we understand why they're doing it and so forth.'

I think it all starts in the offseason. If you just try to pick up and watch three or four films on a team that you don't know very well, from not having played them in three or four years, you can easily miscalculate something whether it's their personnel, maybe you're seeing a guy that's not quite 100 percent and then you get him and he is 100 percent or you don't see a guy for whatever reason, do what he can really do and then all the sudden it hits you and then you get surprised by it. Or scheme-wise, you see something that you should have seen but you just didn't do enough homework on it. You try not to let that happen. That can happen if you only look at a couple games on a team, even though they're the most recent ones.

**Q: When you self-scout or evaluate coaches what are some things you look at? You have a much better vantage point of how all the coaches are doing their jobs. What are some things you look at?**

**BB:** First of all, I think it's an ongoing process. I don't think you do nothing until you get a bye week and all of the sudden here comes a big self-analysis. We do that on a weekly basis. We look at plays we've run, we look at the production we're having or not having and things that stand out one way or the other that are especially good or the results aren't what we want and we try to find a reason for that and correct it, whatever that happens to be. They are all individual analyses.

At the same time, if we're doing a lot of one particular thing, then the evaluation of the production on that is, 'We're doing a lot of that, is that good? Are we getting a lot out of it? Or should we be

180

doing a lot of something else and a little less of whatever this happens to be.' That involves a lot of things. It's plays, it's techniques, its schemes, it's maybe style of play, if you will, so personnel groups, all those kind of things so we try to stay on top of all that. But I think what you really look for are things that once you have enough opportunities to evaluate it – it's hard to evaluate a play whether it's good or bad if you only run it one time. It was good, that's good, does that mean it's going to be good the next time?

Or if it was bad, if something went wrong, does that mean the next time that same thing is going to go wrong or do you believe in the play and you're going to get it right? After you've had a number of opportunities to observe it, you've run it multiple times then you have a fair evaluation. You say, 'OK, we've run this play a bunch of times, these same problems keep coming up. Or this is the issue in this play, we have to change this.' Not that we haven't had experience with those plays before, but again it just gives you sometimes a chance to study it in a little bit more detail.

**Q: How have the guys done preparing for an option attack that most of them haven't seen since college or high school?**

**BB:** I'd say college. I think they're similar principles but it's basically being disciplined. Somebody has to take the quarterback, somebody has to take the pitch, somebody has to take the dive, somebody has to take the quarterback, however they're doing it. They have several different ways that they run it and they use different option combinations which is tough because they're not all the same. You have to have different rules so it definitely stresses the force element - the perimeter of your defense.

On some of those dive plays, they hit so quickly relative to the normal, a guy lines up seven, seven and a half, eight yards deep in the backfield in the I-formation or in a one-back set, like an I-back would. By the time it gets to the line of scrimmage, it's a whole different tempo than the dive guy that's just popping right through there sometimes before they even realize it. That's something we had to adjust to in practice - a couple of times our defensive linemen, the back was already by them before they really realized it. We're just not used to that - the plays hitting that quickly, maybe in short yardage but I'm saying in normal plays, it's a little different look to it. They definitely give you some problems on all those different combinations that they've used.

**Q: When it comes to the self-scouting you guys and a lot of teams do during the bye weeks, what does that entail? Are you involved with that?**

**BB:** Again, I think it is a little of a misconception. We don't just self-scout during the bye week; we do it on a weekly basis. We look at our games that we feel like our opponents are looking at, whatever that constitutes. What are they seeing? Does that affect what we want to do? Do you want to change that? Do we want to not change it? And if we do want to change it, how do we want to change it? That's something that you do every week. The bye week - you have a little bit more time. Maybe if you wanted to not just look at the description of the plays or a written report of the plays, maybe you actually go to those plays and say, 'Okay, not what do they have on paper, but let me actually go look at the plays and see what's happening on our third down or our inside runs or our outside runs or our kickoff returns' or whatever it is.

You have an awareness of that on a weekly basis anyway. You know what you've been doing the last couple weeks. You definitely sit down at some point during the week and look at that. How many times have we called this in this situation? What's our run-pass breakdown? What's our blitz breakdown? How many left returns have we run? How many right returns have we run? What tendencies are we forming? Again, tendencies are like anything else, when it's 50-50, 60-40, 65-35 - how hard can you bank on 60-40? But when it's 90 percent or 95 percent that certain things are happening, now you're getting - that's pretty predictable. And sometimes it's okay.

Sometimes it's kind of okay to - look, Nolan Ryan is on the mound, he's going to throw a fastball. That's no secret. Is he better off throwing a fastball than a change up? Yeah. He's going to throw a fastball; let's see who can hit it. I don't say you have to change up all the time; you just have to know what you're doing. If you want to say, 'Okay, they know it's coming, it's our best thing, we're going to do it anyway, let's see if they can stop it,' that's alright. You just have to know what you're doing.

If you say, 'Well, we think they're not going to adjust to it,' and they do because it's something you do all the time, then you don't want to put yourself in that position. But it's not something that just happens during the bye week. It happens every week. Could you take a little longer look at it during the week? Yeah, absolutely and that's a good thing to do. But it's something we do on a weekly basis.

**Q: I read a comment from Dolphins Head Coach Tony Sparano about the unknown of their offense. That's a team with the Wildcat that you guys saw. How do you prepare for that unknown and does that make in-game coaching more important this week?**

**BB:** I think the players and coaches' adjustments to anything new, of course that's part of every game. They ran a lot of it [the Wildcat] in the past. [Offensive Coordinator] Brian [Daboll] ran it in Cleveland with [Josh] Cribbs and we saw it over the last couple of years. We prepared for it, I think, literally every week. We'll prepare for it this week, we'll prepare for it next week, even if a team hasn't shown it. It's not that far-fetched, you know, because so many teams have run it anyway.

We discuss what our adjustments are going to be to it, how we're going to play it, and then if that's okay, then great and if something happens and we need to adjust it, then we'll adjust it during the game. I'm just saying things like that, like unbalanced line, empty formations, Wildcat formations, defensively four-man line, three-man line with some fourth guy floating around back there behind the line of scrimmage, five defensive backs, six defensive backs, whichever they have shown, I think you still have to be ready and know what to do if they do any of the other things, you know, play a five-down look, cover the offensive lineman with somebody whether it's a defensive lineman or a linebacker walk-up - what we call the diamond front or the old Bear defense, that kind of thing. Those are pretty - I won't say they're standard - but things you better be ready for. If you don't see it this week, you're going to see it next week, if you don't see it next week, you'll see it the week after that. It's not that uncommon.

**Q: Can you talk about the process of scouting an NFC opponent quickly that you aren't familiar with?**

**BB:** It's tough. I think the process starts in the offseason. You get the schedule and you see that you're going to be playing Chicago in a short week. You see you're going to be playing Detroit on a short week, so you try to do your offseason preparations on them and get a feel for what they were like the year before. But, again, with both these teams, it's difficult because the Lions had some new players coming onto to their roster and of course with Mike [Martz] coming in [with Chicago], he brings a new offense - some of the same players, but then how he uses them in the system is different than what you're going to see from the '09 season.

You kind of prepare for that the best you can, but, ultimately, you end up in a short week and you have to try and get a jump on them during the long week, during the Monday night week. You just have to try and do the best you can here on Tuesday and make Tuesday into a Monday and a Tuesday and cram it in there and try to get the players up to speed on Wednesday. I think today is going to be a tough day for everybody. It already has been. What you hope for is that when you come back in here tomorrow on Thursday, is that you are pretty close to being on schedule for a normal Thursday.

If you can do that, then I think you can stay on track for Friday, Saturday and Sunday. That's kind of our goal today, is to get to where we normally are by tomorrow morning. It's a challenge and one of the main things we emphasize to the players is how important everything is this morning with paying attention and the walkthroughs and the films and the game plans and getting on it and being on top of it, even though we haven't had a chance to do as much preparation on Tuesday as we normally would with the Monday game.

**Q: When you are putting your game plan together, how much does depth at a particular position in terms of the number of healthy guys available factor in to how much that position is part of the game plan?**

**BB:** It's a really hard decision to make and that's one of the toughest questions we face as a coaching staff every week. It's not only the depth of that position in the game, but it's also the depth at that position for practice. If you're sitting in there on Wednesday and Thursday saying, 'We think these guys are going to be able to play in the game, but they are not going to be able to practice.' Well, then who practices it? You're putting stuff that guys who aren't in ... Let's say you've got a tight end, so now you're going to run a two tight end play.

So who's practicing the play? Even if you think you're going to have that player for the game, but if you're not certain if you're going to have that player for the game, and you've got only two tight ends and you're working on two tight end plays, now you're saying we might not even have a tight end or somebody else is going to have to learn. Or you say, 'Look, even if that player isn't there, then so and so is going to have to learn how to do this.' We're going to move an offensive linemen - or whatever you are going to do - or we are going to replace that player with a back, or however you are going to run the play and say if he's not there, then this is how we're going to do it.

But it's a tough decision and it's a tough decision in practice, too. [It] is how much time do you want to waste in practice on a play without the players who are actually going to be playing? Is it still worth it for the other 10 guys to see it? Or is it really, you're running a route that a receivers going to run but that receiver isn't practicing.

So do we run the play so everybody can see how the play's going to work without the guy who's going to do it? Or is it not worth running it because the guy running it isn't even going to be practicing? And you go through that a lot. It's no different than on defense. You put in your dime defense, so you've got six defensive backs out there or nickel - five defensive backs - whatever it is. And so in the game if this player was out, then that guy would replace him, and this guy would replace him and we'd put another guy in here. Alright, so do we practice like that in practice?

And then we come to the game, and then this player's here, and now we've practiced in one position, and then we played a game and everybody's playing a different position. Or do you practice with what you have, and you just take somebody on the practice squad? And say you practice that position because so and so is out and everybody else stays where they are because we think this guy's going to hopefully be ready to play in the game. And now again, you are practicing with a guy that's not even going to play, and if in fact he doesn't play, then you're going to have to move them around anyway. Absolutely, and we go through this every single week and so does every other team. We go through that every single week - game-planning, practicing.

And honestly, there are not many practice players. It's not like college where you have a freshman team to run 75 plays a day, it's not like that. Our offense runs plays for our defense [and] our defense runs plays for our offense. You get 30 plays in practice a day and you whiff on 10 of them, it's this - this player's out, that player's out, the guy on the other side of the look team screws the play up, so you didn't get a good look at it. You could lose a whole practice if you're not careful just on stuff like that. Then, pretty soon you go into the game and you've had really 75 percent efficiency in practice instead of a possible 100 percent, so those plays in practice are important and how that gets distributed.

Same thing in a game plan, you work on a certain percentage of your game plan and the personnel doesn't matchup to it by game time and now you've wasted a lot of time on that. Those are tough decisions, they're tough decisions. It's not something that you can really talk about with the press, the media and that kind of thing. It's all things that go into those meetings, planning, practices and all that. There are some hidden costs there, some hidden opportunities.

**Q:** How difficult has this been with the three running backs?

**BB:** I'd say of all the positions, running back is probably one of the easiest positions to tell you the truth because somebody's going to be in there at running back, whichever guy it is, then he does it. If you want to take a defensive back, one of the practice squad backs, for example, and make them a running back during the defensive carry that's really not a problem.

You could take guys like [Kyle] Arrington from the practice squad, somebody like that, and put them in there at running back and let them run plays. And it isn't a big deal. It's a lot tougher to do it at the interior positions: line, linebacker, tight end. It's hard to take a running back, stick him over there and say, 'OK, you play linebacker.' Or take a linebacker over there and say, 'OK, you play tight end.' It's a lot hard to do. That's definitely a big challenge though. It's a challenge for every team. It's a challenge for every coaching staff that makes up the game plans. It's a challenge for the position coaches who coach that position on how to divide those things up and really the assistant coaches, which I'll tell you - I'm not trying to over dramatize it or anything, but I'm saying if you're an assistant coach, there's no way for a head coach to be able to manage all the decisions that an assistant coach has to make.

For example, if you're running a play, which guy do you put in to run the play? Do you put Kevin Faulk in to run it? Let's say it's primarily a play that he's going to be in there for, so you want him to be able to run that play, but now what if he's not in there and you have to put somebody else in. Now, do you put that other player in to have him run it to make sure he knows what to do? This is the second time you've run the play now and it's a little bit of a different look. Or do you put Kevin in there? And now if he's not in there, then now what happens when you put the next guy in? He's never run the play before in practice, so now what do you think of the chances of that being a good play are?

But those are decisions the assistant coaches have to make every single day in practice. Here's how many plays we have and it's not an infinite number. Here's how many plays we have. Here's how many guys we've got to divide them up in between. Here's how many looks we can see. A team like the Jets, they run this blitz, they run that blitz, they run another blitz, they run this coverage, they run that coverage. Well, you're not going to see it against all that, so you have to decide what do you want to see this play against. And who do you want in there running it? What if we have to make a substitution? How does all that work? That's where Ivan [Fears], Dante [Scarnecchia], Matt [Patricia], Pepper [Johnson], Scott O'Brien, and all those guys do a great job of managing that on a staff-wide basis. Scott O'Brien, you lose one guy and he's on six teams, five teams.

A guy like Sam Aiken or a guy like Chung - somebody like that - is in there on five or six teams. You are not replacing one guy; it's one guy on this team, one guy on that team. So when you think about your depth chart and how you're going to place all those guys, that's one of the things you have to consider. Well, if this guy's out, I have to move four guys on this team. I've got to move three guys on that team. I have to move four guys on that. Or can I just take one guy and say, 'OK, you replace Sam Aiken on this team, this team, this team and that team,' or however you are going to do it. That's what assistant coaches ... That's where a lot of those guys make their money right there, is all those decisions as well as developing players at their positions. There's no way to minimize that and there's no way for me to give it due credit either.

**Q: Do you ever install things on Tuesdays, work on it Wednesday and Thursday, but then Friday you don't feel great about it and decide to tell the team to scratch that?**

**BB:** Yeah, absolutely. Absolutely. That happens, I would say, pretty much every week. Sometimes it's on Thursday, sometimes it's on Friday, sometimes it could even be on Saturday. We could say, 'Look, cross this play off. Cross that play off. Cross this adjustment off. We're not going to do that.' Either we ran it a couple times and for whatever reason - either it didn't look good, or we didn't get a run right, or we just don't have enough time to practice it against what we really think we're going to see. We just say, 'That's it.' And we talk to the players about that, too, players - particularly the quarterback, but not just the quarterback.

If we had a secondary or the linebackers and we talked to them at the end of the week and they're like, 'I still don't really feel good about this,' well, alright. You know what? We don't need it. We've got other stuff we can call, hopefully. The whole game isn't just hinged on this one thing. If Tom says, 'You know what, I don't really feel good about his play down here, they do this, do that...' Ok, well maybe if you ran it three or four more times, but we don't have time to run it three or four more times, so you just say, 'Ok, let's pull the plug on it. We have other plays. We have other stuff we feel good about, so let's forget about that one.'

So today, Friday, is the day when you go through the last - we do a walkthrough on Saturday, but Friday is the last day where you really run everything. If something comes up today that's still kind of a little bit dirty, then that's probably not a good sign. But sometimes you have to do it and you say, 'Ok look, we'll take a little more time on Saturday and set it up in the walkthrough. We've got to get this. When this happens, this is the only way we can handle it, so let's go through it one more time and make sure everybody's on the same page.' Again, you get later in the week and you deal with some one-time situations: two-minute, backed up, four-minute, two-point plays and things like that that are just kind of one-time deals that may or may not happen - kickoff return after a safety, you know, all that stuff.

You do it and if you make a mistake on it, you've just got to correct it and move on. I mean, there's no...you throw that out and then you've just got to put something else in. I think the big thing is you want everybody to feel confident and feel good going into the game that what we're going to call, we know what to do and we can be aggressive doing it. If you have that, then you've got a chance. If you don't and you can't play aggressively, then that's not what you want to do.

## Q: You mentioned self-scouting this week. Can you explain what that is and the process behind that?

**BB:** I would say two things, one is your own tendencies - what you're doing in certain situations by plays, blitzes, returns, by down and distance, by field position, by hash-mark, by personnel that's in the game, by the alignment, formation you lineup in - all those things. You sort of looking at what other people are seeing from you and what tendencies you have. I think every good team has tendencies. I think you can look out there at any team in football, in basketball [and] hockey, there are certain things that they do and if they're a good team they probably do them well.

You look at it and say, 'There they go again, that same thing's happening again.' I don't think those tendencies are necessarily a bad thing, but I think there is a point where you want to have balance and do things to compliment it. The other thing is production, where you're actually producing. What plays - how productive are they? Maybe in certain situations - how productive is the play on first down? How productive is that play on third down?

Is it the right side, the left side, man coverage, zone coverage? All those different kinds of things. So you're kind of looking at tendencies and also production. To a certain extent, maybe some that you want to build on or maybe some that you want to subtract and you just feel like it's just taking too much time and we're getting out of it, we need to put our resources into something that's more productive, so those kind of things.

**Q:** Do you put all the plays in a computer and it spits out your tendencies or do you go back and watch each game with the scouts?

**BB:** I think both. I think you can certainly get a statistical analysis pretty quickly. We can pop that out right there with how productive were we in the plays where the tight end motioned or the wide receiver motioned or we didn't motion, wherever you want to look at. More importantly it's kind of looking at all the plays, looking at all the third [and] 3-5's, the third and 6-10's, the short yardages, all the times you're in cover three, all the runs against cover three, all the passes against cover three, all the play action against cover three, all the empty plays.

But actually seeing them is always a little more valuable than doing a statistical look, although that's always a good starting point and a lot times that will trigger something. A lot of those things I think we are aware of on a weekly basis. It isn't like all of a sudden this week we realized cover two is our worst coverage; that's not something that probably just hit us in last week's game, as an example. But it does statistically sometimes point out something and then you go to the film, look at it and say, 'Well yeah we had a lot of production on these plays, but it's a little misleading. They had some missed tackles. It really wasn't that good.

We had some, but it wasn't because it was a great play.' And then there are other things that statistically don't look good, but you look at it and say, 'We're on the right track here. If we just made this block or we hadn't gotten that play called back with a penalty. If something hadn't happened - if this guy hadn't slipped, then we would have been productive there.' So it is a combination of those two things. There's no substitute for actually seeing the play, actually seeing the film.

**Q:** Is it fair to say that you are looking at it and trying to act as an opponent would looking at the film?

**BB:** Well, from a tendency standpoint, sure, absolutely. Defensively, is our tendency to blitz in certain situations, to play in cover one or cover five, to stunt in a certain situation? Of course, if we're seeing that then our opponents are seeing that. Again, it might be something that we might say that's where we want to be and we're

OK with that. Then there also might be a feeling that it is getting too predictable, 'We really want to balance this off with something else.' It gives you a little chance to look at yourself and look in the mirror and see what you're doing, but at the same time [we're] getting ready for Miami and there are going to be certain things that you're going to want to do against Miami, whether you've shown a lot of them or haven't shown a lot of them. That's going to be part of the game plan or the attack against our next opponent. It's good to know where you are even if you decide to stay with a tendency. At least you are conscious of what it is and that's what you're doing.

**Q:** How do you become a game plan coach? When did you see the benefit to becoming an offense or defense that changes week to week and does it take awhile to build a base to be that kind of team?

**BB:** It's a broad question. It's a hard thing to answer. In some respects there's not necessarily one straight answer to it. You can do elements of both. Let me just say in general terms, I think it's hard to change everything every week. I think you can change certain elements from week to week but it's hard to change everything every week. Some teams will run – if they are going to change certain things then other things stay the same. Like maybe their two minute offense, their goal line offense, their red area offense, or their third down offense.

Then they change something else like their first down offense or they change their third down offense but they keep their running game the same, or they change their running game but they basically keep their red area the same. It's hard to change your entire offense every week but I think if you play a 3-4 team then these are the runs we're going to run against a 3-4 team. If you play a 4-3 over and under team well here are the runs we're going to run against a 4-3 over and under. They might be completely different. You see teams do that but if they do that then they probably don't change everything else.

You see some teams pretty much run the same runs every week but depending on what coverages you play - if you're a zone team then they have this set of patterns. If you are a man team then they have this set of patterns. If you are a pressure team then they have another set. If you're a quarters team then they have another set. Now if you mix it up then they mix it up. It's like they have a little block on their game plan. If you're playing cover two we run this. If you're in cover three we run that. If you blitz we run this. Other teams do it by protection.

It's hard to give a specific answer to that. I think what you have to do each week is figure out what their formula is, what they're going to change and what they're not. What their philosophy is in certain situations, on certain plays or certain groupings. Sometimes it revolves around them and sometimes it revolves around the defense.

## Q: How much can watching the games this weekend live help you?

**BB:** Less than one percent, I'd say. At the game live we can actually see what's – but then you have to travel and all that. Now you can get the film just as quickly. But I'd say watching it live versus watching it on TV, you would be able to get a lot more, a lot more out of it. Especially if that's all you had, which isn't really the case for us. But there was a time, live scouting –

**Q:** How has that evolved in your time? The immediacy of the film now.

**BB:** I grew up watching my dad scout games live. They played on Saturday. Sometimes they wouldn't get the films until Monday. Sunday air shipping from wherever the college team was located – Starkville, Mississippi or wherever the film was coming from. It took two days. So, he had that information pretty instantaneously: "Here are their substitutions, these are the plays they ran diagrammed, here's the defenses they ran, here's how they handled these different situations." He had it when the game was over.

So learned a lot on that when films weren't as readily available. I'm not saying they didn't have them, but there was a time lapse there. You're trying to make up game plans, you haven't even seen the game film yet, so you had to rely on live game scouting so it was critical. As technology has evolved it's become less so. Certain things you can get from a game live that you don't get off film, especially things like no-huddle and the communication procedures, things like that. Again, as you play teams through the years and coaching staffs remain the same, a lot of times you kind of know the way it was before and it's probably going to be about the same.

But when you're facing new opponents like we do in other conferences and so forth, it's good to get a live look at those teams and see how they operate, particularly if it's a new staff or they've evolved to something a little bit different than what you're used to. The less you know a team the better that is.

**Q: How has the logging of the film changed? When you broke in you were writing it all done. How much of that is computerized as opposed to what you have to enter in on your own?**

**BB:** You can get a lot of information now that's already preset for you. All the players that are on the field, so if you just want to watch all the plays with no. 79, you can click it and you've got them. Whereas even five years ago, you were, 'Is that 78, is that 79? That's the guy with the tape on his left hand.' You know, whatever picking them out. Things like that are a lot easier now: down, distance, field position, who the ball carrier was, who the penalty was on, all the stuff that basically comes off the play-by-play stats. That's all entered in. It's quicker that way. It's like anything else.

The downside of that is when you do it yourself, you really know what it is and you remember it. When you just see a bunch of crap on the page then you kind of skim through it and you get what you want to get out of it, but it's not like detailing it [and] writing it out yourself. So I think there's still a lot to be said for grinding it out, doing the little things and really processing the information internally as opposed to just looking at it and being able to remember everything that you see at one glance. That's the faster way, that's the way to cut the corner in the end. Yeah, it's faster. In the end, is it better? I'm not sure.

**Q:** How quickly after the games end this weekend can you get the film?

**BB:** Certainly by the next morning; depending on when the game is, maybe even later that evening. A one o'clock game, you can probably get to it by seven, eight o'clock at night.

**Q:** Do you spend more, less or the same amount of time as you did three, five, 10 years ago?

**BB:** I think it depends kind of what my role is that particular year, what areas I'm working with or on. I've worked in all – I'd say since the time I've been here, I've focused heavily on at times one side of the ball or the other or the kicking game, sometimes more spread evenly. Sometimes it varies a little bit from week to week. But I'd say about the same. But sometimes it can be broken down differently. Years that I was working heavily with the quarterbacks, it was a lot of opponent defensive film. Years that I was working more heavily with the defense, [it was] more opponent offensive film. [You're] still seeing the other side, but not in the same kind of depth and detail. The kicking game, that's always a chunk of it. It's just that chunk can vary in size a little bit depending on what the other demands are.

## Q: Is it easy for us to look at things too generally without knowing who ran a wrong route or who was in the wrong position?

**BB:** Yeah, absolutely and that happens to us too. That's why I say, 'Let's take a look at the film' sometimes. It might even look to us like somebody made a mistake but then we look at it more closely maybe somebody besides him made a mistake and he was trying to compensate. I think we need a little closer analysis a lot of times. Sometimes the play calls or what was called on the line of scrimmage might be something that we're not aware of. That could happen in any game.

You think a player did something that he shouldn't have done but maybe he got a call, a line call or a call from a linebacker or he thought the quarterback said something so he did what he thought was the right thing or maybe it was the right thing but that call shouldn't have been made or should have been on the other side. But yeah, I think we need to be careful about what we're evaluating. Like right now, walking off the field, until we get a closer look and fully understand what happened on every play. It's just more accurately to do it. But believe me, I've watched plenty of preseason games this time of year and you're looking at all the other teams in the league and you try to evaluate players and you're watching the teams that we're going to play early in the season and there are plenty of plays where I have no idea what went wrong.

Something's wrong but I don't…these two guys made a mistake but I don't know which guy it was or if it was both of them. You just don't know that. I don't know how you can know that unless you're really part of the team and know exactly what was supposed to happen on that play. I know there are a lot of experts out there that have it all figured out but I definitely don't. This time of year, sometimes it's hard to figure that out, exactly what they're trying to do. When somebody makes a mistake, whose mistake is it?

# 5
# THE NFL

**Q:** When you go into a game pretty light with depth at a certain position what goes into deciding who will be the emergency backup at those positions?

**BB:** Yeah, whoever has worked there. It could depend on what the game plan is or what the role is. Sometimes when you put a player into that position you realize that you're not going to ask him to do everything that you ask the player that normally plays the position to do. So if we have to make this personnel move then we'll be limited in these certain ways and 'Here's how we'll work around that,' or maybe we don't work around that. It depends on what it is. But that comes up somewhere in every game and certainly if you lose a player within the game –

I mean it's one thing to sit here and talk about it on Friday. It's another thing to talk about it Sunday afternoon at 2:00 o'clock when somebody's out and now it's an unanticipated move if you will and then 'Ok, here's the next person we'd put in but what if something happens after that?' And then where it really gets [difficult], I would say the higher degree of difficulty comes in the situational defenses depending on what your depth is but things like goal line or you're dime or sub-defense and then of course in the kicking game where one guy – I mean you have 66 spots on special teams, right? [You have] 11 in 6 different units so that's 66 players. You can't have 66 backups so you've got to have one guy that might backup four or five things, and then if something happens to somebody then that one person say gets plugged in then once you have that second injury if it happens during the game then it's a real scramble.

Sometimes it affects your game plan and sometimes you put the player in and you can run your game plan but sometimes you're limited in what you can do. So for example, if you put an offensive lineman in for a tight end you'd have to change some things in the passing game, maybe in protection, maybe not in the running game possibly or vice versa. If you put another receiver in the game maybe you can run the same passes but you lose that blocker if it was a tight end. You just have to work around that.

**Q:** Along those lines, if you see an opponent going through that sort of problem with depth at a position during a game will you try and test that or exploit that, or do you simply stick with your game plan?

**BB:** No, I think that – no, we definitely try and do that. We try to take an assessment of the team by the time after you've had time to do it – let's call it the end of the first quarter just to pick a time. How's it going? It looks like they're having trouble here or it looks like so-and-so isn't very affective or maybe a player will come off, a defensive back will come off and say 'So-and-so, I don't think he can run,' or 'I don't think he has the stopping quickness that he had the last time I played him,' or whatever. Yeah, they tell us that.

A lot of times they see it before we do. Sometimes if we know about it we try to have people on our staff that observe that and kind of take an assessment of where they are to confirm it with the players. Maybe there's something you can do about it, maybe there isn't, maybe it's just that individual matchup of how that person plays them that can be used to some advantage as opposed to some big scheme thing like 'Ok, this player's limited in something. What play do you want to run?' Maybe it's less of that and just more of 'Ok, we're competing against this player. This looks like a weakness today. Here's how individually we want to block him or defend him,' or whatever the case might be.

**Q: During the bye week how much of a balance is there in reflecting and thinking 'OK, we've got to scrap this because it's not working' and saying 'If we can improve this we'll be alright.'**

**BB:** Look, you have to answer that question every week, not just the bye week, and you do something that doesn't work out well so what are your options, get rid of it or continue to do it and see if you can improve it. That's the judgment you make. If you really feel convicted that you can do it well then you put more resources into it and try to improve it. At some point if it doesn't go well then you might decide that 'We've tried, we've invested a lot of time. We've invested in this and it's still not working. Maybe it's time to move on to something else.' And then you make that decision.

I can't sit there and tell you what the book on that is. I think you evaluate each one individually but that's what coaches do. That's what we do. We evaluate it, we look at it and maybe it's a difference of opinion in the room on the staff like 'Look, I still think we can do it if we just work harder on it,' versus 'We've put a lot into it. Let's do something else. We seem to be on a dead end here,' for whatever the reasons are and there could be a multitude of reasons. That's a whole other conversation but in the end you have to make that decision. It's a bye week decision but it's a weekly decision, too.

You just have to decide what direction you want to go. I think in a lot of cases you can improve things. [For] some teams that's just not their thing. You have to find something else but that's true in every season. Each year I think you have to find a little bit of a different way to win. You can't do everything exactly the same way you did it a previous year. Your team has changed and the teams that you're playing may have changed or you may be playing different teams and maybe that dictates that you do something a little differently than you did it in the past against a different set of opponents. Those are the judgements that the head coach, the coordinators and the position coaches make whether it's an overall scheme thing or whether it's an individual technique thing. It can be a technique thing, too, like

'Look, here's the way we're doing this technique but it's not as affective for us as we want it to be.' Do we keep working on it or do we modify the technique and do something a little bit different for whatever the reasons are; our players, their players, their scheme, whatever it happens to be.

**Q:** Based on your experience are you more likely to stick with what you're doing midseason or switch it up?

**BB:** It depends. I mean we've done both. We've gotten to points, again, it's not even a midseason conversation. It is a midseason conversation but it could be anytime really and just say 'Look, I'm done with this.' I've said that before - 'I've seen enough. I'm done with it. We're going to do something else. We've tried and it just didn't work,' or 'I believe in it. We should be better at it than we are.' It's maybe circumstantial why we don't have production. Eight guys are good, one guy is bad. The next time its eight guys are good and a different guy that [isn't]. If we just get this right we'll be OK but we just haven't been able to do it. Well maybe you keep trying.

**Q: How much of a factor is conditioning in the opening regular season game due to the fact that a lot of players may not play a whole game during the preseason?**

**BB:** Yeah, I think Bob [Socci] it's a really good point. It's something that we've been talking to our players about for several weeks now and just being exactly how you described it. Look, you're not going to play every play of a preseason game but in September you might be playing every play of the regular season game, so here are your preseason plays in preseason but we've got to work your condition level to a much higher point than that because the commands are going to be higher, and I'd say they're even going to be higher this week when we go to a 1:00 p.m. game on Sunday.

Last night's game was indoors, and I mean if we had played that game outside yesterday that would've been even more challenging. I don't know what we're going to get here this weekend but I'm saying potentially a warmer day at 1:00 p.m. tests your conditioning a lot more than a cooler evening does in preseason. All of those things are part of the buildup and we can't get them in preseason but we have to get them in our training camp and the practices to try to prepare for that. I thought that our levels were pretty good there and we executed some plays well at the end of the game that we really needed.

I'd say one of the plays that kind of stood out to me was the screen pass on that last drive where you can see our defensive line and linebackers running to the ball with a lot of effort to close that space down very quickly. I think we tackled them for a loss on that but the energy and the speed that the players were moving with at that point of the game I thought was pretty good, so that's the type of conditioning we feel like we're going to need to win a 60 minute game. It certainly was a 60 minute game last night.

**Q: Over the last three years the three coaches with the most victories happens to be the three oldest in the league in yourself, Pete Carroll and Bruce Arians. Do you think it is a matter of having so much experience that allows for that success or is there some other common correlation between experience and success at the head coaching level?**

**BB:** Well, you know, I think, obviously, I have a lot of respect for Pete and Bruce and honestly I'd throw Mike [Zimmer] in there, too. Obviously, he got a late start in Minnesota, but I think Mike is a tremendous coach. He has always been very good. His units have always been very productive every place that he has been. That's another experienced coach that has gone in and done very well with that team and that franchise. I think that you look at those three guys and they've all done a pretty solid job.

I'd say they didn't come into great situations. They had to build those up, at least in the early part, the early years when they got there. So, I give a lot of credit to those three guys. But yeah, it's something that doesn't seem like a lot of NFL teams are really that interested in. They seem more interested in different types of coaching hires.

Those three have done extremely [well]. Again, I'd throw Mike in there. I know you didn't but I'd throw him in there. I think those guys have done really well. I have a lot of respect for all three of them.

**Q:** Is that a good nod to the value of having experience? Is that fair to say?

**BB:** Well, as I've said many times, players win games and games that we've won here are because we've had good players that have gone out and won them. I certainly wouldn't want to take anything away from the great players that we've had here that have won so many games for us. That's really where it starts. I don't care who the coach is; without good players you're not going to win many games at any level, so start with that.

**Q: When putting together the practice squad do you approach it from a short term perspective as injury depth or do you take a long term approach towards developing players for the future?**

**BB:** [It is] a combination of both. I think, Mike [Petraglia], pretty much the way you described it - that's the goal of the practice squad. It can help you with short-term depth. You've seen us bring players up the day before a game or a couple of days before the game to fill in a spot that we need them. We've kind of also seen practice squad players develop and become roster players after a period of time, so it's a combination of both of those. Sometimes its two-for-one, where a player can give you short-term depth but also be able to develop into a consistent roster player down the road.

**Q: When you see some of your players and draft picks claimed by other teams is that sort of a feather in the cap for those in your organization that scouted them?**

**BB:** Well, we'll see how it all goes but I think we felt like we had pretty good depth on our roster going into training camp and so it's not surprising that other teams in the league recognized some of that and took some of the younger players and put them on their roster.

**Q: Has the preparation for Arizona begun and in general how difficult is it to prepare for the opening game?**

**BB:** Well, yeah, Week 1 is always a tough week to prepare for because just the number of unknowns, the lack of game planning that teams do in the preseason, so we can go back and look at last year. That's a lot of volume of stuff so, look, I know that's a lot of games. There's no way they could do everything in our game that they did last year, plus looking at the preseason, just trying to plug it all in and think what you might get but you know that they worked on some things in preseason that they probably haven't shown in those games, so we'll just have to be ready to attack and defend the way that we want to - kind of generally want to plan to go into the game with - and then have to be ready to make adjustments during the game as we see how schemes and matchups and so forth unfold.

So, after you get past Week 1 at least in Week 2 you can really see what your opponent tried to do in the first game. They didn't hold anything back. They're playing the people and doing the things that they think are the best and you get a much clearer read after that first game, but it's all the same for both teams, but that's part of the challenge of it. I'd say we'll get started on Arizona, really Tuesday will kind of be like a Wednesday for us, so that'll really be our big day in terms of digging into them. We'll get the process started today but like I said, we have a long way to go in terms of really hitting it from Tuesday through Friday this coming week.

**Q: When making final cuts, how much of a balancing act is it to prioritize long-term versus short-term needs?**

**BB:** I think that's a big part of the conversation. I think if you were just picking the team for one game, for the opener that would be one thing. If you were picking the team strictly for next year, that would be another thing, but in reality, you're trying to pick a team for all of those. You've got a game to play, you've got the early part of the season to be ready for. Sixteen games, that's a lot of football, and you need a lot of depth to get through those 16 games, but you don't know exactly where you're going to need it. It's one big balancing act, and you know you're going to have a team next year, so do you want to keep a player this year but you're really looking at where he's going to be next year? You don't think he's going to be a big contributor this year but you really see that player have an upside to improve the following year. Or, do you go with a player who maybe has a little bit of a higher performance now, but a year from now, would somebody else pass him?

Those are all tough questions. I think some of the guys that we've kept here, you see improve over a period of time. Even some guys form last year, like [AJ] Derby and [Tyler] Gaffney, Darryl Roberts, that had a limited amount of time, they were injured, but now have had production out there in the preseason games. There's another group of guys that are rookies this year that probably the same thing is going to happen with them next year. Definitely, Trey Flowers is another guy.

There are several players there that from their rookie year to their second year, weren't really factors on the roster a year ago, but are very much in the competition this year. That's hard. It's hard to do. It's always hard to leave that veteran experience for a little bit of an unknown, but the lifeline of this league and the lifeline of every team is young, developing players. You can't build a team without them, so they're an important part of it. There's uncertainty there. Not all of them develop and then they don't end up being what they might be. Then that, in the end, just kind of becomes a waste of time. Just trying to make the right decisions there, especially when sometimes, the information is limited, but it is what it is. That's what you have to figure out or try to figure out.

**Q:** How difficult is it this time of year when trying to decide whether or not to keep a guy you may want to work with in the future but is being blocked on the depth chart while also worrying that if you cut him he could be picked up somewhere else?

**BB:** That's the 64,000 dollar question. That's what it is. It's been like that since the day I got into this league. From all of the personnel meetings I've ever been in it's a [matter of] a player who's more experienced [and] more ready to help the team now, versus a player that's not as ready now but at some point you think the pendulum will swing in his favor. Will you do that? Can you do that? What are the consequences of making that move? What are the consequences of not making that move? How likely, as you said, is it that you could keep both players in some capacity? That's what it's about, trying to balance now with later.

We're going to field a team in November, we're going to field a team next year, we're going to field a team in 2018. Not that we're getting too far ahead of ourselves, but we're going to be in business in those years, so we have to sort of have an eye on those moving forward and a lot of the other factors that go into that. Those are all tough decisions. They're all things that you really have to think about. It's no different than acquiring – well it's different – but it's the same thing as acquiring a player. So, if you acquire a player who are you acquiring – a young player for an older player, an older player for a younger player, help now versus help later, development versus known performance – and so forth.

They're all interrelated but it really gets back to the same key points. When its close it's tough. If it's not close then it's not really a tough decision. It's a relatively easy decision, but the ones that are close, some people in the room want to have one opinion, other people have another opinion. You kind of have a split camp there and both sides' arguments are good arguments. It's kind of your perspective. Is it today or is it tomorrow? I'm sure every team in the league is having a lot of those discussions about eight, 10 players; five and five, whatever it is, four and four, but that kind of thing.

**Q:** In training camp and preseason games is there an element of just running a particular play just to get a look at it, as opposed to in a regular season game you are running things to execute and score?

**BB:** Right, yeah, that's a really good question and it's a tough balance. I'd say basically you want to just try and run the plays that you know how to run rather than getting into a big game plan thing of "Doing this because they do that", and so forth. That's really not what this is for. On the other hand, to run a play that you just have no chance on then you're probably going to get what you deserve. To just run something into a scheme that just isn't built, that play just isn't built to handle that scheme, then what does that tell you? It tells you that that play isn't built to handle that scheme, which is something you already knew, and it's hard to evaluate players when you just kind of don't even give them a chance.

I think what we want to try and do is have a fair fight, run plays that are competitive, not necessarily some trick play that they aren't prepared for because it's preseason. That doesn't really help us. [We] try to run something that's competitive and see how the competition plays out. One of the things about practice that we can do, and will do with the Saints, is we kind of have a little bit of a set of ground rules.

We'll run these things against this, again, so it's a fair fight and we can evaluate the players, as opposed to putting somebody into a real good or real bad situation. It's more of an evaluation of the scheme than it is the players and we really want to do a good job of evaluating the players. I feel like we have a pretty good evaluation of our scheme. But in order to do that you don't want to make it too complicated and get into too many 'what ifs', and adjustments and all that. Then you lose the integrity of the fundamentals that you are trying to teach, so it's a balance.

It's a lot easier to do it against yourself because you know exactly what you're doing on both sides of the ball. When you're going against somebody else you don't know exactly how they're teaching it or how they're handling it, so sometimes you run into a firestorm that you would be better off not doing, but sometimes that happens. But look, if it happens, it happens, and that's part of football, too.

Sometimes you have bad plays in bad situations and you've got to make the best out of a bad play and not have it be a big play defensively or a turnover offensively. We learn from those situations, too, when they come up, which I'm sure they will.

## Q: What is that integration process like for those new rookies that will soon enter the building?

**BB:** It's huge. They have no idea what they're getting into. It's not their fault. We all had to go through it at some point or another. They're going to get a big dose of what they probably haven't had a whole lot of certainly any time recently. It's a big load. The competition level is going to step up. The volume is going to step up. It's not a scholarship. In college they can't take them away from you. In the NFL you're fighting for a job so it's a whole new ball game. Those guys have a lot to absorb, a lot to learn but just like every other rookie class they'll get through it. We'll have some ups and downs but we'll start the process on Thursday night when they come in. We'll just be grinding away here for the next few weeks.

Q: Do you keep them away from the veterans on the field at all to kind of take them along slowly?

**BB:** No, I mean the way phase two is set up we can integrate them into some things. There will certainly be plenty of times when they're by themselves as a group to go over the things both in and out of football. Regarding football and outside of football that they need. Education on that they need to, I'd say that they're going to need instruction on and so forth and that'll certainly be geared towards them. But they'll work in with the veteran players and their training in some meetings and on-field work and things like that.

So there will be some of that and then they're obviously is going to be a lot of extra and just all of the transitioning. Just coming into a new team from wherever it is that they're coming from and understanding pro football and just the whole transition process. It's a big step for any of us when we do that. Especially for a lot of these guys – some of them haven't made that big of a transition. Some have but some haven't.

**Q:** How do you evaluate balancing who is already on place on the roster and these draft choices?

**BB:** Yeah, well, I think that's a good question. I think that on Monday's waiver wire you're going to see a lot of players on it throughout the league because of players that were drafted or acquired or free agents, whatever it happens to be, that other transactions will offset those or be part of the process so we'll just have to see how all of that plays out. There's definitely a little bit of juggling there. I'd say the main thing for me would be that if the player's circumstances change to the point where you don't really think you can give that player a fair opportunity, then it's in your best interest and his best interest to move on and let him find a better opportunity somewhere else.

I'd say that's not an infrequent situation. It comes up. It's not going to be 20 guys, but there's a player that's going to end up getting stacked behind a few guys and you're going to be able to really give him the opportunity that you thought you would, at a different point of time, then when things change I think that the player appreciates rather than go through training camp, and get halfway through camp and see what is already evident now then that makes it a lot easier for him now to find a better opportunity. When that's the case, that's how we usually try to approach, I think that league wide that's what you'll see from a lot of team. You'll probably see some guys who are not with a team now go to a team based on some teams not being able to maybe acquire a certain position or need in the draft and then looking to a veteran player who's unsigned to possibly fill that spot, or compete for it.

**Q:** How long do you think it took you to insert your program here? Do you feel like it took a couple years?

**BB:** Yeah, probably '03.

**Q:** Because of the personnel decisions you have to make?

**BB:** No, just because of everything. You have to change the culture. You have to change the ... I mean normally one coach is different from the previous coach. You don't see a lot of whoever the first coach is, the second coach is kind of the carbon copy of the first coach, the third coach is kind of a carbon copy of the second coach. I mean you rarely see that. The coach that comes in usually has a different philosophy than the coach that left, so you have to try to implement that philosophy.

That means you're going to turn over a high percentage of the roster because the players that the other coach had don't fit the new philosophy, so a lot of the players are going to have to change in part because of the philosophy and probably in part because of the scheme. Those role-type players, now that role is not needed in the new scheme and a different role is needed, so you get different players, and then just getting your team acclimated to doing things the way that the philosophy of the new program.

You're going to have to go through a lot of tough situations – tough games, tough losses, tough stretches in the season, whatever it happens to be, to build that up over time. It doesn't happen in training camp. I mean look training camp is training camp, but those games don't count. Even in the early part of the season, you might have some tough games, but it's not like playing in January, playing in December. It takes some time to go through that. I don't think there is any shortcut to it.

I know there are a lot of other people in the league that think there is, that after two weeks all of a sudden everything is going to change dramatically, but I'm not really part of that, I don't buy into that. So, I mean we won in '01. In '02, we had a lot of issues. '03 – that was a good football team. '04 – that was a good football team. So I don't think there was any doubt about ... '01 wasn't the best team, but that team played the best, so we won. But I think we saw in '02 more of probably overall where the '01 team was. Just the '01 team played great when they had to in critical situations in big games and that's why they won. You can't take anything away from them. They deserved it because they were the best team. But it wasn't the case in '02.

## Q: Outside of quarterback, is the offensive line the toughest position to have injuries?

**BB:** Yeah, I don't know what number you put on it or something like that. Look every team has some personnel situations that they have to manage one way or another. That's why you have depth. That's why you have all the players you have on your roster to be able to be competitive at all those spots because really you never know where it's going to hit. Again as we talked about earlier, each position is important, each guy is important, each role is important. It becomes even more important when you need it.

If you don't need it, if you don't really get to it, it could be you or I as backups but if you never have to play it doesn't really matter, but as soon as the player has to go in there then we find out how important those are. I think everything is important. You just try to do the best you can to have the best depth throughout your team as possible. Some places you have more depth than others. It's impossible to have quality depth where you're really comfortable with all those guys on your team.

There are too many of them. It's hard enough to have that with your front line players let alone another group of them but you do the best you can. A lot of times you have young players that will be better in time and sometimes that's worth waiting for. I think you have a lot of that in Miami. You have a lot of young players.

You have a lot of guys that are playing well – guys like [DeVante] Parker that have started to come on here in the second half of the season and are going to be really good. I think you've got a number of those guys on that team. Again there's a balance there between experience and knowing what to do and a younger developing player with talent that hasn't peaked yet.

## Q: What are the procedures of releasing a player off injured

reserve?

**BB:** Well once he's healthy, once they're healthy, then you can release them off of injured reserve.

**Q:** So it's on an individual case-by-case basis?

**BB:** Once they're healthy, yes. If you release a player who's injured then you have to designate that he's injured and then typically there would be some type of settlement between the player and the club. So like at the end of training camp for example there are a number of players throughout the league that get released at that point that are waived injured. So say they have a hamstring injury or something and they are going to be out for three or four weeks, not long enough to go on injured reserve, but they're not healthy, so by the CBA ... Yeah, maybe you'd release the player anyways depending on how your roster shakes out.

But regardless, per the CBA, you can't release a player who is injured, so if he's injured then you would waive him but designate him injured, so if somebody else claimed him they would have notification that he's not healthy and then make their own decision at that point. If he's not claimed then he would revert to your injured reserve list, but he wouldn't be on long-term injured reserve because it's a shorter injury, so once he's healthy then he would be released form the roster. That would be the waived injured category.

If it was injured reserve then that would put him out for the entire season, so once you pass that six week mark then you would have the option to either keep him on injured reserve and have him on your roster – and depending on what his contract status is you might have him for the following year, again depending on what his contract says – or if he's healthy then you could waive him off of injured reserve, but you're waiving him healthy. You're not waiving him injured, if you will.

## Q: When you bring somebody in midseason, does their ability to play immediately depend on the position they play?

**BB:** Yeah, no question. When I was Cleveland we signed Mike

Tomczak off the street to come in and start at quarterback. That's hard. That's a lot different than signing a place kicker or a snapper the day before the game to come in and do that skill. And there are a lot of guys in between. When we had to bring Brian Kinchen in after Lonie Paxton got hurt, yeah it's a change, it's an adjustment, but it's not like a starting quarterback when it was Mike Tomczak.

It depends on the player, it depends on the position, it depends on some of the other circumstances surrounding your team and the opponent that week and so forth and so on, but you have to do what you have to do. Each situation is different, you try to look at it and make the most of it, prepare the player the best you can for what he's going to have to do that week, whatever that happens to be. And sometimes you don't know – something could happen in the game that then shifts things a little bit in a way that I'm not saying you don't anticipate but you didn't have time to work on those.

**Q:** With the Rutgers guys like Logan and Duron, who have played together for a long time and know each other very well, they seem to be playing more this season than the last couple.

**BB:** And [Jonathan] Freeny, too – I think he was roommates with Devin.

**Q:** Do you think their background with each other helps?

**BB:** Yeah, sure. There's always a level of trust when you've been with somebody for a longer period of time. I'm not saying there's not that with other players.

It would be the same thing with the coaching staff. Coaching with Romeo for all those years – not that there wasn't a level of trust and a level of communication and reciprocal arrangement with other coaches on the staff – but when it's somebody that's been there that long and you've been through so many things with, it's nobody fault but you just experience more and some things may come up that the two of you can relate to that maybe somebody else can't relate to because they haven't experienced those same things. So, I'm sure that's true.

**Q:** You've brought in a couple offensive players last week. At this stage in the year, what is the process like of getting new players up to speed on the playbook and game plan for the coming week?

**BB:** That's challenging. We do it on a number of different levels. There is just the component of just getting the guy into our organization – here's how we do things. Forget about the X's and O's, there's that aspect to it. Then there is kind of learning what some of the basics are in terms of terminology and formations or alignments or whatever it happens to be, and then it's pretty much game plan-specific. What do you have to learn to play this week and then whatever you can get beyond that in terms of general fundamental foundation building, you do the best you can, but you're usually pretty consumed with trying to get in what we're doing this week.

Here's how we adjusted against the different things our opponents do and then next week is next week. In some of those windows where you have possibly extra opportunities, you try to build a better foundation, a better base, so even though this doesn't apply this week here's what this means because at some point you're going to want to build on that. It's a tough catch-up process, it really is. For a player like Keshawn Martin, who at least from an X's and O's standpoint and probably a program standpoint, too, had some familiarity with protections and adjustments and basic concepts, probably the learning curve for him would have been easier than say a player that comes in with very little in common.

Maybe their routes are numbered and ours are named or vice versa. Or the protections were names and ours are numbers – that kind of thing where you're trying to put together a whole different language, trying to learn a different language as well as what to do but also trying to learn what different words or concepts mean, I think that's probably the hardest part of a new player. As you go through that process with a player, there are some things you'll talk to him about where he'll say, 'Oh I got that. That's what we did here. That's this, this is that; OK good.' Then there are other things that are going to be different that are foreign that are new and those are going to take more time, and you don't really know what those are until you actually go through the process with the player, start talking to the player, get questions, get feedback, quiz him on the information you've given him to try to understand what he's getting, what he isn't.

Some guys learn better by walking through it, some guys learn better by seeing it on film, some guys can look at it on a piece of paper and understand, some guys need to see it on the field. There's that whole process of getting to know the player and his best learning techniques. A lot of different components to it, but obviously you're fighting a losing battle in terms of a race against time that you're just already too far behind in to get all the way caught up. You just have to catch up enough so he can be functional for that particular game and then worry about next week next week.

**Q: How difficult is to separate your roles as the head coach and as the general manager when determining whether or not to bring a player back?**

**BB:** They're all interrelated to me. I'm fortunate that I have input in really all those decisions and I just try to do what's best for the team, that's all. I'm not trying to hurt anybody. I'm not trying to help any individual. I'm trying to help the team. My decisions are based on what's best for the team. I made that clear to the team on numerous occasions in no uncertain terms. My decisions are easy. They're what's best for the team. That doesn't mean everybody likes them.

That doesn't mean everybody thinks that they are the best for them individually or maybe even their unit, but in the end the overall decisions are made for the overall betterment of the team. Sure, there may be some that are right, I'm sure plenty are wrong. Regardless of whatever we think about them, that's the intent behind them. I don't think that's hard. I think that's easy.

Frankly, I think the harder thing is make the decision that's good for an individual player which then really isn't the best thing for the other 52 guys. So you're picking one guy to say, "OK well we'll do this for him so he's happy," but in the end if you've even marginally affected the other 52, I think that's really acting irresponsibly as a coach. I don't believe in that. That's the way I look at it.

**Q: Prior to Sunday's game, Jonathan Kraft said on the radio that the league is looking into expanding rosters. Is that something you'd be in support of?**

**BB:** What are you talking about now? There is a game day roster of 46, there is a regular season roster of 53, and there is training camp roster of 90. So I'm just saying. And there are obviously the rules like the IR designation and things like that that are auxiliaries to those rules, so I'm not sure exactly which part of the roster you're referring to here. I'm just saying there are a number of different elements.

**Q:** I don't think he was specific as to where the roster expansion would occur, but as a coach, where would it benefit you the most – the 46-man, the 53-man or the 90-man roster?

**BB:** Those questions, and look, they're good questions, they come up every year, and I know that the league meetings, those get talked about in one version or another. We'll start with the game day roster. The issue with the game day roster is if you allow all the players to play, let's say you allow all 53 players to play, then you get into some competitive situations due to injuries where I have 53 players but you only have 48 because you have guys that are hurt and that type of thing. So there is a competitive aspect to that versus the argument of, 'Well they're all on the team, they're all being paid, so why can't we use them?'

It kind of goes back and forth on that one. I think one of the issues with the extra players if you will, like going from 46 to some higher number on game day, it gets into the over-specialization. Do you have a long field goal kicker, a short field goal kicker, a kickoff guy, a field goal kicker, extra specialty-type players that therefore just require other extra specialty-type players? So if you carry four tight ends or you carry a lot of receivers or a lot of backs and use formations and personnel groups ... So you have a Wildcat quarterback, you've got a regular quarterback, you've got a backup quarterback, you've got some other type of quarterback, that just forces a similar specialization on defense to match up with that. I don't know if that's really where we want the game to go. There was a time in the National Football League, not that long ago, when the same 11 players played on offense on every play and the same 11 defensive players played on defense on every play. The fans knew all the players. Now it's hard for me, and I'm full time at this, to keep up with all the players, even on the teams that we play, like the Giants, or I'm sure the Giants are looking at us.

There is a lot of roster movement and guys on and off and injuries and practice squad guys and all that, so when you add the practice squad players on the roster potentially because they could be added all the way up to the day before the game, that's other depth that you have on your roster that you can get up to your 46 if you need to. So, you're talking about training camp numbers – I'm not sure in the overall big picture of the league how many of the players of those extra 320 players, the guys from 80-90, from 81-90, that let's say five years ago wouldn't have been on a roster in training camp, although you had the Europe exemption guys and all that. I'd say the 85-90 number, somewhere in there, was what the training camp numbers have been for a while.

You get into that whole how much higher do you need to go than 90 for training camp and what impact do those players really have on the overall quality of the league, although I think without doing a total study on it, certainly my impression is that the injures in the early part of the season – training camp to the early part of the season – is definitely on the incline, so maybe that's something that would warrant further study. And again, I'm sure that the league will take a look at that every year.

But in the end, it comes down to the players that are playing, and I think as you get into the second half of the season, what you usually see at this point is players going on injured reserve that are going to be out for the season because the season is shorter, they have less time to recover, players going on injured reserve, teams bringing in emergency players, whether they bring them in from outside the organization or they bring them up from the practice squad, and in a lot of cases those players that get added to the team or even to the 46-man roster don't play a tremendous amount I'd say overall as a group, although there are some notable exceptions. But overall you don't see those guys getting a lot of playing time.

So when you lose a player and replace him with an emergency player or a practice squad player on your roster, I'd say probably the general tendency of most teams and most coaches would be to take their other better players who are already on the team and use them more rather than take another body that hasn't been with the team and give those snaps to the player that is now out of the lineup.

I think usually you try to find a way to take what you have and just do more with it rather than take somebody that is a lot further away and isn't as familiar with what you're doing and what your system is and think you're going to get them up to the same speed that the guy that you just got hurt was at. Another long answer to a short question, but there are a lot of different aspects to it and obviously there are a lot of other factors involved, like the CBA and the Player's Association and salary cap implications and benefits and a thousand other things, most of which I'm not even familiar with. But it does impact the competitiveness of the game.

**Q:** Is there ever a bad time for a bye week, or do you just play it as it comes?

**BB:** Yeah, whenever it's scheduled, there's nothing really we can do about it, so we just try to take advantage of the time we have and use it the best way we can use it. I don't think I've ever been on a team where anybody was unhappy to have a bye week, whenever it comes. So, you take advantage of the chance to rest, get caught up, take some time analyzing what you need to work on and have a good plan to do the things that can help your team improve during this time and when the team returns to really start in on our preparations for Dallas.

**Q:** Is the bye week as much mental as it is physical?

**BB:** These guys have been going really hard since the end of July. Even though we've had a couple days here and there, training camp rolled right into the opening game of the year, which came on Thursday, so there was a lot of urgency just coming out of preseason and into the start of the season without really any cushion. Then we had an extra couple days there for Buffalo, but Buffalo is always tough so there was a lot of catching up to do that week. And then we rolled right into Jacksonville, so these guys really haven't had much of a cushion from the end of July.

And I'd say usually you get some of that during that last week of training camp and prior to starting your preparations for the opener and all the roster cuts that weekend and kind of Thursday, Friday before the weekend, but we didn't really have that this year. So, this is an opportunity for some of these guys and really all of them, players and the coaches, to after seven games and nine-plus weeks of training camp and football here to catch our breath for a short time and then we've got a long stretch ahead of us.

**Q:** Does the bye week coming in the fourth week affect your self-scouting because you have limited tape on your own players?

**BB:** The self-scouting and really everything else you talked about is on somewhat of an abbreviated basis. It will be the best we can do; we just don't have as much information as we would if our bye was in Week 10 or 11 or something like that. But it isn't, so we'll take what we have and look at that and just do the best we can.

You can't control any of these situations, so whatever the opportunity is, you just try to make the most of it and try to take advantage of whatever time or opportunity that's presented to you and figure out what's the best thing you can do with it. There is really not a lot of thought about, 'Well if it was some other time it'd be this or that.' It isn't, so there is no point in wasting time on that. Just take it for what it is and try to make the most out of it.

**Q: What are Saturdays typically like for you guys? Can it vary based on where you are from a preparation standpoint?**

**BB:** We try not to, yeah, we try not to. We try to take the game, whenever the game is and then work backwards. So, the game, the day before the game, two days before the game, three days before the game, four days before the game - wherever you put the game, we try to work backwards so that three days before the game as a player, as a coach you kind of know where you should be from a preparation standpoint. Two days before the game, you're in a routine, you kind of know where you need to be, these are the things we need to have covered because one day before the game, here are the things we're going to cover there. You know what I mean?

And same thing for the players that in terms of their film study and preparation, they should know physically and from a preparation standpoint - their physical rest, recovery, energy - they should know where they are five, four, three, two, day before the game. So, we don't try to juggle the schedule so one week, two days before the game we're doing this, and as a player you're anticipating one thing and we go out and we have one type of practice, and then next Friday it's a different type of practice, and then next Friday, what is it. It's hard to get into a routine that way, so we try to take the end point and work backwards.

**Q:** What is a day before the game typically like for you guys?

**BB:** Well, it's a review of everything that we're going to do. There are some situations the day before the game that we go over in the meetings or go over on the field in a walk through that we haven't covered prior to that week. Now look, you can't cover every situation in every game that could possibly come up. That would be impossible. But usually over the course of three to four weeks, you can pretty much get them all. Maybe you kick off after a safety, kickoff return after a safety, the squib kick situations, the take a safety on a punt - all those kind of things - just as an example in the kicking game, you maybe wouldn't cover every one of those every week, but you cover two or three of them this week, and then two or three of them the next week, and then two or three of them, so then after a cycle of four to five weeks you would have hit it. Those things don't come up every single game.

You're lucky if it's once a season. But any really critical plays, like a must onside kick or a hands team or having to block a punt rush at the end of the game when you've got to punt the ball and you know they're coming or vice versa - things like that are covered on a more weekly basis. And then we try to pull it all together, so over the course of the week, the players get told about five thousand different things - on this play do this, if they do this we do that, if they do this we do something else, if this happens, this happens, if that happens something else happens. OK, but now we come to the game, like alright, forget about all that, alright what do we need to do here to win? What are the most important things we have to do? We know there are a thousand things we've talked about and everything is important, but in the end, let's get back to what we need to do here tomorrow.

Sometimes you have an extra meeting if it's a late game, a night game or something like that. That's kind of our extra meeting if you will. We do the countdown not really counting on that meeting. Like this week, we have a Saturday night meeting and then we play Sunday, whereas if we played Sunday night, there would be another kind of extra meeting in there. And then that's maybe two meetings instead of one at the end, but normally we just count on the one meeting and work it from there.

**Q:** A lot of kids end their college career and then begin preparation for the combine. Then they have less time in the pro team's conditioning program. How much of a difference does that make when you have them for a full year in your offseason program?

**BB:** I think that's a huge mistake that a lot of those players make, but I'm sure they have their reasons for doing it. We're training our players to play football, not to go through a bunch of those February drills. Yeah, our training is football intensive. We train them to get ready to play and ultimately that's what they're going to do. Maybe for some of those guys another activity in between or a pro day or whatever it is. But in the end, they're going to make their career playing football. We already know that with our guys and we don't have to deal with any of that other stuff. We just train them for football. I think it's huge.

I think there are a lot of players and I think a lot of players learn from that, that they look at their rookie year and feel like, 'I wasn't really as physically as well prepared as maybe I was in college or what I will be in their succeeding years in the league,' and train more for football and train less for the broad jump and three-cone drill and stuff like that. I think a lot of those guys hopefully learn that lesson and intensify their physical football training after they've had that year of, in a lot of cases, I would say non-football training or very limited training for actually football.

## Q: What's the next biggest challenge for all of these new players drafted?

**BB:** The biggest challenge for all these players is to get on our program. For the last six months, they've been a man without a country. They have no team, they have their own individual, whatever it is, situation, and they're trying to figure out, 'How do I best get ready for the NFL?' And that is all 32 teams or however many it is showing interest in them and trying to figure out, 'How do I prepare for that?' Each guy has been an independent contractor; they've been on their own whatever it is: their own trainer, their own training system, their agent, whatever they've been doing.

And right now, that's all changed and they can forget about all that and they need to become New England Patriots. That's what we're going to start getting to work on. They've got to get out of that mentality of 'I'll get up when I feel like it. I'll go to work when I feel like it. I'll eat where [I feel like it]. All that. I'll train the way I want to train.' They're done with that. That will be a huge adjustment for them. I don't care where they came from, I don't care what position they play. None of that makes any difference. They haven't been doing it and they're going to start doing it and they're going to start doing a lot of it.

They're going to be doing it for day after day after day for a long time going forward – if they can, if they're successful. That will be a big adjustment for them. It will be a big adjustment for every rookie because none of them have been doing that. Welcome to the NFL. That will start Thursday. They'll get a big dose of New England Patriots football over the next whatever we've got, six weeks – however long it is. We'll give them everything we can in heavy doses, try to get them ready for training camp and they'll get even more then. The strong will survive. The other ones will fall off. And we'll keep going.

**Q:** The train doesn't stop.

**BB:** Sure doesn't. Sure doesn't. We've got 31 other teams competing just as hard as we are to do the same things. Yeah, we're going to have to outwork people, out-hustle them and just do a better job. That's what our business is. Beats working though.

## Q: When will you take a break or is there no break because of how long the postseason went?

**BB:** As we all know, the downtime really in the National Football League is from the end of OTAs or mini-camp, whatever you want to call it, to the start of training camp. So, last week we had the East-West [Shrine] Game. This week we have the Senior Bowl. Then we have, really our scouts who have been out – our college scouts who have been out – doing the college regular season, then the college bowl games, now the college all-star games, the East-West Game, a couple other bowl games, the Senior Bowl, then they'll come back in with all that.

Then we'll prepare for the Indianapolis Combine. Then we'll have free agency about a week and a half after that, which brings in all the pro free agents in addition to all our own players. Then we'll have the college workouts in March, which even though the draft has been moved back, our assumption is, based on all the information we've gotten from the colleges and the agents and so forth, that those workouts are probably still going to be pretty heavy through the month of March. Then where normally April is kind of a big draft preparation month and the start of the offseason program, which for all teams that don't have new head coaches would be April 21, then that brings our players who are under contract back into the program as we prepare for the draft and of course the offseason program leads right into OTAs and mini-camp.

When your season goes into the postseason as ours did for three weeks, you're behind going into the college draft and to a certain degree, I would say the free agency process. To be honest with you, we're into the 2014 season right now. We're behind, so we have some catching up to do. That's a good position to be in but it's a bad position to be in. That's really where you're at when the season ends on the last day, whatever it is, December [29] this year, then you have those extra three weeks to try to get caught up on the college draft, get caught up on some other things.

We've been trying to win games in the postseason, so now we're actually behind there. The slower time in the NFL is that mid-June to mid-July range. Right now is really not it. It's similar to the college season. Those guys end their season and the next day they're out recruiting. That's just the nature of the schedule. There's not much we can do about that.

**Q: When you hit the ground at the airport when you arrived back here, were you resolute to hit the ground running?**

**BB:** Unfortunately, yes. That's not really the way you want it, but that's the reality of it. Look, there are a lot of coaching changes throughout the National Football League, as it seems like there always are every year. How that will affect our coaching staff, I'm not 100 percent sure, but I don't know; there could be something there. Our players, we have a number of players whose contracts are going to expire that I'm going to talk to one way or another. I'm not saying there's any decision to be made, but there's certainly a conversation to be had. There are a lot of other players, a lot of guys on our team that I have and will talk to personally about their situation or appreciation for what they've done or whatever it happens to be.

Guys have stuff on their mind, whether it be coaches, players, other people in the organization that respectfully will say, 'Coach, I didn't want to bring this up during the season because we were involved in the season, the playoffs, whatever it is, but whatever it is.' You get a lot of things that come up now. On a personal level – and I'm sure that this is true of our players and our coaches as well – but on a personal level, there are a lot of things that come up in the season, particularly as the season comes into the November, December, January range, things come across my desk. I open the drawer, I put them in there and say, 'I'm working on Buffalo, I'm working on Indianapolis, I'm working on Denver, I'll deal with them after the season.'

That drawer fills up and you put them in another drawer. Now it's time to open those drawers and there's a lot of junk in them. There's a lot of stuff that I just haven't dealt with in the last few weeks, even couple of months that you just say, 'I can deal with it after the season. There's more important things to deal with now.' That's where I've been. Now, whether that's my drawer that's opening or some player or coaches or some other person in the organization, they have that drawer too, because they've all been working just as hard as anybody else has to try to accomplish the goals that this team has. There's some of that.

**Q: In regards to practice squad players, how much of their time during the week is devoted to scout team work and what the other team does and also learning your system?**

**BB:** That's a good question. I'd say the majority of the meeting time is focused on what we do and the majority of the practice time is focused on what they do. Those need to merge obviously so we need to spend some meeting time preparing them for practice time and we need to take our meeting time where we're working on what we do and at some point transfer that onto the field to working on what we do, not just what they do. I'd say the percentages kind of flip but they're certainly interrelated and anytime we can practice something that our opponent does that's similar to what we do or sometimes is the same as what we do then we relate it in those terms so we would call the play the same or we would play the technique the same way as we're trying to play it so that even though they're doing the other team's play, they're using the techniques that we would use on our play so that we transfer that back over to us getting better and working on things that we do. So there's definitely a balance there and sometimes there's more of that at some positions or on one side of the ball from week to week than others. One week might be 90 percent of what we do, maybe it's not quite the same play but the techniques are the same, that type of thing.

Maybe another week it might be 40 percent, I don't know. It isn't always the same but that's the merging that we try to get to and it's not easy but that's what we have to do so that's another aspect of our preparation and planning. Like on Tuesdays, that's one of the things that we do is not only to talk about what we're going to do from a game plan standpoint but talk about how we're going to practice, who is going to practice, where, how that person can get the most out of their practice even though they might not even be playing or they might be practicing the other team's plays but they can still gain some experience and execution because it's something that we do, so things like that.

**Q:** With the coaches being on the same team, does that have any meaning to you – to be able to stay on the same team? Based on the way you were brought up?

**BB:** Yeah, I feel a loyalty to all the people that are in the organization. And I'm not saying I'm great or anything, that's not the point. The point is when you're the head coach, there are a lot of people that are dependent on you. Having been an assistant coach for a long time and been the son of an assistant coach for a long time, you know that your future is, to a certain degree, tied to the head coach. It's important to me to be able to hopefully provide some stability to the other members of the coaching staff, the other members of the organization that relate to the football department, the players.

We all know that the first thing that changes is the coach; the next thing that changes is most of the roster. I certainly like the fact that we have players that have been brought up in this system, that have tried to develop in this system, and hopefully they have the confidence to know that they can come back and play in this system again with the skills and the training and the knowledge that they've learned to do it. I mean, I feel a loyalty to them and I think they also feel a loyalty to me along those same lines.

I mean, it's a two-way street. I know everybody has got to take care of themselves and their own needs and all that. I do have a lot of loyalty and respect for the people who work for me and I want to try to continue to provide a good working environment for them to be successful, for us to be successful, so that we can all benefit from that. So yeah, I would say that's definitely important to me and that's the way I was brought up. I mean, when you're an assistant coach and the head coach isn't there, you're probably not going to be there either. That's just the way it is. I learned that a long time ago.

## Q: Do you ever feel the need to talk to the rookies, about if they're not playing as much after being the best players on the team for the last three or four years?

**BB:** I talk to the rookies on a regular basis. The elements of that conversation I think started long before now, going all the way to the spring, going back to training camp. Guys that come from college that were stars on their team, that were getting all the reps, that maybe weren't playing in the kicking game, that had so-called 'special privileges,' with their status on that team, they're in a whole different place, very, very early coming on to this team.

If that's what it was somewhere else, it's a lot different here. I don't know what it was like somewhere else, but my sense is that for some of them, it's a big transition for them. But that transition started a long, long time ago. But, we talk to them on a regular basis about that. Pro football is a lot different than college football. Not just the game, but the whole process of it. Everything we do is a lot different. We talk to them on a regular basis, I'd say at least weekly, if not more. In a lot of cases, it's really daily; it's really a daily conversation with either all of them or groups of them.

**Q:** Why so often?

**BB:** It's because they haven't gone through it. Everybody looking back, which I've heard many times as a coach, 'Well, I wish I had known this,' or 'I wish I had realized that,' or 'I didn't really know that.' They still don't know, but at least we try to do a better job than I did back when I was with the Giants. You've heard that so many times from those young guys that you tell them, 'Look, this is the way it's going to be. This is what you need to be ready for. This is what's going to happen. This is how this is going to work. This is how you need this.

This is how you need to do that.' It doesn't mean it's going to be perfect but at least they've been warned ahead of time, they have an idea of what to expect. A lot of times, you come back and say, 'OK, this is what we talked about. Did it happen about the way you thought it would? The way we talked about it?' 'Yeah.' 'Well, what was different?' 'I didn't expect this or I didn't expect that.' Then we talk about that and move on to the next thing. It's a long season for these guys. There are a lot of hills to climb, not just one. So it's a rollercoaster. Each week is a new challenge and really each day is a new challenge.

I think the better you can prepare them for it, the better chance they have to meet it. But there's still no substitute for experience. Coaches, players, we try to provide that and we do that, that's every year, every group, on and off the field. There are a lot of things in pro football that are a lot different than college, not just the game, not just the preparation but once they walk out of the building there's no dormitories, no classes, not a lot of other stuff. There are a lot of other things. There's regular life to deal with: playing bills and being accountable in other areas of your life that are much less so in college, a lot of that stuff is taken care of for you or you don't have to deal with it at all.

**Q: Is there a way to describe for someone who hasn't experienced it, just the difference in speed, complexity and intensity from what you see from the other side between preseason and regular season?**

**BB:** That's part of it, that's another long conversation that is a continuing one. Yeah, how competitive it is, how different it is. How teams now, the players are so much, other teams have much better scouting report on our players as we do on theirs. The first couple preseason games, you don't even really talk about it much but by the time you get to the regular season and you've seen guys play in preseason or a couple regular season games, you can start to identify their strengths and weaknesses, they can start to identify ours.

The game planning is different, the way that your matchups are. Players try to play to your weakness and avoid your strength and that's something you don't always see I the first two, three preseason games because nobody really cares that much about it. That's a big thing now, the situational football, getting to know the other teams, their personnel, their tendencies, their coordinators, how they do things, how much it changes from week to week, not just out there running around, it's very specific.

Yeah, it's a huge transition from the preseason to the regular season and I'd say it's a huge transition within the regular season. I'd say the games are a lot different now than they're going to be three, four, five weeks from now when there's a lot more evidence in the books. Then teams start dealing with injures and replacements and adjustments and everybody is adding to their scheme. Each week you add a couple new plays, a couple new looks, you add a wrinkle, those kind of things. What looks like a tendency is really just bait for something that they're going to try to setup and show you something they've been doing and do something else off it. All those are learning experiences and it's at a much higher level than what you see in college football, particularly in the passing game, that's the big difference and the kicking game. The kicking game and the passing game, [there are] huge, huge differences from what guys see in college.

**Q: You've done these joint practice several times, and Greg Schiano talked about how you don't want to do them with just anyone, it has to be someone you have a good relationship with. What are some of the criteria that go into choosing who to do joint practices about?**

**BB:** I'd say just the number one thing is that it's not about beating somebody in practice; it's about working with somebody and getting better. We're not here to try to win a drill or trick Tampa on something. That's not the point of it; the point is to work on what we want to work on and work on what they're working on so that we can become better and when we walk off the field we're a better team than we were when we walked on it.

That's the way we practice against each other: we compete against each other, but we compete in a way that we can improve each other – not get guys hurt, not a bunch of piles, not fight, and get all caught up in did he gain five yards, did he gain two yards, did we sack the quarterback, did we not sack the quarterback? We pull off, we don't hit the quarterback, we don't hit guys that are – the same way we wouldn't hit our guys in practice. We take care of each other but we work hard and we set up the drill so that they're fair, competitive drills.

It's not tilted one way or the other so that you can have an equal competition and equal evaluation. We made some plays out there, they made some plays out there and both teams can learn from both those situations. But it's not about going out there and winning the practice; it's about going out there and improving your team and making sure that when the players are on the field, they're kind of of comparable levels, too. We want to compete both athletically and also schematically with players that are their experienced players and that are their best players. At the same time, our younger guys and some of our less experienced guys just aren't ready to handle some of the things that – but they should compete against simpler plays, simpler formations.

They could do something formation-wise or blitz-wise that we just aren't ready to handle with that group of players and so what good is that? We're not ready for it, so okay, they did it because we're not ready for it. So we want to try to compete on an equal level and let the players play and then as they develop and grow then obviously they'll be able to move to that higher level. But you have to evaluate them on what they know how to do first. A lot of things like that go into it and it's just again, working together.

And not just Greg, but the entire staff has just been great to work with – the assistant coaches and coordinators working together and so forth. We've tried to create game-like situations but structured in a way that we know what we're doing and we can get the right people on the field, we can be competitive with each other and not get into a situation where somebody is overmatched or under-matched.

**Q: You started coaching back when there were over 100 players out there but you also had a much longer training camp to weed people out. This is a more compressed type of thing now. Is more players better? I know you also have guys who aren't out there too so at least you have full practices you can run a couple more players available to you. Is it a significant change?**

**BB:** I'd say it's definitely a significant change. When I started coaching in the NFL, first of all, there really wasn't any offseason program or it was very limited. You didn't have the organized OTAs that we have now. When you put in at the beginning of training camp, when you installed your plays, you installed them very thoroughly because it was, I'd say, pretty much the first time they were hearing it. Veterans obviously had heard them before but for the benefit of the whole team, you did it in a very thorough way because it was really the first time. When we go out here the first day of practice, we've already had 13 practices or however many practices we had, granted it was six weeks ago.

There's definitely a level of, from a month of practice, there's some learning and carryover. We might have a couple new guys on the team and all that but I'm saying overall there's a lot more lead-in. The numbers really came from the rookies. That's when teams would bring 50-60 rookies to camp and have a training camp of rookies for a week, 10 days, two weeks, depending on the team and what their philosophy was. [Minnesota Vikings Head Coach] Bud Grant was probably only like two hours. With Dallas and Oakland and some of those teams, they did it for like two, two and a half weeks. Out of those 60, 70 players, whatever it was, they kept 15 or 20 guys or however many they kept to then go to practice when everybody came in and they got rid of the guys who were just kind of tryout guys.

That's where the Everson Walls of the world and guys like that came from. They were just part of a big number and then they made the first cut and got into training camp and in his case, ended up having a great career. That was different. Of course, he had six preseason games plus a couple scrimmages. You had the rookie scrimmage, so you had like 50-60 rookies and then you scrimmage yourself or go scrimmage somebody else a couple times to see how they looked against competition to help whittle that down. So you had the rookie scrimmage and then you had a veteran scrimmage or two maybe and then you had six preseason games.

The preparation for the season really was at the beginning of the season, not in the spring and then kind of jumping to the different points. It was a lot different. Is it better or worse? I don't know. The season didn't start until the end of September, like September 21 or somewhere in that range was opening day. Of course, the season ended a lot earlier too, we weren't playing into baseball season.

**Q: When you're in a situation where you're considering challenging, do the coaches in the booth just have access to television replay or do they have DVR capability?**

**BB:** No, there's no DVR capability. There's a monitor in both coaches' booths and it gets the exact same feed. Whatever the networks feed it, that's what they see, which sometimes is nothing. Sometimes it's what's on the big screen. Sometimes it's what the TV shows, which may be different than what the fans in the stadium see. We try to look at all those. If we have a shot in the monitor of the play, then they look at that. I can look at it on the big screen if it's replayed.

Sometimes you get a couple different looks at it, one of which is maybe the right one you're looking for, like this should or shouldn't be challenged. Sometimes you don't and that's - and then some of them are just really close and it could almost go either way. I think the big part of that is that if you're sure of it, then it's an easy challenge to make. The easiest challenge is [when], regardless of what the play is, you look at the play on the screen and it's obvious to you that the play was called incorrectly. That's no problem. The harder one is when you see the play with your own eyes and you say, 'I don't think that's the way it should have been called,' but can you find another picture of it that confirms what you actually saw? That's a question. And then there are the plays that maybe you think you have a 25 percent chance of being right on. 'Maybe we could get this. I doubt it.'

But it's such a big play in the game and you maybe don't need your timeouts; it's the end of the first half or something and your timeouts aren't that critical at that point and it's a huge play in the game, then maybe you take that lesser percentage chance and say 'Okay, we didn't see the play, we didn't get a real good look at it, but we think it's close. Let's take a shot at it.' Was his arm going forward? Was the ball out? Was it a fumble? Was it an incomplete pass? That kind of thing. It doesn't get replayed up there, but it's a big play in the game, then maybe you just take a shot at it and say, 'I hope it comes out in our favor.'

**Q:** Was the DVR subject something that was ever brought up or did I hear that incorrectly somewhere else?

**BB:** I'm not aware of any DVR system that's ever been in place. The only thing you ever have in the [coaches] box is what the monitor is up there. No coach has an individual monitor. You can't have your own TV or you know - both booths have to be the same. Whatever is fed into the one booth gets fed into the other booth, so there's not any competitive advantage between being at home or having your own equipment or any of that. It's all the same. But as a coach, you're kind of at the mercy of that because you don't really know.

From one play to the next, you don't know what you have to work with. So if they don't replay it - no matter what shot they have - if they don't replay it then you can't make a decision based on it. Sometimes you make a challenge and then you see the play replayed. There's the challenge, the officials go over there, there's a pause in the action and then they play something up on the screen and you haven't seen that and you're looking at it and going 'There's no point in challenging that play, we're not going to get this,' but you hadn't seen that before.

## Q: In the week leading up to a game, do you personally get a lot of one-on-one time with individual players and the new players?

**BB:** The assistant coaches spend the most time with them. So in this case [Donald Thomas], it would be Dante [Scarnecchia, last week with [A.J.] Edds it was Patrick Graham. But I talk to the players, get him on the team, tell him the things we expect for him, what his role is, or kind of what the plan is going forward and then usually talk about that during the week, how it's going, questions, things like that.

**Q:** Do the one-on-one meetings vary from week-to-week based on who you see you need to spend additional time with?

**BB:** Yeah, I would say that it would be fair to say that, about all the players. There's 53 players, plus the practice squad, plus some other guys, so it would be impossible for me to have regular meetings with each player on a regular basis. Some of it depends on that player's situation or that game or whatever happens to be going on that week. [I] talk to different players at different times, different groups - sometimes I meet with a positional group, sometimes I meet with individual players, sometimes I don't. It's not a real set pattern. I try to do what I feel like would help the team and what is necessary. I would say, football, it's an interesting point on how to handle that.

You only have so much time, so how you allocate that as a head coach relative to certain players, groups of players, your coaching staff, other people in the organization - it's one of the challenging parts of the job, it really is. In all honesty, I could sit down and talk to every player about things that I think are important. It's not that I don't want to talk to them, it's just there are other demands too. You try to hit, like I said, the things you feel like will make the most difference or do it in the most efficient way.

In watching other head coaches, being on Coach Marchibroda's staff or Coach Parcells' staff and watching how they handle their interaction with different players and how they do that, I think that's an interesting management part of the job. It changes - it's not the same every day or every week but it's interesting to watch other people do that and as a head coach it's definitely a challenging part of the job - that interaction with the team and your time management with all the different people connected with the team. There's no book on that - at least I haven't read it.

**Q: Is the officiating kind of an unknown in the preseason because of the points of emphasis or even just rust?**

**BB:** I think the preseason officiating is sometimes a little hard to gauge. I think that there is not a ... I don't know. I don't know if there is necessarily a set standard on that. We've seen some very heavily penalized games in the preseason this year; I mean, 20, 22, 25, 27 penalties in a game. I'm not even talking about our games. I'm just saying league-wide there have been some very, very heavily penalized games. And then there're other games in the preseason, we saw a couple - two, three, four penalties. I don't really count false starts. They're penalties, but you've got to call those. [When] a guy false starts, that's not really a penalty the officials are calling. That's the offense jumping or defense running in the neutral zone. You've got to stop the play on that.

That's not really an issue; it's all the other stuff. You don't know in preseason how the officials will handle it. I think some crews – consciously or subconsciously – they call it like they see it. If there're 30 penalties, they're going to call 30 penalties. I think we all know what that does for the flow of the game. I think there are other crews that look at it, or maybe individual officials that look at it and say, 'Alright, it's preseason. We're going to call the ones we've got to call, but we're not going to call everything, we'll be here all night. And some of the guys really, in all honesty, aren't going to be playing in the regular season that are playing out here now, so do we really want to overdo it on that?' I think you probably get both ends of the ...

The pendulum swings all the way on that one. So how a crew handles preseason or how they handle the regular season? I don't know if that's necessarily the same. But I do think there's a certain consistency in general with the crews and things that, if the crews stay the same, which is this season they haven't – most of the referees, at least all the ones we've seen, though I know some crews even that we haven't seen – the referee has a whole new crew. So the referee only calls basically one-seventh of the penalties, or the penalties that fall into his area. And then how the other six guys call them, that's all ...

It might be the same as before, it might be different; depends on who those guys are. So long answer. I'd say short answer then would be I think that's another unknown going into the regular season.

**Q: There are a lot of rookie head coaches in the league this year. When you started as a head coach, what was the toughest part**

## about doing that?

**BB:** I think one of the hard things is just coming into a new organization - if it's a new organization, which it isn't always. Sometimes a coach comes up from within his own organization. But when you come into a new organization and try to kind of get things in a way that either you're used to or you're comfortable with as a head coach - not just the head coach, but the whole program that you're trying to institute. All the support people that are involved in that are important components there, too, because they interact so closely with the coaching staff and the players and the team and all that, trainers, doctors, video people, equipment people, grounds crews, so forth and so on.

There are a lot of moving parts in and around the team. So trying to get all of that coordinated and done in a way that is really efficient, so you don't feel like you're wasting a lot of time on things that in the past were pretty smooth for you wherever you were before, and it feels like you're having time taken away from football, the team and preparation to deal with all of those other things, so that's one thing.

The other thing is just trying to institute your program, what you believe in, the way you want to play the game, your plays, your philosophy, your practice tempo, just all the little things that in some way or another in the big picture, are all connected. It might seem like it is one little isolated thing on a team, but when you tie that in to a lot of other things that are going on, it can be an important component of the whole team-building process. Trying to get all those things to work properly and efficiently, that's a challenge, too.

# Building a Roster

**Q:** What are the considerations that go into acquiring a guy like Chris Hogan as far as his skill set, personality as well as fitting into your scheme after he's performed so well against you as a member of an opposing team?

**BB:** I think probably 90 percent of the process is all the same whether it's a player that we've played against or haven't played against. There are certainly enough, if the players play, there are enough examples in the NFL where you can see how he is going to do against a high level of competition. Through enough games you'll see a variety of schemes and matchups that he'll have to face to have some idea of a projection of how he would be, how you would anticipate him doing for you. That's a much tougher evaluation in college because the level of competition isn't consistent and the schemes aren't necessarily all NFL schemes. I'm not saying it's good or bad, it's just different.

In the NFL, you've got that advantage to be able to see NFL quality players and NFL schemes. I would say that other 10 percent, if it's against your team, then you know the player that you've matched up against and you can evaluate that matchup a little bit better than watching them matchup against somebody else because you have better knowledge of your individual players. There is some benefit to that, but again, I would say in Chris [Hogan]'s case, his situation is a little bit unusual because he didn't have a lot of play time offensively. Some of that came when Buffalo had injuries at the position.

I think Buffalo felt they had a lot of depth at the receiver position and that affected a little bit of Chris's play time. When there were injuries, he played more, but he also played very well in the kicking game which gave us an evaluation, not only of him in the kicking game, but also some of skills that you could see on special teams that maybe weren't as evident on offense – blocking for example. Not that he didn't block on offense, but just the number of times blocking on kick returns that you'd be able to see that in space against good coverage players and so forth. I'd saying playing against a guy gives you a little bit more of an evaluation because you can see him against one of your players and that individual matchup, but I think there is a lot more to it than just that. There's the whole body of work that you want to evaluate, not just one game.

**Q: It seems like you have a bunch of guys now who are 6-4, 270-plus. What is it you like about that body type? Are you looking forward to that?**

**BB:** Absolutely. We'll see how it all plays out. I think that, generally speaking, the bigger they are the slower they run. In that 250-275ish range, depending on the actual individual, is where you usually get those times under five seconds - 4.9, 4.85, 4.8, whatever it is. That speed and quickness with a little lower weight in passing situations usually make those guys a little more active and gives them a little more speed, generally speaking. Not that you don't need inside guys to push and power rush and stuff like that, but those guys have that advantage.

We have a lot of big guys on our team. It seems like every year, the game is getting a little more spread out for us. We're in nickel defense more and more every year - over 50 percent last year. Some of that is being ahead; some of that is teams in our division - Buffalo, you're pretty much in nickel all day against them. That's two games. It's a high percentage of our defense, so that's part of the reason we feel like we need that. It's hard to be in our base defense as much as we were in the past.

**Q: How important is the bottom third of the roster when you're constructing your roster?**

**BB:** I don't think we really look at it that way. I would say the way that I look at it is every roster spot is important. You can number them however you want to number them. I'm not sure who's one and who's 53, but everyone is important and there has got to be a reason for each one and an expectation for each one and a role for each one or a potential role for each one.

What we try to do is based on those criteria the best person that we can have for that spot, that's who we want. We try to make the most out of every opportunity we have. That also includes the 10 practice squad spots because those players are really part of your team, too. I mean they're not on your team, but they kind of are on your team. In a lot of cases they're certainly the next guy – they're in the on deck circle. All those spots, they're all important. I wouldn't single any of them out or dismiss any of them. I think they're all important.

## Q: Is the best way to win in the NFL to have a good quarterback? How important is that position?

**BB:** There are 32 teams. There are 32 different ways of doing things. In our case, we just again try to do what we feel like is best for our football team. And again that's at each position and then at some point there has to be an overall integration because some positions play off each other, even though they're not the same positon. But as you get in the kicking game, tight ends and linebackers and fullbacks and things like that, there is some type of interplay there. Again, all the positions are important.

We want to have the best quarterback that we can. We want to have the best center that we can. We want to have the best left guard, right guard, left tackle, right tackle, nose guard, inside linebacker. I mean we're trying to get the best we can at every position. Linebacker, coach, trainer, video person – you name it – we're trying to get the best person we can at every position in the organization to be competitively the best at that spot in the league. I think that's how you get good, is you get good at everything. You don't just pick out one thing and try to be good at that and then give back that advantage by being bad somewhere else. That's just our philosophy and that's the way that I look at it.

**Q:** You had eight safeties active for the game against Washington. I know a lot of those guys contribute in the kicking game, but is there something about the guys in that position that you're able to use them in various positions? What is the reasoning for having so many active safeties?

**BB:** I think if you take a look at those payers and what their roles were in the game, there were several of the safeties that you're referring to that I don't believe they played on defense. So what their role in the game really ended up being was playing in the kicking game. And as we've talked about, you have those 66 spots that you have to cover on special teams, and when we look at it, we don't look at it as offensive players or defensive players on special teams.

We look at it as who's going to play those positions, and then independently we look at the offensive and defensive depth and personnel groupings and then we try to match them up. In the end, it's really trying to balance all those things and again at this time of the year – well it could be any time of the year really – but when you have injuries involved, when you look at your roster and say, 'Ok these X number of players are out of the game, physically they can't play, then they're out. It's a non-consideration, there's nothing else to talk about.'

Now you take the players that are left that are at your disposal and from a coaching standpoint you make those decisions as to which 46 players give us the best chance in this particular game, and those are the ones that you select, and again to balance out offense, defense and special teams. I'd say one of the considerations would come down to if you could take a player that would have a role in the kicking game that would alleviate another player's role on offense or defense, then there would be some benefit to that even though he doesn't give you depth maybe at that position offensively or defensively, it would help you manage the player that does have that offensive or defensive role in terms of him not having to take on an additional special teams role, if that makes any sense.

**Q:** How has the Patriots approach to the draft and developing players helped the team as opposed to building through free agency, and was that a philosophy you've always had dating back to your years as a younger coach?

**BB:** Well, I think we're all in the business of developing players. I mean nobody plays forever. You always have to restock your team with talent, plus you have the NFL system that's set up in such a way that you can't keep everybody and there's turnover on every team with free agency and so forth. I think, yeah, that's always been important, developing players is definitely important. I think in Cleveland prior to free agency you were able to keep players so a lot of times your team pretty much stayed the same from year to year. Trades were infrequent and it was just the developing of the players that you brought in – draft choices, free agents that made your team in the 70's and 80's.

Over the last couple decades, developing players from Plan B to free agency and with fewer rounds in the draft now – we're not into those 12 round drafts that we had back in '91 or '92, whatever it was – those undrafted players and just the overall opportunity to work with guys and try to develop them, it's been important in the NFL. We did a decent job of that in Cleveland with guys like Wally Williams and Orlando Brown and some of those offensive lineman, Bob Dahl, you know, guys like that that went on to have good careers and Pro Bowls and all that that nobody even heard of, Herman Arvie, when they came out of college, and other positions as well but some of those guys in particular.

So I'd say yeah that's always been important. But you can build your roster in a lot of different ways. Every day is an opportunity and some days provide more opportunities than others, like final cut down day when there are hundreds of players available or the draft when you can select from hundreds of players or even after the draft there are a lot of players to be signed. Those opportunities are really there, some more frequent than others, but you're kind of always working to develop and improve your roster. Practice squad positions, those 10 spots are opportunities for that as well, so I think that's all part of team building.

**Q: When you acquire a guy during the season, how much of that is based on how quickly he can adjust to your system and pick things up quickly?**

**BB:** Having them know what to do to be able to get out on the field is important. We've got to do a good job of teaching it, obviously condensing or streamlining information because you can't get the whole playbook in, and they've got to do a good job of working hard to learn it and specifically learn that game plan, so a lot of times you really try to get them on the game plan first and then the next week you get the next game plan but maybe you can start to add some things to it and eventually over time be able to catch up on the overall nomenclature, terminology, more of a comprehensive understanding.

And that varies from player to player, too – how experienced they are, how much experience they've had in a system similar to ours or things that they can relate or where there is carryover. Each one is a little bit different. Each of us learns differently. Some things we pick up quicker than others, so it is really very individualized between that player and whichever staff members and his position coach are a part of that, getting him up to speed, covering what he needs to know for that game, but also getting him acclimated into all the other aspects of our program, too – not just the plays, but there are a lot of other things they need to learn or fall in line with.

**Q:** With respect to that, what have you seen from the

development of Justin Coleman?

**BB:** Definitely making progress. It's hard for any player when they miss training camp, so there is a lot of ground there that just really never gets made up. You just try to close the gap as much as you can. But it's definitely getting better. Each week it gets better and there is more carryover – kind of what we just talked about. But yeah, he's definitely making good progress. There is just a long way to go. It's a big gap.

**Q:** A lot of times, a player has to adjust his technique when he comes into your system. How difficult has that transition been for Justin Coleman?

**BB:** I'd say not too bad, yeah, not too bad. You have your golf swing and then you go somewhere else and they change your swing – sometimes it's easier, sometimes it's harder. He's done a good job. I don't think it's been a big adjustment for him. We play a lot of ... Our corner techniques are closer to the line of scrimmage – not all of them but a lot of them – so that was something that he needs to work on a little bit. But he's done that. His athletic skills I think are good for what we've asked him to do, so I wouldn't say that's a big problem.

We go over some communication, some adjustments in our system, and anytime you have to do a lot of thinking or you're unsure as to is it this or is it that, that slows you down no matter how fast you are. I think that that's making an improvement. He's made a lot of improvement there and that enables him play faster, play more aggressively and play more confidently. That just gets better every day.

**Q: When you evaluate players in regards to the practice squad, how do you balance having a reserve at a position and also having enough guys to carry a scout team to prepare your team on a weekly basis?**

**BB:** That's a good question. In a way, the players that are on the practice squad are in the same positon as the players who are on the roster but not active. Obviously, you can protect the players that are not active that are on the roster and you don't have as much protection [for practice squad players], but either way they don't play in the game. They practice, but they don't play in the game, so in that way, it's similar. So your depth really is those inactive players and the players who are on the practice squad who are also inactive, even though they're on a little different list, if you will. Sometimes that's a team management thing.

Sometimes there are other reasons for it, but in the end, that's where it is. Then there are some players who are your depth who are not on your roster – they're not on anybody's roster. They're available now. Whether they'll be available in a week, two weeks, a month, two months – that's another story. So, it's a combination of all those places, and honestly there are other players on other practice squads that are potentially available to you on your roster. They're not available to you on your practice squad because you can't go practice squad to practice squad, but you can go from another practice squad to your roster, just like somebody else can go from our practice squad to their roster.

That's all in play. How do you find the right guys, what's the right mix and all that, some of it is the individual player, some of it is the circumstances that are surrounding him. Some of it is maybe your overall read of what the league perception is of that player or your position or whatever it happens to be, and you just try to do what you think is best.

The exception rules on that for the two practice squad players add a little bit of a twist there because there are practice squad players and then there are practice squad exception players, so you're limited to how many exception players you can have, so they're there to a point but only a couple of them and then the rest of them have to come from the other pool. That's another thing for consideration. If you have three exception guys you really want, but you can only have two of them, then which two is it, and so forth and so on.

**Q:** When do you start seriously considering a player for the practice squad? Is it this week? Is it earlier in camp?

**BB:** It could be the draft. It could be a guy that you want to work with that you feel like probably has got too far to go to realistically be ready. You never know. Like we don't try to cut the team in April – I'm not saying that. But realistically, you take players or you bring them on to your team, whether it's draft choices or sometimes it's college free agents – guys that aren't drafted – with the kind of thought that it'd be hard for this guy to make our team, but a year from now, with a year of development and so forth, it might be a different story, and so that's a player you want to work with. Yeah, it goes back as far as that.

It's certainly a lot easier to get one of your players on to your practice squad than it is to get another player on to your practice squad. The fact that a team has a player, a team has been working with that player, they release the player at the 53-man cut, unless another team claims him and then they have to carry him, which obviously frees up somebody else, unless they do that, it's a pretty high likelihood that you would be able to put that player on your practice squad – not 100 percent, but pretty high. Guys that we see get released that we would like to have on our practice squad, the question is, how are you going to get them there? You could claim him, put him on your roster and then maybe move him later or maybe you have to carry the guy as a roster player.

But ideally that isn't maybe what you want to do, whereas it's easier to get our players from our team to our practice squad, just like it is for everybody else. If you really feel strongly about a guy and you want to put him on your roster then that's another story, then he's going on a roster. But in the pool of 320 practice squad players throughout the league, those guys are an important part of your team's depth or every team's depth, and so you want the best ones you can get there, but sometimes it's hard to get them if they're not on your team, or harder to get them.

**Q: How long does it usually take to assess all of those personnel**

## transactions that you're going to have?

**BB:** Yeah, that's a great question. I would say, you know, in the neighborhood of six to eight weeks. Obviously free agency starts a little less than two months from now. We definitely need to be ready by then. There will be some other transactions along the way before then relative to tenders and those kind of things. There are a few other situations that will proceed that, but I would say somewhere in the four to eight weeks category, some sooner than others, some longer than others. But trying to compile all the information on individual players and situations, as well as, as I said, things like responsibilities on our staff and looking at our scheme and you know, maybe a player could fit a little bit better into a different scheme or maybe not as well into a different scheme if we're planning on making some changes along those lines.

That's all part of it too. If we change, then that could affect how the player would fit. Those are all part of the conversation. I would say in the four to eight week range in terms of getting all the information together, being able to really sort through it and then ultimately make decisions in a timely fashion.

Some decisions have to be made sooner than others. Other decisions, honestly, may wait. We've re-signed players here sometimes in April, May, June and we've also released players sometimes in that range. I don't think there's any specific time table but I would say in that four to eight week range is probably when most of the decisions need to be made or at least, even if they're delayed, at least if you've made the decision to delay them. But that's a great question because that's a big part of our offseason right now, is pulling all those things together. It's going to take a little time.

**Q: In terms of the salary cap, it sounds like it might go up a little bit. Do you have a pretty good idea right now what you're looking out right now in terms of space?**

**BB:** I'd say the answer to that question is, look, I'm not oblivious to it, I'm not saying that. I think you get to the end of the season and

246

again, our focus has been on winning games. There really hasn't been anything that affects the salary cap, I'd say in the last two months. I mean significantly. You might bring a guy from the practice squad or whatever but it's not a high monetary issue. Then when you get to the end of the season like we are now, you have different players who have hit escalators, maybe they have incentives in their contracts, there are offseason awards, there are rollovers into the next year's cap.

There are a lot of calculations that go on. Again, I'm not saying this is Earth-shattering news; it's just a lot easier to wait and deal with it when it's all done. Again, in relative terms it's a small amount of money. I'm not saying a half million dollars is a small amount of money in an incentive or escalator, but I'm just saying on a 100 and however many million dollar cap, it's relatively small. So, you wait until that's over. You sort it all out. You have the people who work on that in our organization. We'll get together with them. We'll get a sense of where we are, what some of the issues are going to be, what some of the options are going to be. We have some players that are not under contract.

We have some degree of cap space. We have whatever degree of flexibility we have with other things, we have draft choices, we can make projections on what they're going to cost and you start putting that all together. That's one of the many moving parts that goes with the whole offseason process. I'd say we're not there yet but that will certainly be a big part of the discussions at some point, particularly as it relates to free agency, not so much the draft. The draft will be the draft but there is a salary cap implication to the draft in terms of where you're picking and what those costs will be. Now that we know where we'll be picking we can, because of the format, be able to estimate those costs as well.

**Q:** When you put together your 46-man game day roster, part of it is injuries and you have a good feel of the guys you can count on, maybe he has a foot injury versus a player who has a concussion and it's harder to gauge. How does that affect putting together the roster? Do you add another layer of depth because you're not as certain as you would be about a guy coming back from a physical thing. Do you get what I'm saying?

**BB:** I understand the question. It's probably a lot longer answer than we have time for. First of all, there's no discussion until a player is medically cleared. So if a player's not medically cleared, he's out of the game, it doesn't matter. There's no discussion. Then there's another part of a player being cleared but he's not 100 percent, which that's probably true of everybody in the locker room. But there is a degree of, he can play, he's not injured, nobody is concerned about him being re-injured or putting himself in jeopardy. It's just a question of how effective he can be. At that point, it becomes a coaching decision as to, OK, he can play, just how effective do you think he'll be. A big part of that obviously is practice. We practice – Wednesday is a big day for us, Thursday is a big day for us and Friday is more of a mental review day, it's not as big of a physical day.

By the time you get to Friday, it's not always all that clear because a player can go out there and perform well on Wednesday, he can perform well on Thursday but then those two days maybe take a toll on the player and whatever situation he's managing and then on Friday he's not so good. Then there are other situations where guys will go Wednesday and then Thursday and then Friday and that's easy because you know then, 'OK, that player has responded to every increased level of activity and come back stronger.' So you feel confident that he's ready to go.

The player that goes out there, competes, performs and then the result of that is, I don't want to say maybe it's a setback or maybe it's just, can he really sustain it at that level or is it still going to take another week. Those are the ones on Friday and Saturday that are really questionable. That's the bottom line, is they're questionable. How are they going to respond to the week of work and then where do you think they'll be Sunday. I know everybody thinks that all this is all figured out, but truly it isn't. A lot of it is waiting to see just like the doctors and the trainers are. I know you're trying to find that out too, but I'm waiting to see that as well. I don't know until a player goes out there and does it or even after he does it, what's the result of that going to be?

Those decisions are made a lot of times when we know or when we feel pretty confident what they are. But a lot of times those decisions really go right down to Sunday morning or sometimes even Saturday afternoon. You just have to make a call at that point, you just have to decide what you're going to do: this is what we've got and we either go with it or wait until next week. Again, specifically to answer your question, each case is different.

But until a player is cleared, there's no discussion, there's no decision to make. Once he's cleared, then it becomes a coaching decision as to how effective you think the player can be or you think can be effective for a certain number of plays. Like, OK, this guy can play, we don't think he can play the whole game but he can definitely go out there and play so we need to monitor his snaps. So, it's some combination of all those things.

**Q:** How much input does the player have?

**BB:** It depends. It would depend on the player, it would depend on the nature of his situation. In some cases, a lot. In some cases, I would say, minimal. In some cases, kind of more in the middle. Look, the players want to play. So not very often is a player going to tell you, 'I don't want to play.' Usually it's more along the lines of, 'I want to play, I can do these things.' Sometimes they tell you, 'I can't do these other things.'

Sometimes you have to figure that out for yourself. Because again, a player wants to play, he won't mention, 'I don't really feel confident cutting to my left – I can play, I'll be alright' or whatever it happens to be, because they want to play. Again, my job is just to do what I feel like is best for the team and try to figure out if what he can do is good enough or if we're going to be able to accept that for the good of the team. Not that he won't give us his best, just what is it.

**Q:** One of the big stories yesterday was the release of Texans safety Ed Reed. When something like that happens, what is the process that you go through as an organization to decide if you want to make a move on that player?

**BB:** Well first of all, there's usually, not always, but there's usually an indication of things like that – there's usually an indication that they could happen. Not saying they're going to happen, but that they could happen, and that's one of the things that our personnel department, pro personnel department, does a real good job of, is they stay on top of that. So when you have players who are – whatever their situation is – that we think could potentially become available, then we start working on them ahead of time, so that when it happens – or if it happens – we're not sitting there trying to scramble around and find out the information and evaluate the player on film and so forth.

Most of the time you have a little bit of a lead-in on that if you're paying attention to things that are going on, whether it be some type of internal problem, or maybe it's a player that's had decreased playing time, or maybe there's a contract issue that you can see coming to a head, or you have some indication from whoever that it's going to happen. I'd say most of the time we have a little bit of a head start on that, and then if it doesn't happen, it doesn't happen, and we evaluated the player and the situation anyway. If it doesn't come up then there's no, obviously, action to take on it, but often times it does, and so we try to stay ahead of that. And of course that depends on what our situation is; I mean, there's a lot of players that could be available out there, but if it's a situation where you have a need at a certain position or it's a fit, then you're more interested and more apt to do something than if the player is out there and you have something going on at another position, but not that position, and that could affect what type of decision you would make there. It could be the same player, but it's more sometimes about timing than it is about the player that's available or the situation that you're dealing with on your team at that point in time, which there is always something, whether it's injuries or the type of scheme that you're getting ready to face or that you want to use, and where your depth is at different positions, how to put all that together. I'd say that's kind of the overall process.

## Q: Is there something about the wide receiver position specifically that makes it a greater challenge for new players to catch up to players who have been here?

**BB:** I would say that a lot of players that have come here, however they've come here, have usually commented on the amount or the learning or the adjustments, something, the pace. I'm not coaching any other team in the league so I don't know what the other 31 teams do, but I would say that a lot of the players who come here feel challenged at that position based on…look, we've had an offense that's been in place for 13, 14 years now. It evolves a bit every year, maybe gets modified a little bit, but it's grown. It's certainly – it has a lot more breadth to it than it did in 2000, 2001, 2002.

That means a new guy coming in has to learn – to a degree – 12, 13 years of stuff instead of a guy that's coming in and learning the system from scratch with a new coach and that type of thing. It probably is a lot. I think that's challenging. The move from college football to pro football is a pretty big jump in terms of protections, coverages, blitzes and all those kind of things. You watch a lot of college film, sometimes you only see one or two coverages. You don't see that in this league.

**Q:** Is that something you have to be cognizant of as you try to integrate new players? When Michael Lombardi was at NFL Network he made the comparison to Dan Marino at the end of his careers and they had trouble getting new receivers to play.

**BB:** Sure. I think that's a balance you have to…when you put new stuff in, you have to usually take something out. You just can't keep adding, adding, adding. At some point you have to trim the fat. It's a balance, but at the same time you don't want to take that experience and not take new plays or new adjustments or new things that you do and be able to utilize those skills, because a lot of the players can do it but you have to try to catch the younger guys up. Again, we've done that at a lot of different positions. We've turned over the tight end position, we've turned over the running back position, and we've turned over a number of the positions on the offensive line. Now we're doing it at receiver.

I think it's a little bit of you have to figure it out as you go. You have a plan, you try to do it a certain way but as you get into it, you see how it's going and what certain players are able to do or how quickly they're able to adapt and what's taking longer. You modify your teaching; sometimes you modify your scheme a little bit. Obviously, some of the things we do with Rob [Gronkowski] and Aaron [Hernandez] are different than what we did with some of the other guys we had here. Some of the things we do now are a little different than what we did when we had Kevin Faulk. The team is always in transition to a degree. You have try to figure out where you want to go and how to try and get there. Usually you have to change things as you go along a little bit.

**Q: With the understanding that every player on the team has a role and you want to make sure they do that each week, is there anything specific you hope to get out of the rookies each season because of the age and youthful energy? Is there anything that you want to see out of them over the course of each season?**

**BB:** I think it's more specific to each individual player. I think each player's situation is different. His personal situation and then a lot of times he's impacted by the players around him or the players at his position. Either what he's asked to do or what his opportunities are, that kind of thing. Certainly there's a function of both, but I think they're also related to a point. So, I think each player's individual role and expectations for that player are specific to that player, regardless of what year the guy is or how much experience he has or doesn't have. You go to that player and you talk to him at different points in the spring, in training camp, in the season, maybe at different points during the season, 'Here's what we want you to do. Here's what you're doing well. Here's what you're not doing so well. This is what you need to work on.'

Whatever it is, whatever constructive coaching you can give the player, you give him, relative to his performance and also relative to his role. That covers really everything: training and preparation and performance and position, work habits, attitude, etcetera, all those things. Whatever applies, that's what you talk to him about. I think there are different points in the season where that's a scheduled thing and then there are other points during the season where it's really kind of a weekly thing, where you talk to him week to week about: 'For the St. Louis game, this is what you need to do.' Maybe it was different last week or the week before.

Maybe it's going to be different next week, but you really try to lay it out and define it for them. I understand what the question is about the rookies – it applies to the rookies, but I think it applies to everybody too. I don't think it's just specific to them. I think you try to do that with everybody on your team, including your practice squad players and those guys too because they're still, even though they're not active, they could be active and they do have an important role on the team relative to the team's preparations. So, what you want them to do, how you want them to do it, how they're improving, whether they're leveling off or whatever it happens to be, I think you want to stay on top of that. It's a constant thing for everybody.

**Q: When you put together a roster and you have a third tight end on the depth chart, how much of a blocking assignment is that. How much does it play into a guy winning that job?**

**BB:** It depends on who else you have and what his other skills are.

**Q:** So your extra tackles and all that combine?

**BB:** Yeah. Ultimately, each player has to establish his own value to the team in whatever form that is. Ultimately when you put together the team all the jobs have to be accounted for somehow. It doesn't have to be by this person or that person but somebody has to do it. Somebody has to cover kickoffs, you have to put a kickoff team out there so who is that going to be? What group of people, what combination of people is that going to be? You figure that out and maybe that plays into the final decision.

Or maybe you have that pretty well covered and it's the kickoff return team or it's short yardage and goal-line or whatever it is. In the end, you have to take a look at all those things – they're all factors. That's how we try to put together the team – look at all the jobs that have to be done, try to figure out where our depth is and if there's one void there then you have to figure out how you're going to fill that. Is it change your scheme or find somebody to do it on your roster or find somebody that isn't on your roster to try to do it? Those are the issues.

**Q: When it comes to building depth, do you have a number in mind at the start of the season of how many players you'll need over the course of the season because of the number of injuries that crop up over the course of the year?**

**BB:** No, I don't think so. But I think historically if you look at it, you probably would take your practice squad players, take those eight players and over the course of the year, eventually those eight players will be on your roster. Or if it isn't one of them, it will be somebody, a veteran player that isn't practice squad eligible that will replace somebody on your roster. So I think that's the ball park number. Even though you cut your team to 53, you're really cutting it to 61 when you add the practice squad.

I'd say by the end of the year, you're probably going to get to those 60 players or if not, depending on what your needs are, if you have guys on the practice squad that can move up, it might be them. If you don't have somebody on the practice squad or if there's a better veteran that's available that's not practice squad eligible, he could be an injury replacement during the year. It's a round number but again, you get multiple injuries at the same position, nobody has enough players to stockpile that. I would say that would be the ballpark number. So I really look at it, when we reduce the roster to 61 at the end of training camp, that's really our football team. It's 53 but it's really 61 because as you know you can take a guy the day before the game and put him from the practice squad to the roster and he could dress and he could play in a game. And so could everybody else, so those guys really, they aren't on your team, but they are on your team. Or they are on your team but they're not on your team, however you want to look at it.

**Q:** Dick Steinberg was almost always about taking the best athlete no matter what the need was. With all the picks you have the in second round, philosophically how much would you reach to find that player?

**BB:** I'd say philosophically, that's pretty much where I am always: try to take the player that you feel that's the best player. It's great to say 'OK, we needed this position, so now we have a card to put up there in that spot,' but if that player isn't able to really fulfill that area or that position then you're coming back here the next year looking for the same thing again. Or it's really 'We took him, but we really need better than that,' or 'It wasn't quite what we want.' But I think if you find a player that's good value for your team, you can never have enough good football players. So sometimes you think you have more than what you need at a certain position, but usually that stuff works itself out one way or the other.

You get an injury or two, which inevitably happens in this sport, and what looks like an extra guy that you don't need, ends up being a valuable guy. I learned that at the Giants. The second or third year I was there, we had drafted Lawrence Taylor, we had Brad Van Pelt, and I know we took Carl Banks with the second pick in the draft, and that pick was crucified. 'What a stupid pick. Why would you take Carl Banks? What could you do with him. He's just going to sit there and watch while the other two guys play.' Carl Banks and Lawrence Taylor were really the two bookends to that defense all through the '80s and took us to a lot of victories and two Super Bowl championships. That was another 'stupid pick' that looked like 'why would you do that?' And of course that was with no free agency too, so you only had so many picks, that's how you improved your team, unless you made a trade. But that ended up being one of the best selections while I was there.

Another example of that was when we took Butch Woolfolk and then followed that up with Joe Morris. And that was another 'stupid pick' of 'why take Joe Morris when you had already taken a running back? What are you going to do - get two balls out there and give one to each guy?' Again, Joe Morris really took us to the '86 championship. I think if you believe in your system and you believe in your grades like you said, you've studied that all year, those are the players that you have a conviction on and [you're] probably better off staying with them on draft day rather than trying to regrade a guy five minutes before you pick because of some arbitrary reason. Go with what you believe in.

### Q: What has made the Steelers so good at retooling and restocking over the years?

**BB:** Well I think consistency is a big part of it. I think if I were looking at the Steelers and I was their personnel coordinator, I think I have a pretty good idea of the type of players they would want at each position for their system. And they've maintained that system over a significant period of time so you can look at players - whether they're pro players or college players - and say, 'Okay, this is where this guy would play in their defense or I don't really see what his role would be on defense.' And I'm sure that their personnel department is very well-schooled on what they're looking for and they know what type [of] players fit into their system and what type [of] players haven't done as well with them and maybe why they didn't do as well as they thought they would - we've all had those type of players. But,

I think the consistency and the continuity of their system and the experience of multiple drafts and multiple personnel decisions at the same position in the same system really give you a good formula or good basis of saying, 'Well, this guy did well and this player is similar to him or this player is similar to another play who didn't do as well, [so,] why is he going to do better? What distinguishes him from an unsuccessful guy we've had at that position and vice versa?'

So, I think that's a big part of it, too. I think that's what you try to do in every organization but, really, one of the big things is time. It just takes time. You need to go through a draft and another draft and another draft and another draft and be able to compare players in this year's draft to players in other drafts that were similar but something was better or not as good and try to see the differences and project how one player will do relative to another. So that experience helps a lot. And having a good football team is a good way to stay a good football team [because] you don't have a lot of needs. You can pick the players that fit your system. You can be a little more patient and [Pittsburgh has] done a good job in developing the younger players. It's a credit to their personnel department. It's also a credit to the coaches and their assistant coaches for bringing guys along and having them be productive early in their career and for a lengthy career.

**Q: What is a week like this like, after having a weekend with so many player cuts, to now have the guys you have getting ready for a regular season game? Do you get everything out of the way Sunday and Monday in terms of emotions?**

**BB:** Yes, you kind of have to. It's always a tough time. It's tough to release whatever it is - 22 or more players, depending on how many you bring in in addition to that. Whatever the transactions are to take those players off your roster, that's hard on the coaches. It's hard on the players. It's hard on everybody. Every team goes through the same thing, so you have to get past that and move on. We all know that's going to happen. We all know there is a date for rosters to be reduced. It has to be complied with by every team. Everybody is in the same boat on that. It doesn't make it any easier, but that's just the way it is. And then you put that behind you and you move one. Again, part of the difficulty in the preparation of opening day is not only the unsettling of your own roster but the unsettling of your opponent's roster. They're doing the same thing we're doing and I'm sure they're trying to look at our new moves and figure out who's going to go where and who's going to do what and we're trying to do the same thing with them.

Guys that have played in preseason and now aren't playing, how is all of that going to work? That's part of the preparation, too, and you really don't know how that is going to go until Sunday or today or even maybe going forward. There could still be things happening later on in the week. I'm sure there will be players signed off practice squads and maybe even from other places, I don't know, as the week goes on depending on availability and injuries and so forth. We'll see that throughout the league. That's part of the whole mix of trying to get past your roster and your movement into the opponent and also not only their schemes, but their players and their personnel, too. It's a busy time.

There are a lot of unanswered questions. There is a lot of guesswork. You prepare, do the best that you can, and you have to be ready to adjust on Sunday. I'm sure there will be some things that we haven't seen or players line up in spots that we haven't seen them in before or we've got two or three guys there and [we're] not sure which one it is - that kind of thing. We'll have to see how it goes. It's no different for us or anybody else, but it is more uncertainty than after that first regular season game when you can start to see how the cards are being played.

**Q:** When you guys released Shawn Crable you left the door open saying that if he was healthy he might be back. So now that he's on the practice squad is it safe to assume he is healthy?

**BB:** Sure, yeah. We put him out there. He had to pass a physical and just normal procedures, so we'll practice him. He really didn't get a chance to do much here in training camp, but hopefully he'll have an opportunity to do that on the practice squad.

**Q:** What makes some guys more likely to make the practice squad? What do you take into account?

**BB:** That's another - I don't know if I can give you a straight answer on that, but a lot of things that you consider are one: the depth of your team. Who do you need? Where could you use extra players? The quality of those players; how close one of those players might be to actually playing for you versus being able to [practice]. Being able to practice is one thing; being able to actually be elevated from the practice squad to the 45-man roster or 53-man roster - whichever one it is - that sometimes is another thing, so you take that into consideration.

You have players who are, in some cases, developing. So even though you release the player, you don't know exactly what his ceiling is. So if you think it's high enough, even though he may be further behind other players that you might consider for the practice squad, if you think that player might be able to overtake those guys eventually, that could be another consideration. It's kind of all of those combined. You're trying to improve your roster. You're trying to look at players that can help you, but at the same time, you have to look at the depth of your team. The best thing to prepare for a game is to have quality practices. So if you have good quality practices out there, that certainly is correlated towards better performance on Sunday. So you're trying to balance that relative to your depth and what you need from a practice standpoint

**Q: As you manage the practice squad throughout the year, is it always about guys who are in line to be on the roster or is it about having to fill roles throughout practice?**

**BB:** Yeah, I would say both. I would say both. And looking back, forget about this year, but let's just talk about ... In previous years we've had players on our practice squad that when we look at our practice squad we would say, 'OK these players could be activated, they're our next guy. If something were to happen here, if something were to happen [there] that would be our next guy.' There are other situations where if something were to happen at that position that practice squad player probably wouldn't be the next player, it would be somebody else that's not on your roster. And it could be for a couple different reasons. One is the player's development, like we think he's going to develop into a player, but he's just not ready now.

Other players have more versatility [and] can do different things for you and they can practice in two or three positions and help the other players get ready, but maybe they are not quite, we just don't feel they are quite at the developmental level to be regular roster players and again sometimes that changes over the course ... as the player improves, sometimes that changes. Maybe you don't think he's going to be, and then he is and we know we've certainly had players like that. I've had players like that in my career in the past, like the Keenan McCardell's in the world that, when we had Keenan in Cleveland I don't know if we thought this guy [was] going to be one of the top receivers in the league.

We thought he was a good receiver, and as he kept getting better, then pretty soon you start to say, 'maybe this guy can help us' and then look at the career he had. It was magnificent. Troy Brown — back when he came into the league — not the Troy Brown we all remember. Players improve. Hard work, technique, physical development and all those kinds of things, there's a lot of room to develop. And we certainly can recite a lot of offensive linemen that fall into that category. We can also recite a lot of them that are on the practice squad that never played in the NFL. If you really feel like the player is a player and you don't want anyone else to have a shot at him, you try to find a way to keep him on your roster. And if you're kind of not sure, then that's probably why they're on the practice squad.

**Q:** How extensive are the tests you put somebody like Rosevelt

## Colvin through before you sign him?

**BB:** The workout is pretty much the same for all the players other than the position specifics. Obviously, what a linebacker would do is different than what a running back would do and that's obvious. We don't run the marathon because if you sign the player you want to go out and work with him the next day. You don't want to get a workout that is so extensive that it sets them back going forward. But you want to see what kind of condition and playing shape they are in and evaluate their playing skills.

Regardless, if it is a player you know or you aren't familiar with, through experience we have worked out enough players at all the positions to have some kind of evaluation of if it was a good workout or not. If you are familiar with the player, then it is relative to the last time you saw him. Was it better? If he is coming off an injury, maybe it is better; but maybe it is not as good. Then, you go forward with that information, make your decision, put him out on the field, start practicing and evaluate him in a football setting.

It is a lot different working a guy out by himself on a field with no one else there than putting him out there with 21 other guys and playing football. The workouts - that is all we can do so that is what we do. Once you get a player on the field then you can start evaluating his playing performance. That is how the process works. It is not scientific; it's subjective. You go with what you see and what the evidence is there in front of you. It is not complete, but it's what you have so that's what you use.

## Player Evaluation & Scouting Prospects

**Q:** When a player like Elandon Roberts only has one year of college production what goes into scouting that player?

**BB:** Yeah, that's a great question. Really, that's a tough one. You're like, if this guy is so good, why did he not play? Why wasn't he out there? So that one year of production, regardless of who - [Rob] Gronkowski, same thing. One year of production. [Rob] Ninkovich, one year of production. Rob was the same thing. Rob didn't play at Purdue and then when what's his name, [Ray] Edwards got suspended, he played the first half of the season. Edwards was out like four games, five games, so Rob played. Rob had a bunch of production and then got drafted in the fourth round. Elandon [Roberts], kind of the same thing. Got into the starting lineup, played and was very productive.

So it's a great question. It's like, is that production circumstantial? Is that production real? Is this guy really on the way up, or was that the peak, and is it going to come back down? I guess the one that sticks out the most for me would be Coach [Nick] Saban's story about [Jack] Lambert. When he at Kent State, speaking of the Steelers. You know, how Lambert couldn't get on the field. He was a backup linebacker and didn't play. The kid in front of him [Bob Bender] was really their leader, he was kind of the heat and soul of the Kent State defense, Nick played quarterback on that team and through a series of circumstances, that's another long story, but we'll skip through all of that. Anyways, the kid dropped out of school, went to work for Mick Jagger, he was a security guy on tour with the [Rolling] Stones, and Lambert became the starting middle linebacker. He probably would have never played had that not happened, and you know, you have a Hall of Fame player.

Sometimes things take a turn, and then once they get that opportunity and they get in there, the Tom Brady's of the world or whoever, you can't get them out of there. Lou Gherig, it's just, you know. So is that one, or is the other one of, 'Ok, well that was the high water mark,' and it never gets close to that point again? It's really a tough question. Obviously, the more you have to go on, probably the better chance you have of making the right evaluation. The less you have to go on, the more, 'Is this a one-year flash or is this the start of something that's going to be at that level you saw for a short amount of time?'

There are certainly a lot of examples of both, but Ninkovich, it's the same thing. It's a very - I mean, forget about him being at Miami and at New Orleans and all that, but just his college career. He didn't play until his senior year and the only reason he played his senior year is because the kid ahead of him got suspended. Then once he played, you're like, this guy's pretty good. But Elandon had tremendous production last year. He had tremendous production, and I'd say about his production, some guys make a lot of tackles, a lot of them are downfield after four, five-yard gains and that kind of thing, but Elandon had a lot of plays that were not always tackle for losses, but they were plays on the line of scrimmage as opposed to dragging a guy down after he's gained six yards. To me, there's a kind of difference in those types of tackles, in that kind of production.

**Q: You mentioned that Cre'von LeBlanc is a guy that has a knack for finding the ball. How do you evaluate a skill like that versus something more traditional such as speed or size?**

**BB:** Well, it's a valuable skill. That's a good question. Logan Ryan is another guy that did it in college. He has done it here. Some guys have a real knack for that, other guys not as much. Sometimes it's a little bit acquired, sometimes it's just instinctive. The best example I ever had was Everson Walls. He didn't technically do hardly anything right from a fundamental standpoint. You would never take another player and say 'Look, do it the way Everson's doing it. This is the way you would want to do it,' but in the end [he had], I don't know, whatever it was 56 career interceptions. It was a lot, it was over 50. He did things but he could find the ball and he had a great instinct for quarterbacks, routes, pattern combinations and so forth, so certainly it wasn't a speed and measureable thing. You would have released him on those measurables.

That's why he wasn't drafted, but as a football player he's productive. When I was in Detroit, Lem Barney, [was the] same kind of thing. Len probably had better measurable skills coming out but at that point he made a lot of plays and he made them on his instinctiveness, ball skills, awareness, etc. Ty [Law], I mean Ty was a first round pick, but Ty had that, too. There are a lot of first round picks that don't have that and he had that. It's definitely an important skill and it really probably separates good from great players, or average to good players. It's not the easiest thing to evaluate and sometimes some of those plays are circumstantial more than they are great instinctive plays. They're fortunate the way they happen, but when a guy starts making enough of them then you know it's something a little special. It's tough to evaluate.

**Q:** How much has that evaluation changed over your time in the league? How likely is a scout to tell you that a player may lack certain measurable skills but that he just has a knack for the ball?

**BB:** Every year. I think there are those guys every year, and I think the hard part is, in your question Dan [Roche], is taking it from the college level to the pro level. So, you can be a good instinctive college player and have it not be good enough in the NFL, or it might be good enough in the NFL, and sometimes there are other factors that become the overriding factor; speed, quickness, explosion, those kinds of things that maybe those guys just can't get quite close enough to make those plays at this level that they made at a different level.

Coming out of college and those things, it's one thing and then seeing that transfer – I'm not saying it doesn't transfer – but transfer it to the level of high-production maybe like it did at the college level just isn't always the case. A lot of those guys end up coming up short just like a lot of the size and speed guys that have the physical talent end up coming up short because they may not have the instinctiveness or awareness or whatever it happens to be, whatever adjective you want to put in there, to do it at this level, whereas in college or high school, whatever, there are measurables; their size, speed, power and all is just enough for them to be better than their opponents. Once that playing field levels out a little bit here then the instinctiveness, awareness, anticipation, those kinds of things, they become more of a factor. But it's a tough thing to evaluate. You need time.

**Q: When looking at players at the running back position, how do you balance the potential for a big play versus the consistency of a more pedestrian pickup on a regular basis?**

**BB:** That's a great question, Phil [Perry], and you can kind of say a little of the same thing about the receiver positon, too. A player that maybe only catches a couple passes a game, but if he catches them because of his playmaking ability, you know, might be for big chunks of yardage versus a player who catches more passes for less yardage, but maybe [an] equivalent amount but off of more catches, so anyway, that's a good question.

I think a little bit of it is the philosophy of your offensive system and what you're trying to do, and how much those plays mean to you. How important it is to have a big play versus how important it is to have consistent, maybe lesser plays, if you will, and maybe how likely the player is to break those big plays, but it's a tough conversation when you have that situation and I think you just have to go back to what your real goals are from that particular player and the role that you envision him having, how likely those are to occur. But it's challenging when you have that kind of tradeoff, you know, one's good, the other one's good, which one's better?

If you can only afford one, and look if they're both good enough, [then] you're probably going to afford both of them, but if it's one or the other then philosophically that puts you into a tough choice, and that probably would be decided based on a bigger philosophy that you have for your either overall team or offensive unit.

**Q: Over the years do you feel like your offense has had one philosophy in particular in regards to that type of evaluation or has that evolved over time?**

**BB:** Well again, I think it depends on the quality of the player. I mean, Corey Dillon had some good runs, but I don't think he was known for the 70 and 80-yarders, at least not when he was with us, but as far as a big, durable, tough consistent runner that gained positive yards, and again that kind of player is going to have some short yardage carries and so forth where his average is going to go downward, you know, when he makes a two-yard run it's a great run, but when you run for two yards on first down it doesn't feel like a great run.

And then we've had other players that were maybe a little more explosive, probably like [Shane] Vereen, who ripped off some long runs, you know like the Jets play where he went 70 yards for a swing pass. It wasn't a run but it was the same kind of thing. I don't know if some other backs would have gone that far with it, but they add a little different value to the team, but again, if the players are good you're probably going to find a way to have both of them. It's that kind of, you know, I don't want to say – it's where you get that lifestyle.

So you know like when we had [Jeff] Demps, in our opinion in the end we just didn't feel like the threat of the big play – even though he had some, we saw him in the preseason on I think it was a punt return and a couple other plays he got – in the end we just didn't feel like those plays would offset the other things that we needed other players to do, or that he didn't do as well as other players, which is why we kept them. But that didn't mean that the plays he had didn't have value or they weren't important, but in the end we just ended up going with a different direction, so I think it depends on the level that we're talking. I mean the concept is, I clearly understand, I think it's the level of the performance of those plays that you're talking about. That's an interesting discussion.

**Q:** Can a player's intelligence overcome some of his physical deficiencies on the football field?

**BB:** Maybe the way I see it is if a player understands what you're telling him and he works hard to try to improve on it then he gets better. If he doesn't understand or doesn't want to understand what you're telling him then how does he get better? Even if he works hard he's probably not going in the right direction. Being able to understand what we're doing, how to do it, and then being able to understand how to do it better, how to improve, wherever that is, whether it's in training, in the weight room, technique, preparation, any of those areas, if a player understands what he can do and he works at it then he's going to improve.

But I think that's the most important thing to me, not what he can do outside of football on some other occupation. I care about that but I don't really care about that. I care about whether he can do it in a football context.

**Q:** How difficult is it to evaluate players that come from smaller schools and have played against lesser competition?

**BB:** It's a tough projection. You evaluate the film. A lot of times they're just better than the players they're playing against. How would that compare when they play against higher competition? Sometimes you can see matchups at that level that are comparable. Sometimes those guys play in an all - star game, like Jimmy [Garoppolo] did, which gives you a little more of a level playing field, if you will. You evaluate their physical skills and see whether those are comparable to the players at your position.

A guy might be a great player at another level, [but] when you look at him physically and you say 'Well, he's well below what we have in terms of size, speed,' whatever other measurements you have. Even though he's a good player once you put him up against other good players it just might not be that competitive. So, I think those are all things you kind of look at but it's hard when you're looking at one level trying to compare it to another. That's why it's a lot easier to evaluate pro free agents than it is college kids because you see them playing in the NFL. You see them playing against the same guys that we play against every week, so it's much easier to make that evaluation. But we're all looking at the same film, we're all looking at the same player, we all have the same opportunity to take that slice of information and figure out whatever we figure out with it. Yeah, it's definitely a challenge.

**Q: Going back to the scrimmage you held at practice on Friday, what kind of evaluation are you able to make from that as opposed to just individual team drills?**

**BB:** Well, that's football. The big part of football is being able to change. The situation changes every play. It goes from first-down, to second-down, to third-down, the ball moves, you go from offense to defense, to special teams. You don't go out there and punt six punts in a row like you do in practice. You punt it once and then maybe the next thing you do is a kickoff return, so I don't know. It's doing things like that. It's getting players to understand the situation and then apply the call and the technique for that given situation. So, we do things in a lot of one-on-one drills. When those situations come up in the game you want to carry those techniques into the game situation and do it.

A lot of times that doesn't happen because players don't remember to use the techniques that they've worked on. They don't know when to apply it or they forget to apply it and they kind of lose track of it and that type of thing. This is football. It's as close as we can get to it. The drill work is good. The repetition is good. That's how you build your fundamentals. That's how you build your execution, but at some point you've got to play like we're playing and that's good, too. It's good for the coaches; handling all the substitutions, making adjustments on the sideline, seeing the game on the down and distance basis, seeing it live as opposed to making corrections on film. Not that we don't coach on the field, but when you don't know when it's coming, when the down and distance changes, we need work on that, too, so it's good for all of us.

**Q:** When in the course of your career did teams start to identify guys coming out of college that could be just core players on special teams as opposed to offensive or defensive guys that you just stick out there?

**BB:** I think it's kind of always been that way Bob [Socci], from my experience. Going back to when I was with the Colts we had a couple of guys who were just primarily kicking game players and certainly with the Giants; guys like Reyna Thompson, when I was here in New England; [Larry] Whigham. With Cleveland certainly we had Bennie Thompson, guys like that. I would say those groups of players – Whigham maybe more than the others – didn't play a lot, played some on defense or offense, but they were really primarily special teams players. Tony Bertuca back in Baltimore; those guys were core special teams players.

The more guys you have on the team, the more you can specialize. The fewer guys you have, the more you have to double up on the roles. It's nice to have a guy that can do everything – be a good offensive or defensive player, maybe a backup player and then play well in the kicking game. Sometimes it tilts a little more one way or the other; guys more of an offensive or defensive player and a little less in the kicking game , or more of an impact player in the kicking game and maybe a little lesser on offense or defense.

Those are some of the difficult roster decisions that you have to make. We've probably taken more of those type of guys. [Nate] Ebner didn't even play defense in college; Slater was a special teams player. [We] drafted a kicker in the fourth round, a long-snapper in the fifth round. We probably do more of that type of thing that most teams do.

**Q:** What does the unknown factor revolving around every new player, such as Joe Thuney, do for a player in terms of being able to define his own role and position on the team?

**BB:** Right, I think that each situation is different. You can change jobs but you're still doing the same job but it's different working for a different organization. So, what we do, what we ask our guys to do in different positions, is going to be different than what somebody else asks them to do. I think that is just inherent and whether that is our style of play, or the timing of the passing game for an offensive lineman is different for us than it might be for another team. The running game might be a little different than it was, like it was definitely different than what they did at N.C. State, that I know for sure.

Regardless, there are some changes that are just different and that's just part of going to a different team and some players adapt to those easily. Some of those have new techniques, some favor the player's moves, some of them sometimes maybe aren't as good as what the system they were in before. That happens too, sometimes. Those things are always hard to predict until you have a player and actually work with him in your system, some players play multiple positions in another system but then when you try to do that with a guy in your system, it doesn't work out as well for whatever the reasons are now. Maybe it's just whatever you're asking them to do – the processing, the nomenclature – I don't know. Sometimes it works out good, sometimes it doesn't. Until you actually get them in that, I don't think you actually know how it's going to go.

Maybe a guy does well at one thing but maybe he isn't as comfortable doing something else. Sometimes it takes a while to figure that out. Some guys aren't asked to do a lot and then once they are asked – the Mike Vrabel's of the world, played linebacker at Pittsburgh, and then here he played – run around at free safety at practice, played offense, played defensive end, played linebacker, played inside linebacker. He embraced it and it kind of opened things up for him. That's not always the case with everybody. I think it's very hard to know that for sure. Look, if the guy's played multiple positions in college, let's just say, or with another team, it gives you some idea that he can do it. You can evaluate how he is doing it but it's not always the same when you do it. Even though it looks the same on paper, it's not quite the same. Teamwork; a lot of teamwork is involved. I'd say look shortstop, shortstop, and right. Bases are the same; you line up the same players, shortstop, and shortstop. You start getting out there with 10 other guys versus another 11 guys and they're all moving at once, there are a lot of things involved there. It's a little bit different.

**Q: How much do you factor an offensive lineman's ability to play multiple positions when deciding to acquire them as opposed to just their skill set?**

**BB:** I think there's a place for both. Somewhere along the line you're going to need versatility, but everybody doesn't have to play a lot of positons. If they can just play one well, there is a lot to be said for that. But you've got to be able to play it pretty well. Steve Neal never played anything but right guard for us. That was it. He played right guard good – it was great. Mike Vrabel played everything from free safety to tight end, so that was good. I don't think it's either or but somewhere along the line somebody is going to have to have some versatility. You just don't have enough guys to have depth at every position.

But at the same time you're going to put some players out there that need to play well, so being able to play six different positions isn't as important as having one guy who can do one thing well, whatever that is. The less you can do probably the better you need to be able to do it. The more you can do maybe you can be not quite as proficient in one area, but your versatility creates some value. No matter how versatile you are, eventually you're going to have to get in there and do something, whatever that is, and if you can't do it very well, then really how much value is the versatility?

**Q:** Obviously you take talent into consideration, but what other factors do you look at when evaluating a guy from a smaller school, like Malcolm Butler?

**BB:** It's a pretty long list. It starts with I would say just the overall program. The commitment in a Division I program is pretty much 12 months a year in terms of offseason training, offseason summer program, class schedule, practice. It's every day. It's like being a professional player. Not quite the same, but between your class commitments, your academic commitments, your football commitments, your offseason training and all that, you're always going. You have to do a lot of things just to be able to be compliant – your grades have to be up, you can't be missing stuff.

Like the NFL, you have to be here every day, you have to be accountable, you've got to be dependable, so in other programs, that just isn't required or not anywhere near to the same degree. Level of competition is obviously a big gap. You see a lot of talented players at a lower level of competition, but then when the competition changes and it's a little more equal, are they really able to compete at that next level? Do they have the competitiveness, the drive, the whatever it is to go out there and outwork and outcompete and out-tough the guy that has just as much talent as they do versus just being better than everybody else and going out there and just being themselves but they're just better than everybody else. That doesn't really last.

Schematically the same thing, teams that don't have as much time, don't have the same kind of resources, the game is narrower, fewer coverages, you're defending less, you're playing with less defense, a couple of coverages, that kind of thing, and now you come into a more expansive system and you've got the volume of we've got more, there is more on the other side of the ball. When you start putting all those together, it becomes really exponential the number of variables – playing one position versus both sides, inside, outside, factoring the kicking game into it, all that.

So there is the on the field, there is the talent and I'd say there is the overall program and being a professional, being a solid, dependable consistent player, which is what all great players are – they're consistent. They're not just making one play. Those guys aren't the great players. They might have highlight plays, but the great players are the ones who can sustain it over a game, over several games, over seasons. Those are the guys who stand out. It's hard to measure until you put a guy in that situation.

**Q:** Marcus Mariota ran a different system in college. What do you see when you watch him and is it harder to evaluate quarterbacks now because of the spread offense?

**BB:** It's definitely harder to evaluate, there's no question about that. Look when I came into the league, you go to the combine or you interview quarterbacks and you talk about reading the coverages, reading the safety, reading the middle linebacker, understanding where the rotation is or if there is a rotation or if it's split safety coverage or all those kind of things. Now you go to the combine they tell you about reading the end, reading numbers, we have three guys out there and they have three we throw it, if they have four ... So it's an addition game. Reading the end, reading the tackle, that was a different concept.

When I came into the league there was no quarterback reading the defensive tackle, like you've got to be kidding me. Different type of offense, but that's what they've been brought up on. The thing I've learned about all that is guys learn what you teach them. If you teach them to do something different, then they learn something different. Some learn it better than others, quicker than others, it comes easier. All of us are individually different on that, but just because a player has been taught one thing definitely doesn't mean when you teach him something else that that's going to be a problem or that he can't do it. You don't know that that's how it's going to turn out, but I wouldn't just rule that out out of hand. Just because a guy hasn't been asked to do something doesn't mean he can't do it.

Then you have to make the determination if it's like that, a player coming out of college, you have to make the determination of how you think he'll be able to do the things you ask him to do, whether it's learn them, execute them, physically change a little bit so he can fit more into that type of style that you're looking for, whatever it is. You just have to make that calculation.

It's an inexact science. Some guys do, some guys don't, some guys you judge right, some guys you misjudge right. It's a lot easier to scout them in the NFL because you see them against the same people we play against. You see them in a similar environment in terms of the routine, the schedule, the length of the year and so forth and so on. There's a lot more in common even though each team is different. When you look at guys coming out of college there are a lot more variables and the level of competition is a lot different, too, so it's a little bit harder.

**Q:** Do you think Mariota is making that adjustment?

**BB:** The offense he's running is definitely not the offense he ran in college, so there's no question about that. But yeah, I think he's done a good job. He's hitting a lot of passes, hasn't turned the ball over a lot, has had his share of touchdown passes, makes his share of big plays, reads coverages.

I think you see him throwing the ball to the right spot. I don't know exactly what he's being told to do but generally speaking it looks like he's throwing the ball to the right spot, throwing it where he should be throwing it. I think he's coming along well. I'm sure they have a lot of confidence in him and he's shown toughness coming back from an injury and taking some hits and all like every quarterback does. He's done a good job for them.

**Q: When you're scouting or evaluating players, is part of the process envisioning what role they'll have on special teams?**

**BB:** It's envisioning what role they have on your team in every sense of the word role. How they would play on offense, defense, special teams, kind of how they would fit on to your team, how they would fit in the weight room, in the meeting room, in every place they are, what they need. I'd say every player needs something – usually a lot more than one thing – and whether or not you feel like as an organization you can give that player what he needs, whether that's scheme or a certain type of training or whatever it is. So, yeah, all that is a part of it. Just trying to figure all that out: how he fits with you in small areas, very specific areas, and then in relation to the big picture.

When you have a team, you have to manage all the aspects of your team. There's the financial aspect and the salary cap we have to manage, an age [aspect] and there's a transitional aspect to our team. I mean, there's going to be turnover; that's the business we're in. Understanding where that turnover could occur, it's all part of the management. So yeah, everything. We try to – I'm not saying we do a great job of it or do it perfect or anything, but we definitely take it into consideration, talk about it and try to do the best we can with it. Sometimes you can have control over it; sometimes you have to give something up to get something else. Maybe it solves one or two problems, but leaves something else that's maybe not quite the way you want it but it's the best you can do.

**Q: He's obviously a smart kid in the classroom and on the field. Is there always a correlation there?**

**BB:** No, no, definitely not, absolutely not. There just isn't. Some guys are football smart and they're not smart in other ways. Other guys get 1500 on their SATs and can't get a double-team block right. No, that definitely, in my experience, sometimes it correlates, sometimes it doesn't. I don't think you just take it for granted. I think a smart guy can learn. Some guys learn – it's just like all of us – some guys can learn electronics, some of us can't. Some people can learn something else, some of us can't. I mean, we're all wired differently. Some guys, football comes really easy to them; they can see what all 22 players are doing, can see what all 11 guys are doing on their side of the ball, how it all fits together. It's easy for them. For other guys, once you get past their assignment, the big picture, the overall concepts, how it all fits together, sometimes that doesn't come so easy for them. Depends on what position they play, but they're all different. But I would say in his case, he's a smart, instinctive football player and the rest of it is good too. I mean, so is Grissom.

**Q:** What is it about the Stanford program that David Shaw and Jim Harbaugh before him run that has these guys NFL ready in terms of being mentally capable as well as physically?

**BB:** Well I mean, I'm sure when Jim [Harbaugh] was out there, he probably ran as close to an NFL program as – that's what he knew. That's Nick [Saban] at Alabama or Greg [Schiano] when he was at Rutgers or Pat [Hill] when he was at Fresno or Kirk [Ferentz] when he was at Iowa. You know those guys that have gone back into college football from the NFL a lot of times just take whatever they did as an NFL program, so the players are kind of accustomed to those demands. I mean, it's different because they're going to class and all that, I get that, but just the football part of it: the meetings, the walkthroughs, the offseason program, all the demands of the program, the training, the film study on their own, all those things, whatever they are.

Then when they come into this league, a lot of times it's an adjustment, but it's not as much of an adjustment. I don't know. I can't speak specifically to that program, but from what I understand – we have Cam [Fleming], we have Tyler [Gaffney] – we have guys you can talk to about that. They didn't seem to be overwhelmed by our program. I'm not saying that wasn't a jump, but not like we might see from some other guys – terminology, all that stuff. But if that's what you're used to, it maybe doesn't seem all that bad.

**Q:** With the evolution of defensive football to counteract offenses, is Jamie Collins, to a degree, a prototype of what more

**players will be? It seems like fewer linebackers will be on the field and there's a greater need for versatility. You played two linebackers for a huge chunk of the season.**

**BB:** Yeah, well two or more, depending on how you classify them. Look, Jamie Collinses don't – it's not like there's two or three dozen of them in the draft every year. We're lucky to have one. Was Lawrence Taylor a prototype outside linebacker? Where's the next Lawrence Taylor? Those guys don't grow on trees. So, I don't know. I think that's part of building your team is trying to anticipate where your team is going and to a certain extent where, especially defensively because you have to react to what they put on the field. Defensively you have to be able to defend those things.

How do you construct the defense so you can handle the different challenges that you have? I think if you look at the numbers statistically, the amount of five defensive backs that are on the field, you'll see numbers shift dramatically but particularly this year. You can see a trend, but there's a spike. There's only a very few number of teams, maybe four or five, that were under 50 percent nickel. So, when you talk about what defensive system do you run – virtually every team in the league, the defense they play the most is nickel. Five defensive backs, whatever version it is. There are five DBs, put it that way. Whatever the rest of it is, you can look at that separately.

That's certainly not the way it was 10 years ago. I'd say we were in the 30s, 30 percent, high-30s. Now that number is doubled. We're almost, I think we're in the 70 – where's our stat guy [ESPN Boston's Mike Reiss]? But you know, I think we're in the 75 percent range of nickel defense this year. Now you know, we've been ahead some, but we've also played a lot of multiple receiver teams. That's flipped a little bit for us too. We've seen less nickel than a lot of other teams have. We go back to some of our other teams five, six, seven years ago, when we had a lot of three-receiver sets on the field, we saw more nickel than any team in the league.

Now we're seeing, I'm not saying less than anybody, but we're certainly in the bottom quarter of teams that play us in nickel because we have a decent amount of two-receiver sets. Or, they just chose to play us that way, whatever it is. But I think the trends are a little bit – we're kind of going in an opposite direction there with what some of the league trends are.

**Q:** Is that almost advantageous? People used to talk front to back in terms of numbers – 3-4 or 4-3 – now it's from the back.

**BB:** I think it's certainly something you have to be aware of. When we put in the 3-4 in 2000-2001, there were three teams running it. It was us, Pittsburgh and I don't know where the other team was. So, if you wanted a nose tackle, there were plenty of them out there. If you wanted a 3-4 outside linebacker, there were plenty of them out there. Guys like – [Roosevelt] Colvin was a good example at Chicago or even [Mike] Vrabel, those 3-4 outside linebackers, but there's nowhere to go. New England was a good option for both of them because the guys Mike was playing behind and Rosie was trying to play a 4-3 walked off the line linebacker to a defensive end in sub situations. But it wasn't really a clean fit for him. So he had a much cleaner fit in the 3-4. You look back five, six years ago and you've got 16, 17, 18 teams playing 3-4.

You go to the draft board and think, 'Here's a nose tackle. Who needs a nose tackle?' Well eight teams in front of you need a nose tackle and there's two nose tackles. It's something you have to figure out where you can get the players to play in your system. Sometimes you just can't get them so either you have to change your system or modify it or play with lesser players if you want to maintain system. That's definitely a challenging part of it is keeping up with that, trying to stay at least even with it. Hopefully ahead of it, but at least even, but it's a lot easier said than done.

**Q:** You mentioned that there are a lot of qualities that you like in Jimmy. Can you give us an idea of what those are and is the ability to throw the deep pass one of them?

**BB:** Well I'd just say in general without getting into any specifics or we'd be here all night the general qualities a quarterback needs to have are being able to manage the game, being able to do what the team needs to win, be accurate, be smart and be productive. I'd say he's done those things.

**Q:** Was there one thing that perhaps separated him from the other quarterbacks you brought in?

**BB:** I don't know. Each player has their own, everything that comes with that player, you can't pick and choose – take this guy, give it to that guy. Take that guy, give it to this guy. Whatever the guy is, he is. And that's what you draft. You draft the total person. That's what we do.

**Q:** You spoke of the level of competition. How significant were his performances in the All-Star games?

**BB:** I don't think it hurt. I don't think it was, I don't think it hurt him. I don't know how much it helped him, but I don't think it hurt him, let's put it that way. It's certainly a better level of competition. The game plans are simple. The defense can't play two coverages or whatever it is. It's not like that's some very difficult – it's not really what a quarterback does, but it's a better level of competition and so forth. There's some value to it, but it's not a real game, if you will.

**Q:** How about the interaction that he has with an NFL staff? Is there anything you can glean from that?

**BB:** I'm sure when you coach those All-Star games, you're able to spend a whole week and you can certainly learn a lot about all the players, their ability to process information, how important football is to them, how attentive they are, how much they're really putting into it. If you ask them to change something form what they've been used to doing – how adaptable are they? How set in their ways are they? How coachable are they? Those kinds of things. You certainly [can] gain all that when you don't do it and you're looking at it from the outside. I think it's a lot harder to evaluate that. But I think it's a big advantage when you coach those players over several days.

You tell them something and go out on the field. Do they correct it? Can you move on? Does the pace slow down? Can they not correct it? Can they get it without really going over it on the field? Can you just tell it to them in the classroom and they make the adjustments? You learn things like that. You get a better feel for specifically what you're asking them to do and how well they do it. When you're watching don't know exactly sure what they're being told. You have to kind of think you know but you don't know for sure. It's always easier to evaluate the players you coach than somebody else's players.

Certainly the coaching there is a little bit different than what is in college and there's an exposure to the pro staffs. But, the overall complexity to the game, that's the bottom line. The complexity of the game is a lot different than when you're competing, having game plans and that kind of thing, as opposed to an All-Star game, especially at that position.

**Q:** How big of a difference is there projecting a quarterback, who like you said have to process so much information, than it might be at another position?

**BB:** I think all the players coming into this league from college have a lot to learn – some more than others. I don't know exactly what he was told there anymore than what I know exactly what Dominique [Easley] was told at Florida. I have an idea, but we'll just have to see what happens when they get here. That's the way it is with all players. I don't want to assume anything. We'll give them all the information at the same rate and see how they learn it. Some guys may need a little more time. Some guys may need a little less time. In the end, they usually can get it one way or another if they work and it and put the time in and work at it. If they don't, then they probably won't learn it as well.

## Q: What attributes can you see in a player in the 3-cone drill?

**BB:** I think it gives you some evaluation of a combination of his lateral movement and vertical movement. We can see the vertical movements in the 10s, the 40s – 10-20-40, that's all one drill. The shuttle drill, for the skill players, which is a 60-yard test but it's all vertical. The 20-yard 5-10-5 change-of-direction drill is really a lateral drill. The L drill or 3-cone drill combines a vertical and lateral element with it. Once again, I think you always want to keep in mind in those drills, whichever ones of those you're talking about, ideal conditions, ideal start, nobody lining up across from you, nobody hitting you when you try to release and run 'em. Nobody hitting you at the finish line. Nothing to think about -- no play, no snap count, no defense, no offensive adjustment, no anything. It's just a straight timed measurement, which is fine, because otherwise when you put all those other variables in it, it would be really hard to manage it. It is what it is. It is a time measurement that isn't really a football-specific drill because of all the variables in football that are not a part of it.

**Q: You've seen a bunch of tight ends who have a basketball background and you have Jordan Cameron this week. Is there something those guys have in common that you see when you're defending them?**

**BB:** I think the biggest thing that I've seen with basketball players through the years is their hands. Those guys have to have good hands. They obviously handle the ball a lot and it's on them quickly. They're cutting and it's a short pass and a lot of times it comes at good speed or bounce passes and trying to get it around the defender. They have to be able to react to the ball very quickly. It's a lot different than football, seeing the ball travel however many yards to you. If you're coming out of a cut, it's still not like in basketball where the passes are, a lot of times, very short, very tight and you have to reach out and extend and get the ball away from the defender, like you do in football situations rebounding the ball.

It's not about – you can't let it come into your body. You have to go up and aggressively take it. I would just say in general that basketball players, and certainly basketball players that have come into football that I've coached or I've observed, one pretty common thing is their hands and their ability to handle the ball aggressively, cleanly and it gets on them quickly but it doesn't seem to affect them like it does other players sometimes where the ball is on them and they can't quite find it and adjust to it. Those guys seem like they're used to it. They've done it their whole lives and they're used to it.

**Q:** Have you spent any time scouting basketball players?

**BB:** Sure, yeah. We've seen those guys through the years – guys with football backgrounds than end up playing basketball. I'd say I've had many conversations with [former Head] Coach [Bob] Knight about that when he was at Indiana. I would say that the big thing for most basketball players is, in general, they're quicker than they are fast. When you get out there and time a lot of those guys in the 40-yard dash, they're slow. They might look fast on a basketball court, but we have such a much bigger field that vertical speed, especially for those positions – there aren't many linemen playing basketball so you're talking about skills guys, receivers and DBs, those type of positions, that most of them don't have the speed that we, at our level, they don't have the speed to play.

They have quickness and a lot of times they have exceptional quickness but when it just comes to straight, flat-out speed, I'd say that's where a lot of times, in the scouting part of it, the deficiencies come up. You go see a basketball player and say, 'This guy has great hands. This guy has great quickness. This guy is strong, he's competitive.' Then you go out and time him and he runs 4.75-4.8 and you're like, 'What are you going to do with him?' What corner in this league is – they have to be able to run faster than that or if they're receivers, they have to able to run faster than that. I've seen that several times. Like I said, I've been in a couple of those situations with Coach Knight at Indiana, like 'Hey, I want you to take a look at this kid, this guy he's this, he's that.' And he was, but then you go out and put a watch on him and he's just not fast enough to play at this level. It's generalities but that's my general experience with it.

**Q: How do you know when a guy who is relatively new to the system here, like Austin Collie, is ready to be in a game day**

**situation? Is it just from practice or the conversations you have with him?**

**BB:** That's a really good question because there are always things that no matter how many walkthroughs, meetings, film sessions, conversations you go over with somebody, there are things that happen in the game that you don't cover or they happen a little bit differently. So, when are they ready? I mean, they're never 100 percent ready. But there's a difference between being ready and when you put the person in there and feel like, well there's just too many things that can and probably will go wrong because they're just not prepared enough for those. We know there are going to be one or two things that are going to come up that we haven't covered, they're just going to have to react to and hope it's the right thing. I'd say in Austin's case, that the first week he was probably, we probably could have played him. I don't know.

He certainly worked hard. He's a smart guy. But I would say that there was a lot of growth from week one to week two. I think we all felt – myself, Josh [McDaniels], Chad [O'Shea], the quarterbacks – that he was much further along the second week. he'd heard it the second time, he'd repped it more, he was more familiar with the terms and things like that, even though in the [Saints] game, we were in more of a no-huddle offense and the week before, against Cincinnati we were more calling the plays in the huddle. But regardless, he just seemed quicker, had fewer questions, was more confident, played quicker, played faster so I think it's a combination of all those things. It's seeing it on the practice field certainly, but it's also when you ask questions in the classroom and go through it, that the player can respond to them quickly and with confidence and you know he knows it.

Sometimes giving the right answer isn't really comforting because you just don't have any confidence that, maybe it's a 50-50 guess or maybe they say it but you're not sure if they're sure, whereas there are other times when you feel sure. Crossing that bridge – which I don't know if I'm really answering the question, but it's kind of a judgment thing – but crossing that bridge, once you're across it, you feel like, 'OK, we're pretty confident he's got it.' Yeah, there are going to be one or two things but we have experienced players that one or two things might come up and they could make a mistake on them. But I think from week one to week two, we saw a definite, much more solid player in terms of communication, understanding, decision-making, reactions and hopefully that will continue. But that's a fine line.

The answer to that question, what it looks like on Wednesday, what it looks like on Thursday, what it looks on Friday, maybe even what it looks like on Saturday, sometimes changes with a new player. Sometimes it crystallizes and it becomes more solid and sometimes as you from first and second down to third down to red area to two-minute, that it unravels if you will. The wheel spins faster and what they had on Wednesday, I don't want to say forgotten, but maybe gotten confused with some of the things that come up on Thursday, Friday and Saturday.

So, a lot of times you really don't know the answer to how that's going to come out until you get the full body of work in and can make a better decision. But I've seen it go both ways. I've seen guys come in the first day on Wednesday and we're saying, 'OK, it looks like this guy's got it.' Then by Saturday, it's, 'Well, what he had on Wednesday, that's all running together with the other stuff.' And vice versa, sometimes it looks bad on Wednesday and doesn't looking very good on Thursday but by Friday and Saturday, somehow after multiple reps and multiple meetings and all that, that it finally settles in and it makes sense. It's certainly a very individualized type of call and I don't think there's any book on that. You just have to try to figure it out the best you can.

**Q:** Is it common to get a lot of consistency from all your scouts on one player?

**BB:** I would think it depends on the player. If the player's consistent, I think it's common. If the guy is, for whatever reason not, then you see a lot of fluctuation. Sometimes that could be scheme changes or injuries or something that's nagging him. It could be a guy who gains experience and does better. It could be a guy who maybe is a senior or whatever the circumstances are, slumps a little bit or his production slows down. Especially at the receiver position, we know a lot of that is a function of the quarterback.

Sometimes that looks like it's reflected in the receiver but a lot of times there are other things going on or a change in offensive scheme and things like that. They're all different. I think we have plenty of guys that are consistent and then there are other guys who some things are better than others. Some are strong at one thing, not so strong at another. It's harder for a scout to evaluate that. Do you evaluate the good things? How much do you take down the down things? Can you straighten out the things that aren't good or are the things that are good more circumstantial? Are they going to be able to translate to the next level? Are his strong points going to outweigh his weak points? Are weak points going to outweigh his strong points? You get all types.

**Q: Is it fair to say that the skill set that slot receiver would have is why you look to those guys more to flip to the other side of the ball like Troy Brown and Julian Edelman, maybe not so much with Matthew Slater because he seems like he's more of an athlete?**

**BB:** Sure, yeah, I think they're reciprocal. There is an element of playing strength that you need inside there, that you may or may not have with perimeter receivers, but I think you need that playing strength inside where there's blocking or tackling or just dealing with forcing the run or collision in the slot, getting collision by linebackers and bigger people, stuff like that. There's an element of short space quickness that you have to work in in that position whereas the further out you get, generally the more space there is to work in whereas in the slot there, you have a lot of people around you - you have guys in front of you, you've got guys outside, you've got guys inside and sometimes it can get a little sticky in there. There isn't a lot of clean space to work, so having quickness and having the ability to get through those spaces or defend in them, to be able to move laterally quickly to be able to defend those areas, it's a similar skill set, [yes].

## Q: Can you talk about what went into making Julian Edelman a two-way player and does he remind you of what Troy Brown has done in the past?

**BB:** There's obviously similarity between two guys that played in the slot and moved to the other side of the ball. We've been working with Julian for, I don't know, it's been several weeks, post-practice, one-on-ones, mixing him in on some scout team work, mixing him in on some defensive work, some things on post-practice, had a few snaps in games, has had a lot more snaps in individual practice and also in our team practice sessions. Obviously, we don't have a lot of numbers there and he's done a great job of trying to step in and learn what we're doing and try to do it to a competitive level and he's definitely done that.

He's a smart guy and he does have a little bit of an instinctiveness and also a set of skills that are conducive to both spots - what you want physically from your slot receiver is pretty similar to what you want physically from your slot corner or vice versa. I think the fact that he's played in there gives him some understanding of what that position is from the other side of the ball, which helps him play on the defensive side, as it did with Troy. Troy had obviously a great understanding of the slot position offensively and why the slot receiver would cut down a split, why he would widen it out, why it would stem a certain way because that's what he did.

He was able to flip that over, which isn't the easiest thing in the world to do; it's easy to sit here and talk about it, but it's sometimes hard to go from thinking about techniques on one side of the ball and now you're on the other side of the ball and now you're thinking about them all in reverse as a defensive player. Julian has had a good presence for that and I think has adapted to it pretty well.

**Q:** How much does his experience tackling on special teams help him tackling in the secondary?

**BB:** Well it's really the same thing. Tackling in the open field, using your leverage, knowing where your help is, whether it's a defensive player inside of you or the sideline outside or wherever it happens to be. You're in some of those same relationships in the kicking game, no question. I don't want to say tackling is tackling, but tackling is tackling. It's leveraging the runner, knowing what you're taking away, knowing where you're light but counting on your help from that position, whether it be a player or the sideline. Fundamentally, keeping your head up, wrapping up, doing all the fundamental things you do on contacting to get a guy on the ground. There's definitely carryover.

**Q:** Along that line, is there a chance that when you switch a player like that, is there a chance that his aptitude for the new position suggests that his potential is greater at his new position than returning to his old position?

**BB:** It's possible. It's possible, yeah. Not to dig too deep, but that's kind of where it was with Steve Neal. We started with Steve Neal and we put him on defense - that was a brilliant coaching move. We had him there in training camp for a couple of weeks and he kind of got worse instead of better. Finally, when we moved him to offense, he was so far behind from never playing football, from now shifting over to offense in the middle of training camp that it was again, impossible and he was put in a really tough position there. I think we saw enough that when we resigned him at the end of the '01 season and brought him back, we felt like he would be able to develop more on the offensive side of the ball than on the defensive side of the ball. Sometimes it could work out that way.

**Q:** Do you see that with Julian Edelman?

**BB:** I don't know. That's a good question. I'd say that's a good question. He's certainly been competitive, I'll say that. He's been competitive. I think the question with young players always is, when does it start to level out? Any player, at any position. And once it starts to level out, you have to say to yourself, 'Okay, is that good enough? Is that leveled out or that small incline, is that good enough?' If it is, then great, you can leave him there. If it isn't, then 'Okay, are we going to come up short there?' As long as the curve is climbing, where is it going to stop? Well, I don't know. Is it going to stop here? How far up is it going to get?

As long as it's moving in that direction..; think you kind of have to [have] enough time, enough experience, enough reps to where you can try to make a decision as to whether you think that it's leveled or it's going to continue to improve. I think we're too early in the running to know that so we keep going until we can figure it out.

## Q: Talking about LaDainian Tomlinson and age, when you're assessing a player, do you consider age?

**BB:** I think you have to look at it. It's still a relevant thing. There are some players that are 40-years-young - the Junior Seaus of the world - and there are other players who look old at 28. I think it depends on the individual player and all the factors that go into that player. I think any time a player, in general, gets over 30, I think you have to start looking at it as a year-to-year type of thing. That doesn't mean that 30 is their last year, but I think I've seen enough players after the age of 30 decline quickly, that I think you have to be aware of it. There are a lot of players who can extend that - again, the Junior Seaus of the world, the Vinny Testaverdes and those guys who were almost timeless.

They went from 30 to 40 and were still pretty much at the same level, or certainly at a high level, let's put it that way. I don't think there's any set formula there, but I think you've got to start keeping an eye on it at a certain point. I think the way I look at is whether a player is closer to the beginning or closer to the end of his career, let's put it that way. Whether that is this year, next year, two years from now, three years from now, but there is a certain point where a player is closer to the end that he is to the beginning. And then if a player is closer to the beginning than the end, then you hope in that during that time there will be improvement and he will make strides physically and experience and his performance and he'll peak and continue to rise and improve as a player. But then there is some point where that is going to start to go the other way, and once that happens, I think it's pretty clear that at some point, the end is closer than the beginning.

That can change and it can change quickly. I've seen guys and I can think of several examples of players that were Pro Bowl type performers one year and out of the league or close to out of the league the next, or two years later. It can go in a hurry. As the head coach [of] a football team, I think you have to be aware of that. You don't want it to happen. You don't predict that it's going to happen, but when it does happen you've got to be prepared for it.

## Q: What characteristics do you look for when drafting a 3-4 linebacker?

**BB:** I wouldn't be cautious at all. Anytime you like a player I'm happy to draft them. When you feel like a player's a good fit for your system and can do what you need them to do, based on whatever the other options are that you have, I am happy to take them. I don't care what position the guy plays. I think it would be wrong, and I've said this many times before, that it would be wrong to characterize our drafting philosophy as 'we're going to take this or no we're not going to take that'. That's just not true. You can say that, but that's just not the way it is. We're going to take the player we feel is the best for our football team and that's the guy it's going to be, whatever position it is or isn't.

But for inside linebackers, outside linebackers, depending on how you want to classify them, those guys need to be able to do the things that their job entails. For a player at any position, really, to be a productive player and to be picked probably in that area you would like for him to be able to play all the time. You'd like for him to be able to play on first down, second down and third down. It's hard to draft linebackers and players like that - defensive linemen, running backs, tight ends or whatever it is. It's hard to draft those players that don't contribute on every down. If they don't, then they really need to be exceptional in the area that they're in. You draft a guy in the first round that does one thing really well, but then you've got to go get somebody else to do something else, then that's a high price to pay, especially for that role, if you want to call it that.

So that's kind of the battle you're fighting there. Find somebody that can play every down, like Jerod Mayo, play as well on first down, second down, third down, fourth down. You want to have him in the game in every situation. If you're comfortable with that then it's an easy pick.

**Q:** Is Jon Beason an example of a new age player?

**BB:** Jon's really a good player and that's the guy we talked about that we looked at hard in the draft. He runs well. I mean, he's playing very well. He makes a lot of tackles and makes a lot of plays. He's big. He's physical. He's got good speed and quickness. He's a very good pass defender, along with [Jonathan] Vilma. I would say those are probably the two best defending inside linebackers that we've played against in a long time. They cover a lot of ground. Jon can play man. He can play zone. He drops deep, but he's also a very good run player. He's a physical tackler. He's got good instincts. He finds the ball. He sees holes. He knows when to run through. He knows when to play over the top. He protects himself well. He's really a productive player for them and he's playing behind a good front, too.

Those guys in front of him, [Hollis] Thomas, [Damione] Lewis, [Julius] Peppers, [Landon] Johnson and all those guys - [Everette] Brown, they are very good, too. It's hard to be putting a lot of guys up on the linebackers and run them past the guys on the defensive line, so sometimes you end up blocking the guys on the front and you don't quite get to the linebackers and they're the beneficiary of that, too. That being said, Beason makes a lot of plays on his own, too.

**Q: You talk about guys that can play the X, the Z and the slot. Is it just mental? Is that why it is so hard for a guy to be versatile enough to play all three different spots or do you need to be that versatile physically, too?**

**BB:** No, there're definitely physical skills that are involved, there's no question about it. It's hard to play on the outside of a formation without a lot of speed because you don't really threaten the vertical part of the field for those guys; they sit on you and don't have very many routes. It's hard to play in the inside part of the field without some quickness to find those spaces because - usually, when you line up in the middle of the field - there is at least one guy, if not two, that are on top of the formation that are deep, so it's hard to run by them because they're already so far back there. Again, it's being instinctive.

Like a basketball player, knowing when to pull up, when to drive to the hoop, when to pull up for the jump shot, when he can make it to the basket and when he can't and when to pull out. It's all that stuff. And some guys have an instinctiveness and a capacity to do that without even being coached. You run a play and say this is what we're going to do on this play, "boom", "boom." [Then] you go out there and run a play and something happens that you didn't even talk about, some guys will do what they're supposed to do and other guy's will, 'Well I should do this, but here's what they did so obviously I can't do that, so I adjusted into something else.'

And it's the right thing to do. Lawrence Taylor was like that. Lawrence Taylor knew what every player on the field was doing. I'm not saying he was a coach, but OK, well, 'I'm here, this guy's here, that guys there, so obviously that guy's got to be over there, that guy's got to do this.' I think guys that try to memorize plays, 'OK, I run this on that play. I run that on this play. I do this on some other play.'

And then it runs together and they kind of make mistakes. Whereas, 'OK, I run this, well of course I've got to run this because that guys here, that guys there and that guys somewhere else. So where else would I be?' It's just easy for them. It's just natural. Some players have a great capacity for it [and] other guys - you tell them to key one guy [and] they come off after the play and you say, 'What did that guy do?' 'Oh, I didn't see him.' Well. that's the guy you're keying, but sometimes that happens. Some guys see it, some guys ... Brady, I mean from day one, Brady, you ask what happened after a play and he'd tell you eight things that happened. I dropped back, the lineman flashed in front of me, the linebacker dropped wide, this guy slipped, he was over here, the other guy flashed on this side, I stepped up, this happened, that happened.

You go back and watch the film and there are the eight things that he said happened [and] that's what happened on the play. You can see every one of them. This guy was pressed and then he backed off late, this guy rolled down. Like I said, Lawrence [Taylor] was like that, too. Lawrence would go out there, come in after the series and say, 'Coach, they're not blocking it the way you said they were going to block it. Here's what they are doing. Instead of him taking me, he's helping. I can see that guy looking for me, so if I come inside, the centers going to come off and he's going to pick me up.' You can look at the film and say he's right. You could never get that from the sideline.

**Q:** Just judging by the names you're throwing out there, I assume that that kind of adaptability and having that both physically and mentally is really rare?

**BB:** Yeah, that's what makes them special. That's what makes Tom Brady, Tom Brady. That's what makes Randy Moss, Randy Moss. That's what made Lawrence Taylor, Lawrence Taylor. They just have that sixth, seventh sense. It's like Brady, you see a guy coming at him from the backside and you say, 'he doesn't see him coming and look out he's going to get hit.' And he either ducks or throws the ball right before the guy gets there and makes those kinds of plays. You see running backs, you think somebody's going to come in there, and clean him up from behind, and at the last second they stop or they duck and the guy goes right over the top. And you think, 'How did he see that guy?' But they just know. Emmitt Smith was like that. You watch him run, you get the end zone film, he's got the ball and you're saying, 'There's no hole there,' and he finds four or five yards out of it.

He sets up a block, squirts through, gets his pad down and it's second and five. Where's that yardage? We had this defended great, there's no place to go and he ... So some of those runs, some of those three-, four-yard runs that those great backs make, they're some of the best runs I've ever seen. Barry Sanders, that guy could gain four yards and it would be a spectacular play. It's not just the 80-yarders, it's the ones when there's nothing there and the guy creates a four-, five-yard gain out of literally nothing - three or four guys miss blocks, but he finds some way to take what little there is and make something out of it.

**Q:** When you have guys at the combine and have guys in for free agent visits, looking at video and explaining what you were doing on this play so valuable?

**BB:** I think there's something to be said for that. But on the other hand there are guys that can, when you watch film, look at it in the classroom and look at it in a book, they'll give it to you chapter and verse, forwards and backwards. And then you get out there on the field and spatially here's the same stuff we went over in the meeting, here's the same thing we watched on film, and it happens on the field and they don't recognize it, or they're late to recognize it. And then there are other guys that don't understand it in the diagram, they don't really understand it.

But then you get out there spatially and say, 'OK, when this guy is here' ... Oh, OK. We all have different ways of learning. It's interesting how that happens. I'm not saying everybody's like that, but sometimes you can get misled by that. You think, 'Well, somebody comes in and they can draw 100 different plays.' But then you get out there on the field and they miss. But you get guys like Brady and Moss and guys like that; they get it at every level. You diagram something, 'Oh, yeah I can picture that.' You see this play? When this guy is here, you go there. [They respond,] 'Of course, I would go there, what else would I do?' It just comes easy to them. They get out there on the field and they make adjustments during the game, they just instinctively know what to do. Sometimes they see it a lot quicker than the coaches do and that's good for us.

**Q: In New York you had a linebacker, Carl Banks, that was very good covering the tight ends. It seems now in the league finding that linebacker is a challenge. Can you talk about that challenge?**

**BB:** I think Carl Banks, of all the players that I've coached, was probably better at playing over at tight end than anybody else. Certainly, in the running game he was extremely good at playing against tight ends and the blocking schemes that go on the tight ends side, which are multiple because there's an extra guy over there and that's what the tight end position does. It creates an extra blocker, an extra gap and an extra other combination of schemes. As far as pass coverage on the tight ends, he wasn't really asked to do that all that much in New York. I'm not saying he didn't do a good job of it at times, but that wasn't really a big specialty of his and I wouldn't say, to my recollection, there were all that many times he was asked to do it.

I think there were a couple game plans that he was, but I would say probably in 16 games that might of come up once or twice a year at the most. Having a linebacker who can cover a real good pass receiving tight end, it's pretty unusual to see that in this league. Certainly, some guys are better than others, but it's a tough matchup against a real good receiving tight end. If you put a defensive back on him, then the tight ends have a size advantage, a lot of times, 20, 30, 40, 50-pounds - depending on how big the [defensive backs] you put on them [are]. And usually when you put linebackers on those real athletic receiving tight ends, they have significant speed and quickness advantages and that's why tight ends are hard guys to match up on.

You've got Tony Gonzalez, just to pick a name, it's almost impossible for any team to matchup with a player like that. He's just got size skills against [defensive backs] and speed and quickness skills against linebackers. On top of that, he's a great route runner with great hands, so even if you're on him it still might not be good enough. That's a hard position to matchup against.

**Q: When you see a defensive end in a 4-3, what attributes might you see in that player that leads you to believe that he can play the outside in a 3-4?**

**BB:** I think the positions are fairly similar. Most of the 3-4 outside linebackers in this league are better going forward than going backward, but still at times they do have to do that. You get an opportunity to see them sometimes do that in their scheme, depending on what that is. Moving laterally and being able to slide down the line of scrimmage and contain plays, [those are] sometimes things that the defensive ends don't have to do so their lateral movement and their backward movement in a 3-4 are a little bit different than a defensive end's more forward movement in a 4-3 front.

There are a lot of coverage adjustments too that they have to be aware of that mentally a defensive lineman doesn't have to worry about. Sometimes that can affect a player's aggressiveness [because] he has a lot to think about in the coverage. They run a simple play, but he's worried about a lot of other things, whereas defensive linemen have less to worry about from a coverage standpoint.

**Q: You talked about watching film with Ray Lewis in college. Was he above average then?**

**BB:** I would say exceptional. Exceptional. I think when you watch film with players, like I did with Ray that day, you think back over the number of times I've done that and some of the guys that really stand out, there's a handful of them. You really remember those and how impressed I was coming out of Miami after spending the day with him. You watch a guy play, but you don't really know what's inside there, but when you sit down and talk to him and he can recall and tell you about things [like], 'This was what this play was.' 'This is this.' 'This is what I'm keying.' 'This is what happens.' 'This is the situation.' 'We check to this.' 'They did that.' 'This is the game plan.' 'We made this adjustment.' I mean, all those things.

You really have an appreciation for this guy - who knows a lot more than what he's supposed to do on the play. He has a great concept of the defensive scheme, of the opponent, of situational football and all of those things. It was really impressive. There's probably a handful of guys like that that I can think back to but he's definitely one of them.

**Q:** A long time ago you mentioned Lawyer Milloy as being one of those guys. Who else?

**BB:** [Devin] McCourty was one for sure. Guys start telling you what the nose is supposed to do on a particular stunt when he's playing corner and stuff like that. Usually you don't get that. I'd say Devin was a guy, sitting down with him...and I know a little bit about that scheme from Coach [Greg] Schiano and what they do and so forth, so you kind of [say], 'What's this guy doing? What's that guy doing?' and kind of keep going and say, 'Well alright, so he understands what the linebackers are doing. He understands a couple adjustments. Ok, now what about this?'

**Q:** Do you walk out of a film session like that and hope nobody else asks the guy about that stuff, or do you know it's going to be out there?

**BB:** I think this league has got a lot of pretty good people evaluating personnel on every team: scouts, coaches, personnel people and so forth. I assume in the end, probably pretty much everybody knows [or] can find out whatever they want to know anyway.

**Q:** Why does that seem so rare for a guy to know what everybody else is doing? Is it that difficult?

**BB:** Let's just say a lot of players don't...some players just know what they do, which is ok. I'm not saying there's anything wrong with that. You can talk to some guys and you ask them what the defense was and [they say], 'Well, here's what I do on that defense. Here's what I do on that play. This is what my assignment is. If this happens I do this. If that happens I do that.' 'Well, what does the linebacker do?' 'Well, I'm not really sure, but here's what I do.' I'm just saying it's different. When you're a middle linebacker it's certainly helpful - [Jerod] Mayo, Ray Lewis, guys like that that really have a good understanding of not only what they're doing, but what the line is doing, what the secondary is doing, why we can't play this coverage against this formation, why we can't run this line stunt against this type of blocking scheme.

Then they'll never call those things. They won't put your team in those bad situations because they have such a good understanding of it. Or maybe it's something that you would do, but not in this particular situation. There are a lot of things in football that are good calls, but if they're done at the wrong time, they're really bad calls. It's not that the call is bad, but to do it at that particular time wouldn't be the right thing. Having an understanding of all that and having a feel for the game - Pepper [Johnson] is another guy. [To] just go through the whole game and not do something but then get to the one critical time in the game where it's really the right time to do it and then make that call and put your defense in an advantageous position, that's what good football players do. I would definitely put Ray in that category.

**Q:** When you're evaluating a guy like Geneo Grissom coming out of college, how much stock do you put in his performance at a position you don't plan on playing him at? If you decide you're going to play him as a lineman, how much weight does his senior

## year at linebacker carry?

**BB:** Those are good questions, and they're the questions that we have to answer. That's the reality of it. You take what you have and then you try to figure it out the best you can. In Geneo's case, really he played four-technique his junior year, and then he played some as an edge rusher in passing situations as a defensive end. In his senior year, he played more as an outside linebacker, and then he played both inside and outside because they have two other good pass rushers there, so he was kind of the guy that got kicked inside on a lot of those sub-situations and played actually over the guard or in a three-technique. He's done a lot of different things.

I think when you look at a player like that, you think, 'OK what do we want him to do, how does he do that?' Maybe the other things you can use, maybe you can't, but how's he going to do on the things that we want him to do. It goes back to a guy we talked about a little earlier this year – [Willie] McGinest. When you watched Willie play his senior year at USC, he played defensive end, he played defensive tackle, he played up, he played down, he played middle linebacker one game. I can remember him being the Mike linebacker. We didn't really envision him in that position, but it spoke to his versatility and his athleticism to be able to do that. But they were trying to move him around to create different matchups, not let the offense key on him and so forth. Coach [John] Robinson used him in a lot of different spots.

I think some of those for us – I mean, I was in Cleveland at the time – but we would kind of discard and say we're not going to use him there. But there are things you see a player do at a different position that you recognize athletically, he can run or he can take on blocks or he can cover a seam route or whatever it is, and maybe there is some application for that to other positions. Sometimes you look at a guy play a position and it's totally different, like [Julian] Edelman – the position he played in college is not one that we would want to play him at, so it's almost a total projection. And they're all in between.

# On His Own Players

**Q:** How unique is Patrick Chung's ability to cover different positions like he does against receivers, running backs and tight ends?

**BB:** Yeah, Pat [Chung]'s got - he's got really good skills, very tough, very good tackler and he matches up against a lot of players. I think I've said before Wes [Welker] was a hard guy to cover in the slot but - and I'm not saying he shut Wes out - but I mean he covered Wes. Wes had his plays, too. But he covered Wes competitively in the slot in one-on-ones out here many times. That was a good battle. Wes was good, Chung was good, but I'm just saying that's a pretty high level of player to cover. Those were very competitive matchups. Like you said, he's been on receivers, he's been on fast tight ends, he's been on big tight ends, he's been on backs.

He's got good quickness, good strength, instinctive, tough, mentally tough, physically tough, very good tackler. Guys can catch passes on him but usually he tackles them so that keeps some of those plays from becoming bigger plays and that's important, too. He can play zone, he can play man. He's a versatile player for us. He helps us in a lot of ways and he plays in the kicking game and you've seen him make plays on special teams as well. He's one of our best conditioned athletes. He's able to play a lot of plays and able to play them at a high level.

**Q:** Patrick Chung lines up often close to the line of scrimmage and seems to do well defending the run. What is it in his skill set that allows him to have success doing that?

**BB:** That is his skill set. Yeah, he's great at that; finding the ball, getting through traffic, fitting in the running game, covering in traffic. He knows all of those kinds of things. He's really good at that. When we had him before he left and then he came back and you know we just weren't able to put him into some of the positions that he should've been put in. We had other things to deal with. We were trying to deal with other things on the defense and we've been able to

I would say play him in a much better way in the last three years than we did when he was here the first time. I think our utilization of him has been better.

He's been pretty much the same player but I think we've been able to utilize him better the last three years and he's done a great job embracing the different responsibilities that we've given him, which he has a lot of different things to do on the defense within the game or from game to game. So he handles those responsibilities very well in addition to this responsibilities on special teams, which again, when you start talking about guys like Lorenzo Alexander and [Patrick] Chung and guys like that that not only are impact defensive players but they're impact players in the kicking game, that's a lot of added value.

**Q:** You said you have utilized him better on the field in his second stint here with the Patriots. What goes into that process of getting a player to reach their potential? Is there a moment where something just clicks and he finds his proper role?

**BB:** I mean every situation is different. Every player is different. I mean I told you what the sequence of events was and after Philadelphia released him I talked with Pat [Chung]. We had a long talk about what our situation was, how I saw it going forward, how he saw it going forward, how it was different from the other years that he was here and I would say that's the way it has been. Things change.

## Q: How would you evaluate Malcolm Butler's tackling ability?

**BB:** Well, I think one of the biggest things is just the desire to tackle. I think I've coached a lot of defensive backs and Malcolm will go in this category of when a guy catches a pass on you they really want to tackle him and tackle him hard. And I think you see that. There's a certain type of defensive back I think that has that mentality. If they catch one then 'I'm really going to try and tackle a guy as hard as I can because he caught one on me,' type of thing. I think you see a lot of Malcolm's tackles like that. Tackling receivers is different than tackling running backs. That's a challenge for any defensive back really because of the skill those players have running the ball and usually they can face up the defender. But you know, Jonathan Jones is kind of like that, too.

He's not the biggest guy but kind of like Malcolm he's tough and wants to tackle and knows how to use his size and his quickness usually to tackle low but to be able to get those guys on the ground and wrap them up. I'd say a lot of it is desire, some of it is technique, and then there's definitely an element of playing strength that comes in there. But desire's probably number one. Guys that really want to tackle are usually competitive tacklers. Guys that don't want to tackle aren't going to be good tacklers.

**Q: Can you talk a little bit about what Kevin Faulk means to this franchise and are there any guys on this roster that remind you a little bit of him?**

**BB:** Well, I mean that's a pretty high bar. You're talking about Kevin Faulk. We have guys like James White or [Shane] Vereen going back that had similar roles and had production. Kevin's pretty special. As I said this summer, I think many impressive things about Kevin, amongst them would be that I thought he played his best football in the biggest games, the most critical situations, the most critical plays. The times when we need him the most is when he came through with some of his best plays. The Carolina Super Bowl, the two-point play, I think it was the only time he scored all year, but what bigger play is there than that?

So, I'd say that's kind of typical of Kevin. I can still see him converting on third-down or punt return situations, getting him in a nine-man, handling a short punt, or blitz-pickup so that we could make the play to somebody else but him stepping up and making the block that we needed on a critical third-down or two-minute play to be successful. I think Kevin's one of the great, great examples - and

I've tried to point this out to players that I've coached throughout my entire career - Kevin's a player that came in; I mean first of all, out of all the great running backs that have come out of LSU, which have been a lot of them, he has pretty much got every record. I mean [Leonard] Fournette might break a couple of them this year but he has pretty much been the best guy down there of all the great ones they've had. His role in the NFL was different than that and he accepted his role, he embraced his roles, and he was the best that he could be in those roles and he's a Hall of Fame player. Instead of sometimes trying to make a role different, instead of embracing the role that your team wants you to have and needs you to have, some players want a role that they want to have and then sometimes that's a little bit of a conflict.

I think Kevin was a great example of coming in here he started off as a returner and was a great runner, but kind of worked his way into more of a third-down sub back but he always had good run skills and he had a lot of good runs for us. He was great in the passing game, he was great in the return game when we needed him, he was a great leader. When we had backs like Corey Dillon he was a great - or Antowain [Smith] or guys like that - he was not only a great compliment to them but he was a great mentor to them in terms of preparation and dependability and a lot of little things. Just taking care of a lot of little things so the example and the leadership that he gave to the team was exceptional. It really was, and to a degree a little bit below the radar.

Not a big out front team captain and that type of profile, yet the undercurrent that he had was arguably as strong as any. Kind of like Troy Brown; a little bit different than Troy Brown but kind of like Troy Brown. So, [he was] a really, really special player. [He] had ball-security issues, had blitz-pickup issues when I got here. He came in, "Coach what do I need to do?" "Kevin, here's what you need to do." He worked very hard at it, became very good at it. It wasn't an attitude of like "Well, look, here's what I'm good at. Here's what I want to do. What do I need to do to help the team," [and he'd] go out there and do it. You're probably really lucky as a coach if you have a couple of guys, we've had a lot of guys like that, and he would certainly be up there at the head of that class. And honestly I think it's great that he has been recognized for that.

I don't even know how many games he started in his career but I would venture to say not all that many, yet you're talking about a Hall of Famer player that let's just say wasn't even a starter but that doesn't really matter. When the game was on the line he was always in the game and he was always in the eye of the storm, and that really speaks more to me to the value of the player than whose name is in there on the starting lineup on the first play of the game. You've got 59 minutes of football left. I don't think that's the most important play yet that's what a lot of people want to relate it to. Really the most important plays are the game-winning plays at the end of the game. Who's in there for those? That's what you really want to know.

**Q:** Troy Brown had a memorable quote when he was retiring that you can't outrun father time. What do you see that allows Tom Brady to be competitive against father time?

**BB:** Tom works really hard, he takes great care of himself, and he works really hard physically to be ready to go. I have great respect for the way he competes off the field in terms of his preparation physically and as far as knowing our opponent and the game plans and all of that. That's a big part of it. I would just say in general, not about any specific player, this is not directed at anyone, but I think at the beginning of each year, I always try to remind myself to just go back and be objective and look at each player objectively – not judge them on the past, but judge them on the current year.

I know you guys don't like to hear that and I talk about that probably ad nauseam, but every year is its own year, and some players get better, and some players kind of stay in a fairly consistent area and other players decline for one reason or another. That's something that I don't think ... I learned a long time ago that you don't take that for granted, you go on what you see. The players who are on this team this year earn what they get based on their performance, as have the ones in the past – not based on some other resume or some other year or whatever. It's what the player does or if there is an injury situation, where you project him to be, but you can't dream about that, you have to be realistic and evaluate it.

I've had players that honestly one year were as good of players at their position as there were in the league, they went to the Pro Bowl, they were really good players, and the following year they weren't, and in some cases they were maybe a year or two from being out of the league. And vice versa, guys who don't play or who have very little to no role on your team and all of a sudden they go to a very prominent role – Tom Brady as an example.

I think you just have to constantly evaluate each individual player, you have to constantly evaluate your team, whether you were good at something last year or even at one point in the season, doesn't mean that you're going to always be good at it, doesn't mean that when you run into a matchup and you haven't made the improvements that you need to make that it's going to be good enough against somebody else.

A lot of times you don't find that out until you get into the game, so it's a week to week thing. I know this is a very long answer for a simple question about one player, but I think it all for me is the same. You've got to continue to evaluate each guy, your team, the different units in your team, figure out how to get better, why you are having problems, what needs to be corrected, how to maximize what are not your perceived strengths but what are your actual strengths, how to get the most out of that, or the individuals, whatever it happens to be. And it is constantly changing and constantly evolving, and I think that's what I learned.

But certainly there is a point in each player's career where I'd say at the end of the year, you've got to look at that player with the idea of, well let's see where he is next year, because Troy's quote certainly has a lot of truth and application to it, for all of us.

THE BIG BOOK OF BELICHICK

## Q: How have you seen Rob Gronkowski evolve and improve as a blocker?

**BB:** Experience. He goes up against a lot of different guys at that position. It's tough. Tight ends have to face anything from 300-pound guys to those 260 to 280-pound defensive end/outside linebacker types to the guys that are a little bit smaller and even faster, like the Von Millers and the [Elvis] Dumervils to occasionally in sub defenses, blocking defensive backs. They have a wide range of guys that they have to block on various plays. A lot of that is really experience. It's a lot different blocking a defensive end that weighs 300 pounds then it is blocking a sub safety that's 210 but is fast and quick and all the guys in between. I think that's one of things that he's learned, it's not just X's and O's, it's who the guy actually is and how he would deal with a blocker like Rob. I think not knowing who to block, I don't want to say that's the easy part but that's kind of the easy part. We can 'X' and 'O' it and get the right guys on the right guys but actually getting them blocked based on who they are and the way they play, that's a little different story.

## Q: Related to the defensive linemen groupings, can you talk about Vince Wilfork's versatility and how he has handled that?

**BB:** Vince is a very versatile player. I think he has handled it well. He's a smart guy. He's a good technique player. He can do a lot of things on the front. Again, like a lot of players, though, in college that play the one-technique and the three-technique, the three-technique is pretty close to the inside shoulder of the tackle and the one-technique is a shade on the center. So in a 3-4, that's pretty close to those two positions. A lot of teams play that on their over and under defensive sets anyway. I don't think it's that major of a deal, but Vince is a really versatile guy. He's smart. He line stunts and understands protections and pass rushes, and reads plays very quickly

- blocking schemes. He's excellent at all of that and provides great leadership for the other guys on the line. He not only plays his position, but helps the other guys play better. I think that's really the mark of an outstanding player: a guy that can elevate the play of the players around him, either with what he's doing or in doing things that help other guys and give them better opportunities. He's very unselfish about that. There are a lot of plays that get made that he is a big factor in causing the play, even though he's not the final guy that makes the tackle and gets the credit for it.

**Q:** When you shift him outside is he still able to maintain that impact that he has on the interior?

**BB:** I think he's a tough matchup for most offensive linemen. There are a lot of guys he has a size and power advantage on. And a lot of the guys that might have a chance to match up with his size and power, then lose on his quickness. Again, he's a tough matchup. The best thing against a guy like that, really, on the offensive line is when you have two people that can - initially at least - step to him. A center and a guard and then the guard comes off on somebody else or the center comes off on somebody else. But at least you can initially start to control him and then the one guy can hopefully take him over. We see that a lot. Like this week Kevin Williams is a good example of that. You can't leave two guys on him, where you're not blocking somebody else, but initially you're probably going to have a number of plays where two guys step to him to try to control him and then one of those two guys will come off for one of the linebackers at some point.

**Q:** Is that why it works having him at end? Since you have a linebacker next to him so he can't be doubled?

**BB:** You've got a guard who's got a linebacker over him, so that guard can help either on the end or the nose, depending on the play. But eventually he's got to get to his blocking assignment or you're going to have an unblocked guy there. Again, to start the play a lot of times, if two guys step at the defensive lineman then that gives one of those guys an opportunity to kind of fit the block and take it over. I wouldn't call it a true double team. I don't see a lot of true double teams. But as far as initially fitting the play, that's how it works.

# On Opposing Players

**Q:** Is Antonio Brown one of those guys that you simply cannot cover one-on-one?

**BB:** [He's] very difficult. He's got a tremendous skill set, very quick. He almost always can create separation in his route. He's a very good technique route-runner so he does a great job of setting up routes. He does a really good job of getting on top of the DB's [defensive backs], almost stepping on the toes before he goes into his route so they can't get any kind of - they can't really anticipate it.

He does a great job of stacking the defenders where he gets a step on the defender then he kind of cuts him off so that the defenders like a full man behind him so he can use his body to protect the ball on the deep balls. He's hard to jam on the line because of his great quickness and then as I said, when he gets that half a step on the defender, not that he necessarily outruns everybody on the field, but once he moves in front of them and stacks them then he is on top of them. The skills with the ball in his hand as a runner are exceptional. You see that on the punt returns. You see it on a lot of those under routes, catch-and-run plays, so you don't want to back off of him and let him catch it and break a tackle or if you get up on him he runs behind you.

That's a problem and he's a good intermediate route runner, too; in-cuts, comebacks, curls, things like that. He has great quickness coming out of cuts so he's very, very hard to cover. And he's seen a lot of double-coverage, too. I don't think that really bothers him either. He knows how to beat that. When you double him I mean at some point he attacks one guy so it really becomes single coverage. He takes the other guy out of it and then he beats that guy. So he's tough. He's really tough.

**Q:** Does Troy Polamalu freelance more than other players at his position? Is he unpredictable because he takes more chances?

**BB:** I'd use the word instinctive. He's a very instinctive player. You can say that he's guessing, taking chances, but I'd say he's right most of the time; most of the time he makes the right decision. Whether some of those plays are called blitzes or he just blitzes on his own, I don't know exactly how they do it. But there are times where you look at it and say, 'That's not really where you're supposed to be.' But where he is, is the right place to be. He's right in the middle of the play or he's doing something that's disruptive to the offense. However that's orchestrated I don't know, but you can't just let him run free and ruin the game.

Just because this is where they're supposed to be isn't necessarily where he is. He's very, very instinctive. He has a great nose for the ball. A lot of times he winds up in the center-guard gap, sometimes he winds up in a tackle-tight end gap, sometimes he's 20 yards deep, sometimes he's out in the flat, sometimes he blitzes off the edge and sometimes he lines up in one of those places and runs somewhere else as part of the disguise. It's really hard to tell even where he is, whether he's going to stay there or not when the ball is snapped. He has excellent timing and really has a good feel for the game; makes a lot of plays. Even when he plays close to the line of scrimmage, he plays very strong. He can definitely hold his ground, even against offensive linemen.

When he gets blocked, it isn't like they knock him out of there. He can penetrate and take up a couple blockers or hold his ground here very competitively for a guy his size. He's fast, he can make a lot of plays from the backside. He's a good tackler; strong and very, very physical but very instinctive. Call it whatever you want to call it, but he knows where the ball is or where it's going and he gets to the right place at the right time way, way, way more often than he's wrong.

**Q: Last week you talked about Champ Bailey and his ability to match up with anybody. Does this secondary present that same physical skill set that they can cover all types of receivers? What does that do for your set of receivers? Does that put more**

pressure on them to be more precise in their route running to gain separation?

**BB:** First of all, I think Champ Bailey is in a class by himself. I don't want to start comparing guys to Champ Bailey, the guy has been to 11 Pro Bowls. I'd say he's pretty close to the gold standard at corner over the course of his career. There aren't a lot of guys I would compare to Champ Bailey. These guys are long, they're big. They're extremely long, 6-4, 6-2, 6-3 corners. You just don't see those very often. To see them on one team, they're just hard to get away from. They're big, they're physical, they take up a lot of space. A lot of guys just aren't used to working against that size player, 220-pound corners. There just aren't a lot of them out there. I think that's a challenge because it's a little bit unique.

They're also good tacklers, good run-force players. For the quarterback, it's harder because it's no different than playing against a taller middle linebacker, a guy like [Brian] Urlacher or somebody like that in there that's 6-4, 6-5 in the middle of the field. Their range and their height just make those throws in the middle a little tougher. Throwing the ball outside on a 6-2, 6-4 corner, it's a little different deal getting it over them or trying to run some high-low combinations out there. It's just a much bigger guy. They do a good job. Again, it's not just them, it's the entire defense. They have a good pass rush, they have good coverage players. A lot of times the guys aren't open, the quarterback has to hold the ball a split-second longer, the rush is there. Sometimes the rush is there right away, the quarterback is forcing the ball, defenders don't really have to cover them very long.

They do a good job of putting pressure on the passing game, covering them, they're a good run defense, they're strong, they're very active, the linebackers are fast, [K.J] Wright and Bobby Wagner and [Leroy] Hill all run well, they pursue well. [Kam] Chancellor is like a linebacker, he's another 230-pound guy so they drop him down so they're playing a 4-4 sometimes. Those guys are big and they run well and they're physical. You look at their defense, I don't think you get real excited about saying, 'Oh, let's do this, let's do that.' They've done a pretty good job of defending everything over these five games.

**Q:** Would it be tough to speed them up?

**BB:** I wouldn't say that we've seen a lot of that against them. I would say that they're not the most complicated defense in the league. I don't think that their thing, to run 70 different blitzes and 10 different fronts and all that. That's not really their game. I doubt that playing fast or in a no-huddle, I doubt that would change their scheme too much because they have enough things to keep you honest but it's not like every defense that's ever been created. They do what they do, they do it pretty well. I can't imagine that they would have a hard time getting to those defenses because that's what they do, that's the core of their defense. They don't have a thousand different things over there.

**Q:** In the secondary, with Champ Bailey, is he somebody capable of by himself changing the way he's playing a receiver in the look he gives a certain receiver or even the tight end?

**BB:** I would start by just saying with Champ, to me he's one of the few corners in the league that really can match up against anybody. He matches up against the Andre Johnsons of the world, the big, strong, physical, fast guys. Then he'll match up against quick, real good route running, quick receivers, guys like that too. [It] doesn't really make any difference.

You can watch him match up against whoever they want to put him on, whether it's Mike Wallace or whether it's Calvin Johnson, through the years; I'm not just talking about this year. At times, he's been on tight ends, like when he would be on [Tony] Gonzalez back in the day and things like that. So, I think he's really capable of being physical and standing in there and banging with the big guys. He's got enough quickness and length with the little guys to match their quickness and give them a problem and stay with them, or if he gets his hands on them and jams them, he can destroy the route right off the bat. He's a very instinctive player, so he has a good sense of what the guy is trying to do and what their tendencies are and things like that. He's on a lot of routes just because he's experienced and he's smart.

I think he can cover, I'd say there aren't too many corners in the league – it would be hard to think of who the next one would be – who like him could match up as well against any type of receiver. Some guys do well against some type of players and have a little trouble with another type of guy. It looks like to me like he does a pretty good job against anybody – on whoever the other team's best receiver is, if they want to match him up, which sometimes they do, sometimes they don't. They don't always match him but at times they will. He can match them or not match them or he can take whoever comes out and do a pretty good job with it. Man, zone, he's a good Cover-2 corner, he's a good one-on-one corner, he's a good zone corner, tackles well, he's a good run-force corner, he's pretty much a prototype corner in terms of having a full set of skills, does everything well, plays the ball well, very good hands, but he's a strong tackler and a good run-force player too.

**Q: Andre Johnson has had the kitchen sink thrown at him coverage-wise. What is it that's allowed him to consistently make big plays and be productive?**

**BB:** They've got so many other players that you just can't throw everything at him on every play. You might be able to limit him a little bit, but you have a lot of other things to worry about, but he's a good receiver, he's good at everything [and] I think that's the hard part. He's very good down the field. He's an excellent deep receiver. He's got great size and speed and goes up for the ball — post patterns, corner patterns, go routes, play-action, bombs down the field — he's good at those. He's got good quickness in and out of cuts on those intermediate routes, those 20-yard in cuts, the 18-yard comebacks, the post corner routes and things like that. He's a strong runner with the ball in his hands, so they give him slip screens, slants, crossing routes and things like that, like Terrell Owens' type routes.

It's a 3-yard route and it's 25 yards by the time he gets tackled. You can cover him on one thing, but it's hard to get him on everything. He's really dangerous with the ball in his hand, but he can get open. He overpowers the smaller guys. He outruns some of the bigger more physical-type corners. He's a tough matchup no matter who you put on him because of his route tree and his skill set.

**Q:** Schematically, how much do they do to free him?

**BB:** A lot. You don't really ever know where he's going to be. He's all over the place. He can be the perimeter receiver on the outside, on the strong side, the weak side. They put him in the slot. They motion him out of the backfield. A lot of times he's stacked with another receiver, so it's not just him by himself, it's him and somebody else that they switch release, double inside, double outside and make it hard to leverage him.

He gets moved around quite a bit and he's a good blocker, too. He does a good job in the running game. Whatever he is, 220-225, he's a man, so whenever he comes in and cracks on linebackers and safeties he can get them, and on some of the little corners he stands there and covers them up and there's no run force. They like to run the ball outside and he's effective there, too. Those aren't in the stats, but he's good at that.

**Q:** You do the same stuff with Randy Moss and move him around, does that mean he's smart?

**BB:** Yeah, absolutely. The number of different things he does, the positions he does them from and when you watch the film where everybody is asking where do we lineup and all that, they go out there and run it. Clearly, he's smart, knows the different formations, the different routes they ask him to run from those different formations. It doesn't look like it's a problem.

They don't have a lot of mistakes in the passing game, kind of like when you watch Indy, New Orleans and teams like that. You see the pattern, there's good distribution. They have good passing concepts. Sometimes you watch plays and you have guys running together and it doesn't look like it's a very well designed route. You hardly ever see that with Houston.

**Q:** Can you talk about Ed Reed and the mind games he plays?

**BB:** I don't think there's anybody any better in the game, or I've seen anybody any better than Ed Reed in terms of disguise, ability to read the quarterback. [He can] anticipate plays, sometimes it's route, sometimes it's formations, sometimes it's what the quarterback's doing. And on top of all that, he's got a tremendous burst and acceleration to the football, great hands, timing and ball skills.

When you put it all together, he gets around a lot of balls. I think the quarterback has to know every time that ball leaves his hand where Ed Reed is because that guys makes ... He can play sideline to sideline. Usually, you feel better in two-deep defenses than one-deep, but really with Ed Reed back there, I think you almost feel better in one-deep because he can cover the whole field by himself, and you don't have to worry about the other guy covering half of it. He really can handle the whole thing back there. When I was in Hawaii with him for a week at the Pro Bowl and got a chance to work with him - I mean, I know it was the Pro Bowl, but work with him on a daily basis in practice, and really watch him up close, and tell him what to do, and watch him do it, and that type of thing - that was even more impressive.

He's a rare, rare player at that position, as good as any I've ever seen. I know there are a lot of guys that have had a lot of interceptions there, the Paul Krause's and the Darren Sharper's, guys that I'm not taking anything away from them. But this guy, he can do it all back there. He can play corner if they want him to play corner. He blocks kicks. He returns kicks. He returns interceptions for touchdowns. He scoops up interceptions for touchdowns. He's always around the ball and that's usually bad for the offense when he is. He's a great football player.

**Q:** Will Drew Brees change plays frequently or will he look for

**matchups post snap? How much work does he do at the line to get them in and out of plays? How important is the disguising chess match that you'll do defensively?**

**BB:** That's a real challenging part of playing New Orleans here and their offense. I would say that they certainly have the ability to change plays. He will, at times. You'll see him change plays or change protections. I wouldn't say that it's something you see him do a lot, but he certainly can do it. I think they're a team that plays at a pretty high tempo: quick counts, they come out and they go fast a lot of times, not all the time but enough. I think that the pace that they go at, even though they're not really a no-huddle team per se, they have a very fast tempo.

I think that's a very challenging part of playing against them. Does he change them? Yes. Can he change them? Yes. Does he do it a lot? I wouldn't say it's... we've seen other guys do it more. But I would say that he does it probably when he needs to, like if they're in a play that's a bad play, he can get out of it. But he plays at a fast tempo and you don't have a lot of time defensively to see your assignments, communicate them and do them because it all happens in a hurry. They give you a lot of different looks so you have to react to it pretty quickly.

**Q:** So you have to get lined up, you can't be playing games and trying to disguise?

**BB:** I'd say that's pretty accurate. You have to be careful about trying to do too much with him. You better be able to get to what you have, which does mean that a lot of times you have to show what you're in, in order to match up against their different looks because they create a lot of different formationing and like I said, detaching the tight end, detaching the backs, they use a lot of different personnel groups with the multiple tight ends – all their backs play, all their tight ends play, all their receivers play.

They run them in and out of there in a hurry. Then get lined up and get to go, you have to be ready to play when the ball is snapped because he does a very good job of, when the defense, when they miss somebody, he finds them. They get a bunch of plays every week on I would say, defensive mistakes or alignment errors that he recognizes and just gets the ball to whoever it is and then you're chasing him. That's a big challenge.

## Q: What has made Tony Gonzalez so consistent over the years?

**BB:** Yeah, he can pretty much do it all. He's really a receiver. He's a tight end, but he's not really a tight end; he's a receiver - great ball skills, hands. He's got that ability — like a basketball player — to position the defender out and use his size to box out the defender. I think the quarterbacks, obviously, that he's played with know that and they put the ball in a place where he can only get it and he can pin the defender behind him and he can go up and take the ball. He's got a great patience in the passing game. He sets up routes, runs a lot of double moves. But he's got quickness out of his break.

He's got good speed, exceptional hands. He's obviously a smart football player. He knows how to run routes and get open and set them up. Double-covering him is hard because he'll attack one guy or the other, so you're really only ending up with one guy on him and he can defeat that one guy. He's not just going to run in between two guys and get covered. He'll pick out on or the other and attack them. Whatever aspect of the passing game you want from him, red area, third-down, big plays, possession passes, play action, you name it, he's really good at all of it. And having spent a few days out there with him out there in the Pro Bowl after the '06 season, when you are just around him on a day-to-day basis, you really have an appreciation for how skilled he is, how athletic he is, what kind of ball skills.

There were times out there I remember where he would come out of a break and the ball was almost on him and he would just turn around and snatch it. He would never see the ball leave the quarterback's hand, it was just on him quick, and 99 percent of the receivers would have dropped it. He makes it look easy. He's really exceptional.

**Q:** One of the best battles you had against Tony Gonzalez was in 2004 when he matched up against Rodney Harrison.

**BB:** You are talking about two real competitive guys and I'm sure they both took it as a great personal challenge to play against each other. But we're in different matchups this week. [Tony] Gonzalez is in a different offense and Rodney Harrison won't be playing in this game, so it'll be a different matchup for us.

**Q:** If you played zone against Tony Gonzalez, can he stretch that, too?

**BB:** Look, over the course of his career, he's gone up against a lot of zone defenses. He's gone up against a lot of man defenses. He's caught a lot of balls against both of them. There's something to be said about playing zone; you've kind of got him surrounded and you're not in an isolated one-on-one situation. It depends on what route they have called. And there's something to be said being man-to-man on him; at least you are close to him. At least you got a guy that's fairly close to him — maybe he doesn't cover him every inch of the way — but you don't have the space you have in between your zones for him. I think it depends on what the situation is, what type of play you're trying to stop, what kind of play they happened to have called, like it is in a lot of things in football.

We run the same play and run it against five or six different defenses and we had five or six different defenses on the play - rattle adjust, ball go to a different person or something like that. That's why you build the route concepts the way that you build them. At the end of the season, you go back and you look at [inaudible]. Here, we're throwing to the Y. Here, we're throwing to the Z. Here, we're throwing to the X. Here, we're throwing to the fullback. Here, we're throwing halfback. Here's the Z making an adjustment on that route. Here's the X making an adjustment on that route. Here's a blitz. Here's an adjustment by the back.

Here's an adjustment by the receiver. Here's an adjustment by the tight end, so you run the play 25 to 30 times in the year, and you go back, and look at it at the end of the season, that's why you have everybody doing what they're doing on the route. If this happens, you go to this guy. If that happens, you go to that guy and maybe he changes his route a little bit, depending on the play based on the coverage, or technique he is being defended with. That's what the passing game is. If they're in this, a lot of times the ball will go somewhere else. If they're in that, a lot of times the ball … It's not like high school when you say, "OK, I'm going to run a down and out and I'm going to throw it to you.' That's not the passing game in the NFL, it just doesn't work that way.

# On Peyton Manning

**Q:** You've prepared to face a Peyton Manning offense more than 20 times in your coaching career. Is there one common thread that stands out to you over the years about how those preparations and then the game have unfolded?

**BB:** I guess Manning.

**Q:** In terms of the offense itself, the way the games have unfolded.

**BB:** Each game is its own game. The offense, they've done a good job of utilizing their personnel and what those particular players do well in different systems, different teams, kind of similar system. Peyton does a great job of getting the ball to the weakest point of the defense, whatever defense happens to be. He's great. Obviously he's a great quarterback – best quarterback I've coached against. He does a tremendous job. They have good players and they have a good system. I'd say that's a common thread: good players and a good system and a good quarterback.

**Q:** When you say best quarterback that you've ever coached against, not that you need anything to get your motivation going, but how much does that stoke the competition of what you do?

**BB:** The competition is there every week. Every team has great players, great coaches. Every team is hard to beat in this league. There's no – everybody is tough. It's been the same, like relative to the [Joe] Montanas and the [Dan] Marinos or [John] Elways or whoever. I'm not taking anything away from any of those guys, but this guy is tough.

**Q:** What separates him from them?

**BB:** He's just good at everything. He's good at everything. I see no weaknesses in his game.

**Q:** What is it about Peyton Manning that makes him so hard to defend? Has anything changed with him this season with

## Knowshon Moreno gone?

**BB:** I think it doesn't really matter who is out there with him. Whoever it is, he finds a way to utilize them. He's had different players at different positions and different combinations and guys have been out and other guys have been in and all that. But no matter who it is out there, he does a good job of finding ways to utilize the skills of the particular group that is out there relative to their defensive matchup.

It seems like he causes every defense a problem every week for the last 15 years or however long it's been. You have to know who the other people are out there. Everybody has to do their job to defend them. You can't just stop one guy or one thing. But he does a great job of utilizing his players, his resources relative to what the defense is giving him and what looks best – a combination of his personnel versus where the defense is soft. He's good because he does everything good. Really I don't think there are any weak points in his game.

He's very smart. He has a great understanding of concepts and timing, game management, clock management, situational football – third down, red area – great utilization of the field from sideline-to-sideline and attacking the deep part of the field, very accurate, great decision-maker, quick release. He has very few negative plays, plays where something happens that just a quarterback might be able to keep the team out of. He very rarely puts his team at risk on plays like that, where there's an unblocked guy right at the point of attack or those kind of things. He's always able to get to something else that doesn't create a problem, is somewhat of a soft entry point to the defense one way or another. It's pretty much everything really, I don't think there are any weaknesses in his game.

**Q:** Knowing how much Peyton Manning has done at the line over the course of his career, how much more do you see this group and coaching staff doing as they play more together and get comfortable?

**BB:** I don't know, you'd have to ask them. I don't really know. I don't get the sense that they change every play, if that's what you're referring to. I think if they have a play called and they get a bad look, that they get to something better. That's what I think they do. So how many times does that come up? I don't know. When it comes up, then they do something about it. I don't see them run a lot of bad plays into plays that just have no chance. I don't think they go up to the line and call a different play four or five times every play. I just don't see that, but you'll have to ask them.

**Q: Was there a temptation to do something more against the run? A thought of putting an extra man in the box and if you choose to do that, how do you weigh that against taking another man out of pass coverage? Was that kind of part of the strategy you have to determine how you're going to play this game?**

**BB:** I think when you're up against Peyton Manning you have to be really careful about telling him what you do. We tried to have a good disguise package. I mean, not that you're going to fool him, he can definitely figure it out. But we tried to disguise what we were doing. I thought progressively as the game went along, that we were more competitive defensively. Obviously a big part of the score in the first half was the poor field position that we had, combined with not great defense either. We were able to hold them to one field goal there, but then on their third touchdown drive, they took it, I want to say like 80 yards down the field, whatever it was, it was a long, solid drive.

The first drive was 10 yards, the second drive we hold them to a field goal and then their drive right there at the end of the second quarter that went the whole length of the field, that was kind of the one that really, I think, hurt us the most. We tried to at halftime just talk about how we could play things better rather than just scrap everything that we were doing and try to go to a different look and all that. Because one thing with Peyton is when you go to a look to take one thing away, you just push the problem somewhere else. You don't eliminate things, you just push it to another part. They came out, they took the wind in the third quarter and we were obviously still concerned about the passing game and so we didn't want to pack everybody in and just invite them into throwing the ball because they did have the wind at that point.

We kind of stuck with our game plan, fortunately we made a few plays. We turned the ball over, we were able to stop them and get the ball back. Our offense converted those opportunities and then the fourth quarter, we finally got to the point where we made it a one-score game and then we kind of felt like we were back on even turf. We had the wind advantage and we were able to come back and sort of have a fair fight there.

### Q: For a rookie, playing Peyton Manning for the first time or first couple times, do they get star struck?

**BB**: No, I don't think it's star struck. I just think their offense is kind of unique and the way they handle it and all - you don't see that every week. If you haven't played in this league, you probably haven't seen it at all. I think talking to our younger players through the years, guys like [Brandon] Meriweather and [Jerod] Mayo, talking about the first time they played them, it certainly helps to play them once. There is no doubt about it. The timing, the tempo of the game, Manning's quick release and his ability in the pocket to get rid of the ball so quickly and to scan the field - like Brady - like we've talked about. But competitively, you don't see too many quarterbacks at his level. Having played him before, I think that's certainly helpful for young players. As much as you can talk about it before the game and say this is the way it's going to be and all that, but until they get out there and experience it, it's not quite the same. [Brian] Hoyer's done a real good job for us this week, I'll just say that up front. He's done a great job of running the Colts offense for our defense, running the scout team, and I think he's run the plays, made the decisions and given our defense the looks that are probably most similar to what Manning would do. He's done a nice job of that.

**Q**: Do you have him specifically do everything that Peyton Manning would do - the barking down the line and all that?

**BB**: We do it in our terminology, of course. He doesn't want to run a lot of bad plays, so if it's a bad play into a bad defense, then he's going to go to something else and that's pretty much what Brian's done for us. Whatever plays we have called, if our defense happens to be in a look that we think Peyton wouldn't run that play against, then we have him go to something else. We don't know exactly what it's going to be of course, but it's the process and the flexibility they have at the line of scrimmage that was well simulated.

**Q**: Is the pace hard to simulate? I know a couple of the players said that until you get out there, it's almost impossible to know what pace they are going to create.

**BB**: Yeah, especially because they change the pace. They have an ability to play fast, they have an ability to play at a moderate rate, and sometimes they can slow it down and go to the line and make a bunch of calls and snap the ball with one or two seconds left on the 40-second clock and wait and get their look. It's a problem for the defense because if you show it early, then if he sees it early he can change it. But if you're not ready to play when they're over the ball, then they can snap it right away and then you're out of position. It puts some stress on you from a timing standpoint of disguises and showing what you're going to do. If they don't like it, then they try to get to something they prefer against that particular look.

### Q: Why doesn't Peyton Manning get sacked?

**BB**: Because he gets rid of the ball. He throws it away. The only way to sack him is for somebody to come that he doesn't expect - the guy's blocked and he beats a block and Peyton's not thinking about him or for some reason he just doesn't see him. If he sees him coming, he'll get rid of the ball. And he has a quick release anyway, so he's the kind of guy that...Historically, we've seen people blitz him and the blitzer comes clean from the center guard gap or right from the line of scrimmage and he still gets rid of it and sometimes for big plays. Kind of like the Miami game; they tried to come after him there at the end of the game and they tear screened him [and he got a] touchdown. So you have to be careful with him.

## Q: How has Indianapolis's offense expanded since the first year you played Peyton Manning?

**BB:** I think they've definitely expanded it over a period of years. But they do a good job of having the things they need. There might be something that they haven't run in a year or half a season - or whatever - for the situations that didn't come up, and then they pull it out when they need it and they get it against the situation, or the look, or the coverage that somebody springs on them. They know how to pretty much beat everything and they have their ways of doing it, so whatever defenses you run, that'll trigger concepts that they'll use against them. You might not have the exact formation, or they change their personnel groups around, but they attack - whether it's split safety coverage, or post safety coverage, or pressure, or four-man line, or three-man line, or stunting, or two-gapping - whatever the defense's system is, they have ways they want to attack it and then when they see it that's kind of what they go to. I wouldn't say they have a lot of changes. It's kind of the exact opposite of the Miami offense. They don't motion a lot; they kind of sit in the same formation. They want to see where you're at and then they'll go ahead, go to work and dissect it. That's sort of the challenge that we have there. I would say the things they've expanded their offense with were things that they felt like there was a need for, they found a better way to attack something than they had in the past and they go do it that way.

# On Opposing Coaches

**Q:** From your experience going against Wade Phillips's defenses, how much does he change up the second time you face him? Did you notice a difference between the first time they faced Pittsburgh and the second time they faced Pittsburgh?

**BB:** Yeah, definitely. Look, Wade is a great coach. He's one of the great defensive coaches in the league over the past, really 40-something years, 40 years, however long it's been. And he does a great job. He does what he needs to do. If he needs to change, he'll change. If he doesn't need to change, he won't. But regardless of what he does, he stops people. He doesn't give up a lot of points. They turn the ball over. They play great situational defense, and that's the way it's been ever since he's coached defense as long as I can remember through the National Football League and all the different places that he's been. We've played against him in multiple spots as a head coach, as a coordinator, but the thing in common is his defenses always play well. They're always well-prepared. They're hard to run against. They're hard to throw against. They turn the ball over, and they play smart, situational football. So he's got a lot of different tools in his bag. Whichever ones he decides to use, we've got to be ready for and deal with. So I'm sure he'll make whatever adjustments he feels like he needs to make, and they'll be challenging for us. They always are.

**Q:** Did you learn anything from Bill O'Brien when he was on your staff?

**BB:** Yeah, sure, I think I learned a lot from Bill. Bill and I spent a lot of time together and it was good. Bill has got great leadership skills, without a doubt, great leadership skills. Watching him, observing him handle in-game situations or practice situations or meetings or that kind of thing, I think he did a great job of that. I'd say I definitely took some things from that. Overall just preparation of the team offensively, things that we talked about in terms of what to do, when to do it, how much of risk to take, when to take it and so forth, managing in-game situations that we had, like any offensive coordinator or defensive coordinator over a multi-year period you have a lot of those end-of-the-game or critical situations that you talk back and forth on of what's the best thing to do, how do we best manage the situation. He had a lot of input in that as Josh [McDaniels] does now or Matt [Patricia] does, Joe [Judge], for those situations.

But I think Billy has really got a good mix of all those things – leadership, toughness, command, intelligence, decision making, poise – and again, nobody could have gone into a tougher situation than Penn State and do what he did in two years. I mean whatever he had to deal with here I think was a fraction of that in a total picture of it. You talk to the players that played for him there, people that were there with him, the job that he did there was just spectacular. And he did a good job for us, too – I'm not saying that – but he's had multiple opportunities here along the way from here to Penn State to now Houston and same thing when talking to players that come from down there, the amount of respect they have for him, just watching the way his team plays, going through four quarterbacks last year being 9-7 dealing with some of the things he's had to deal with. I think he's done a great job. He's a great coach.

## Q: When he was here as a player, did Mike Vrabel strike you as the kind of guy that would go into coaching?

**BB:** Yeah, absolutely. Mike and I talked about that a lot. He'd give me advice and I would tell him, 'Mike when you're a coach and you're calling the defenses, you should go ahead and do that. Here's why we're not going to do that. Or that's a great idea. We can do that, that's good, I'm glad you brought that up.' Mike is not afraid to make a suggestion, and we've had a lot of good discussions even when he was at Ohio State or when he was in Kansas City for that matter, we would bump into each other from time to time, but when he was Ohio State particularly when he got into coaching, we discussed a lot of ... My daughter was out there at that time – Amanda was at Ohio State – we saw Mike and we would talk about different things, whether it would be X's and O's or managing players or practice tempo or whatever it was. It could be general coaching things. I think Mike has a great mind for it, great passion for it. He's got great playing experience, so he can draw on things that honestly I can't. I've never played in this league.

I can't draw on those, so I think there is definitely some advantage to that. I don't think that's a ticket. There are a lot of other things that go into it, too, but if it's used properly I think it's valuable. Mike was a great player. He's played different systems, he's played different positions. He's played offense, defense, special teams. He's played end, he's played linebacker. He would play free safety in practice for us probably once or twice a year, especially when we were up against a guy like Ed Reed or somebody who you really didn't know what he would do. You would just say go back there and go with what you see and if you want to gamble, gamble. Mike, he would love that. He would drive [Tom] Brady crazy doing that, like, 'He'll never be there on that pattern,' but it's Ed Reed – you didn't know where Ed Reed would be. He was usually wherever the ball was. He somehow got there. So Mike did that. Again you could just see his overall passion for the game, whether it be playing multiple positions, playing offense, defense, he had a great awareness of the total game and loved to play it, loved to play tight end. If we'd be up against a big receiver, he would go in there and take a couple plays at receiver.

**Q:** Have there been many guys like that where you can tell right away that they would make a good coach?

**BB:** I think there are a lot of guys that probably fall in that category, but I would say Mike probably as much as anybody. Even when he first got here, that was only his fifth year in the league or whatever it was, you could even kind of see it then and his career wasn't even half over and he was already thinking about coaching.

You could kind of tell when he got done playing that's what he was going to do. That came up pretty early. But he had a real passion for not just knowing his position but understanding the total game. He was always very good on things like being able to anticipate what the offense was going to do, hearing a call and then that call coming up later – maybe not even that game, maybe it was like the next year we played them – a guy like Peyton Manning who is making checks at the line of scrimmage or things like that.

He had a lot of those little things that you never see on film but somehow he knew them or he figured them out or anticipated them and made a lot of instinctive plays or plays based on experience and just knowledge. Mike was really tough. He was a tough football player. I'm sure that comes across in his coaching as well. I don't think he babies them. I don't think there's a lot of sitting around eating marshmallows. That's not really his style. Mike played hard, he coaches hard, and I think the players respect him because he puts in as much work as he demands. I don't think he would ask anybody to do anything he hasn't probably done more of.

**Q: To me, it seems that head coach Sean Payton has a very good offense. With the coaching fraternity, how much do you share with him? The coaching tree has some connections there.**

**BB:** I don't really think that's that significant right now. What Coach Payton and I have talked about is what we want to try to get done and I think that really centers around taking the things that we've installed and they've installed and work them against a different scheme and different group of players and try to evaluate those. This really isn't a game plan, what plays we run against the Saints or what they run against us and that kind of thing, trying to create advantages or use schematics to give your team an advantage. It's more evaluating individual players against different matchups and letting your players learn the execution of the plays against a different type of defense or against a different type of offense than what we're seeing over the last two weeks from ourselves. I think all those learning experiences are valuable, individually and for different units on the team, how to handle different problems and obviously things that we'll be facing over the course of the year, and that's really what it's about. We're not trying to do anything that they haven't prepared for or vice versa.

That doesn't do us any good to go out and see something that we haven't worked on and know that we're not prepared for it. We already know that. What's more important would be to go out there and do the things that we've worked on, that we should know how to do, that we have a good foundation on and see how we're doing. And I think that's what they're looking for, too. So, that's kind of the way we've structured the practices. We've had a good working relationship with the Saints and with Sean, his staff and the entire organization, and we just want to get better, they want to get better, and we want to work with each other so that we can both do that. We've been able to do that with them several times before, so hopefully we'll be able to get that again this week.

## Super Bowl Media Day: (on if there is one attribute that the opposing coach [Pete Carroll] has that they wish they had)

**BB:** Well, I think when I've watched Pete's teams play through the years – most particularly with Seattle – the thing that impresses me the most and the thing that I guess I would like to do a better job of is just the way that his teams play for 60 minutes. They play from the opening kickoff to the final whistle or the final gun. They play from the snap of the ball until the whistle blows at the end of the play. They play extremely hard down after down after down, week after week, year after year. They compete relentlessly as well as any team or any organization I've ever observed.

They just compete relentlessly on, not even 60 minutes – it's even longer, like last week against Green Bay. But it's from the opening kickoff to the final gun and they're just never going to let up in any phase of the game: offense, defense, special teams, the receivers, the defensive backs, the linemen, the quarterback. Everybody just competes at such a high level for every single second that they're out there, and I think that's a great credit and attribute to Pete and his staff. The players they brought in there, they're just relentless in the way that they play. And so I think that any coach wants his team to play that way and I think that Seattle and Pete really are the model for that. They do a better job than anybody. And I'm not saying that there aren't other teams that are in that category or very close to them, but I put them at the top."

## Q: What have you seen from Rob Ryan over the years in his development as a defensive coordinator?

**BB:** I think Rob is, when he was here, he wasn't a coordinator. He coached the linebackers then he went to Oakland as the coordinator. He was the coordinator in Oakland and Dallas and now obviously New Orleans. But I would say that the characteristics of his defense have remained pretty much the same throughout the years that I've seen him and when we've played him, which hasn't been every year but it's been a few times. He's sound fundamentally and he does game plan things from week to week that try to attack the opponent's weaknesses. Depending on what you do and how you do it and what he has available, what resources he has, then he's going to come up with some type of individual game plan for you that may or may not look like something that he's run in previous weeks. That's specifically based toward what the offensive opponent is doing and what the personnel matchups are that week. I think that's a pretty common thread so what's different is what happens with those matchups and those schemes because they change from week to week. That part of it is different but the common part of it is that he will change to create what he feels like is an advantage for his personnel and his scheme.

**Q:** Do a lot of coaches change like that?

**BB:** Some do and some don't. Some coaches run their system without a lot of changes from week to week and other coaches make some modifications and other coaches make, I'd say, bigger modifications in the game plan based on that type of philosophy. I would say Rex [Ryan] has a similar approach at the Jets. It's different but it's similar in that there are some weekly game plan adjustments that gain, you may or may not have looked at it because if he hasn't faced somebody like you, then you probably haven't seen them. If he's faced similar problems then you might have seen some elements of those but the matchups may be different.

Like Rob uses several different players on the inside part of the defense: he uses Malcolm Jenkins, he uses [Chris] Carr, he's used Roman Harper in the there, obviously [Kenny] Vaccaro. Sometimes it's a couple linebackers, sometimes it's nickel, sometimes it's dime, sometimes it's one guy, sometimes it's another guy. It depends on who they're matching up on. Right there is a bunch of combinations just from a personnel standpoint. Is it five DBs, is it six DBs, is it three safeties, is it four safeties, is it three corners, is it four corners? And you can just go on from there. That's the way they do it.

**Q:** Do you find it to be a trait of success to be able to change from week to week?

**BB:** Ultimately, whatever you do, you have to be able to do well, whatever that is. If it's running the same thing, if you do that well, then that's good. If you can change up and do that well, that's good. It depends on what you're able to execute. Anything can look good on paper or look good in a meeting room, but it's what you can actually get down on the field. If you can do it well, then it's successful and if you can't do it well, then it's not successful. There are plenty of examples of both, there are tons of examples of both.


**Q:** You've been here for 14 years and Marvin Lewis I think is 11. Longevity in the NFL coaching wise, how do you view that? You're the longest-tenured head coach with the same team and he's the second longest tenured head coach.

**BB:** Yeah. It's kind of surprising, really. It is and it isn't. When I came into the league, that's the way it was: coaches coached for a long time with the same team. They had a consistent program. There was always turnover, but not like there is now where guys coach for a year, year and half and the team makes a change and brings in somebody else. Wheels spin pretty fast in that and along with it goes all the changes – head coaches then therefore coordinators, position coaches. I mean, you go to the Combine and it seems like every year a third of the coaches are wearing a different jacket than they wore the year before when you saw them. From that standpoint, it's a big change from what I was used to, the way I was brought up on the league, brought up in football.

We all know it's a production business; we all know that you're not guaranteed anything for very long. But the way things turnover in this league and in pro sports in general... It turns over pretty fast. It's pretty amazing, really. On the one hand, it seems like a long time given the quick turnover that we have now. On the other hand, given the way I was used to it, it doesn't seem like it should be that way. But it is what it is. Marvin is a good coach. He's done a good job. He's been very consistent.

The last couple years, taking a young team into the playoffs back-to-back years with a rookie quarterback, second-year quarterback last year... He transformed that team over the past few years, won with different guys, won with Carson Palmer, won with... winning now. So they've had different ways of doing it, but the common thread is that he's been there. Mike Brown-Marvin Lewis has been a good owner-coach combination. They've done a good job of acquiring personnel and coaching them and winning games. The consistency says something. We've seen that at other organization like Pittsburgh for example: a lot of success through the years with not a lot of changes.

**Q:** Is there anything that characterizes what Wade Phillips defenses are all about? Is there anything that stands out from his

## defenses in San Diego and Dallas and Houston?

**BB:** Yeah, I think he's pretty much kept the same system through all those. Their 3-4 is really more of a one-gap 3-4 than a two-gap 3-4. They shade those guys and they play a pretty high amount of man coverage, which he's done in the past. It varies a little bit but they play quite a bit of man coverage and then they go to their sub defense which is a dime defense in this case, where they bring in [Quentin] Demps at safety and whoever the third corner is, they've had a couple injuries but whoever that third corner is and move [Glover] Quin down. It's not a myriad of formations and different personnel groupings and all that.

They basically have the same guys on the field for a high percentage of the time. This isn't the most complicated team we've ever seen but what they do, they do well. They're well balanced, they do enough things to keep you off balance to complement what they're doing so they're not just setting one track. They have a lot of multiples and variables but it's contained within the system. They do it every week; you have to deal with it every week. They're not going to let you off the hook, they're going to give you the variables every week, you're going to have to decide how you're going to handle them and sooner or later you're going to see them.

## Q: In what ways have you seen Mike Martz put his imprint on the offense?

**BB:** Everywhere. The way they break the huddle. From there on, it's Mike Martz. They shift. They motion. They use a lot of different formations. They run the concepts that he's always coached - the passing concepts, the running-game concepts they have. Mike has a great set of complementary plays so if you stop one thing, then he's got the complementary play. If you're stopping one, then you're really not going to be able to stop the other. It's always a bit of a guessing game with that. He's got a scheme that's very challenging to everybody on the defense: the coaching staff, the front, the linebackers, the secondary. And, of course, it all goes to the quarterback and Jay's done a great job of executing it, making the reads, seeing the receivers, seeing the things that you need to see in his offense to make it run, and Cutler's done a great job of that.

And at times when things haven't been there, he's been able to get away from the rush, extend the play or make yards and run for first downs, positive yardage and things like that. So, the offense itself is tough and they have a great quarterback running it and a group of explosive players - backs, tight ends, receivers - that give them a lot of weapons to choose from. And they use all of them. Everybody gets the ball; everybody's been productive. It's not the receivers or the tight ends or the backs, it's all of them, and it's the quarterback - he's their leading rusher. You've got to watch out for everybody all the time. That's hard to defend.

**Q:** It used to be that it seemed you annually matched up against Mike Shanahan. Is Norv Turner similar to Mike Shanahan in style?

**BB:** They are both every formation oriented. Norv gives you a lot of different formations. The thing about Norv is the deep ball. He's a great deep ball coordinator, coach, whatever you want to call it. His offense is very effective getting the ball down the field. Their receivers have great height, average per catches. They always have. It's been consistent through the years, even going back to Dallas. It seems like as much as you talk about 'We can't give up the deep ball. We can't give up the deep ball.'

He finds a little different way to scheme it up against you and then you get one up and just about the time that he's catching it, you realize that, 'Uh oh, they kind of got us on this one. We're in a little bit of trouble here.' That really sets up everything else - the running game. The deeper you go to take those plays away, the easier it is for the quarterback to dump the ball off to Gates and Sproles or [LaDainian] Tomlinson, or Emmitt Smith, or whoever it has been. You end up giving up a lot of 10, 15, 20-yard plays that are two-yard passes because everybody is so conscious of the deep ball. You can't let them throw it deep and you can't let them run the ball and you can't send everybody back there and let them screen and check down you to death either. So he does a great job, really, of attacking all the levels: the deep level, the intermediate level, and the line of scrimmage level in the passing game.

They've had some big plays like in the Jacksonville game they hit Sproles coming out of the backfield on an angle route and it goes for 50 yards. It wasn't a long bomb but it was a 50-yard play because they gave Sproles a little too much space and you got loose on the inside part of the defense. That's what he does and he does it consistently. They're at the top of the league in offense and it's easy to see why. Their third-and-10 conversion percentage is 40 percent or whatever it is. That would be a good percentage for a team on all third downs and they get it on third and ten-plus. Rivers does a great job throwing the deep ball. They've got big receivers that can go get it, plus their tight ends are like big receivers, too. Norv does a great job with his scheme. So they're good.

# 6
## SPECIAL TEAMS

**Q: How much emphasis is placed on creating big plays in special teams when you go into a season and how much do those plays swing the momentum either for or against a team?**

**BB:** Well, sure I think those big plays are always good plays for momentum and, you know, just put a little spark into the team. Honestly we're always trying to make them. We've never tried to do anything but make plays. I'd just say the more playmakers you have out there then the better chance you have to make them.

Sometimes you end up with players who are just fulfilling a role out there, which you need that, but when you actually have playmakers, guys in the return game that you can count on to make blocks, or you can put one-on-one to make blocks on their good players, or in coverage guys that can't be single-blocked and have to be double-teamed. If you only have one of those guys then they double team him and you're back to kind of treading water.

If you have more guys than they can handle then whichever ones, one or two they might double, then you've got good opportunities with other players. So, returners that can make plays with the ball in their hand, blockers that can block good players, coverage players that have to be double-teamed and then obviously good specialty play from the snapper, kicker, punter, and punt returner or kickoff returner; those are all the keys.

**Q:** Is there a common denominator in terms of their mentality that allows certain guys to excel on special teams?

**BB:** Well, I don't know if it's a mentality. I mean it is to a degree, the aggressiveness, trying to make plays as opposed to just trying to stay in your area of responsibility. I'd say that just the instinctiveness of being primarily a space player, recognizing how much space there is between you and the runner or how much space you have to defend from the guy you're blocking to where he has to get to the runner, can you get around the guy to the backside to make the play, do you have to go to the front side, or do you have to go through him?

Obviously, the combination of speed and explosiveness, their strength, is the combination that you're looking for. So, if you have to take people on you can take them on and if you can run around them or avoid them you've got the speed to do that as well. So, it's a combination of space ability, speed, power, explosion, quickness, and just judgement in space which is different than making inline judgements or close quarter type decisions. Those space judgements are your speed, their speed, the angle, what's between you and the guy, whether you're blocking or covering.

Those are all kind of instinctive qualities that we coach, we have guidelines on, we try to explain fundamentally what you want to do but each situation's a little bit different. The player has to make that decision as to whether he can make it or not make it and so forth. So, it's a lot of instinctiveness on all of those plays because each one of them is different. You just have to have a good sense and a good feel for where you can get to with your skills versus what obstacles you encounter along the way.

**Q: How much can special teams contributions factor in and push a player on to the roster from the lower end of the depth chart?**

**BB:** 90 percent. I don't know? It could be 100 percent if it's good enough. It's just a question of how good it is relative to what the role is on offense and defense. There's some balance in there, but the more a player can do, the better he can do it, the more value he has. So, if he can only do one thing that's good is that enough? I don't know, it might be, it might not be.

You can't have a whole roster of guys that can do just one thing. Somewhere along the line somebody has to be a role player in offense or defense and play in the kicking game. We just don't have enough roster spots to have all offense, all defense, all special teams. It's not like college where you dress 80 or 90 guys.

## Q: Where would you rate your special teams progression after one preseason game?

**BB:** First of all, I don't think you can really rate anything in preseason. You spend a lot of time in practice and in meetings trying to prepare your team to particularly do the fundamental things in the preseason games that will serve as a base for you throughout the game, no matter what the actual scheme is. Whatever running play you run, it's about the fundamentals of blocking, and whatever defense you play is about the fundamentals of taking on blocks and tackling.

Whatever pass play you run is going to center around getting open and catching the ball. It doesn't really matter what the ratings are. It's more of what are we doing, how can we improve it, are we doing something that doesn't look like it's going to be productive for us, are we not doing enough of something where we think we can find more production? It's really just trying to get better on a daily basis, and if you're better day to day today and then in your games during the week, and again I don't think that's necessarily reflected in the final score. You could score well, but that doesn't necessarily mean you're doing things well.

Or you could not score well and you could be doing things OK. I just think that's really more what it's about. In the kicking game, yeah, we had three penalties - 12 men on the field, we hit their gunner out of bounds and our gunner didn't get back in bounds fast enough when he went out of bounds. So, those are all penalties that we can't afford, that cost us field position, that we can learn from, and hopefully if they don't happen again then these were lessons well learned. They shouldn't have happened in the first place, but they did and we've corrected them. We've made sure everybody understands exactly what we need to do so that we're not in violation of those rules and I think all three calls were good calls - I have no issue with the calls - but what we did allowed them to make the call against us, so we have to not do that or do a better job of it. Maybe we didn't coach it well enough.

So, in any case, we've got to get that corrected along with a lot of other things. We definitely have some things to work with in the kicking game. We looked at a lot of young players. Very many of the players that have played a lot in the kicking game for us or even with some other teams that are on our roster didn't play very much - some didn't play at all in the kicking game against Green Bay.

So this week against New Orleans and going forward, those guys will get more opportunities and we'll start to evaluate them. We wanted to look at a lot of the younger players against Green Bay [and] we did. Some of those guys really helped themselves and showed that they could possibly compete for a role in those units. Some of them didn't show up quite as well and they're going to have to turn that around pretty quickly or we'll run out of time. So, that's where we're at in the kicking game.

**Q: Are kickers different from other players in that they're not really building up to the season; they're already game ready? Just wondering how impressive that field goal was last night, even though it was in mid-August.**

**BB:** I think there is definitely an element of timing and consistency with the kickers, and like every other player pretty much in this league, anybody can go out and there's enough talent for almost all the players in this league to go out there and make a highlight-type of play. That's why they're in this league – they have that type of ability. It really comes down to consistency, and training camp and preseason games are an opportunity for all our players, including our specialists, to build that consistency. I just don't believe in judging players on one play.

I know that's what a lot of other people like to do, but I don't personally believe in that. I think it's a bad way to evaluate players, or a team for that matter. There is going to be a lot of kicks in the season, a lot of punts, a lot of snaps, a lot of punt returns, kickoff returns – all those plays – and preseason games are an opportunity for us to work on our timing and consistency at those positions and that's what those players do. It was a good operation. Steve [Gostkowski] made a really good kick last night, but if it hadn't gone that way, it wouldn't be the end of the world and there will probably [be] one that doesn't go that way just because our timing and execution overall in any phase of the game is not where hopefully it will be in weeks going forward.

It's part of the process and it's part of what training camp and preseason games – the value of those for the building of your team and timing and consistency. There are going to be some good things and there are going to be some things that are not so good. Either way, I don't think it's the end of the world. You build on the ones that are good, you correct on the ones that don't work out as well. And there are going to be those, and you try to learn from those and improve it. We've had highlight plays in practice and we've had plays that weren't very good, and we need to improve those. It's a long haul. There is a lot of work to do, a lot to digest. I wouldn't personally overreact to any one or two plays good or bad, one way or the other. There's a lot more to it than that.

**Q: Specialists have become better, kickers are better from longer distances and punters are stronger. Are all those hidden yards in special teams even harder to come by than they were when you were a special teams coach? Does that make those plays even**

## more vital?

**BB:** I think it kind of evens out. Their punters are better, our punters are better; their kickers are better, our kickers are better. I think it's all relative. But yeah, certainly there's a lot more coaching technique, I'd say, sophistication in the kicking game than what there was 15, 20, 25 years ago, no question, or 35 years ago when I was coaching special teams. A lot of it is the same, but a lot of it is different. Some of the rules have affected it. Also just the evolution of seeing things work, seeing schemes evolve and for lack of a better word, copycatting them. As we've talked about before, when I came into the league, as an example, there was no spread punt. Nobody would spread and if they did, the first thing anybody would do was rush them.

That was because the snappers weren't involved in the protection so you were a guy short. Now every team's snapper is involved in the protection. Every team spread punts, even against rushes. That really, I would say, started when [Steve] DeOssie went to Dallas and they did it with Steve. Other people saw it and found guys and started teaching it and got comfortable with it.

That's a scheme and a thing that's involved – I'm not saying that the snappers are that much better now than they were in the '70s or in the early '80s but once Steve and once that became – Cardinals did it, there were two or three teams doing it – once that was effective then everyone was looking at it saying, 'We should be able to find somebody who can do that. Give us an opportunity to have two split guys and not get them held up from a tight position on the line of scrimmage.' I think there are other things like that, other aspects of the game that have schematically evolved, just like we've seen on offense or defense whether it be blitz-zone schemes or multiple receiver sets and so forth and so on. That's a little bit of an evolution and sophistication of the game.

**Q:** Whether it's Jacoby Jones in the Super Bowl last year or the plays that you guys made in 2001, so many postseason games between evenly matched teams come down to the kicking game. Do you anticipate we'll see the same things over the next few weeks with games turning on that?

**BB:** Well, who knows what the difference in a game in a close game is going to be. But certainly the kicking game is always an important part of every game and any close game, especially when you have points involved, which we have with the field goals but potentially in a return game or blocked kick or that type of thing. Those are kind of bonus points.

I don't think you ever go into the game thinking, 'We're going to get seven points from our punt return team or we're going to get seven points from our kickoff coverage team to recover a fumble and run back for a touchdown.' Those are kind of bonus points you don't really count on. You hope you get a couple of them over the course of the year but statistically that's about what it's going to be. So, a big play in that area is a huge play really because it's like bonus points. I mean really I've always had a great appreciation for the kicking game. I think that I was fortunate when I grew up when Coach [Wayne] Hardin was the coach at Navy, he emphasized the kicking game a lot.

Plays like the quick kick and some plays in the return game and so forth that kind of caught my eye as a kid and always sort of stayed interested in. I had an opportunity to coach it and I think it's one of the great things about football is it brings that third element to the game besides offense and defense. It adds the kicking game, the specialists, all the different rules and strategical situations that can occur on kickoffs, punts and field goals and fakes and all those kind of things, field position plays. I think that's an integral part of the game. Of course, back when the game was invented and even back into the, let's say the '30s and the '40s, [Robert] Neyland at Tennessee and a lot of his disciples followed the old rule of thumb on field position: inside your 10, punt on first down, inside your 20, punt on second down, inside your 30, punt on third down.

You didn't punt on fourth down until you got the ball outside of the 40-yard line, until you got close to midfield. You played defense, you played field position. Of course, we see a lot less kicking now than we saw back then and of course we see the specialists now that we didn't see back then too. So you had the Sammy Baughs of the world, or all the single-wing tailbacks for that matter, that were punters first, runners second and passers third. The game, I would say, has gradually taken the emphasis off of that part of the game but it's still a significant part of the game.

I personally would love to see the kicking game remain as a very integral part of the game so that the kickoffs are returned and so that extra points are not over 99 percent converted because that's not what extra points were when they were initially put into the game back 80 years ago, whatever it was.

**Q:** Would you be in favor of –

**BB:** I would be in favor of not seeing it be an over 99 percent conversion rate. It's virtually automatic. That's just not the way the extra point was put into the game. It was an extra point that you actually had to execute and it was executed by players who were not specialists, they were position players. It was a lot harder for them to do. The Gino Cappellettis of the world and so forth and they were very good. It's not like it is now where it's well over 99 percent. I don't think that's really a very exciting play because it's so automatic.

I don't know how much excitement there is for the fans in a touchback. It's one thing if it's a great kick, it's another thing when, let's just say for example, over half the kicks are out of the end zone, then I wouldn't really say it's a great kick. It's kind of almost a normal part of the game. I personally would love to see those plays be the impact plays that they've been. As you mentioned, where would last year's Super Bowl have been without the 108-yard kickoff return. The play that that added to the game was a spectacular play. I mean forget about who you're rooting for, but just as a fan of the game, it was a spectacular play in the game that I think all fans – unless you're a 49er fan, but you know – that all fans objectively love to see those plays as part of the game.

**Q:** You have such a great voice and command and you've been doing it for so long – I know you just want to coach the football team – but will there be a point in your career when you want to help at the level when you can help shape the game?

**BB:** Right now I'm just trying to help our football team prepare for the playoffs. I'm not here to solve the world's problems. I'm just trying to win a football game.

**Q:** Were punts on first down common back then?

**BB:** Sure. Well, inside your 10, yeah. Inside your 10, sure. Absolutely. That was like [Robert] Neyland's – it was a rule. There was no decision. It was, you're inside your 10, punt on first down and play defense. [You] wouldn't take a chance on turning the ball over if you had bad field position. Again, it was a running game and there were less first downs but that was very – and again, all of his disciples which were numerous, that yeah, I would say back in the '20s, '30s…and then you get the players like Don Hutson that, everybody talks about how great of a receiver he was, and he was, he was the first great receiver in the National Football League, he was a great kicker too.

That was another important part of his job. Back in those days, you had to have a kicker, you had to have a punter and the punter was probably the most important position on a lot of teams. That kind of took priority over, like I said, passing or running for the single-wing tailbacks for us.

**Q:** You mentioned not being able to count on getting seven points out of your special teams on a weekly basis. But was there something about that 2001 team that maybe gave you an idea that you can't count on it but there was something different about that team in terms of their special teams ability?

**BB:** I think anytime you have a unit on your team that's playing well you hope you're going to get production from them, whether it's your offense scoring a lot of points, whether it's your defense creating turnovers and scoring points, whether it's your special teams creating field position or scoring points. I'm not saying that they all impact the game. You can make a big play in the kicking game and it not result in actual points on that play but it could lead to points, like LeGarrette's [Blount] returns did. Those weren't scoring plays but they led to points or vice versa.

It's no different than having a good kickoff coverage play and then you go down there and make a stop on defense and then you get the ball back at midfield and you're knocking on the door again. Kind of like what happened in the Baltimore game. We made the fourth down stop and then we punted and they returned it and they were on the 35-yard line or whatever it was. I'm just saying it's hard to create runs in football. You see them all the time in basketball, as an example, but in football they're harder to create. The way you create them is you score, you have a good kickoff coverage play, then you get a stop or a turnover on defense, then you score again, then you have another good kickoff coverage play.

That gives you an opportunity to be able to string a few points together. Conversely, if you can make a play on the kickoff return, it really does a lot to negate your opponent from being able to create that momentum. Even if you don't score, if you have a good return, you make a first down or you don't make a first down, you punt the ball to them, they're 80 yards away from the goal line, statistically that's a hard place to score from. Not that we don't see those drives, but percentage-wise it's a hard place to score from: 80, 85 yards away from the goal line.

I think those plays are huge momentum plays and the field position eventually, statistically, will result in the point differential. They're huge plays. But they don't always result in scores. But I'm just saying the ones that do result in scores: interceptions for touchdowns, fumbles for touchdowns, kick returns for touchdowns, blocked punts for touchdowns, at the end of the year, how many of those are there on average in the league? A couple a team. So, if you get one that's points that you generally don't get so it's great to get them.

**Q:** Do you coach when the right time is to take a risk like you said with the touchback being so common that somebody is eight yards deep in the end zone, now might be the right time or look to take it out? Do you and Scott O'Brien coach that?

**BB:** Yeah, we do. Of course we do, we definitely, yeah. It's not just do whatever you feel like doing.

**Q:** Or trust the returner's instincts.

**BB:** I would say that the way that it is in the National Football League now, I would say for the most part if you have confidence in your returner and your kickoff return team, what's the downside to bringing it out? They get you on the 15, they get you on the 16, wherever they get you. You don't get back to the 20-yard line so you lose a couple yards of field position, whatever that's going to be, three, four, five yards. But you get the opportunity to make a big play.

You get an opportunity to get the ball to your returner and if you feel confident about your return team then that's what you're willing to risk. You're willing to risk a couple yards of field position for an opportunity to return. The other thing I would say is a little bit overrated in my opinion is how the deep the ball is in the end zone. Everybody wants to talk about, 'Well, it's three yards deep, it's four yards deep, it's seven yards deep, it's two yards deep.' That's true and that's great but that doesn't say anything about the amount of time the ball's in the air. The hang time of the kick is, to me, more about than the depth of the kick.

You put a ball nine yards deep in the end zone with 3.8 hang time, I don't see any problem bringing that out. You put a ball one yard deep in the end zone with 4.5 hang time, that's a whole different ballgame. Again, that's where it comes into judgment by your returners, by your short returner who is helping your deep returner gauge how deep he is, how long the ball is in the air and again, how fast the coverage team is. Not all teams cover at quite the same rate. Some teams have faster guys, some guys have bigger guys: more linebacker, tight end, fullback types.

Other teams have more DB, safety, corner types. I mean there are a lot of things that come into play there but I think that the general rule of bringing the ball out of the end zone or not is to me, is saying how deep it is in the end zone is missing 50 percent of the boat. I think that the hang time of the kick is as much, if not more, important than the depth of the kick. I would say to a certain extent also where the returner has to go to get the ball.

It's another thing for the returner to have to run sideways and handle the ball versus being able to catch the ball coming straight ahead, step into it and create his momentum back up the field, which again, a good returner can negate or pick up, I would say, some extra yardage there by his timing of the catch and his momentum going forward versus catching it over his shoulder, going sideways or going backwards or whatever it is then that's just like added hang time.

**Q:** You just never know what the makeup of your team is going to turn out to be. Is that a learning process throughout the season and all of the on and off field that's happened with this roster it seems like they've weathered it a lot better than maybe the 2009 team?

**BB:** I think it's an ongoing process. I think it starts the first day of OTAs and the first day of training camp and goes all the way through the season. Really your roster is constantly evolving, even if it isn't evolving it's evolving because your younger players as they spend more time on the roster and their role becomes let's just say bigger, in some cases, not all or as the roles shift on your team from week to week or through the course of the season based on whether it be injuries or performance or whatever it happens to be that it's constantly evolving.

The chemistry and your team relationships are changing throughout the course of the year. When do you know what it is? I don't know. I'd say certainly you know a lot more by midseason than you know in May or August or September, let's put it that way, because you've been through it more.

You've been more battle tested. You've been through more weeks of preparation. You've been through more real games, regular season games. You've been through more whatever ups and downs, whatever challenges your team faces over that period of time, which every team faces a number of them. You get a better feel for individually and collectively they'll deal with those. I don't know if there's a set date but you certainly know a lot more about your team I would say in midseason, let's just call it the seventh, eighth game whenever that is – end of October, early November – than what you know in September or August or the spring, which is why so many of the early predictions are usually so far wrong because nobody knows.

You see teams that finish at the bottom of the league one year finish at the top of the league next year. You see teams that finish at the top of the league one year finish at the bottom of the league the next year. That's because there are so many changes and variables that occur during a football season that until they occur you just don't know how it's going to go.

**Q: I noticed you signed another separate long snapper. When did the position become someone who only snapped as opposed to a player who played another position as well?**

**BB:** I'd say probably by the '90s.

**Q:** What is the perceived skill? Why would you use a player who doesn't have other responsibilities, rather than someone like Rob Ninkovich.

**BB:** I think the risk that you run is when you have a regular player doing something like that, if something were to happen to them, then who is the replacement? It's such a key position that it's hard to have two people who are regular players to do it, let alone one. The snapping end of it, I think the guy who really changed the game was [Steve] DeOssie. When Dallas had him, they went to the spread punt formation. He was able to snap and block. Prior to that, most teams kept their ends tight at least against rushing looks.

When they brought 10 guys up to rush, they would bring them in tight and Dallas got to really the spread punt and the center snapped and blocked which up to that point was very unusual. Some teams tried to do it even from closed formations. He was able to do it and once people saw him able to do it then they felt like it could be done, which I'm not sure that collectively coaches felt that way.

**Q:** Like Guy Morriss here, he was the first one to only snap.

**BB:** The difference with Steve [DeOssie] was they were able to spread the ends and he was able to snap and block so it was eight against eight in protection. I'd say up until that point, it was usually nine against ten. You only had nine blockers, the center wasn't responsible for a man, so you had nine blockers against a ten man rush. Once they split the ends out then that cleared it up for the punt team because you only had to block eight instead of 10 and if your center could get one and when they start looping and twisting and getting out there wide and everything – it's not that easy.

It became more of a premium to where if you could get a snapper to snap the ball accurately and block then it certainly takes a lot of pressure off your punt protection and it helps your punt coverage. Especially in this league where you can't release them downfield until the ball is kicked inside. When you have to bring those guys in tight, and then they jam at the line of scrimmage and then you get nobody down there. That was a big change in the game and that was in the mid '80s. But I'd say by the '90s, then most teams went with a pure long snapper.

Even the teams that had them before that, like when Steve was with Dallas and later with the Giants, they just weren't doing the things that he and then his successors did. In a lot of respects, Steve really changed, in my opinion, he changed the punting game in the National Football League and ultimately in college as well. He was the first one that really allowed teams to do that. People copied it and then other snappers came along, and guys like the Todd Christensen's of the world who were regular players and good snappers were ultimately replaced by the 'specialists'.

Of course, as the rosters expanded, then that made it easier to be able to afford to carry a snapper – and also returners, all the specialists. When I came into the league in the mid-70's there were very few specialists – a lot of kickers or punters or returners and snappers also played other positions. Progressively through the years, the kickers and the punters, they started to have their own positions and then snappers and now in a lot of cases returners, that's all those guys do is return. Some of them play other positions but snappers, kickers and punters now are pretty much their own exclusive club.

**Q: Why have coaches gone to the decision where a separate player has to be a long snapper as opposed to training someone else on the team to take that role?**

**BB:** I think, really, that's just the way of the world now. It certainly didn't used to be like that, but you can say the same thing about the other positions as well. It wasn't that long ago, at least in our lifetime, where you had punters that did other things besides punt. You had kickers that did other things besides kick, and you had snappers that played in a different position other than long snapping. But, you don't see it much in college and that's where our players come from, [so] you don't see it too much professionally.

When you can afford that situation, then you can certainly actually have an extra player, if you will, on the team, but really, no team has it to speak of, or very marginally if they do. It was not that long ago where, even on the Pro Bowl squads, where if you didn't have a long snapper on your team, [then] you were allowed to add one, but, really, nobody would have one, so they just include it as a separate position. That's really, I'd say, been in the last five, eight years. So, it's definitely a different skill.

I think there are some issues with it even though a lot of players did it in the past. I'm not diminishing that at all. You take players that play other positions like offensive line or linebacker [and] they wear the big pads and the things they need to play their position - to play center or guard or middle linebacker or nose, whatever the position is, tight end even - where some of the deep snappers have come from in the past and just to try and do it with that type of equipment is limiting.

I think there are a lot of things that play into it. If everybody's roster was 35 players and you had to do it, I think you'd find someone that could do it, especially with the rules now about hitting the center. I think that's made it a little bit different for the position compared to what it was before those rules were in place. Really, the interesting things about that is, not only are they just pure snappers, but I'd say in a high percentage of the cases in punt returns, those players aren't even blocked.

The returns are set up so that those guys aren't even accounted for. They're blocking all the other guys except that one. So, literally, they're snapping and, I'd say, overall over the league, they have a minimal impact in the coverage game. It truly is a specialty. But if you can do it well, you can have a 10-year career. You don't have to do a whole lot else. You can just do that well and have a 10-year career, maybe longer.

## Q: What is the impact of losing a player who is a 'big 4' player on special teams versus a starter or a full-time guy?

**BB:** That's the issue on special teams. When you lose a player on special teams, you really lose a starter on four teams at least. Sometimes you have one person that can replace that player so it's player A in for player B. But a lot of times you have a combination of players where you either have to move somebody around or you use more than one player to replace that guy.

It just depends on the player, but that's the challenge on special teams as a special teams coach, especially when it happens during the game. You lose somebody and then, 'Ok, it's the kickoff team, the kickoff return team, the punt team, the punt return team.' It's hard during the game, usually, to have one player that does all four of those. Maybe the next week if that player is out if you have one person that can do that, you might be able to do that and make that guy active. But normally during the game you end up having to juggle some balls there. 'Ok you're in on this team. You're in on that team. You're in on something else. You're in here, but now you're moving to there.' It's one of those deals.

That's why we try to use guys at different positions all through training camp, work them at different positions in practice. A lot of times on your punt team you have maybe one guy on the inside and he's the first guy in, so if you lose any of your interior people he'll be the first guy in and you bump somebody else over or he plays all the way across the board. And then you have your first gunner and then on the punt return maybe the same thing: one inside guy, one end, one vice guy, that type of deal. There are some moving parts there. It's definitely challenging.

**Q:** Obviously you've had some special teams production the last few games. Can you talk a little bit about what kind of game change that presents for this team going forward?

**BB:** We all know how important the kicking game is. We put a lot of emphasis on it with the players. I think Scott O'Brien does a tremendous job. I think he's as good a coach as any coach I've ever coached with. We try to be good at it every week. It's a combination of scheme and individual fundamentals and technique. Of course it always comes down to the specialists. If your returners and your kickers and your snappers - if those guys do a good job, then you gave a chance to be good.

If they don't do a good job, then it's hard for the other 10 guys to overcome that. It's hard to be a good punting team if you can't punt. It's hard to be a good return team if you can't return. The specialists play an important part of it, but at the same time, you have to have a core group of guys to go with them. I think as the season goes on, the weather, I think, usually affects the kicking game before it affects anything else: the passing game or the running game, whether it be wind or moisture or temperature or whatever. It affects how far the ball goes, what direction it goes in, how high it's up there and so forth. That's always a big part of the game, too, the conditions and how it affects the kicking game first and then the passing game second. All those are challenging.

**Q:** You've had guys like Sam Aiken or Larry Izzo in the past that have been special teams captains or almost been like assistant coordinators. Do you have anybody who has kind of assumed that role this year?

**BB:** I don't really think there is anybody I would put in that category. But Larry Izzo is off the charts. We're lucky we had one Larry Izzo, let alone try to have two of them. As far as a leader and a special teams captain and a playmaker and as productive a player as Larry was in his career in that role and the leadership that he gave in it was just exceptional. I've never been on another team that really had anybody at that category. So anything below that could be really good, he was just exceptional. But I don't really see that this year yet. We're still growing and we're still coming together.

But there really haven't been one or two individuals that have just stood out in that area. Our specialists are still pretty young. Stephen [Gostkowski] has the most experience, but Zoltan [Mesko] is a rookie and Jake [Ingram] is in his second year, so those guys are part of it. A lot of our core players are young players as well. And we have a lot of guys that play on one or two teams who are good special teams players, but they don't play on all of them, like [Patrick] Chung and guys like that that a year ago they were on everything but this year they're not. They're only on some selected teams.

That's [Alge] Crumpler and [Rob] Gronkowski on kickoff return, guys like that. [Jerod] Mayo on the punt team - guys that are just on one or two teams that are important guys, but it's hard for them to be the core four-team guy when they're only on one or two of them. I think it's a good group. I think they work well together and they've been productive, but it just doesn't have that dynamic of there's the one flag carrier. At least not yet.

**Q:** I remember hearing that whenever you have a special teams score, it results in the team winning the game something like 90 percent of the time. Are you familiar with that?

**BB:** It's a high percentage. I think anytime you get what I would call 'bonus points,' whether it's a defensive score or special teams score, the correlation between that and winning is high. I'm not sure if it's 90 percent, but it's definitely high. In the National Football League, when you have roughly half of the games being decided by a touchdown or less, if you can get those seven points that basically you can't count on, but when you get those bonus points, that tilts a lot of games right there. There's no question those are huge plays, whether they come on defense or special teams. There's just not a lot of them, so if you can come up with one, that give you a big edge. Statistically anyway, it gives you a big edge in the chances to come out on top.

**Q: Pierre Woods has been your leading tackler on special teams. Does his production on special teams get noted and does it help a guy get on the field more?**

**BB:** Oh absolutely. It's interesting, a lot of players think that their role on offense and defense - if they're not starters - their role on offense or defense comes first and then the role on special teams is secondary. It's actually just the reverse of that. When a player has a significant role in the kicking game, then as an offensive or a defensive coach, as an assistant coach and when you're putting together a game plan, you absolutely know that those players are going to be available at the game. And whatever role they have on offense or defense, you absolutely know they'll be available to do that, versus if you set up a role for somebody else, maybe you think they're a good player on offense or defense, but they don't have a role in the kicking game, then they can't get active for the game then they have no role on offense and no role on defense.

So actually, a player's best way to develop a role on offense and defense is to either excel in that area or have a role in the kicking game, which then makes them available for a more significant role on offense and defense. At least that's the way I've always looked at it and that's the way we approach it here. It's interesting how that works. A lot of times you have better offensive or defensive players who are inactive for the game, or maybe not even on your team because of other players who are better in the kicking game because you need players in that role for your active roster on Sunday. Then that leads to more opportunities on the offensive and defensive side of the ball. Pierre's played defense for us in the past and he's done it at different times during the year this year, as have players like Patrick Chung, Sam Aiken, Brandon McGowan and guys like that.

Sometimes those roles change a little bit from week to week, but they're definitely important and when the whole package gets put together, as to who's going to be at the game, who's going to play, who's going to contribute, some of those players that contributed in the kicking game contributed on offense and defense, and some of the players whose primary roles are on offense or defense have to contribute in the kicking game. That's part of what putting together a team is about.

**Q:** Given how important it is to have depth in certain positions on game day, why wouldn't you want a position player to just handle snapping? Why has it become so specialized because it seems like it just takes up a roster spot?

**BB:** It gets into a bind there. One, is the skill level of it. Two, is the injury factor and, three, is just the ... I think there are some other smaller things that add into it. For example, if you look at these offensive linemen, you just look at them out there on the field, they've got shoulder pads on that would protect them from an 18-wheeler, so then to be able to have the flexibility and the motion to be able to bring their arms over their head and snap the ball through the legs and all that when they have pads that are that restrictive, that's a problem.

Little things like that. As specialization has increased at the NFL level it's also increased at the other levels: college and even in high school. You go to a high school game now and a lot of times, you see the team's best player do everything, but there are other players that - they have their own snapper, they have their own punter, they got their own kicker, they've got a guy that just does that, so those guys improve and they can be more competitive at the next level. But it's definitely a roster consideration. Another thing is the injury factor. Now again, I understand in the 60's and the 70's the guy snapped, he played linebacker, he caught passes, returned kicks - that's just the way it was.

We've seemed to evolve into a different stage here, but you have a snapper in there who plays linebacker and he's out for a couple series with a sprained ankle, now who snaps? You really need two snappers now, not one. That's a consideration, too. It's a consideration on the holding. A lot of teams used to use backup quarterbacks. Even in some cases, wide receivers as holders. Same thing, you have a punter, a snapper and a kicker that can spend an hour a day working on that timing and that skill and you have a quarterback who at the end of practice comes over and holds 10-15 kicks. If you've got a punter that can do it, you probably have a better operation with him doing it along with the fact that a quarterbacks out for a series with a sprained ankle, so who's your next holder?

So you come down to the player of the game and you don't know who your holders going to be on a key play like that. If you can afford it, I think you do it. If you can't afford it, if the roster was 36, 38, there would be some cutoff there that you would have to start doing that. You cut it down far enough and you end up with two-way football, but that's specialization. I don't know if the fans would want to see that or don't want to see that. That's an interesting question. Do they want to see 50 guys out there playing or do they want to see 30 that they know and can keep track of?

**Q: If you have to make a change at holder on the field goal operation, how significant is that? Is that something after a couple days of practice, you feel confident going into the game if you had to?**

**BB:** Whatever we have to do, we'll do. Again, our players, from day one, know that – I mean, everyone is responsible for more than one position. We just can't have the luxury of a backup for every single spot. Especially when you look at the kicking game, you have basically 66 different starters on those six units there, in addition to offense and defense. That's part of everybody's job is to be responsible for more than one, or in some cases, multiple positions. Who knows who is going to be called on to do what when? Like Steve [Gostkowski] had to punt last week.

Again, that's part of the NFL. You don't have that many guys on your roster and you need to be able to compete in the game and function with guys that can't go. I think we've prepared for every situation we can prepare for. That goes all the way back to training camp or in the spring when we have guys playing multiple positions where sometimes there's a perception that we're moving a guy. But we're not moving anybody necessarily, we're trying to build our depth for him and our team. You get into a situation at this time of year, sometimes those things pay off.

# Punt/ Punt Return

**Q:** What did you see on Danny Amendola's kick return to start the second half in terms of his decision making after he fielded the ball and what the guys up front were doing to help him along the way?

**BB:** We had good blocking on the return. Danny [Amendola] did a good job of setting up the blocks. We had two double-team blocks on the play and both of those doubles were very good. We got the three and the four both kind of moved out of there so there was quite a bit of space. [We] did a good job on the kickoff blocks. [Barkevious] Mingo and [Patrick] Chung had big blocks on the back side to get Danny through and Danny did a nice job of running – broke a couple tackles, beat the kicker. There was a little traffic there where he couldn't really just get through clean at the end. I think they got him on like the 20-yard line, but again, a well-executed play.

I think we've had several of those set up, not several, but we've had a few of those set up that looked like they would be pretty good, but we didn't get a chance to return them because they were touchbacks against teams like Pittsburgh that touchback a lot. I thought we might have a chance to get started and I think the players really worked hard and felt like this week with [Dan] Carpenter that we would have a better chance to actually get a chance to return the ball and bring it out, which we did. They did an excellent job of blocking, and as I said, Danny set those blocks up well and then did a good job of finishing the run.

**Q:** In fielding the ball at the three-yard line, I'm assuming there's really no choice but to field the ball?

**BB:** Well I think you saw Buffalo do that – let the ball hit on the two-yard line and bounce in. Right?

**Q:** Is it generally too risky there to let the ball bounce?

**BB:** We almost always want to catch the ball, regardless of where it is. Once it hits the ground, there are a lot of things that could happen. The ball takes a lot of funny bounces, it's not a round ball, so we want to try to handle the ball when we can handle it. Decision making at that position is a big part of the position. Some of it's the returner, some if it's the short returner. They have to work together on that. But it's also a function of the hang time of the kick and the direction of the kick. For example, if the ball is kicked to the right and you have a left return on, the depth of the ball might be a little bit different. Your judgement and rules on that might be a little bit different than it would be if it was kicked right on a right return as an example.

Again, there are a number of factors that come into play but in the end, decision making and ball handling are the most critical things on that play along with not getting penalized. Unless you have good ball handling and don't get a penalty – if you get a penalty, you're not going to have a long return, or a good return for that matter. If you don't handle the ball well, your chances of having a good return are very much diminished because the timing of the play now is off. If you can handle the ball, make good decisions and not get penalized, you at least have a chance. If those things are bad then you pretty much have no chance to have a good play or have good field position.

**Q: In defending a play like yesterday's when the punter dropped the ball and ran for 16 yards, what is the fundamental coaching technique for those players so that can be avoided?**

**BB:** I'd say there are a couple things involved for. One, that wasn't unexpected, we actually practiced that play last week in practice. That honestly wasn't – I don't think anybody was surprised by what happened. I think just the particular call that we had on and just the way the play unfolded led to a favorable play for them and a bad play for us. I think it starts with coaching. We've got to do a better job of coaching that play. We can't let that happen. We can't get the fourth-and-13 and not end up with the ball on the next play.

It starts with me. We've got to do a better job of coaching. We've got to take care of that and we will. With the players, there's always an awareness. Sometimes, they can be put in a tough spot of trying to stop a guy from going downfield and also having vision on the punter and the play so I think that could be better.

It could certainly be better coached, so it's like a combination of the two. In all honesty, there was some good fortune involved on that, again, the way the way the play turned out. But again, that's our fault. We created an opportunity and they took advantage of it. That's just not good enough on our end. It's really a combination. It should never happen, but it happened and we've got to keep that from happening again.

**Q: We know that certain positions have their own positional coach. Where do placekickers turn for that level of expertise? Do the special teams coaches have a level of knowledge about placekicking despite the fact they themselves may not have been kickers in the past?**

**BB:** I certainly get where you're coming from. I don't think that's the case here. I can't speak for other teams. I think Joe [Judge] is very knowledgeable about the techniques of kicking. I know when I became a special teams coach and coached special teams for many years as an assistant coach and I continue to be involved with it as a head coach, but for many years as an assistant coach that's one of the things I had to learn. I had to learn how to coach those individual specialists; the snappers, the kickers, the punters, the returners. I don't think it's any different than coaching any other position.

Things you don't know you need to learn and the things you do know you need to be able to teach to the players, however you've acquired that information. And some of that certainly comes from the players, especially when you coach good players at the position that you're coaching. You can learn a lot from them just like I learned a lot from many of the players that I coached going back to people like Dave Jennings as a punter or Carl Banks or Lawrence Taylor or

Pepper [Johnson], guys like that as linebackers for the Giants. However you acquire that information you acquire it. You have to be able to convey it and teach it to the players and recognize technique or judgement.

I mean look, there's a whole host of things that go into performance but all of the things that are related to those, but you know, be able to figure out which ones are the most important, which ones need to be corrected and so forth, but I think Joe is very knowledgeable in that, as was Scott O'Brien. I've had a lot of experience with that myself. But that's what coaching is. If you don't know it then you've got to find out. Nobody knows everything.

I mean no coach knows everything about every position. Maybe if a guy has played it for a decade he might be well-versed in that position but I'd say for the most of the rest of us that haven't done that, things you don't know you've got to learn. You've got to find out. You've got to figure it out.

**Q: You guys have fumbled three punts in the last four games. Is that ultimately an individual responsibility or is there more to it than just the guy who fumbled the ball?**

**BB:** Well, two of the plays were muffs where the ball wasn't caught cleanly. The one last week we had possession of the ball. That could happen on any play. It wasn't the catching of the punt. It was running with the ball, so I'd say that would go in a little different category. In the end we've got to handle the ball cleanly on the exchange and get possession of the ball. That's the first job of the punt return or kickoff return team when you put them on the field is to gain possession of the ball. That's number one; we've got to do that.

**Q:** When you look at muffed punt, do you look into factors like blocking that could have given the returner more space to make the catch?

**BB:** In the end, each punt is different, each play is different, so there are no two things that are the same, but at some point the coverage is going to be down on the returner. I mean it could be a great hang-time punt, it could be good coverage, it could be not great blocking, but if the punter hangs the ball up in the air long enough the coverage is going to be down there, so there are going to be situations where you can never just say, 'OK we're going to eliminate everybody in coverage.' It's just impossible.

At some point that's going to happen. At some point there are going to be situations where the coverage isn't down there, there will be some grey area, there will be some [punts] where the coverage definitely is, and that's part of the returner or returners if you happen to be in a two-deep situation like on kickoff returns bringing the ball out of the end zone or on punt returns where you have two deep, then you have a communication element involved between the two players.

If you only have a single player back there then that's part of his responsibility is to make that decision. I mean I don't know how you could ever take the decision making part out of it. If the ball is short or if the ball is up in the air long enough, there is no way to prevent the coverage from getting down there. It's just impossible.

**Q:** With Australian punters coming into the league, has the teaching and philosophy of when to field punts changed, or do you still tell your returners to stand on the 10-yard line and if it goes over your head let it go?

**BB:** That's a really good question and I think there are a lot of factors that go into the coaching of that positon and that situation that you described, but among the things that the returner has to consider is where the ball is being punted from and how close the coverage is to him and how apt they are or what kind of position they're in to be able to down those balls. We've all seen a lot of plays where the returner runs out of the way and the coverage player comes down there, turns around and catches the ball on the three-yard line or whatever.

I think it's definitely a challenging situation. First of all, it's a lot different when a punter punts the ball from his own 40 and the ball is carrying 55 yards and hits on the five-yard line from when he's on your 40 and the ball is being punted straight up in the air and it comes down on the five-yard line. The trajectory of the ball and as you mentioned the technique of punting it where it has a backspin if you will or kicked in a way that it's less likely to bounce forward, then you've got to think about catching the ball inside the 10 as opposed to letting it be downed on the one or two and the chances of it going into the end zone are probably not very good. So, there is that whole situation.

I think a good returner can tell by the way the ball is traveling, not that you can predict at 100 percent, but you can get a pretty good idea if it's going to bounce or if it's going to kick backwards based on the way the ball is spinning. So that can play into it. The wind can play into it. And then there is the whole philosophy like we talked about before with kickoff returners that if you have a great returner, and you handle the ball, assuming that you don't fumble it, that you handle the ball in that kind of situation, what's the risk and what's the reward. You might lose a few yards of field position versus giving that player an opportunity to return a kick and possibly make a big play.

So are you willing to trade a few yards of field positon for an opportunity at an explosive play and handling the ball, and I think that a lot more returners are given the green light on that maybe than what they were in decades earlier let's call it. I think that's part of the equation, too, taking your returner out of the game just because the ball goes inside the 10-yard line, not saying that's wrong, but it's also a decision you're making to limit the playmaking ability of potentially one of your explosive players.

Long answer to a short question, a lot of different factors, I think every team probably gives their returner certain guidelines. I think the more trust and confidence and experience that player has, the more willing you are to let him make the right decision based on the actual kick and what happens on that play as opposed to just a generic set of rules. And then there are some situations that are cut and dry, depending on the score, time and situation of the game, there is not really a decision to make. Here's the way it is and we follow those rules. But it's certainly an interesting point of discussion, and I don't know that there's any right or wrong answer to it other than whatever has been identified and communicated to the returner by the team. But there is certainly variability on that subject.

**Q: Do you coach players to score if they have a chance on an onside kick? It looked like Rob Gronkowski wanted to do that.**

**BB:** Well again, it depends on the situation in the game. In that particular situation with the Colts out of timeouts and the amount of time that was left in the game, all we had to do was kneel on the ball, so you don't want to take any needless opportunities or chances in trying to advance the ball. Ball possession really wins the game in that situation. But again I think that play was a little bit unusual because Rob was moving forward. He kind of made the play on the run so it might have been a little more awkward for him to go down than to just catch it and keep moving forward.

The most important thing in that play is obviously just ball security, is securing possession of that ball. A lot of times it's going to the ground and securing it, but on that particular one it was probably actually easier for him to do it the way he did, and he handled it very cleanly. Those are the plays we talk about a lot. They don't come up all that frequently for any individual team. Maybe if you watched all the games over the weekend, you'd probably see a couple of them every weekend, but for your individual team, when that play comes up, it's kind of a game-winning play. It's kind of like the Hail Mary pass that goes into the end zone – if you defend it you win and if you don't you lose.

The onside kick is maybe not quite that dramatic, but it's pretty close so if you can make that play then you can run out the clock and end the game and if you can't make it they have that chance to score and you've got to stop them on defense. The execution of that play is critical when it comes up. It just doesn't happen all that often. But when it does, everything you've done in the previous 59 minutes all hinges on the execution of that one play.

**Q:** It might be overlooked because of the result, but what role did Ryan Allen's actual kick play in what happened?

**BB:** It wasn't overlooked; it's the most important part of the play. That is the play. That was a big emphasis point, for Ryan especially in those conditions, with the wind to get the ball up there, not so much for the wind to carry it but just to get the ball up there to make it hard to handle. That's a tough ball when it's high. People are around you, there's wind, it's knuckling a little bit, it's cold, which a cold ball is a little bit harder to catch anyway. Just to make that as difficult as possible.

We got the play at the end of the half on another mishandled ball into the wind, but with the wind, the hang time, the difficulty of the catch is, I mean, that's just what you try to do as a punt team is put pressure on the returner with your coverage, with your kicking, whether it's making them run for the ball or putting it up in the air. You try to pressure that specialist. I thought on the flip side of it, Julian [Edelman] did an excellent job of handling those balls on our end, which they did the same thing. They got them up there and there was some traffic and with the wind, against the wind, inside the 10 or around the 10-yard line, some tough judgment decisions.

That's another one too. You're back there on the punt and it's high and the ball is drifting. That ball wasn't but the whole idea of is it inside the 10, is it outside the 10? You kind of lose track of it in a situation like that it's a little bit harder to judge rather than just on a normal day where you can plant yourself somewhere and it's over your head [or] it's not over your head. Now it starts drifting and then it forces another part of the decision. I wouldn't minimize that at all. I would say it's the most important part of the whole play. If that ball wasn't as high and difficult to handle as it was, then it probably would have been caught.

**Q:** There were a few snaps were the ball moved in the wind. Are you learning a lot about Ryan Allen's hands?

**BB:** Ryan has good hands, yeah. I don't think that's ever been an issue. He has good hands. I'd say overall, for the most part, not 100 percent, but for the most part, a lot of our punters here have had good hands. But again, it's kind of like throwing the ball in these conditions. When you get into November, December, January, ball-handling is crucial or could be. Not every day is like the Denver game but ball-handling is crucial.

There's nothing more important – this might sound stupid but there's nothing more important for a punter than hands because without good hands, handling the ball and being able to place and drop the ball properly on your foot, no matter how strong your leg is, you're not going to be able to punt consistently. You can't really be a good punter, not a really good punter, if you don't have good hands. So, the Dave Jennings and the Tom Tupas and guys like that I've coached that were, even [Sean] Landeta, those guys had really good hands, not only catching the ball and handling the snaps but being able to place the ball properly on their foot so that they could have the contact that they needed to punt it. I don't think, when you're evaluating a punter, one thing you don't want really is a punter that doesn't have good hands.

It's just hard to punt the ball consistently – no matter how strong the guy's leg is – if he's not a smooth ball handler. That also comes in play as a holder too, which that's something that Ryan didn't do but has done and has done a good job of. That's something that's had to gain experience in and learn to do but I think he has the hands and the ball skills to do it. Look, punting is kind of like passing. It's not like being on a pitcher's mound or being on the driving range and just teeing it up with nothing around and throwing the fastball or teeing off whenever you feel like it. You have to handle the ball, you have to deal with the rush and then there are a few punts where you're backed up and you're looking for hang time and distance but there are plenty of punts where that's not the case. You're trying to kick the ball but not kick it into the end zone. Or you're trying to kick the ball based on what tendencies they have on their return, maybe away from the return or to where your gunner is singled or whatever the strategy is.

There's a lot of situational punting that comes up for the punter that, honestly nobody ever talks about. But it's way more than 50 percent of the game. It's not just standing back there and hitting the ball and see how high and far you can hit it. Those are, it's like drives, those are a few shots on a round of golf but you're hitting a lot of other shots that aren't drives off the tee box. I think that's what a punter's job is, but that's really a small percentage of it. That's what they would all like it to be, but that's really a small percentage of it. Hands are huge, huge. Jennings probably [was] as good as anybody – well Tom Tupa. Jennings and Tupa [were] as good as anybody.

**Q: The coffin corner kick seems to be almost nonexistent now. What are your thoughts on the evolution of that aspect of the game and situational punting, and the art of angling the punts out of bounds deep in opponent territory?**

**BB:** That's really an interesting question. That's a trend that has kind of changed gradually through the years. Now it's, as you said, almost extinct. Similar to the punt formations that I saw when I came into the league which almost never had detached guys, split receivers, gunners, like we call them now and how that evolved to tight punt to one split guy to two split guys to now where you almost never see the gunners in tight unless you have the situation like we did where you're punting with a two-score lead with under two minutes to go in the game or something like that.

I think the Aussie style punting, the ability to kind of put backspin on the ball, to have the ball hit and generally bounce back away from the goal line is just a higher percentage than trying to angle it for the corners. Also, angling those corner kicks is also a little bit of an issue in protection because now you're not protecting the punter where you normally are to try to walk right down the middle behind the center. You're kind of shortening the edge, you either have to catch the ball behind the center and then walk to the angle to shorten the edge or you have to offset a couple yards to one side so that when you kick the ball it's behind the center but now the center has to snap it a couple yards sideways.

I don't want to say it's tricky, but it's definitely a little bit different going with the corner and it just seems like the punters now are more experienced and they're coming in with a better, they do a better job of executing the Aussie style punts with the end over end where the ball a lot of times hits and comes away from the goal line, fewer touchbacks than they are just directional punting in general, specifically directional with the coffin corner. You hate to see that art, as you put it, lost from the game but you don't see it much anymore. Now you see a lot of guys and [Dolphins punter Brandon] Fields is a good example of that, not so much in Sunday's game but over the course of the year.

Of course, he kicks in pretty good conditions. [Giants punter Steve] Weatherford is another guy that's a good directional punter, that a lot of their punts land out of bounds or a yard or two from the sideline that really pins the returner back. Those guys have so much confidence and they're so good at doing that. They don't have those shank punts that if you're trying to put it on the sideline and you hit it off the side of your foot and it's a 15, 20-yard punt but if you do it right and you hit the ball right, then it's a 50-yarder but no return which would obviously lead the league every year if you could be consistent on that. Those guys are pretty good at it.

I think there's still an element of that directional kicking but it's certainly not what it used to be and it's changed a little bit. I think the other part about the Aussie punting is it forces the returner to make that decision around the 10-yard line or wherever the ball comes down. Those guys try to drop it down in the five or 10-yard line area now the returner has to make decisions whether to catch it, whether to let it go, handle the ball if it's less than ideal conditions and also the possibility of having guys kind of standing right there when he catches it to distract him or be ready to get on the ball if he muffs. Whereas, as you know, when you coffin corner it, it takes the returner out of play. I think the combination of all those things is why it's shifted the way it has.

**Q:** Julian Edelman said the thing that helps him the most on punt returns is getting a good read as soon as the ball is in the air of the blockers in front of him. What makes him so good and what goes into a unique punt returner?

**BB:** A punt returner can't be watching the guys run down the field when he's catching the ball but while the ball is in the air there's a short amount of time there, a second or two, where he can start to get an idea of how the coverage is getting displaced as opposed to a kickoff return where everybody is in their lane and starts down the field. On the punt team, by the time the ball is snapped and the blocking occurs and guys get off the line, it's not usually just the wave of guys. There is some kind of displacement in the coverage. You can get a feel for what kind of depth the gunners have. I think that's what a good returner does, is he takes the ball off the punters foot, sees it start to pick up the flight in the air, takes a look at how the coverage is starting to unfold, come down the field and get a sense of what the opportunities might be and then as the ball is coming in, he has to get a feel for how close or how dangerous those guys are to hitting him when he catches the ball, whether to fair catch it and that type of thing. So, a lot of decision making there in a pretty short amount of time. Some of that depends on what the return is and what we're trying to set up and what we're trying to do. There's definitely a lot of judgment and decision making involved there, no question. I would say the biggest thing for Julian is, one, he makes good decisions and two, he's aggressive. He'll take it to the edge but for the most part he's done a good job of not putting himself in harm's way but at the same time being aggressive and making the plays that he can make. He's had a couple balls that have, like last week, bounced and he saved us some yards on those without overexposing himself or the team to a turnover. There's a fine line between saving a couple yards and taking care of the ball. But when you can do both that helps the team.

**Q:** Is it safe to say hesitation is something you can't have at that position as a returner?

**BB:** I don't think that's ideal but I'd say sometimes it's better to make no decision than make the wrong one, let's put it that way. If it's make the wrong one or not make one, sometimes you're better off just getting away from the ball rather than trying to catch it in traffic or catch it on the run or put yourself in a spot where you could lose the ball.

## Q: You have a history with left-footed punters. Why do you like them so much?

**BB:** You know, I've been asked about that before. I think it's a coincidence really. I don't go into it with an attitude like, 'We have to have a left-footed punter.' I know it's been that way. Lee Johnson was here when I got here. We had Tom Tupa at Cleveland. Tom didn't punt in the NFL, he punted in college and we brought him in and he became our punter. Of course he punted for us here when I was at New England in '96. He was an excellent right-footed punter. I coached Dave Jennings at the Giants and he's one of the best punters that ever punted in the NFL.

I had a long relationship with Sean Landetta as well; that's another good right-footed punter. I don't really have any preference toward left-footed punters. I know it's worked out that way, I can't deny it. But, I've also had the opportunity to coach and be with a lot of good right-footed punters too and I was more than happy with them. I loved Tupa, loved Jennings, loved Landetta. Even going all the way back to when I was involved with the special teams at Baltimore, with David Lee and at the Lions with [Herman] Weaver and John Stufflebeem who we brought in who ended up with a long career in the Navy and didn't play professionally other than in training camp. They were all good right-footed punters too. I would say coincidence.

**Q:** Is the spin different when you talk about a left-footed punter?

**BB:** It's totally different, yeah. It's like facing a right-handed pitcher or left-handed pitcher. It's backwards, it's totally different. But, the basic rotation of the ball is fundamentally the same, it's just backwards. If you were able to flip that over which you can do, just like on a camera if you were able to flip that over, it would be like a right-handed golfer or a left-handed golfer, the mechanics and everything are the same, it's just reversed.

**Q:** Is there any reason why you prefer punters to be holders in the field goal operation?

**BB:** You want your best holder to be the holder. I think that the key thing in the NFL now is just with the opportunity of your specialist. Again, the game has evolved from when I came into the league. Most teams had kicker, most of the punters played another position and I would say all of the long snappers played another position, either center or linebacker or tight end or whatever it was. Then punters became pretty much specialized so every team carried a kicker and a punter.

Occasionally you had a guy who could do both but that was more the exception than the rule. Eventually, teams started going to just pure long snappers. Like Steve DeOssie, who came into the league as a linebacker/snapper, kind of ended as a snapper and was one of the best snappers in the league. He was part of that transition and in that era where teams went and committed fully to a long snapper that played no other position. You've also seen that now in college. Most college teams have a pure snapper as well as a pure kicker and a pure punter.

I just think that when you have that situation, if your punter can hold, then the amount of snaps and time that those guys get to practice together, work together, meet together, watch film together, watch slow-motions films, concentrate on the technique as opposed to the backup quarterback or somebody like that who has a lot of other responsibilities. It's just a time – if your holder can be your punter, then the amount of practice time, consistency, preparation time that those guys have together just so out-weighs what it would be with any other player – receivers have been holders. Then you go through the whole thing, if it's a position player like a defensive back or like it was back in the '60s, a Jimmy Patton or a receiver and something happens to them, now whose your backup player because those guys are regular players.

Not only do you have to replace them at their offensive or defensive position, you have to replace them in the kicking game so it just cuts into your depth. Back when you had 36, 37 players, that was a whole different ballgame. Everybody doubled up in one way or another. I think that's the way it is on most teams. Most teams punters are the holder and the snappers are the snappers and kickers are the kickers. That's the way it is in college so we're recruiting players that are in that very specialized phase themselves.

**Q:** Has it always been like that since you've been at the Patriots?

**BB:** Yeah, I think even going back to, not the Giants because Dave [Jennings] didn't hold and Sean [Landetta] didn't hold but ever since then, [Tom] Tupa held at Cleveland and so I'd say from somewhere in the early-'90s that that was more the norm. Prior to that, some did, some didn't. Danny White held for Dallas for years and so forth. There was kind of that transition there from maybe '85 to the early-'90s. I'd say by around '95 or so, it was pretty much one snapper, one kicker, one punter on every team. Also as the roster numbers have creeped up as well, that's made it affordable. When you're down in the 30s then it's a lot tougher to carry one of each of those; that slices into your roster pretty good. The rules have made it much easier to do.

**Q: What are some of the traits you look for in a gunner?**

372

**BB:** Well, some combination of speed, strength and quickness. The more the better of all three, but that's a tough position to play. You have to deal with two guys. You have to be strong enough to deal with them or quick enough to deal with them or fast enough to deal with them and then there's all the techniques of not only dealing with the double team but also the punts, the returns, the rushes, the wind conditions, knowing where the ball is, trying to defeat two blockers and then locate the ball and the returner and the different returns and so forth. There's a lot of technique and skill that's involved beyond just the physical part of it. I think you need some combination of those three elements to deal with consistent double teams out there.

**Q:** Do you also need a certain mentality?

**BB:** Be aggressive. It's a tough spot to play. As I said, if you're good, you have two guys out there a lot. Two guys get you at the line of scrimmage and are trying to keep you from getting downfield – it gets pretty physical. It's a physical battle out there. You definitely have to have a high level of aggressiveness to deal with that.

**Q: Would you mind stating the obvious and tell me how much Julian Edelmanhas improved in that short amount of time and how much commitment it takes for a young player to go out there and correct something that he shows up as a little deficient to start with to the point where he looks great now?**

**BB:** Well, I certainly wouldn't use that adjective. Catching punts, there's a lot to it. Unlike kickoffs - where the ball usually tumbles end over end and the movement on the ball is much more limited - when a ball's punted, left-footed or right-footed - which is another thing, we have a left footed punter at camp although we've had both - [it's] spinning the opposite direction.

So depending on how the ball comes off the punter's foot, a lot of different things can happen. [With] the nose turning over, it lengthens the kick. It drives it away from to the left if it's a right-footed punter. If the nose doesn't turn over, it's shorter, it breaks -

kind of a curveball - to the returners right. Tumbling balls tend to be shorter. There are balls that tail. There're balls that are tight. Then you have directional punts that go with that, in addition to all the plus-50 situational punts, whether we're rushing plus-50 or returning plus-50, whether it's a real downing situation like it would be on a rugby punt type of thing, where the ball's kicked end over end compared to maybe [when] they're punting from their minus-40 and the ball carries down to the 10 yard-line.

So there are a lot of different situations. In addition to that, there are a lot of different types of balls that you have to field, just like a hitter has to hit a variety of pitches over the course of a three-game series from a couple of different pitchers. You've got a lot of different types of punts that can happen and then through the wind with all that, or the sun, or the lights, or whatever. So some of that is experience; certainly, a lot of it is concentration. Some of it is natural ball-handling skills. Some guys just handle them better than others no matter how much coaching.

Like I know where the ball's going to break, I can read it, but you don't want me back there catching it. So you have to have some skill to go along with it. But Julian [Edelman has] worked hard. He's been out there every day. He's caught punts. He's caught kickoffs. He's caught a lot of plus-50 situational balls, directional punts [and] so forth. There are a lot of things for him to work on. He's worked at them. He's gotten better at them and he's got a long way to go and - as we all know - catching punts or punting in this stadium at the latter half of the season is very challenging. That's a tough enough skill when everything is perfect in a dome, but doing it out here in the conditions we see in November and December - that's a whole new ballgame, too.

As we go forward, whoever those players are, that's why we try to practice outside a lot - even when the weather's not perfect - to try to get used to those situations: rain, snow, wind, crosswind, kicking with the wind, kicking against the wind, fielding the ball and so forth. There's a lot to it. He's obviously getting very well-coached by Scott

[O'Brien]. I don't think anybody or could help a player tell or tell a player anything in a kicking game than Scott could, so I think that's been a big benefit to him as well.

## Q: Can you talk about what the skills you that you have to have as a special teams coach that translate well to a head coaching position?

**BB::** I think the big thing for a special teams coach is your dealing with basically with every player on the team other than the quarterbacks. Every player - receivers, tight ends, linemen, linebackers, defensive backs, specialists - you deal with all those players in one phase of the game or another and they have different personalities. They're different. They are all important, but they're different. They see things differently and sometimes they learn differently or you have to teach them differently. At the same time, you work with all the players from the veteran players to the rookie players and all the guys in between.

That's a spectrum too where there are some players that special teams is very important to and there are other players that maybe look at it like kind of a necessity: "'I have to do this and maybe this will lead to other opportunities." And there are some players that really don't want to be involved in that aspect of the game. But, as a coach, you have to coach everybody. So you are coaching the different positions, the rookies to the veterans. Some guys are very passionate about that particular part of the game and I've coached other players who weren't very passionate about that aspect of the game as much as they were their offensive or defensive roles. There are a lot of challenges in that.

For me, it was great training to be head coach when I was a special teams coach with Floyd [Reese] at Detroit and working on it at Denver, Baltimore and, of course, at the Giants. So those eight years were great training for me. Once I became a head coach, in working with all those different types of things, as opposed to coaching one group of players like the linebackers, tight ends, quarterbacks or whatever it is, it really broadened out.

# Kickoff/ KOR

**Q:** We know that certain positions have their own positional coach. Where do placekickers turn for that level of expertise? Do the special teams coaches have a level of knowledge about placekicking despite the fact they themselves may not have been kickers in the past?

**BB:** I certainly get where you're coming from. I don't think that's the case here. I can't speak for other teams. I think Joe [Judge] is very knowledgeable about the techniques of kicking. I know when I became a special teams coach and coached special teams for many years as an assistant coach and I continue to be involved with it as a head coach, but for many years as an assistant coach that's one of the things I had to learn. I had to learn how to coach those individual specialists; the snappers, the kickers, the punters, the returners. I don't think it's any different than coaching any other position. Things you don't know you need to learn and the things you do know you need to be able to teach to the players, however you've acquired that information.

And some of that certainly comes from the players, especially when you coach good players at the position that you're coaching. You can learn a lot from them just like I learned a lot from many of the players that I coached going back to people like Dave Jennings as a punter or Carl Banks or Lawrence Taylor or Pepper [Johnson], guys like that as linebackers for the Giants. However you acquire that information you acquire it.

You have to be able to convey it and teach it to the players and recognize technique or judgement. I mean look, there's a whole host of things that go into performance but all of the things that are related to those, but you know, be able to figure out which ones are the most important, which ones need to be corrected and so forth, but I think Joe is very knowledgeable in that, as was Scott O'Brien. I've had a lot of experience with that myself. But that's what coaching is. If you don't know it then you've got to find out. Nobody knows everything. I mean no coach knows everything about every position. Maybe if a guy has played it for a decade he might be well-versed in that position but I'd say for the most of the rest of us that haven't done that, things you don't know you've got to learn. You've got to find out. You've got to figure it out.

**Q: Statistics have shown that a large number of the kickoffs for your unit that are returned by the opponent are resulting in them being stopped inside the 20-yard line. How much of an emphasis do you put on that for your kickoff unit?**

**BB:** Well, I think that's a very big play. Obviously, there's only two times when you kickoff. One is after you score and the other is at the start of a half, but good play in that situation is really kind of a momentum play and it sets up the coming series for the defense. It's hard to go on a run in this league, but that's one way to do it, is to score, have good kickoff coverage, good field position, make a stop on defense and now the offense is in pretty good position to score again.

So, the kickoff coverage really gives you an opportunity to possibly string a couple of points, some points together if you can play good complimentary football. Our guys take a lot of pride in it. Joe [Judge] and Bubba [Ray Ventrone] do a great job of coaching it. We have a good kicker, we have good coverage players. They work together and we do take, as I said, those guys take a lot of pride in it and they put a lot of effort into it and it certainly helps us. I mean defensively, the thing you hope for the most as a defensive coach is good field position. Sometimes you get it, sometimes you don't.

You've got to go in and play regardless of where you go in at, but it's always good to have good field position. It certainly gives you a lot more options defensively in terms of play-calling and game management. That's where I think it becomes very helpful for the defense. Obviously the same thing is true in the punting game and our coverage in both phases this year has been good. The return game's been another story but yesterday was the best we've had on that so hopefully that's heading in the right direction.

## Q: What is the thinking behind kicking off closer to the sideline as opposed to the middle of the field where the returner may traditionally line up?

**BB:** Well, I think what most teams try to do on the corner-type kicks is to force you as the return team to either take the ball right up the sideline where you catch it, which means you have a limited amount of space to work on, or to bring the ball all the way across the field which means you're doing a lot of running without gaining yards and there's the potential that you could really get caught inside the 10 or really get pinned down there deep if somebody's able to cut off the returner before he can get all the way across the field. And if you put hang time on that ball that makes it tougher to come across the field with.

On the return end of it if you know where the balls going to go then you could set up a boundary return even though you're running into pretty tight quarters there, but you could set it up and get the blocking angles the best that you can and just try to take the ball up the field the shortest distance. But if you're not sure where it is and if the kick goes away from where you think it's going to go, so if you set up a boundary return one way and the ball ends up getting kicked the other way, now you've kind of got all of your guys out-leveraged, and again, your choices are to either take the ball straight back up field with not enough blocking or bring it across the field to where your blocking is but you've got a long way to go. It definitely can put you in a tough situation on that.

That happened to us in the Carolina game where they kicked it over to the corner and James Develin had to field it and he obviously was our short returner, not the primary guy, so it kind of limits what you can do if they can get the ball in the right spot or in a tough spot. It really limits your options for the return team. Obviously, the best option for you in the kickoff return is that the ball is straight down the middle of the field with not very much hang time. That's the best returnable ball. The toughest returnable ball just on the kick alone - forget about the coverage, that's a whole other discussion - is a ball with good hang time that pins you in the corner. You just have a lot fewer options there.

**Q:** Is there statistical analysis that has shown that an offense will have a tougher time starting with the ball on the 20-yard line as opposed to the 25-yard line, and is that why with the change in touchback rules this season there has been a bigger emphasis on those lofty kicks that are designed to force the return team to bring the ball out of the endzone?

**BB:** I think that's part of it. Yeah, I do. I think that's part of it. I'd say, you know, also part of it is just the matchup with your opponent and what they're strength is in the return game and so forth. You know, I would say over the last couple of years because of fewer and fewer kickoffs were returned, it made decisions tougher for teams, made it tougher for teams to carry guys on the roster whose strength was on kickoff or kickoff return, whether that be the returner, or a coverage player, or a wedge guy or something like that because you just weren't getting very many shots at it.

And so if you have a real good kickoff returner, how many times are you going to get to return it? In some games you're probably not going to get to return any. Again, especially depending on where some of those games are being played, a little bit less of an issue where we are because sooner or later those balls aren't going to be touchbacks but if you're kicking in a dome or you're kicking in the south consistently, those are pretty heavy touchback games.

That's one thing there, so I'm just saying that explosive kickoff returner that maybe could make a handful of plays during the year that would change the game, can you really afford to carry that guy for the number of opportunities he's going to get? Overall, generally speaking the level of returner in the league has probably declined a little bit on kickoffs because the opportunities that they have and so it's become more of a punt and punt return game. Not to digress, but when I came into the league on special teams you had six phases. Every phase was very competitive, so field goal protection, field goal rush, kickoff, kickoff return, punt, punt return - now that's really down to just two phases; punt and punt return.

Field goals - it's very hard to block a field goal because of the rules. You can't hit the center, you can't jump, you can't overload, you can't do much of anything. You just have to make a great play to somehow split the coverage or have a bad kick or both to really affect that play. It's not impossible but it's hard, so field goal protection isn't what it used to be and the field goal rush has really been taken out of the game. Then when you start touch-backing the kickoffs you take the coverage players out of the game because you and I could cover a lot of the kickoffs when they're nine, 10, 11 yards deep in the end zone. You don't need anybody to cover them and the same thing with the return game.

They don't block because there's no return, so it's become a punt and punt return game and that's where a lot of the emphasis now has to go in the kicking game because that's where most of the plays are. As the kickoffs I think are coming back into it, at least it seems like they are this year more, then that increases those opportunities and probably the value of some of those players that play in that phase of the game. It will be interesting to see how it goes. We're only a couple of weeks into the season. We'll see how it all plays out, but in looking at a few other games it looks like there are a lot of teams that are doing some of the directional, corner-type kicking with good hang time. Just kind of popping the ball up in the air and making teams bring it out, which isn't surprising. That's exactly what happened with the college rule.

**Q: On the kick to the up-man the other day, what do you look for from the guys that are back there in that position?**

**BB:** It depends on what scheme you're trying to run and really what you're trying to do. I'd say they're not all the same. Some teams have big offensive and defensive linemen back there. We've had them back there before. I'd say that's more of a wedge-blocking scheme. There is certainly an element of ball handling that goes on back there like what happened on that play or squib kicks and things like that. I think depending on what kind of returns you're running, also obviously what personnel you have available, but what type of returns you're running and what you're trying to defend in terms of the types of kicks you're getting, how much movement is involved are all considerations as to who you would put back there.

## Q: How do you feel like the coverage units have performed?

**BB:** Well, I think it starts with the kickers, like it always does. Nobody can cover bad kicks. That's tough for anybody. When we get good kicks, good hang time, which Steve [Gostkowski] has given us really good kickoffs - not just the touchbacks, but also the hang time on the kickoffs. Ryan [Allen] has given us a lot of good balls to cover. We got beat in the Carolina game, I don't know it was like whatever, a 20 or 25-yard return, and that was a combination of a number of things. We also had one in the Pittsburgh game that got called back. And Geneo [Grissom] has drawn a couple penalties on coverage the last couple weeks, so some of that is good coverage, you get in good position to make the play and they have to block you. That's part of having good coverage.

The big thing has been the kickers, and I'd say overall the coverage units, the kickoff is probably a little ahead of the punt right now, but that's been OK, too, and Ryan has really punted the ball well for us. Joe [Cardona] has given us a little bit of coverage from that position, which there's usually not a ton of, but he's helped us a little bit there.

I'd say overall, it's been alright, but I mean, this will be a big challenge this week. We're not really sure who the returner is going to be, and that is always, like there is not going to be big scouting report on whoever they put back there, so we're going to have to figure that out a little bit as we go. They're a big, strong hold up team. A lot of times they've used defensive linemen to hold up in the past, and they have some good inside players that are tough to get away from, so that will be a challenge for us, for our units to get off the line of scrimmage and to get good distribution down the field.

**Q:** When Steve kicks one five yards out of the end zone, are you still reviewing the film on the kickoff coverage the same way?

**BB:** You can only see what you can see on those plays, so a lot of times, there isn't a lot of contact in terms of playing blocks, playing leverage, getting off blocks. Sometimes that part of the play doesn't really happen. But definitely, you're evaluating the get-off, you're evaluating the overall lane distribution and the players recognizing what the returns are. I'd say that's become a little bit of a game within a game - probably not that anybody cares, but I'll just take a minute to talk about it anyways.

If you think you're going to get touchbacked - they're kicking off with the wind or whatever - and you see a return or a type of return, it's really probably not what they want to do. Like they're going to double team these two guys and the wedge is starting to go over here, but it's a touchback, so you've kind of got to scout it, you've got to defend it, but in the end, I don't even know if they really want to run that. It's almost like a fake return, or maybe a guy is going to line up one side and you're going to cross block, but you're not really sure who they're cross blocking because they don't actually get to the blocks.

So, you're kind of trying to figure out what it is, when really you can't see the full development of the play. And then again, as the return tem, you're sometimes showing something that isn't really what your intentions are because it's a touchback play. You see it's a touchback or you anticipate that it's going to be a touchback. So, you go against a team that has a good kicker, like our kicker, and we see three or four middle returns and the ball is five yards out of the end zone, and then now OK we're kicking off into the wind and they feel like they have a chance to return it and they run a side return - stuff like that. So again, it's kind of a bit of a game within a game in terms of you sort of see it, but you don't really see it.

As you're scouting your opponents it's something that well, here's the return they're trying to run, but you don't really see their return, but then is that really what they're trying to run or are they just trying to give you an illusion that this is what it is when really when they have a chance to return it, you're going to get something else. Joe does a good job of that. Joe Judge does a good job of that - breaking down those kinds of things. It used to be that way on PATs. You're seeing a little bit less of that. You see the PAT rush because you couldn't bock them, so teams would sometimes put two or three guys on one guy and just try to run over somebody, just to get a good hit on him or something.

And now when you actually have to block a field goal, now you get into something where you really feel like you might have a chance to block it and the rush is a little bit different. The fact now that all those kicks are a little more competitive, you're seeing more of whatever the team is trying to do to rush it. You're seeing more of a rush rather than one or two or three guys just deciding to, well we're not really going to get this, so let me just tee off and smash this guy because he's been blocking me all day. So let me just go ahead and smash this guy while he's just sitting there. I don't really think that's what the game is about.

But it's kind of taken that out of it and made it more of a competitive play rather than that type of play. But it was kind of the same thing on those PATs. You look at the PAT rushes like well this is a big middle rush team, they're really trying to do this or do that, but then when you get into a field goal situation, it's not that at all. It's a little bit of a game within a game there.

**Q:** The onside kick in the Rams-Seahawks game, I think the rule is if the ball hits the ground first you can't fair catch it, but if it doesn't you can fair catch it. How much do you rely on your players' instincts in those situations?

**BB:** I think those are things that you start with in training camp. You go over first of all, basic fundamentals, then you go over rules, and then you go over situations, which sometimes rules are part the situation, sometimes they're not – whether to stay in bounds, whether to go out of bounds – that type of thing. That's all part of it. It's all part of the conversation – knowing the rules and playing within the rules and knowing the situation and playing the situation to our best advantage. And that starts back at training camp.

We go through a period of training camp where we don't really get into a lot of detail on that, and we gradually build on it, but then as we get into the last couple weeks of training camp – like the Saints was a good opportunity for us to get a lot of situation work down there against them. The following week against Carolina, we were able to build on that, so we build into those situational plays, and a lot of them came up in those games actually. The halftime and end-of-the-game situations in our preseason games, there were some good learning situations there that we were able to talk about and build on – not just what we faced, but had we been on the other side of the ball how we would have played them, what we would be thinking, what our calls would be.

Look, you go out there, you can play for 59-plus minutes and it all comes down to one play or one situation, and whoever handles that situation better could end up being the victor. They're critical, you just don't know which ones are going to come up, you don't know the exact circumstances of it, but you try to cover your bases the best you can.

**Q:** Do you think there's been any change in philosophy from a kickoff return standpoint since the kick got moved up? It seems like before that a kick three or four yards in the end zone would result in the returner taking a knee and now it seems like the opposite.

**BB:** Yeah, oh no question. I think there's a much different mentality. Again, it comes back to a philosophy. If you have a kickoff returner, or a guy that you feel like is capable of making a play, then you're risking three, four, five yards of field position, whatever it is. Even if it doesn't go good, let's say he gets out to the 16, 17, whatever it is, versus him having a chance to make a play. You're just taking the ball out of that guy's hands. Is there a little bit of field position risk?

Yeah, there's arguably a little bit but if you feel that your return matches up well enough against their coverage or your guy is a guy that you just want to get the ball in his hands and you're willing to take that four or five yard, whatever it is, field position loss in exchange for the opportunity to make a play, then absolutely that's the tradeoff. So yeah, you're seeing guys come out from seven, eight, nine, nine-and-a-half yards deep now that you probably wouldn't have seen awhile back. That whole rule has had a lot of different dynamics to it.

Also relative to the college rule, which is the 35-yard kickoff but then the 25-yard field position. But then you see a lot of college teams now going with – of course they have the wider hash marks – but they're going with the cross field kicks, more hang time, kind of forcing the return team to bring the ball out and trying to nail them down inside the 25, rather than just banging it away. There's definitely some, not that I really care about the college game, but it's interesting because you're evaluating the kickers and the returns to a degree.

So you're looking at the strategy and how all that shapes up relative to our game where I'd say for the most part kickers are just banging away. Again, when you tell a kicker to just bang away, sometimes those kicks that are coming down seven, eight yards deep in the end zone have 3.8 hang time too. So it's not the same. There's a difference between two yards deep and four or five hang time and nine yards deep and 3.8 hang time. I'd rather be nine yards deep. I think there's a tradeoff there and I think the returners are definitely aware of that. The guys that are going for distance, trying to touch back it, yeah, the balls are deeper but also, many of them are with less hang time and sometimes significantly less hang time. That changes it too. It's not all about how deep the ball is. There's certainly a hang time element involved as well.

**Q:** Is using Matthew Slater as the guy who tells the return man whether to stay in or come out a nod to his special teams knowledge?

**BB:** Yeah, sure and experience. The guys that we've had back there and [Shane] Vereen did that, Kevin Faulk was a guy that did that for us, guys like that. Sure, that's a big part of it. Especially in conditions that are less – it's one thing in a dome where you're getting the same conditions every week. But here, between the wind and again, the hang on the kickoff and the coverage team and knowing who you're playing against, what you're return is. Again, if you're trying to run a sideline return and the ball is deep in the end zone and it's away from the return, you have a long way to go to get to where you want.

That's different than a ball that's kicked deep on a middle return down the middle where you're a lot closer to where you want to be. Again, there's a lot of things that go into making that judgment, more than just, 'Well, the ball is this far deep in the end zone.' It's what's the rest of the play and how long is the ball in the air.

**Q: How important is the role of the guy in front of the returner, who is telling the returner whether or not to come out? Is that role more complicated than we might realize?**

**BB:** Yeah, I'd say that's definitely a key role on the team. It's sort of like, if you will, the personal protector on the punt team. It's the last line of defense for the returner. There's the judgment on ball handling, but even if it's just a normal kick and we know who is going to get it, the short returner usually, depending on what the return is, has different responsibilities. Sometimes he cleans up on blocks, sometimes he's assigned to a specific guy but usually when he's assigned to a specific guy he normally would have to weave his way through some traffic, like the wedge or another coverage player to get to his assignment.

You don't want him blocking the first guy down because there would be too much penetration. Normally he's on more of a second-level player or he's looking to take some kind of leakage from, say if you were on the right return, maybe he takes the leakage from the left side so that nobody catches the returner from behind but he has to make that decisions of 'Is the guy close enough or can we bypass him and go to somebody else?' again, that all gets into the relationship between him and the returner and the track that the returner is on, being able to know where he is, know who you have to block, who you don't have to block and then making decisions in terms of getting to your man through traffic, so that you can get to your assignment without screwing the returner up. I'd say there's definitely a lot to that position.

It's a hard position to play. It's kind of a combination of being the fullback in the running game but you're dealing with a lot more space and a lot more decision-making. Sometimes those guys are reading three, four, five, different people on one play, depending on what happens, 'Somebody shows, they take him. If nobody shows, then I'm blocking this guy but I have to work my way up to that guy.'

**Q: Have the kickoff rules diminished the role of the kickoff returner in general? Some of the guys that you would say are critical to the return, has that changed?**

**BB:** Statistically there are definitely fewer kickoff returns on a percentage basis and total numbers than what there were before they moved the kickoff restraining line back to the 35-yard line, which was what they said was their attempt to have fewer returns, which there definitely are but there are still plenty of them. I think as the season goes on, particularly in places like this, where the weather is cooler and wind conditions become more of a factor, that there are fewer touchbacks in the second half of the season than there are in the first half of the season. It becomes more of a factor later on in the season, but there are fewer of them, no question about that, absolutely.

# 7
## X'S AND O'S

**Q:** In Week 4 they ran a few plays from the wildcat formation. How much time do you need to prepare for that wrinkle in their offense despite the fact it may not be used often?

**BB:** Well, that's what they do. Between the wildcat, the unbalanced line, the kind of two different option packages, that's kind of what they force you to do. They sprinkle those plays in, they make you work on them, but they also have I'd say some of the more conventional plays but they also have the speed sweeps and things like that, reverses and quarterback runs that are wildcat runs but it's a quarterback that actually runs the ball instead of a running back or wildcat guy. So they have a lot of things like that that force you to make adjustments even though they're essentially running the same play but they get to it in different ways.

Again, whether you want to call them wildcat, unbalanced line, option, but all of those things; they all kind of fall into the same category. And with them you're not going to see anything like 30 times. You're going to see they have five of these, six of these, five of these, six of these, maybe eight of something else, maybe two of something else. But that's kind of what they do. Yeah, it definitely stretches you and forces you to prepare for those things that you're going to get a handful of times in the game. You might get them more if you don't stop them but that's what they do and they're pretty successful at that because they do force teams to eat up a lot of practice time working on things they're going to see only a couple of times but then they're on to something else.

**Q: In reference to the James White screen play that you mentioned, is it a little more difficult to call a screen play like that down in the red area due to the compacted space that you have to work with?**

**BB:** I mean that's a good question, Phil [Perry]. I think it depends a little bit. But you know, for the most part on the screen once you get past the - maybe call it the first five to eight yards from the line of scrimmage to five-or-so yards down field - that's really where all the action takes place.

You get the ball to the screen back and then you have one or two blockers, three blockers, whatever it is to block two or three guys whether it's a slip-screen to a wide-out or a back-screen. You've got a couple of blockers, you've got a couple of defenders and say whether the ball is on the 20-yard line, their 20 or your 20, it's probably going to be about the same space where those blocks occur. How much the deep guys get run off, I mean not as much obviously in the red area, but they're usually not the main factor on the play. The main factors on the play are the guys that are close to the line of scrimmage. Like the play that [Ryan] Shazier made, I think it was in the second quarter, we actually kind of had two blockers there. We couldn't quite get him. He made a nice play.

He kind of knifed in between us and broke it up, but had we gotten him I think it would've been quite a few yards on that play. Again, it's usually really about getting the runner started and getting them I'd say, once you get them more than four or five yards down field then a lot of the rest of it takes care of itself. It's getting them to that point cleanly.

**Q: In regards to Dont'a Hightower's blitz that resulted in the safety, we've heard that referred to as a 'hug blitz' before. What**

## goes into the timing of a play like that for a pass rusher?

**BB:** Well, the best thing about the good hug blitzes are when the linebacker can anticipate them. If he can anticipate that the back's going to block then it's really like having another blitzer. Then the huggers really like another blitzer. The linebacker's thinking about coverage and then he just doesn't anticipate it or doesn't see it as quickly, then there's some time lost between when the back blocks and then how long it takes the linebacker to become part of the rush.

So, anytime you can anticipate it if you run a certain type of a play where you think you're going to get the back to block and then he does and the guy who's got the back just comes right in on top of the guy who he's blocking, then he can get there almost as fast as the blitzer can. It's hard for the offensive line on those kinds of plays because they sometimes lose that coverage player especially if he doesn't come right away. Sometimes they lose him in all of the traffic that's going on there around the line of scrimmage.

## Q: What is the advantage of having the strong side linebacker up on the line of scrimmage more?

**BB:** Well, it all depends on what we're playing against. We've played a lot of nickel. Last week we played less nickel because the Browns were more of a two receiver team, or in some cases one receiver. Again, defensively whatever you do a lot of cases is a function of what the offense does. You just can't go out there and start calling defenses.

You've got to know who they have on the field, what personnel group they have on the field, and obviously down and distance plays a little part in that. But based on who they have on the field there's a certain matchup that I would say almost every team in the league, if not every team, is going to follow to a point. [If the] teams in base defense then you're probably going to see some on-the-line linebacker. If we're not in base defense then you might see less of it.

## Q: What did you see from Martellus Bennett and Rob Gronkowski

## when run-blocking out of the two tight end formation against Buffalo?

**BB:** Those guys are both good blockers, so we're comfortable running behind them in really any situation. They're good at the point of attack, they're good on double-team blocks, good at blocking the force. That's always a tough position. I mean it's a tough position on a lot of levels but it's a tough positon in terms of blocking because there are times that they're blocking safeties, guys that are good run players but quick and athletic and then there are times when they're blocking linebackers and then there are times when they're blocking defensive linemen, anywhere from the 260-270 pound defensive ends to occasionally some of the bigger five-techniques that push closer to 300.

So there are a lot of different levels of power, athleticism, technique. Some of those blocks are in-line blocks, some of them are space blocks. Occasionally they have to pull and things like that. At times they're even involved in perimeter plays like flip-screens and those type of things where they're blocking in space against corners. So the variety and the matchups that they have as blockers is pretty extensive. It's pretty difficult really to be able to matchup against all of those and execute them. But those two guys do a real good job of it. They're both long, have good strength, good feet, and they're both smart players that know how to use their leverage and understand where the play is going and how to use the proper technique to block it.

**Q: The wildcat formation on offense was a big factor back in 2008 when you played Miami here at Gillette Stadium. Was that kind of a fad that has phased itself out of the league now?**

**BB:** I mean you see it from time to time. It looked like Buffalo might've run it a couple of plays last night with [LeSean] McCoy. Yeah, all of those things - the wildcat, unbalanced line - things like that; I mean you've always got to be ready for them.

**Q:** What did you learn from that game in 2008 about it and how your players reacted to it?

**BB:** I mean it's really just a lot of elements of the single-wing offense. We just missed some tackles. Obviously didn't have it coached very well. [We] didn't coach it very well, didn't play very well. It's not unstoppable. We just didn't do a very god job on it that day.

**Q:** That formation was prevalent with the Arkansas Razorbacks at the time but did it come completely out of the blue that week in the NFL?

**BB:** Well, again, the coach for the Dolphins [quarterback coach David Lee] was at Arkansas when [Darren] McFadden ran it. Again, no matter how you slice it up it's just putting the quarterback into the equation into the running game which creates another gap, if you will. So, if you play eight-on-seven or seven-on-six then once the quarterback is part of the play, now you're eight-on-eight, you're seven-on-seven. There's no extra gap. You've got to account for him. That's what Mike Shanahan did with the Broncos offense with all of the bootlegs.

You had to account for him, so even though you could be eight-on-seven, once you accounted for that bootleg guy now you were seven-on-seven, or whatever the numbers were. You always lost a guy. It's really just a numbers game and those teams that run those type of plays - it seems like Navy that run a lot of option, run a lot of quarterback plays like they did with [Keenan] Reynolds. You run out of guys on defense. You can't outnumber them. You just run out of people. There are different versions of it but it's all the same concept. It's adding another guy in the running game that the defense has to account for that you lose a gap, which was the single-wing offense.

**Q: When you are playing in a nickel defense what goes into the thought process between alternating amongst three cornerbacks and two safeties or two cornerbacks and three safeties?**

**BB:** Right, yeah, it's a good question. It's really a good point. Some of it is the matchups, some of it at times is what we're doing and if we're doing something that one player versus another one is maybe better at, whether that's man coverage or zone coverage or blitzing or playing the run, whatever it happens to be. There could be other reasons for that as well, too, as part of just the overall matchup. Not necessarily one-on-one, it could be that, but it also could be more of a scheme thing or maybe anticipation of what they would be doing against that personnel group. So, I'd say it's a combination of all of those things that could change week to week. It's hard to go into games with a lot of different groupings.

I think that's because you have to have those backups in case one person gets hurt, then what do you do with that group? Do you just throw it away or do you have to have somebody else practicing so that you can maintain the group? So, it's hard to go in with multiple groups and have them all backed up, so a lot of times we might go with one or the other. If you do that with multiple groups then you have to figure out some way to adjust if you don't have all the players in that group for one reason or another. But that's all part of what we look at each week with our matchups against our opponents and again, not just the individual size, speed, personnel strength and weakness [of the] matchup but also from a scheme standpoint what our players do well, what position we want to try and put our players in based on the types of calls or defenses that we'll be running.

## Q: Is Andy Reid the type of coach that will script plays in sequence?

**BB:** Yeah, absolutely.

**Q:** How does that make them a different type of matchup?

**BB:** How does it make it different? I mean probably half of the teams we've played do that, so it's not really - you prepare for that just like you prepare for other situations.

**Q:** Is it a matter of them scripting a certain amount of their best plays or is it too simplistic to look at it that way?

**BB:** You'd have to ask him about exactly what those plays are. I wouldn't necessarily say that when you go up against a script that it's necessarily a team's best plays. It's the plays they want to start with and there's a lot of things those plays can do. They can set up other plays, they can force you to show defensively what type of adjustments you're going to make to certain personnel groups, certain formations, and it probably helps them plan for maybe how they want to call other plays in the game or which plays come next, whether that's the one that they set up or whether it's based on your defensive adjustments and which of those next plays they want to attack that adjustment with.

I'm sure a lot of times it's with the idea to get the ball to certain players. Offensively you can control who has the ball. Defensively you can't control that. You just have to put your guys out there, but you don't have any idea where the ball's going or whose going to get it. Offensively you have some control over that. Those things all play into it. Each game's different and whoever's doing the script probably has different reasons and different philosophies on why they do what they do. That's defensive football. You're on the other side of the ball - you defend what they give you. When you're on the offensive side of the ball you have some control over - well you have control over who's in the game, you have control over kind of where the ball's going and how it's going there. We see it all the time. I don't think it's like there's only two teams in the league that do a script or anything like that. I think it's pretty common every week.

**Q: How have they generated their downhill running game without incorporating a tight end?**

**BB:** Well I mean you pretty much turn on any college game on Saturday and that's what you're going to see. There are dozens of college teams that don't even have a tight end on their roster, don't even recruit tight ends. You spread them out, if they bring a lot of people in then you throw the ball. If you walk out there on them then it's fewer guys to block and more space for the runner. [Chris] Ivory gets good blocking, but he doesn't need a lot of blocking. The run he had against Miami, he must have run through like seven different guys. It could have been me and you out there blocking for him on that play. He didn't need any blocking. So that's part of it. But [Bilal] Powell does a good job, too. He's quick. He hits the crease in there, so they're different styles.

Powell is more of a space runner, and Ivory, he can run in space obviously, but he's a power back. He runs through tackles and has got great balance. But they do it from more of a spread set — one to no tight ends on the field. There is not usually more than that, so one at the most. [Quincy] Enunwa is not a tight end, but he's a bigger guy, so when you look at Enunwa blocking a defensive back, that's a mismatch. He's bigger than most of those guys, whereas if you put a tight end in a game, usually the guy he's blocking is comparable. In Enunwa's case, if you put a corner on him then he gains an advantage on that. So I'd say there is a little bit of that, too.

## Q: You guys have been using a lot of motion right before the ball is snapped. What is the advantage of doing that?

**BB:** Usually when you put a player in motion it's to either gain an advantage somehow on the defense or it's to force the defense to communicate and adjust after they've already made their call and you've come out of the huddle and lined up. I'd say it would fall into one of those two categories.

Sometimes you do it just to force the defense to deal with something, change of strength or a tight split or a wide split that goes from one to the other, where the tight end aligns, which we know is important when teams are setting their front, their linebacker locations and trying get ready to set up their gap control. If you're trying to gain an advantage, that's one thing. If you're trying to in general force the defense to communicate and be ready to play one thing when you're actually going to snap the ball and do something else, then there's some subtle advantage to that that's hard to measure, but you know from experience that it's taking place and it puts more stress on your opponent.

**Q: Scheme-wise is there anything in particular you have to defend, like tempo?**

**BB:** Tempo is a problem. But I'd say the biggest thing with their offense is they make you defend the whole field. They run from sideline to sideline, they run up the middle, they throw deep, they throw outside, they throw inside, they throw short catch-and-run plays, they throw balls that are over the top behind the defense, they throw the intermediate routes, the over routes, the in-cuts, the outside scissors, sail-type routes. There is really nothing that you can say, 'Well we don't have to worry about this or that.' You do because they run it inside, they run it outside, they throw it short, middle, deep, they have a lot of misdirection plays so you can't over-pursue because they have plays that force you to defend the backside of the plays. I'd say that's really the strength of their offense. On top of that, they go really fast and try to wear the defense down or force the communication issue on defense so if you aren't aligned properly or you aren't able to get your assignments – even if you're aligned right, if you're not able to get your assignments done quickly the way the plays come off, there's space in there, somebody gets free, they do a good job of finding it. They're used to playing fast at that tempo more so than the defenses are because there aren't a lot of teams that do it like that. That's a lot of challenges for the defense this week.

**Q: Understanding you can't control it, how much does it catch your attention when there is a late change to your referee assignment, especially when the crew that you're getting is being demoted from a primetime game?**

**BB:** It's not anything we have any control over. We've had Pete [Morelli's] crew twice this year already and really haven't had any problems with them – once in the preseason and once in the regular season. I thought in terms of the communication and all the things on the field, there wasn't an issue with them. Look, there's whatever, 17 crews? We get them all. I don't think any of them are to me noticeably one way or the other. Each game has its own dynamics and close calls and some go one way, some go another way, but overall I think that they do a pretty good job of balancing the crews out. However they do it, I don't really know, that's not really my thing. Those groups, they're professional, and I think overall they do a pretty good job – not perfect, like all of us.

**Q: What are some of the advantages and disadvantages of going up-tempo?**

**BB**: I think Chip and the Eagles do a great job with it. We've basically played them every year, or practiced against them, and they make it really hard. The speed that they go at, it's hard to get much communication in. It forces you to kind of simplify things defensively. You just don't have time to get some of that stuff called or can't get the right group in, or you only want to run it against certain looks, but the time you have to communicate is short. Generally speaking, they're a lot better at it than you are because they do it more than you do.

Defensive communication and adjustments and being ready to play at that speed is hard. On top of that, the Eagles have just a tremendous group of skill players. They're literally two deep at every position or more – running back, tight end, quarterback, receiver. I mean, they have two floods of groups of really good skill players at all those positions. That makes it really tough because they have so many good players, so many explosive guys.

**Q: What makes Rob Gronkowski effective as an outside receiver? Have you thought about using him more in that role considering the depth issues at receiver?**

**BB:** Sure, it's a possibility. It creates a different kind of matchup, and depending on who is covering him, it puts that player in a less comfortable position. But the closer you are to the middle of the field the more route options you have. You can go inside or outside, it's really the same thing at that point when you're right in the middle and you have a lot more variety in what you can do.

When you're outside your route tree, you can't get to the other half of the field basically unless it's a long-developing over route or something like that. So your route tree is in more of a confined area. I'm not saying it's good or bad. It's just different. I think there are places and advantages to, whether it be a receiver or tight end – I mean, they're all receivers – backs, tight ends, receivers, there are advantages to being outside or somewhere in that slot area or inside if you will. So it depends on what you're trying to do, who you're matched up against, what you're trying to run.

### Q: Is there still a lot of zone blocking in the running game?

**BB:** That's all it is. That's it. It's the same zone blocking we saw in Denver when Coach Kubiak was there with Coach [Mike] Shanahan. It's the same zone blocking we saw in Houston when Coach Kubiak was there. It's the same zone blocking we saw in Baltimore last year. It's the same zone blocking this year. Fundamentally it's all the same. Now it could be a different personnel group. It could be a different look. It could be same variation with the formationing and tight end on, tight end off, two tight ends, no tight ends, etc., but it all comes back to the same [thing].

You've got to be able to stop the outside zone play against these guys or it's going to be a long, long day. And the plays that complement it – obviously the boot plays and the play actions that go with it, which a lot of those play actions are home-run kind of play actions. Like they're not looking to run play actions and throw the ball two yards out into the flat. That's not really their idea of play action. If they hit you with play action it's going to hurt. It's not going to be a two-yard gain, not many of them anyways. And that defeats the whole extra guy in the front. The proverbial eight-man fronts really don't help you against them because you've got to cover the quarterback on boots.

You might have eight bodies there, but if you don't have an eighth guy to cover the quarterback or seven or whatever it is, you can't outnumber them like defenses try to outnumber teams in the running game. You've got six, they've got six, you've got seven, they've got seven, you've got eight, they've got five, you've got six. You can always put one more in there, but then when you have to account for quarterbacks on those boots then you lose that guy so your seven-on-six becomes six-on-six. And that's the foundation of the offense. They do a good job with it.

**Q: Chandler Jones leads the league in sacks, but often it seems like he's not the only guy getting pressure on the quarterback. Can you speak to how important it is to have a good pass rush from the entire front?**

**BB:** Again, that's really important. There is going to be a handful of plays that you can probably identify and say well that was a great pass rush by a certain player and that basically dominated the play, but there are far more plays that are collective – they're done on a collective basis, whether it's coverage that forces the quarterback to hold the ball a little longer or people in the throwing lane or, as you mentioned, a player that's providing a little bit of pressure initially on the quarterback but he slides to get away from him and that puts him closer to other rushers, that type of thing. It's usually more of that situation that's more common to have guys that their production in the play is a function of what somebody else is doing in the play and really team defense.

Now that being said, the closer you are to the ball more often, the more chances you're going to have of making plays, and I'd say Chandler has definitely done that. He's put himself close to the quarterback on a number of occasions and sometimes he makes the play, sometimes he forces to somebody else, but he's around there quite a bit, so he certainly is getting a high level of production there because of that.

He's been really active and productive, but probably one of the best things Chandler has done this year is play the run, and a lot of times he's playing it from the edge but there are certainly other times when he's played it from a three technique and much closer to the ball and he's done a good job of that, too. I'd say his whole game has been good and he's performed well on a consistent basis all year and that's been great to see him play that way and have that kind of production and consistency.

## Q: Do you defend a receiving tight end like Jordan Reed differently than you would defend a more traditional tight end like Jason Witten?

**BB:** Each player has their own individual strengths and weaknesses, whatever those happen to be, and I think you always want to be aware of what the player's strengths are and take those away. If you can gain an advantage where you feel like you have an advantage in that matchup you want to take advantage of that when you can or if you can. Again on that side of it, sometimes when you're on offense, you keep players out of situations that you don't feel are strengths for them.

That's what good offensive coaches do with their players. Reeds' case, I think he's obviously one of their best players. They have a lot of confidence in him. They go to him in a lot of critical situations, he comes through. They move him around, he's all over, he at times plays receiver positons where he's split out and detached from the formation. That's fairly common. He's in close more than he's split out, but he's split out more than a lot of tight ends are. When you face guys like that, you've got to figure out the matchup that you want to be in that you feel comfortable with. And he's made plays down the field.

He's a very crafty route runner, knows how to get open in tight coverage. He's a big target, catches the ball well, has got a big catch radius, so you can kind of put the ball away from the defender where he can get it and the defender can't, and he can come up with it. He's good in the red area, good on third down. He has quickness to separate from man coverage. Yeah, it's just trying to find the best matchup, but again, a lot of times it's hard to jam him or disrupt his route because he's extended as opposed to being in-line. But yeah, he does a lot of things well. I'd say in their running game, they use their tight ends but a little differently than say the Dallas offense as an example in the way they block. A lot of times they don't force players, or extended players, so that's really compatible with the skills of an athletic tight end. It's similar to [Tyler] Eifert when Jay was at Cincinnati. I think Reed is kind of Eifert in the Cincinnati offense if you will.

## Q: What's the difference between a West Coast running game and a traditional running game?

**BB:** I'd say that's all kind of changed. When you go back to Paul Brown, that is the offense. What the running game was in the 70's when he was in Cincinnati, late 60's and 70's when he was there, what it was throughout the league is a lot different than what it is now. Even in San Francisco when [Bill] Walsh was there, it was a lot of two backs. Now most every team has one primary runner in the game. Very seldom do you see two runners and so that has obviously been a big change. So it just depends on where you want to draw that line.

We're going back call it 30 years of West Coast, Ohio River offense, whatever you want to call it, and that running game has changed. I think what has probably stayed more consistent is the passing game concepts and then whatever running game you have, then you adapt that with that kind of Ohio River passing game, whether it's zone runs, whether it's gap runs, whether its 12-personnel runs, whether it's 21-personnel runs. But the pass concepts I would say there is a lot more carryover.

When you go back to what Coach Brown did, Coach Walsh, those are primarily two-back sets with some one-back sprinkled in there. Now you see teams that have West Coast background, even when

Mike [Holmgren] and Andy [Reid], but they've kind of transitioned as they've gotten further into their careers, they've kind of transitioned into more one-back offenses as well. But I think in the passing game, I think those core concepts kind of have stayed more constant than the running game.

**Q:** So do Alfred Morris and Matt Jones split their carries?

**BB:** Yeah, some version of that. Some games it's more than others. Maybe it's a little bit of a who has the hot hand type of thing, but you're going to see both of them. [Chris] Thompson is more of a third-down sub back, but he's a good runner, too. They also use Morris and Jones some on third down, especially when Thompson hadn't been out there, those guys have played in that role, so I think there is a comfort level of using each of those guys on every down, but probably it looks like Morris and Jones are more early-down guys and Thompson is kind of their sub guy, but there is definitely some carryover. It's not cut and dry. There is some carryover here.

### Q: How does the deep coverage by Devin McCourty and Duron Harmon help your cornerbacks, if at all?

**BB:** It helps them, but I think as a corner, you don't count on that help. I mean, you count on it on inside routes, but you don't really count on it on go routes, but if they can get there on that … The big part of that position is the quarterback. If the quarterback controls the free safety by looking him off, looking one way and throwing the other way, then that corner is probably not going to get any help. Now there are other components of that – the pattern, the protection – the quarterback's ability to do that and so forth.

So I'm not saying that's a given, but again as a corner, it's not like when you have a half field safety and you know that guy's going to be back there at least on your half of the field. A middle of the field safety, there are some guys that can get over and guys that get great jumps on the ball and are instinctive and all that, and Duron and Devin have given us some of those plays, but I think as a corner, you can't just sit there and say I have help over the top. You might, but you can't really count on that. Then there is a certain field position where you don't have it for sure. Once the ball gets to the 35, 40-yard line going in, the ball is not in the air that long. You're just running out of space. So the plays that he's more effective on in those field positions are the seams and the in-cuts and those types of things.

Again that player, he's the quarterback of the defense. He sees the field, he defends the deep part of the field and gets to the ball based on his recognition of the routes and the quarterback and the overall matchups. Sometimes that affects him, too. It's hard to know exactly where that's going to be when you start talking about outside the numbers. Inside the numbers, that's one thing. Outside the numbers, you just can't count on them. I'm not saying those guys can't get there. Our guys have gotten there and have made good plays out there, but you can't sit there defensively and say, "Well he'll be there for that play," because if the quarterback looks him off, he won't be there.

## Q: How does the defensive line play into the rushing of your inside linebackers? Is there coordination between those two units?

**BB:** Yeah, there definitely is, and that takes a lot of communication. When you bring players inside or especially when you walk them up into the line, you never really know how the offense is going to block it. Sometimes they take it from the second level with the back picking up one of those guys and then sometimes they push all the linemen down and put the back on the end of the line, so you can just kind of get a wall of bodies in there or possibly be able to penetrate it. And then we get up there, sometimes we come, sometimes we don't.

We fake that one way or another, but there is definitely a lot of communication there and being able to not only get it right, but then get it right depending on a couple of different looks from the offense including running plays, we have to be able to fit our gap responsibilities based on different blocking schemes and so forth.

When we're coming up inside, that changes things a little bit. There is definitely a lot of communication, and one of those things that probably the more you do it the better feel the players get for it because it's a little bit different. You can talk about it and you can walk through it and all that, but it's a little bit different when it happens on the field. It's definitely important for us to get everybody on the same page on that against a variety of different things the offense can do. It's not like it's just going to be one or two plays. We have to get it worked out against everything.

**Q:** What are your thoughts on Jamie Collins and Dont'a Hightower in that regard?

**BB:** They do a good job. No, I'm not talking about them. It's pretty easy, whoever the guy is blitzing, he just hits the gap and goes. That's really the easy part of it. It's getting everything else coordinated with everybody else. If you're a defensive tackle, you're used to seeing certain blocking schemes, but now if you blitz a guy up the middle, that blocking scheme might vary a little bit because of the linebacker that's trying to penetrate the middle of offense. But that's being caused by something. It's not something maybe the defensive lineman would normally see or would expect to see because that doesn't usually happen. But when it does, now that changes his read a little bit. Again, it changes the blocking or the offensive assignments on the play. The more experienced the players get with seeing how those changes occur and then what they should do against them, it's just part of the whole learning progression.

## Q: What did you see on the touchdown pass to Rob Gronkowski? It looked like a guard pulled on a play action pass, but stayed in pass protection.

**BB:** Well, I think it definitely opened it up. Rob released and kind of got in behind the linebackers pretty quickly and then Tom [Brady] got the ball out in a hurry. There was some space there between the linebackers and really [Reshad] Jones, who was on the backside, so it was kind of away from the safety.

Rob was lined up on the right side and he kind of ran away from the safety on his side and caught the ball in front of Jones behind the linebackers and then broke that tackle and then got a big block from [Brandon] LaFell and finished the play. I think the play action definitely had an effect on the play. That's one of the best things about play action is the opportunity to really get receivers into some open space.

When you just drop back and throw, whether you're throwing against man or zone, for the most part the defense is usually going to be fairly close to those guys – either matching them in zone or running with them in man-to-man. Sometimes when you have a good play action and you're able to displace the defense and get the linebackers coming up or the secondary going back or get the linebackers or whoever running inside while your receivers are running outside you can create some space in the passing game that you just couldn't – I don't want to say couldn't – but it's much harder to get on a drop back pass.

That's the advantage of doing it and the running game helps the passing game, the play action passing game. And then the play action passing game helps the running game in terms of keeping the linebackers from running up there quite so fast. We tried to have those plays kind of complement each other last night – the off tackle runs with the pulling guard and the protection that looks as much as we could make it look like a run, but it was a pass and we had guys running out. Actually I think those runs in the first drive helped that pass and then hitting that pass helped some of those runs later on in the game where the linebackers weren't quite up on the line as quickly as I think they probably would have been if we hadn't hit a play like that.

### Q: Why are the first 15 plays such a big deal as far as how the game might go?

**BB:** Well, I think it depends on the game. I don't think that's necessarily true every week. I think some weeks it's true, some weeks it isn't. It just depends on the way that team tries to approach it. Some teams have a game plan, whether it be on offense or defense, and they kind of start out playing that game plan, like Dallas did. You could see that game plan the first series. Halftime adjustments, I mean that's ridiculous. Why wait till halftime? There it is. The first series of plays you can see what they're going to do, so you better start dealing with it.

There are other teams that maybe anticipate that you're going to play a certain way and they script the plays, and a lot of times the scripts are to break their tendencies like, OK we've done this so we're going to start the game and show this but do that. We want to get the ball to this guy because we want to try to get him going, so we're going to put this play in. So maybe those first few plays are just how they want to start the game. Maybe that's not really the game plan at all. Maybe that's just they want to break their tendencies, they want to show you something, they want to throw a deep pass to back the corner off so they can throw in front of him. They want to throw a quick pass to get the corner up so they can throw behind - I mean whatever.

So sometimes those plays are significant in terms of, OK here's the way it looks like they're going to play us. Sometimes it's not. Sometimes a team will come out and play zone coverages the first few plays to see what kind of formations you're using, see kind of how you're trying to attack them offensively, and then once the game gets going, then OK, here they are, let's go after them - that type of thing. It doesn't always declare that way. A lot of times those first few plays are just a little bit of mirage. You've got to be careful about this is what it's going to be when really that's not what it is at all. That's just the way they want to start the game. That's not really the way they want to play the game. I don't think there is any set book on that.

**Q: How important is it to read the timing in the front to allow the shooting of the gaps to occur?**

**BB:** That's a position again similar to linebacker that I think really some of the physical testing and all just doesn't do it justice. I mean, you talk about vertical jump and bench press and 40 speed and all that, when you're playing safety or linebacker and you've got 15 bodies in front of you doing a lot of different things, play action, run, pull, misdirection, there are a lot of different things that can happen, a lot of schemes. Some players are very quick at being able to sort that out and be moving at top speed and recognize exactly what's going on and then other players who may have timed speed or great physical testing numbers but just aren't able to mentally see everything and process it and sometimes even anticipate it and react to it that quickly.

There is sometimes a big gap on that. It's a very hard position to sometimes evaluate because there is an instinctiveness and awareness and just a kind of feel for all that's going on that it's a lot different than playing corner where sometimes you just lock on one man or you've got a two-to-one read or something like that. At safety you've got a lot of bodies and a lot of things to sort out - same thing at linebacker. Yeah, the ability to recognize that and make the right decision quickly because if you make the wrong one and it's a play action pass and the guy is behind you, you can give up a lot of yards in a hurry.

Patrick and Jordan, they do a good job of that. Really, all of our safeties do. Tavon [Wilson], he does that well, too, and Devin [McCourty] and Duron [Harmon], even though they play back more than they play up, they all do a good job of that. [Safeties] coach [Brian] Flores does a good job of coaching that group. They react well.

**Q:** When you bring new players in, do you have to change the way you run the hurry-up offense? How important is the conditioning factor when you're doing that?

**BB:** Conditioning is definitely important, and it's important for everybody. It's important for the big guys obviously because it's the big guys, but it's important for the skill players because they're the ones who are doing a lot of running – run 40 yards come back to the line of scrimmage, run 30 yards come back to the line of scrimmage. The conditioning part of it is important and of course it's not just the conditioning but it's also the thinking part of it. It's being able to think quickly, make decisions, if Tom [Brady] changes a route or we call a play and then they run to their look and then we need to change it there is some quick thinking, quick decision making that needs to go on.

That's really part of the conditioning process, too. It's definitely challenging to do that with new players. There are a lot of things that can happen when you're trying to go fast and you don't have a lot of time to think or communicate. You kind of got to know what to do, so terminology and communication and anticipation of all three of us, four of us, whatever it is, we all kind of see the same picture, but we all need to see it the same way. We don't have time to talk about it because the ball is being snapped and we're going to go. That part of it is challenging. You also get some defensive looks that obviously aren't the way you're going to practice them.

They're struggling to get lined up, they're kind of scrambling, they're moving late because they're communicating on their end of it, too, so normally when you huddle up and run a play, you're going to be where you want to be and they're going to be where they want to be, and then you execute it from there. When you're going fast, that's not always the case. Sometimes they're kind of where you think they're going to be and sometimes they're kind of scrambling at the last second – a linebacker or a safety or someone will get to where he needs to be on that call and it happens late. Sometimes it works to your advantage, sometimes it doesn't, but it's still being able to identify it and see it and all be on the same page in a short amount of time.

It's challenging for guys who have done it multiple times, and it's even more challenging for guys who have less experience in that. There's no doubt. And you hear one word or two words or whatever it is, only a couple words, instead of calling out the whole play – the formation, the protection, the play, the blocking, the route. Now you're just sometimes saying a couple words and that tells everybody what the formation is, what the blocking is, what the route is. Sometimes it's two plays. The terminology, it's cut down to make you go faster, but you have to remember a lot more things where if you just hear a normal play normally that will tell everybody what to do.

You use three of four words to call a formation and you use words to call out the backfield action, the run blocking, the protection, the strong side route, the weak side route, maybe what the back's route is or what some auxiliary route is just to tie that in. Now it all just becomes one thing.

**Q:** You have used a lot of no-back formations. When did that become a big part of your offense, and what is the reasoning behind it?

**BB:** I think we've kind of had that empty backfield. It really started back in the 80's, when I was with the Giants with David Meggett. It was kind of a mismatch type of formation where you get a back either out on a linebacker, or if they don't put a linebacker on him and they leave a corner on him, then one of your receivers inside gets matched up on a linebacker. So, unless they are in a substituted defense, where they can match up across the board with DBs, you can usually get a linebacker outside on a back extended away from the formation where a lot of linebackers don't play a lot.

Or if they keep the linebackers inside, then you have your receivers working against those guys on the inside part of the field and the corners are outside on the backs. I'd say that's kind of the basic overall philosophy of the formation. We've used it quite a bit through the years. And our quarterback does a good job, Tom [Brady] does a good job of that, and Josh McDaniels does a good job of creating matchups from different formations. That's one of the ones we use.

**Q:** With the way the league is trending with the passing game,

## how much do you expect that Tom Brady is going to be throwing the ball on the majority of plays?

**BB:** Well, we go into each game trying to game plan and do what we think is best and then as we get into the game sometimes that can change a little bit based on how the game is going situationally and also what the matchups are or what's working and what isn't. I think when you look around the league, last year there might have been two teams in the league – maybe it was one, I don't know – but not many that threw the ball less than they ran it.

So, basically every team is over 50 percent passing. Some teams were up around 70 percent if I remember correctly – like the Bears, teams like that. That was last year. But that's the kind of the general trend in the league. A lot of plays are based on run-pass checks in the league, so teams get into more coverage positions, sometimes that invites the run and vice versa. It's really hard to go into a game and say we're going to do this this many times or do this that many times. Each game is different, and as you get into the game it just depends on how the game is unfolding and the score and the situations, but also how the matchups are working with the personnel you're facing and what type of defenses or coverages or pressures they're using and how you want to try to attack those.

That's kind of a long answer to a short question, but the bottom line is if it works out that we're balanced, that's fine, it's great, but if it works out that we're favoring more of one than the other, then if that's working that's fine, too. We had a game against – it was circumstantial, but the Buffalo game in '08 or when we played Buffalo in the rain here a couple years ago, those were games that were tilted very heavily to the running game because of the conditions of the game.

You can draw up all the pass plays you want, but when the conditions are such that you really can't execute them, then you have to find something else to do. We want to try to take advantage of our skill players and all of our players on offense – our run blockers, our skill guys in the passing game, our runners in the running game. So, however we feel is the best way to do that and gives us the best opportunity, then that's what we're going to try to do on a daily basis. And it changes from week to week. We'll just have to be prepared for the game to go however it goes, and then once we get into it adjust and do what we feel like is best in that particular situation.

**Q: When a defense shows what it's trying to do or lines up late in the play clock, is there a way to combat that as an offense, or do you have to wait to see where they're going to be first before you decide what to do?**

**BB:** I think it becomes a cat and mouse game. If you go quick, then if they wait to stem, sometimes they wait too long, and the ball is already snapped. If you go late, then they have time to do that. If you mix it up, then it's a cat and mouse game. Do you want to stem late but they might go quick or do you want to show it early but now they go on a longer count? And that's where good, instinctive players can, whether it be on the offensive side of the ball or the defensive side of the ball or it could be the punt team or the punt rush team, it's all the same really. It's just kind of that timing element.

There are some players that have a real good feel for that – guys like [Troy] Polamalu, Rodney Harrison. There would be times where those guys would line up on the line of scrimmage like they're going to safety blitz and they'd be in the deep half on the other side of the field. But if the quarterback was going to run a quick count, they could kind of sense that and get out of there, and if the quarterback was going to try to read it out, they'd stay there and then right at the end bail. They would be checking into a play for one defense but they were actually in a totally different defense. There are some guys that are really good at that.

Quarterback, same thing – they can see whatever the key is and they don't really care where some guys are, or maybe they get fooled by somebody that's really out of position, but it shouldn't matter. But the cadence and the disguise and all that, it's all part of it. Just like shifting and motion and defensive stemming and disguising, it's all just part of keeping the other side of the ball off balance, but being able to do it in a way that you can actually execute what you're trying to do. It doesn't do any good to disguise something and not be able to get to the guy you're supposed to cover or get to the gap you're responsible for or block the guy you're supposed to block. You fool them, but you can't execute your assignment, so there's that balance.

## Q: What are the dynamics of having two big tight ends together in the red zone?

**BB:** Well, I think the main thing in the red zone, whoever you're throwing to, somehow that person has to create some separation with the defense, and it's hard because there's not very much space and the defense is taught to get on those guys quickly. So, whether it's quickness, size, I'd say ability to catch the ball away from your body with great hands consistently, maybe a person that excels in a particular route, the technique of it like a fade or a slant or some type of push-off contact play to create separating.

But it's hard to get open down there and there's not a lot of space. If the defense drops seven against five or eight against five, which teams are doing a little bit more of that, going with a three-man rush to get that extra guy in coverage, it's just really tight, so any player that can separate, whether it's size, quickness, hands, technique, makes them a good red-area receiver.

I don't think it has to be a tight end or not a tight end – it can be anybody – but the ability to do that is what makes them good. Obviously, bigger is better, particularly when a lot of throws in the red area are at the back end line, high up by the cross bar on the goal post – those high throws in the back of the end zone. That just gives the quarterback a little bigger target, but the guy has got to have good hands to be able to bring the ball down and make a tough catch. Just being tall might help, but without good hands, jumping skills, timing, concentration, then that's only one component of it.

## Q: Does it make it more challenging to defend a team with man-

### to-man when they're using no-huddle and going up tempo?

**BB:** Any team that changes a lot, there are going to be moving parts no matter what you do, unless you can just leave the same players out there throughout every personnel group they have. I mean, you could, but then that creates other problems, and then you've got some matchup issues. If you want to get matchups, then you substitute with them. If you don't care about the matchups or you're comfortable with the matchups or whatever, then you don't substitute and you play your guys out there. But I think in this league, it's pretty hard not to get mismatched somewhere along the line if you keep the same 11 players on the field all the time. I'm not saying you can't do it. I'm just saying you've got to deal with some matchups.

If you can live with those matchups or you can somehow neutralize them, then great, then you can do that. If you can't, then somewhere along the line, you're probably going to have to substitute and change the matchup. That's your choice defensively. You don't have to matchup, but if you don't, then you have to deal with their receivers against your linebackers or their tight ends against your DBs [defensive backs] or whatever it is.

**Q:** Were matchups big when you were first breaking in?

**BB:** No, because the same 11 guys stayed on the field in all situations. It'd be third-and-20, and they might flex a tight end out, but basically had the same guys on the field, and you had the same defense on the field, same 11 guys. The nickel defense was originally, like George Allen brought in a safety for the Will linebacker. It was the same exact defense. They just had, in their mind, maybe a better coverage player playing that position. There was no change in the defense. The ball was on the one-yard line, you'd still have two receivers out there. It's just regular offensive formation. You didn't have the goal line. The roster sizes were different. You didn't have the specialization that you have now.

You had 10 less players, so you didn't have multiple tight ends. You didn't have all those extra guys. You had a couple backups here or there, and they played in the kicking game. And you had a long snapper and you had a kicker and a punter that played somewhere else for the most part. That transitioned pretty quickly. That was totally different. Now, [there's] bigger roster size, more specialization, more matchups on one side of the ball, more matchups therefore on the other side of the ball. It's totally different.

## Q: For your linebackers, is that the primary point of emphasis – making sure they don't get sucked into the run play?

**BB:** Well, it could be. It depends on what the defense you're in is and it depends on what play they run. Some plays are the responsibility of, it depends what the coverage is and what the formation is and what the play is. It's not always the same guy. It's not always the same guy in the same play. That's why practice is so important. We go out there and practice and play and we have one defense called, but if we had another defense called and they ran the same play, then that's where the other guys say, 'OK, if we were in this other defense, you would have this guy, you would have that guy, you would be the force guy, you would whatever.'

We can't run the same play against five different defenses. We just don't have enough plays in practice, not even close to that. We have to be able to recognize the play. But if we happen to be in a different call, it could change the assignments. It could totally change them. Or if they flip sides on the play, then all the guys that saw it on this side would now be seeing it on the other side. It's whoever's responsibility it is, that's who it is. But it could vary based on what we're in, what formation they run it out of and what the actual play is.

## Q: If you're in man-to-man, should play-action have any impact on the secondary? Or is it as effective as it would be against zone?

**BB:** That's a great question. In a way, no, but where the conflict comes is you still have to have run-force in man-to-man coverage. You can't just play man-to-man and not account for the run responsibilities. The conflict comes when you have a – and you try to avoid those conflicts. Obviously, defensively you don't want to have 'I'm responsible for this gap, but I have to cover this guy over here.' That's the recipe for disaster. The responsibilities tie together, but your run responsibility and your pass responsibility when they're in conflict or when you're a step late on that, then yeah, you have the guy in man coverage, but if you're a step late covering him because you're trying to get to your run responsibility or vice versa, you're standing there waiting for the pass, but you're late getting to your run responsibility then that creates seams in the run defense. So, it's all those.

But that's the way it is on every play. It doesn't matter who the opponent is. That's inherently the offensive and defensive – that's the battle. The offense is trying to get the defense to, if they stop one thing, they shouldn't be able to stop something else. Or, 'We're trying to put this player, whoever it is, in some kind of a conflict and if we don't get him on this, then we'll get him on that.' Or, 'Here's what we think he's going to do,' we'll be able to get him on whatever the complementary play is. It's obvious on a play like a reverse where you're chasing a play down from the backside and that guy's got – but the same thing holds true in all the other positions in the interior part of the line as well. Man-to-man theoretically everybody should be handled. It's the conflicts in the running game that potentially present problems on that.

### Q: How important is communication post-snap on defense in defending their route combinations?

**BB:** Yeah, I'd say on defense it's almost always an awareness or a visual communication or recognition. You see a player crossing, you anticipate that based on the call maybe somebody else will take that guy. You kind of, sometimes you see it, sometimes you anticipate it. We play in front of a sold out crowd here so the idea of me yelling routes to you and you yelling them to me – that might happen on the practice field, it might sound good, but the reality of it is, you're not hearing much on Sunday. So, you have to be able to visually communicate it without actually saying anything or in some cases, even doing anything. Just by your teammate's body language or by the reaction you anticipate and then once you start to see that then you know that it's happened the way you had practiced it or had talked about it happening then you're able to adjust to it. There are a lot of different levels of communication. There's the verbal communication, there's certainly the signaling before the snap, whether it's on defense or offense relative to crowd noise and so forth. On the road offensively, at home defensively, so the communication is kind of always an issue. It just depends on which side of the noise you're on. Then there's a post-snap communication between a quarterback and a receiver, a quarterback and a tight end [or] running back, running back and an offensive lineman, a pulling guard.

Then the same thing defensively, with pass rush games, linebackers, defensive linemen, secondary players, linebackers that when you see something happen the way you've anticipated it then that's kind of a communication if you will that then your assignment corresponds to that. If it doesn't happen that way then that can sometimes be a little bit of a scramble or a void somewhere along the line somewhere that then you try to adjust and react to. But that whole process is really in the end, that's the backbone, that's the spinal cord of football is all that process which can be emphasized differently depending on exactly which part of it you're talking about or where the noise is coming from, where the communication is coming from. But in the end, when you put it all together, that's really what connects everything on the football field is communication, understanding, anticipation, reaction, being able to do all that at a high level, at high speed, in a short amount of time. That's the hard, that's it. If you can't do that, it's going to be a long day. If you can do that, then you have a chance to play at the speed, the game speed that you need to play at to win.

**Q: When a team uses misdirection on trick plays, how does that**

## dictate the defensive call? Is there a relationship between the two?

**BB:** As long as I've ever coached, every defense, you have to take care of those responsibilities. I've never coached a defense where you tell the players, 'Well, we don't have a reverse on this play if they run it, that would be a touchdown. Or if they run a halfback pass, nobody is responsible for that and that will be a touchdown. Or if they run an end-around, we don't really have that play.' I just don't think you could coach like that. Somebody has to be responsible for plays over, plays over there. If they start over there, then somebody has to be responsible for a play back there.

If a guy reverses his field or they run a reverse or they throw a double pass or the quarterback peels out of the backfield. Whatever it is, there are fundamental responsibilities and those plays are part of the responsibilities. You just don't see them as often. I would say that's the thing. I don't think our defense or probably any other defense is designed to say, 'Well, if that guy runs a post pattern, we're not going to cover that.' Or, 'If that guy runs a reverse, we don't have that.' Somebody has it, but if you don't see it very often, you aren't thinking about it or maybe you're not respecting it enough and then it comes and it hits you. Then you don't see it again for another year, but the damage is done. That's the way I would characterize those plays.

Not that there's not a way to defend them, not that there's a magic to the play, but it's a play you haven't seen that we're not practicing against because I'm sure the ones that they've already run, they're probably less inclined to run those. They're probably more inclined to run a new play that they're working on and that's the one that we'll have to react to in the game. That's the challenge of those plays. The challenge on the other side of it is the execution. Some play that you don't run very much, it's calling it at the right time to get maybe a look that you think will be good against that and then being able to execute it well.

But I would say that the Bengals have done a very good job of executing those plays. Like [Mohamed] Sanu's passes. He throws the ball as well as a lot of quarterbacks do. He's very accurate and he's got a great touch and arm, but his accuracy is very good. So, they run those plays and it looks like, you see it's [number] 12 but you kind of think, 'Is that a quarterback?' 'No, it's the receiver throwing the ball.' So, they execute them well and they have a good design to them. But I don't think it's a case where you don't – you have the play defended, but you have to actually execute the defense of the play and it's a play you haven't seen or worked on so that sometimes can cause a problem.

**Q:** When you're in the red zone, does the running game change at all – how you can call plays and what plays you're more likely to call?

**BB:** I think it changes a lot from the standpoint that the defensive backs really become linebackers, especially as you get – obviously it's different if it's on the five and if it's on the 20. When the ball is down there inside the 10 or certainly inside the five-yard line, those safeties are linebackers. You're not really blocking linebackers anymore, you're blocking spots and somebody has to get them or you have to run over them. It's as simple as that. I think your running game down there involves a lot more in terms of your receivers blocking run force or formationing to get the run force out of the way or having free guys.

You don't mind having a free safety as the unblocked guy on a running play and you get to the line of scrimmage and he tackles you and you gain 10, 12, 15 yards, whatever it is. Down there on the goal line it's a different story. Those guys can make the play at or behind the line of scrimmage, especially if the play isn't a quick hitting direct play. So you have to account for them. Defensively that gives you a lot more opportunity to stunt, pinch guys inside because you have extra force players, so forth, they're a lot closer to the line of scrimmage. I think it changes the running game quite a bit, I really do.

**Q: What's your thought on Rob Gronkowski's impact? Obviously he's one of the best players in the league at his position.**

**BB:** No argument there. I think he's a good player.

**Q:** How does he open up more things for you in your offense?

**BB:** I don't think he opens up anything. I think that when the matchups are favorable and Tom [Brady] sees that, that's where he'll throw the ball. When it's not, I hope he doesn't throw it to him and we throw it to someone else where we have a better matchup. Look, the more things they have to defend defensively, the harder it is for any defense, we all know that. If you can run the ball, if you have multiple options in the passing game at multiple levels, then that makes it harder to defend and everybody benefits form that. It might be one guy one week, might be another guy another week.

Again, I think there's a perception out there that in the game plan it's, 'Well, we're going to throw the ball to this guy on this play and we're going to throw the ball to that guy on that play.' It just doesn't work that way. I don't think any passing game, unless you want to throw a screen pass or something like that. You have four or five guys out in the pattern and depending on what the coverage is and how the matchups go, there are certain guys you want to throw to and there are certain guys you don't want to throw to based on what they're doing. You might hope that you get a certain matchup and if you get it, great. But if you don't get it, you don't want to tell the quarterback to throw the ball to two or three guys standing there, just because that's a guy you want to throw the ball to. I think that's ridiculous. We would never do that. I don't know if other teams do that, but that's not something we want to do.

**Q: What makes that stuff that you mentioned, like the stretch play, hard to defend?**

**BB:** Well yeah, because they're running wide so you have to defend the boundary. You have to defend the backside on the boot, so it gives you a lot of width; it forces your defense to handle a lot of width. Then when the defense stretches, the backs, when they hit that third step, they're looking to get downhill. I don't want to say cut it back, but they cut downhill. If your defense doesn't get wide enough, they hit the edge. If they get too wide, the back comes downhill. You can't let the backside go because of the amount of bootlegs that they run. Even if you bring an eighth guy into the box, so to speak, against seven, that eighth guy has to take the quarterback. He doesn't have to, but you better have somebody on him.

So if the eighth guy takes the quarterback, then you don't have him to chase those plays down from the backside. That's how they keep you honest. It's not different, but it's similar to the zone-option, read-option program because in that, it's the same thing: they hand the ball off to the running back, but somebody has to take the quarterback on the keep. Well, in their offense, somebody has to handle their quarterback on the boot or you let him stand out there by himself and throw. That's not a good situation so he accounts for the extra guy you could potentially bring down into the front. It forces you to play seven-on-seven or six-on-six or however the formation is displaced. That's how they handle the numbers game, which is a good concept.

**Q:** Does that fall to those guys on the edge a lot, to stay at home?

**BB:** Well, to be sound, somebody has to have it. It doesn't have to be the same guy every time, but if you send one guy down then you have to leave somebody back. If you leave one guy back, then you send the other guy down. You have to fill your space in there. But I'm just saying, they've made plenty of big plays where the backside guy has tried to chase the run down, it's the pass and the quarterback whether it's [Matt] Schaub or [Case] Keenum or whoever it is, [T.J.] Yates, is standing out there with nobody pressuring him, has all day to throw and he's looking at receivers 20, 30 yards downfield, that's not a good place to be defensively. I think somebody has to take it or you want somebody to take it.

**Q:** How much pre-snap disguising can you do with Peyton

### Manning?

**BB:** You better do a good job of it or it's going to be a long day. You have to.

**Q:** Does it come to a point where you say, 'We better stop disguising and just get into what we're trying to get into'?

**BB:** I mean, you can do that. it's just a question whether you can hold up in it or not. I'd say the odds of that aren't great, to be honest with you. I mean, usually when he sees what it is, he gets to the play he wants to get to. I would say they've hit a lot of big plays on plays like that.

**Q:** He just figures this is where it's coming from?

**BB:** He sees the blitz, calls a tear screen to Demaryius Thomas and he goes 75 yards for a touchdown. You can be in whatever you want to be in, but if they have a play to beat it, and it's well executed, which it frequently is with Denver, you're just playing right into their hands. They've been waiting all day to run the play against that situation. You tell them, 'OK, here we are, we're going to be in Cover-2 zone, go ahead and run your best play,' well they will. Or 'We're going to be in man-free or we're going to be in blitz or we're going to be in man-under two-deep, what are you going to do about it?'

They can usually do something about it. I don't really think anybody has had a lot of success playing them that way. If you just out-personnel them at every position across the board and say, 'We're all just going to lock up on one guy and we're going to take everybody and we don't care that we they know where we are because we're that good.' I just don't think anybody has been able to do that. They've scored like, I don't know, more points than anybody in football. I'm just saying, it's hard to do. Somewhere along the line, they have a good matchup, if they know exactly what you're in.

I don't think anybody has played them that way very effectively in whatever it is they've tried to play: man, zone, blitz, man-free, two-deep man, two-deep zone, three-deep zone, three-man rush. If you tell them what you're in, I think you're probably not going to like the way it's going to end up. Now, you know, sometimes it's situational. Then you have to, sometimes you have to live with that. I don't think down after down, anybody has really had that much success doing that.

**Q:** Is there an art to defensive masking that goes on? You can't just have guys running around.

**BB:** No, absolutely it's got to be coordinated as a team. Yeah, you can't have one guy disguising on things and somebody else disguising somebody else. a good quarterback would probably be able to figure out what you're trying to do and see that one guy is way out of position. You have to be very well coordinated on that because what they do with the cadence, they make it hard for you to do that. Sometimes they run up and snap the ball real quickly, so it forces you to get lined up.

Other times they go up there and they delay and check the play and get into a formation that kind of makes you declare so they can see what you're in and then get to the play they want to get to and go at a very slow pace. It's hard to over-disguise because if they go quick then you could be way out of position. [Peyton] does a real good job of that, of changing the tempo to kind of force the defense to show what they're in so he can get to it and then obviously the plays they go quick on, they don't really care what the defense is in because they're kind of all-purpose plays. No matter what they're in, they have the answer on the play somehow.

**Q:** Do you want the players to avoid listening to his checks at the line because they could change or are dummy calls?

**BB:** We'll see how it goes Sunday night but I would say normally at home, it's hard for the defense to hear the offensive calls. It's hard for the offense to hear them. It's hard for the defense to hear them. It's hard for the defense to hear the defense's calls, if there's crowd noise, which sometimes there is, sometimes there isn't.

But I would say it's the same thing playing on the road that it's hard enough for us to hear what we're trying to tell each other when the quarterback is turning around and actually talking to the guy and you're standing five yards away to try to hear them, it's pretty difficult. I mean, that's been my experience. For example, when we used to play Indianapolis in Indianapolis, you could hear what he was saying there but here it was much harder to do that, I would say most of the time. You could never count on it, let's say that. You might hear something because it was quiet at a certain point but you could never count on, 'Well, we'll be able to hear this or we'll be able to hear that' because there are too many times when you just can't. Crowd noise is just as big a problem for the defense as it is for the offense, in trying to communicate.

**Q: How much does your approach change in covering running backs out of the backfield from game to game?**

**BB:** It could change a lot depending on who the players are and how the offense uses it. Some offenses involve their running backs a lot in the passing game. Some of them use them more in protection and to run the ball and play-action, things like that. Some guys, they're go-to guys in the passing game on third down or getting them the ball in space. Protection is another thing that varies from back to back. Some backs can do a lot of different protections. Some backs it looks like teams just use one or two protections with them so that they don't have a lot of different assignments.

I think each week when the linebackers see who the backs are, or the secondary if they're involved in it, you definitely take more time to go through the scouting report with the backs, how they're used in the passing game, what kind of skills they have, some examples of them using those skills, whether they're deep receivers, whether they run a lot of option-type routes, whether they're guys that can get open, whether they're more catch-and-run type players, check-down receivers, things like that.

Usually the player's skills will be complemented within the offense. If the back is a good route runner, they'll probably run him on some man-to-man type routes. If the back is more a catch-and-run guy, they'll run receivers deep and let him be the check-down type guy if it's zone coverage and things like that instead of asking him to win in a lot of one-on-one situations if that's not really one of his strengths. It's definitely a key coaching point, particularly for the linebackers and it could be in sub situations, if you have a DB that's playing down close to the line of scrimmage but covering those guys, what they do, how they do it and what their skills are. There's a wide, wide range from real good to almost non-existent, guys that some teams hardly ever throw the ball to those players. So knowing who is in the game and what they're capable of doing and how we want to do defend them is a key point every week, very important.

**Q: On the idea of running on a two-back set compared to two tight ends with one tight end on each side of the line or two tight ends on the same side of the line, what does that give you as an offense when you have a two-back set in the running game versus two tight ends? Is that a different dimension that's a positive or are they equal in terms of the benefit they give you?**

**BB:** You're talking about two backs and one tight end versus one-back and two tight ends?

**Q:** Right.

**BB:** There are still two receivers in the game?

**Q:** Exactly.

**BB:** Well, I think when you, just fundamentally, when you have one back in the backfield and you have four on-the-line receivers, that gives you an ability to get into the defense potentially with four people. Or even if it's three of them, sometimes the defense isn't sure which three of them it is. One tight end could be in it and the other guy could be in protection, that type of thing. I think you're able to attack the defense from the line of scrimmage a little bit quicker and with a little less predictability, depending on who those players are, of course.

That's certainly a factor. But as far as your running gaps, I mean, you can put more width at the formation by having a guy on the line, whether it's four on one side and two on the other side of the center or three and three. You just have a wider front, which there are some advantages to that. By having them in the backfield, you can create that same four-man surface or three-man surface after the snap so the defense doesn't know where the four-man surface or three-man surface is. The fullback has to – he can build that from the backfield. And then there are also, let's say, a greater variety of blocking schemes with the fullback in the backfield because he can block different guys and come from different angles. He's not always behind the quarterback. He could be offset one way or the other and create different blocking schemes and angles that it's harder to get from the line of scrimmage.

Also, depending on who your tight end is, it can be a little bit easier to pass protect seven men because two of them are in the backfield instead of us having one in the backfield. And then when you start running guys up the middle in the gaps and things like that. I think fundamentally it's a little easier to pick them up when you a have a guy in the backfield that can step up and block him from the fullback position as opposed to a tight end in the line of scrimmage who probably isn't going to be able to loop back in and get him, so the line is probably all going to have to gap down or not gap down if the guy drops out and all that. It just creates a different – it creates some advantages, I think, and it also creates some things you have to deal with.

You just have to decide how you want to deal with them. Obviously when you have a guy in the backfield, it's harder to get those two receivers vertically into the defense in the passing game. They're usually running shorter routes to the flat or checking over the ball or those kind of things, short crossing routes – versus having that fourth receiver on the line of scrimmage who can run some downfield routes, again depending on who the individual person is. The skill definitely changes what you can do with that guy.

So, I mean, I think those are the things that come into play. Some teams are very settled in one type of offense or another, so all of their plays and their rules or their adjustments come from that particular set. And other teams use multiple looks to, say, run the same plays or the same concepts to try to give the defense a different look. It's harder for them to zero in on what they're doing. But they're able to do similar things from different personnel groups or different formations. That's a long answer to a really short question, but I hopefully that helps a little bit.

## Q: The Eagles are in the process of making the switch from a 4-3 to a 3-4, as you had to do. How difficult and challenging is it to do that?

**BB:** I don't know. I think it depends on what you're doing. I personally never felt like it was that big of a deal. People called us a 3-4 team when I was the defensive coordinator with the Giants and Lawrence [Taylor] rushed 85 percent of the time, so everybody treated us like we were a four-man line, but to the media and the fans it was a 3-4, and vice versa.

Guys have to play on the end of the line of scrimmage – whatever you want to call them, linebackers, defensive ends, crash-ins, whatever term they have – guys have to play inside of the outside guy on the line of scrimmage and they're some version of 5-technique, 4-technique, cutback players, however you want to call it. So, I don't think the spacing is – it's important, I'm not saying that, but I don't think it's that big of a deal. We play an even front, we play on off front. I'm sure Philadelphia will do the same thing, even having not seen them. I'm sure that we'll see an even front from them before it's all over. I don't think it's that big of a deal.

## Q: Is tight end traditionally a difficult position to acclimate yourself to in this offense because of the number of responsibilities?

**BB:** I think it's one of the most difficult positions in any offense. Any time you change formations, that player is really at the heart of the changes. You usually, the backs are usually in the backfield, other than some empty plays. The receivers are usually detached, other than some close formation plays. Normally the tight end or tight ends, they're involved in a lot of the formation variations, which then involve them in a lot of different assignments. Basically they're involved in the passing game, the running game, pass protection, blitz adjustments, all the multiple tight end personnel groups like goal line and short-yardage and four-minute offense and things like that in addition to their, as bigger players, their roles in the kicking game.

It's really hard to get around, you might be able to get around a part of that, but not too many parts of it. Or else the guy is a receiver or he's an offensive lineman. That's really what it comes down to. Sure, that position takes a lot. It takes a lot, there are a lot of assignments, there are a lot of adjustments. They have a lot of different responsibilities.

**Q: When Tom Brady is at the line making calls and you have a guy like J.J. Watt, is it common to call for a double team or is that something that's already set up?**

**BB:** I think it depends on how you have it set up, how that play is set up or how your game plan is set up. We've faced guys before, I'd say guys you have to game plan for – the [Dwight] Freeneys and the Jason Taylors and guys like that – whether they're inside or outside guys and you just have to decide how you're going to handle them. First of all, if they blitz then you have to pick up the blitz and the double team really doesn't exist.

But if you have an extra guy, if you can get the extra guy to where that player is or if you can take a guy who would normally be in the pass pattern and let him either bump the guy on the way out or just block him and lose him in the pass pattern, so there are a lot of different ways you can try to get help in the passing game, if they don't blitz. If they blitz, you need all the guys that you have to pick him. You don't want to be double teaming one guy and letting somebody else come free. Again, there are a lot of different ways to do that, but I'd say those are basically what your options are if you want to definitely try to get help, get your line slid that way or keep an extra guy in on that side.

**Q:** How difficult is it for offensive linemen to communicate on the fly with that sort of stuff?

**BB:** I'd say it's more visual communication and you just have to have your rules. All five guys have to see the same thing. So if one of them sees it differently than the other one, it's probably going to be a problem. When to pass them, when to bump them, when to stay with them, when to, even though this is the next guy here, sometimes you have to push past that guy to the next guy outside of him but you have to trust that the guy behind you is coming over to get the guy that's on you.

But that's the way your rules tell you to do it. Sometimes you have to pass up a guy to go block another guy, being confident that the guy behind you is going to take that guy that you're passing up. Things like that. It's about all of them seeing it the same way. But the communication of, 'I've got this guy, you take that guy,' is really, I don't think there's a lot of that – it just happens too fast. You just have to see it and be able to know that, 'OK, I'm getting bumped by him and I have to push back because somebody is coming around or I have to push back away from the protection because somebody is taking me off the guy I have so I can go get somebody else.' That's how you have to block those games.

**Q: What's the biggest difference scheme-wise between a big nickel, three safety secondary and a standard situation with a nickel secondary where you have two safeties and multiple corners?**

**BB:** I would say the ability of that fifth defensive back, that third safety vs. the third corner, what the skills of that player are and what you're playing against.

**Q:** Do you see less of the big nickel because of the passing games, just as a simple generalization?

**BB:** Again, I think it depends on the team and it depends on the player. Like the Giants, they really play the third safety. We've played it that way with [Patrick] Chung in the past. I think if you have a true third slot receiver, a guy like whoever it is, whether it's [Wes] Welker or [Davone] Bess or [Jeremy] Kerley or whoever you happen to be playing, then it's who you want matched up against that guy and what your options are, who you want to put on him. Running game can factor into that. Again, who that player is, sometimes that – like a bigger slot receiver or is it a smaller, quicker guy? Is it 12 personnel, is it two tight ends and that inside receiver is more of a tight end type player. And who are your players, who are you talking about putting on them relative to the matchup? Some teams like to put the same guy in there and do everything with one guy and then there's continuity to the defense. Other teams like to match up to try to get the player they want matched up against the other team's guy that he's going to be facing. It depends, there are a lot of variables.

**Q: Yesterday Mike Lombardi said that ever since he's met you all you've cared about is tight ends. Obviously an exaggeration, but why is the tight end position so important to an offense?**

**BB:** I just think a tight end is involved in a lot of plays. He's involved in the running game. He's involved in the passing game because he's in the middle of the field. He's involved in pass protection. There's really no way, there really aren't hardly any plays where that guy is out of the play. He's a central guy in pretty much whatever you want to do. And the more versatile he is, the more things he can do, then defensively the harder he is to defend. If you have to defend a guy in the passing game, then that's an issue. You have to worry about them running behind him, that's an issue. You have to worry about his speed, that's an issue. You have to worry about him breaking tackles and catching short passes and turning them into long plays. The more versatile any player is, the more valuable they are. At that position in the middle of the field – with skill players are involved in every play, they give you more options.

**Q: What goes into the decision when it comes to three-man fronts**

**and four-man fronts? Do you practice both during the week? Do you go into the game saying 'this is what we're going to run' or do you wait and see what happens?**

**BB:** Your spacing on defense, it could be either or both. It just depends on how you want to play the game. If you want to play it in one look, then you practice that look. If you want to have a couple multiple looks, then you practice multiple looks. You get into the game, you might keep them multiple, you might favor one or the other. Again, we go into the game and we prepare for what we think we're going to see, but we don't know what we're going to see. Then you get into the game and you find out that you may be getting a little more or a little less of this than you thought and that may alter what you want to do or it might not. There's no set formula on that.

**Q:** When you have a situation like last week when you have to change on the fly, the game is obviously going on -

**BB:** You make that decision during the game. You decide whether you want to do what you decide is best for the game even though your personnel might not be ideal for it or change to maybe what your personnel fits but may not be ideal for what you think they're doing. You just have to weigh that and decide what you think is best.

**Q:** What is Matt Patricia's role in that? Does he step away from the sideline and get away and figure it out? How does he handle that adjustment?

**BB:** I basically talk to those guys at the end of every series. I talk to Scott [O'Brien] in the kicking game, maybe not after every play but you know, after a series of plays or whatever - our kickoff coverage or our punt protection or whatever it is. At the end of the series, I usually talk to Billy [O'Brien] and Matt or other coaches, it could be Dante [Scarnecchia] or it could be somebody else about the series that happened. We talk about what we need to do or what they're doing and what we can do about that, whatever it happens to be. That's part of the whole. We talk about that on the headset too. It's hard on the headset too because if we're on offense, we're calling plays, we're substituting people.

That's not really the time to have a philosophical conversation but when you come off the field after we've scored or we've punted or whatever the situation is, okay, next time we get out there, do we want to go no-huddle, what do we want to do the next series or what are we going to do the next time they give us a certain look or what are we going to do in the next third and medium, third and long, second and long? If there is a particular situation that we're not doing well in, what are we going to do the next time that comes up? It's the same thing defensively - what are we going to do if they put three receivers in the game, what are we going to do if they tighten the formations? Yeah, we talk about that in between series.

**Q:** When you come together with the coordinators and coaches, do you initiate the conversation about what you see or do you ask what they're seeing or is it a case by case basis?

**BB:** Yeah, all the above. I rely a lot on them. We talk, it's not like we've never talked about this stuff before. We talk about it going into the game. 'Look, this what they do well, this could be a problem, what are we going to do about this?' Or, 'We're not expecting much of this but if they do it, what's our answer going to be?' Or, 'We're concerned about these matchups, how are you going to handle those?' Then you get into the game and you talk about it. You say, 'Okay, we were concerned about this matchup and it looks like it's still going to be a problem.' Or, 'I think we kind of got that under control but this might be a bigger issue than we thought it was over here.' Or, 'We expected this type of a game plan but they're really doing something, they're mixing in some other things with that and not just staying with what we thought they were doing to do.'

Again, that changes during the game too. Where you are in the first quarter, second quarter on that by the third quarter that sometimes they shift away from something. You see, 'Hey, they're really trying to go to a certain guy.' So you try to decide how you want to handle that. Like in the Philadelphia game, they started going to [Jason] Avant, they were feeding it to him. There was a point where you recognize, 'Alight, they're obviously looking for this guy now, he's got six, seven catches, we have to start paying more attention to him.' DeSean Jackson went out of the game. I'm just saying, things like that happen in the game that you talk about them then. I talk them out with the coaches and they talk them out with me, however you want to call it.

**Q:** Do you look at the Polaroids as much? Bill O'Brien and Tom Brady obviously rely on them.

**BB:** The pictures are definitely an aid. You can sometimes get a lot out of picture. Sometimes you can't really get anything out of it. It depends on what you're looking for and when it was snapped. There's certainly value to those. There's also value to seeing what you see. That's what we all do. Definitely if I ask Dante [Scarnecchia] about what happened on this blitz or what happened on this blocking scheme, that's what he's looking at. If I ask Chad [O'Shea], 'What happened on this route?' Then, 'Hey, we got jammed' or, 'The corner did this and the safety did this and that's why we ran it that way.' I can't see all 22 players at once but I can focus on whatever I'm focusing on but that may or may not be an issue on that play. We definitely talk about those things.

**Q:** Is that a real coaching skill, if you're Chad O'Shea on field level to watch your receivers and see what kind of leverage they're getting and see how it works in combination in live time? To be able to process and assess what's going on accurately?

**BB:** It's a skill but I think it's a realistic expectation too. That's what we do out there in practice every day. We watch the play and then after that you tell a player, right there at that point in time, 'Look, when that happens to you, then this is what you do. You did this but you really need to keep it tighter. You should have done this or you should have done that.' We do that on a daily basis.

**Q: You often hear that the defense has someone to spy the quarterback. Is that concept something that you agree with or is that overstated when you hear that talked about by analysts?**

**BB:** Depends on what the defense is doing. If they assign a player to spy the guy, I don't think it's overstating it; that guy is spying. If they don't, then it's probably overstated.

**Q:** From what you've seen from the Broncos this year, how much have defenses done that with the quarterback?

**BB:** They've seen it some, they've seen it some. The teams that, whatever they do, they basically do what they do and then they might have some modification or variation off it, but it's still - if you watch the Bears, it's still the Bears' defense. If you watch the Jets, it's the Jets' defense. You watch Kansas City, it's Kansas City's defense. Not every play is a pass play. Not every play the quarterback scrambles on, so sometimes things will be called and you're not really sure what they would have been if that would have happened. The only plays you can really evaluate are the ones that actually get to that point. If it's a running play or if it's an option play or it's something like that, I have no idea whether they're spying or not.

**Q:** What makes a good spy if you were to adopt that?

**BB:** You need somebody that can tackle the quarterback. Depends on what the quarterback's skills are. I don't know if you want to spy [Ben] Roethlisberger with the same guy you'd want to spy Michael Vick with. It depends on who the player is. There's no point in spying him if you can't tackle him. Whatever those skills are, you probably better find somebody - if you're going to put him on him, you better find somebody that can do it.

**Q:** What are the pros and cons to using a spy?

**BB:** If you can get it done, then hopefully that eliminates that player as a runner. But you're playing with 10 players, then you have one less guy to do whatever else you need to do. It just depends on what your priorities are.

**Q:** Is there any negative impact on the defense when you do that?

**BB:** Yeah, you have one less guy. You can't cover a receiver and spy the quarterback at the same time. You either spy the quarterback and don't cover the receiver or you cover the receivers or cover a zone and don't spy the quarterback.

**Q: When you're defending Denver's running game and Tim Tebow is running the option, are there Wildcat elements to it, like how you would defend Miami?**

**BB:** Yeah, absolutely, that's what it is - that's part of what it is, it's not all option, but there's definitely an element of that in the running game. They have several different, I'd say, concepts - not really packages, because you don't when they're going to be in them and when they're not because they don't change personnel. It's not like seeing a running back or a receiver come back and stand behind the center - a different guy - it's always the same guy. They can either be in it or not be in it at their discretion so you have to be ready for it even though that's not what they're doing, and then you have to be ready for it and that is what they're doing.

It definitely has a Wildcat option element to it, no question about it. But they also run a lot of plays that I think we would say are conventional plays, if you will - whatever that is, you know, plays that are more familiar to all of us. They do both and that's part of the problem; you don't know when you're going to get one thing or get another. They don't substitute necessarily to get into it, so you just have to figure it out. Sometimes at the line of scrimmage or sometimes after the ball is snapped you have to figure it out. They create some problems on that, no question.

**Q: Obviously you practiced Matt Staler and Julian Edelman on defense leading up to the game. Have you ever had an instance in your career when you've had to move an offensive player to defense or vice versa because of an injury or whatever and the guy hasn't been able to practice that position?**

**BB:** I don't think so. I think we at least got him in there for a little bit. We were playing Larry [Izzo] at safety in preseason, Don Davis at safety, whenever that was, '04. I don't think you just take a guy, I guess you could, but I wouldn't recommend it. Even [Rob] Gronkowski, we use him in our end of the half type defenses or

Randy [Moss] or Keyshawn [Johnson], or guys like that in the past. We've always practiced those things - showed them where to line up, what to do. You don't know exactly what the offense is going to come out in, it's maybe one of two things so there are some adjustments and little bit of understanding what the situation is. We've always practiced that.

**Q:** Was that different maybe when the rosters were smaller? Did you have to bring up more guys on each side of the ball just for emergency situations?

**BB:** I don't think so. I think going back to when I first came into the league, you just didn't have as many personnel groups as you have now. A lot of times, those 11 guys never left the field. Like the Hail Marys from [Roger] Staubach back in the '70s, it's just their regular offense, a guy running a go route. It wasn't all those guys together jumping it and tipping it and that type of thing. When I came into the league, you rarely saw - you saw a tight end, you saw two receivers, you saw two backs.

Whatever, you had four backs, those four replaced those two, those two replaced the other two. If you had two tight ends, then your tight end replaced the other tight end. There were no two tight end sets. Even in goal line, short yardage on the one yard line, you still usually had two spread receivers, there were no third receiver. There were a few teams that played some nickel defense, like the Redskins when George Allen was there but it wasn't really nickel, it was just the defensive back came in for a linebacker. They played the exact same thing but it was just a DB instead of a linebacker having those coverage responsibilities so he was maybe a little more athletic and had a little more coverage skill.

If something happened to him, they would just put their linebacker back in and just run the same thing. It really wasn't until like in the late '70s to early '80s when you had teams running two tight ends and one back and even starting to get into three receivers. I remember being with the Giants in '81 and we didn't even have a nickel defense. That was a big step. I can't remember what year it

ALEX KIRBY

was, maybe it was '82 or '83, we were like 'Okay, we're going to put in the nickel this year.' It was like 'Oh my God, this is going to be a big step, how are we going to do this?' and terminology and all that. We didn't even have that. You had maybe if it was third and ten, you had a third and ten call that was different than your first and ten call, I'm not saying that but as far as substituting guys in. Therefore, what we have now in terms of depth is more of an issue. There were fewer players than but honestly there were fewer positions. Now there are more players but you have three receivers, you have two tight end sets, you have all your five DBs, maybe your six DBs, you've got your pass rush guys, which is the whole, it's like college football where it's expanding rosters to go on and on.

You've got your backup punter, you've got your plus-50 punter, you've got your short field goal kicker, you've got your field goal snapper, you've got a punt snapper, you've got an onside kick guy, you've got four tight ends on this formation, you've got five wide receivers on this formation - it's just more and more substitutional groups if you have more and more players. It gets further away from just the 11 guys that you had out there. You can take it all the way back to the '50s in college football when you didn't have free substitution, guys went both ways. You look at some of the old defenses there, why were teams playing a 5-3 and a 6-2? Because it was the same guys that had to play offense.

You had to take your offensive players and put them on defense or more importantly, you had to take your defensive players and then fit them onto offense. If a lot of fullbacks looked like guards it's because they were linebackers on defense. The game, in terms of substitution and all that has expanded tremendously. Your depth now, you have to have, if you're a three receiver team, you don't go to the game necessarily with six receivers or if you're a two tight end team, you don't necessarily go to the game with four tight ends, so you can't have a backup for each guy like it used to be. You have to have either different personnel groups or one guy backing up multiple spots, stuff like that.

438

**Q:** Was it Washington that kind of spurred all the different packages?

**BB:** I'd say they were ahead of the curve on that, yeah. George Allen was ahead of the curve on that. I think he also was one of the guys that started to take the middle linebacker out. They would take their outside linebacker, [Chris] Hamburger and slide him into the middle. You had a Sam, Mike and Will and your inside guy a lot of times was the least of those three coverage players. If you took your Will and bumped him into Mike and then put a DB in, which a lot of teams do now, similar thing, you'd just have a more athletic, better pass coverage on the field. Allen was, I would say, ahead of the curve on that. Once the multiple receiver sets came in then defensively you have to match those.

Really defensively you have to match what the offense does. If you can just put one group out there and defend everything, great. But it's hard to do, it's hard to do. They bring in bigger people, well somewhere along the line, you're probably going to need to match it with bigger people. They keep bringing in smaller people, like in the '80s when Mouse Davis and June Jones and those guys ran the run and shoot offense where you're in four wide receivers on every single down, the 3-4 defense just wasn't built for that. The 3-4 defense is built for I-formation.

Now you match that with another DB or maybe two more DBs, depending on how you want to play it. But the more of those guys they put out, then you have to have somebody to put out there and match them. Defensively, you don't control that. Offensively, you control who is on the field, you control what formation they're in and to some degree you control who gets the ball. Defensively, you don't have control of any of that so you have to defend whatever it is they do.

**Q:** We've seen a lot of examples of offensive players going to defense and playing that way. Is it harder to go defense to offense because of skill sets?

**BB:** We've seen [Mike] Vrabel play tight end, we've seen different guys play fullback, [Dan] Klecko and Dane [Fletcher] played it this year. We've had different guys doing that, Bryan Cox did that. Again, a lot of those guys, like Klecko was a high school fullback and defensive lineman/linebacker. Again, those are kind of compatible, a fullback and a linebacker, that has kind of been a traditional two way player, that has been the complementary position - outside linebacker/tight end complementary position, wide receiver/corner. Again, a lot of the corners coming out of college football are converted wide receivers, I'd say a good chunk of them are. Of course, you have a great player in high school, you put him at wide receiver. Now he goes to college and he doesn't quite have the hands or the skill set to be a top receiver, there are other receivers on the team that are better but he's a good athlete, he's a good player, he's big, he's tough - you put him over on defense.

That's the complementary position there. I don't think that that's necessarily - let's put it this way, at whatever point a coach takes a player from offense and puts him on defense, there is usually a reason for that. I would say the reason usually is that he's not enough of a playmaker on the offensive side of the ball. What coach is going to take your best playmaker and put him on defense? You just wouldn't do that, all the things being equal. If the guy can't catch but he's a good athlete or he's everything but he doesn't have great hands, at some point you get a receiver who is a better pass catcher and you put this guy over on defense.

You get a guy who is big and strong and tough, but he's just not elusive enough runner, he just can't run over everybody, you can run over guys that are smaller than you but at some point when everybody is the same size, you just can't run over those guys and he doesn't have the elusiveness then you put him over on defense and you get a more elusive running back. Whether that's at high school, college or wherever it is, and I tell the defensive players all the time, 'Don't kid yourself. If you were a big enough playmaker, you would have stayed on offense. Either at the high school or the college level they would have put you out there and you'd be out there having 100 yard receiving game or 150 yard rushing games. You'd be doing that. Don't kid yourself.' It's like the defensive specialist in basketball, if you were that good of a shooter, you'd be the point guard but you're not so start covering these guys or we'll get somebody else in there.

**Q:** We've heard you joke before that you started Stephen Neal on the defensive line and that didn't work out and Matt Light at right tackle didn't work out. Has there been a receiver that you tried to flip to the other side of the ball as a security measure and it was a disaster?

**BB:** There are plenty of them, yeah. Some guys just don't, the other side of the ball, they're just, I don't want to say one-dimensional players but their specialty is on one side of the ball and that's all they are. But that's okay. There are a lot of good players that don't have secondary positions - Tom Brady. That's okay if you're really good at your one position. Conversely, a lot of the defensive players - why does a coach move a defensive player from defense to offense? It's usually speed. That's generally what it is.

If the guy runs well, which is Steve Neal, the guy ran a sub-4.8. Where do you get a guy that weighs 300 pounds and runs a 4.8 that is tough and physical and all that? You want to try him on defense. But he just wasn't a defensive player or at least he wasn't in 2001 and I don't think he ever would have been. But you give it a shot. To play with a lot of guys that can't run on defense, that's probably not where you want to be on defense. You have a good football player, he's tough, he's physical, he's smart, he uses his hands well, he has good power he has good balance but he doesn't run well, what do you do with him? You make him an offensive linemen. That's his last stop. I tell the offensive linemen that too - 'If you could run, you'd be on defense.' Why are you on offense? Because you don't run well enough to play on defense. Most of the time, that's the truth. Not in Steve's case, but I'd say most of the time, the defensive players run better than the offensive players. The offensive players have more skill, ball skills, than the defensive players or more elusiveness.

**Q:** You guys offensively seem to be successful running the no-huddle. Are you running it as much as you were earlier in the season?

**BB:** We've kind of go in and out of it. If we feel like it's advantageous, then we'll do it. If we don't, if there are other reasons to not do it, then we won't. It's not a set formula. Obviously if you're behind and you don't have much time, that's one thing. But other than that, it's a question whether you feel like you're getting an advantage versus what you're giving up by not huddling and not substituting and all of those things. [You] just have to decide what you feel is the better option there.

**Q:** When you do decide to go to it or away from it, is it more based on the defensive personnel or the down and distance?

**BB:** I think if you're in it, you're kind of in it regardless of down and distance because you can't really control the down and distance. If you run a play on first down and you're going no-huddle, it could be second and one, it could be second and 10. Unless you want to get in it or get out of it based on one play then you kind of lose the tempo of it. I think if you're in it, you're in it. If you're not in it, you're not in it. Again, it just depends on what you're trying to gain from it and then what you give up by not being able to substitute, not being able to call a play, not being able to utilize motion or things like that.

Again, you can't run every play that you have from no-huddle unless you had a much smaller selection of plays. But the plays we have in our game plan, not all of them are no-huddle plays. I don't want to say it takes you out of it, but it would take you out of certain plays during that sequence. If you want to be out of those, or you don't care about that then you gain the advantage of the tempo. If you want to be able to do some of those things, then you have to be able to huddle up and go back and do it. It really keeps you out of the no-huddle. We use them both. They both have advantages. We've had production doing it both ways. We try to do what we think is best for that particular situation in the game.

**Q:** To go back to our no-huddle topic, when Tom Brady is calling the plays, is he getting them one right after the other or do you guys typically have a series that he knows, say the next three are going to be this and he already knows what he's calling? Or does it happen right after the last one?

**BB:** Definitely the latter occurs, but it's a combination of things. We go on the field with usually an idea of what we want to try to do in that series. It isn't just, 'What am I going to call here?' 'We're going to line up in this formation and run this play and then if that play goes okay then the next thing we're going to do is this and the next thing we're going to do is that' and that kind of thing. Now, you get a 40-yard gain or you get a holding penalty, then obviously that could change things. But it's kind of one play sets up another or one play complements another in some way, whatever it is, whether it's a formation or look or maybe you want to move your players around so they have to adjust to it.

Or maybe you don't - maybe you want to leave them there so you see it the first time and then you kind of can see it the second time - is it the same or are they doing something different? It just depends on how you want to do it. We talk about that and assuming things go according to plan, then the plays would probably come off about as we planned on it. Of course things could change or sometimes the play goes to another hash mark and you have to flip the play or something like that. At the end of the play, then it would be called into him, yes. 'Okay, let's get them into this formation and we're going to run that play,' and then he would communicate that to the team.

But a lot of times there's an anticipation of what's going to happen, so it doesn't really catch anybody by surprise. But again, occasionally sometimes things change and something might come up that we didn't say going onto the field 'this is something we're going to want to do.' But now the situation has presented itself and then we would call that formation, call that play. It's a combination of both.

**Q:** Getting back to the safeties, in terms of communication, when there's confusion is there one player who has the final say to get everybody on the same page?

**BB:** When you have communication with somebody else, it's a two-way street. Safeties have to communicate with each other, they have to communicate with other players on the defense - the players to the outside of them and also have to coordinate things with the linebackers. It's a combination of all of those. Sometimes it's more on one guy than another depending on what the call is, what the formation is. Ultimately, the two safeties have to communicate. That communication extends to the perimeter. In some cases, the secondary has to coordinate their communication with the linebackers. In some cases they don't but in some cases they do. Then it all has to be coordinated. I'm not trying to give you a run-around answer but it depends on what the defense is - not every defense really involves the linebackers and the secondary. Some do, some don't.

Some really involve the secondary and the linebackers are kind of, I don't want to say on their own, but their element of it is self-contained. It just depends. They communicate with the outside linebackers and the defensive ends in terms of run-force. And the corners depending on who's responsible for the end of the line run-force in the running game. Then you have coverage adjustments and assignments. Some of those are between the secondary, some of those are between the secondary and the linebackers [and] some of them are clearly separate.

**Q:** At some point, it's better to be on the same page.

**BB:** It's always better to be on the same page. It's always better. It's better for us all to be wrong together than for half to be right and half to be wrong. We're better off if we're all wrong. That's right. If that makes any sense. It appears that we should be playing in this set, but we're playing something else. At least if we're all playing the same thing, we have a better chance of executing it than half of the guys are in the right thing and half the guys are in the wrong thing. They usually don't tie together. That's not a good combination. That's true of everything too - it's offensively, special teams, we're all better off wrong together.

**Q: When you have tight ends like Aaron Hernandez and Rob Gronkowski, with the skills they have, how much does that open up for you from a diversity standpoint offensively?**

**BB:** I think that's the nature of any offense. You can't move your five linemen, you can't move the quarterback, you usually have a running back in the backfield so the players you move are your receivers or your tight ends and we've always done that. Both Aaron and Rob are versatile players, they can do some different things, they have different skills and they're smart.

You can move them around and give them different assignments and they're able to handle that. But that's part of the nature of the tight end position I think. Whether you're talking about [Antonio] Gates or [Anthony] Fasano or whoever we play next, that's what most teams do. It is part of the formationing, in a lot of cases, you set your defensive front based on a tight end's location, you set your secondary rotation based on the tight end's location so maneuvering those guys around, putting them in different positions, having them do different things, that's what creates problems for the defense. I think all teams do that to some degree.

**Q: What is it about the 3-4 defense that has been near and dear to you throughout your coaching on that side of the ball?**

**BB:** At the Browns we played a 4-3.

**Q:** Other than the Browns, what is it about the 3-4?

**BB:** We won two Super Bowls playing a 4-3. In '01 and ['04]. Second half of the '01 season, we played 4-3 after Bryan Cox and [Ted] Johnson got hurt.

**Q:** 3-4 has been historically presumed to be your preferred defense.

**BB:** In all honesty, most people thought we played a 4-3 at the

Giants. Lawrence Taylor did a lot more rushing than he did pass dropping. He was probably 90 percent of the time, 80 to 90 percent of the time he was the rusher in the defense. Now not every play was a pass, but certainly in passing situations and on a lot of pass plays, he was the designated fourth rusher which really put us in what amounts to a 4-3. I think honestly that's something that's a media fabrication. There are a lot of different alignments out there, you see 4-3 teams use odd spacing, you see 3-4 teams use even spacing. You have same... look, you have 11 players. You can put them in various positions. Whether you want to put it in the pregame depth chart as one thing or another I think is a little bit overrated. You play different fronts, you play different spacings and you teach the techniques of your defense and that is what is consistent.

The techniques that are taught in the different defensive systems, whichever ones you want to talk about, are consistent within those systems. And those teams go from a three-man line to a four-man line or a four-man line to a odd spacing line or overs-to-unders or unders-to-overs or over-wides or whatever you want to call it. They'll continue to play the same fundamental techniques that they've been teaching for the entire year, for the most part. I think that's what teaching defensive fundamental football is about. It's about fundamentals.

Wherever you put them, you have to put other people in complementary places however you decide to do that. It's pretty straightforward really. You can't have them all over here and none over there. You have to balance it off at some point. It's more the teaching and techniques and the fundamentals that you teach your defensive players more than it is the 3-4, 4-3 lineup that is so important to put on the flip card.

**Q:** Would it be more accurate to look at it as a two-gap versus a one-gap then?

**BB:** It's all the fundamentals and sure, that's part of it. There are techniques in terms of how to play your front, how to defend the number of gaps and the ways that the offense can attack you, particularly in the running game. So how you want to do that? In a normal set you have eight gaps - seven blockers and eight gaps - so how do you want to defend that? Do you want to defend it with seven people or do you want to defend it with eight? That's really what it comes down to. And every time you spread a guy then the defense spreads a guy, so eight becomes seven. Then seven becomes six. Depending on how many guys are detached from the formation, then that's how many gaps you have. You decide defensively how you want to defend them in the running game.

Do you want to defend them with gap control? Do you want to two-gap? Do you want to try to overload the box with extra guys and play eight against seven or seven against six? Those are all the choices you make. With every decision, there's going to be an upside, there's going to be a downside. There will be advantages to playing certain things, there will be disadvantages to playing [them]. So every system has multiple coverages, multiple fronts to adjust to, different problems that the offense presents.

**Q:** If 3-4 and 4-3 is overrated like you said, is the important thing to look for players that have skills that can match up against a variety of things that you'll see throughout the season?

**BB:** Again I think there's certainly a lot to be said for flexibility. There's also a lot to be said for playing well at one position. I think if a player plays one position very well, there's a lot of value to that. If a player plays multiple positions at a good level, maybe not quite as good as a guy who plays one position at a little bit of a higher level, that versatility is worth a lot as well. How do you value those? I don't know. I think you have to have both. We've had plenty of good players who really just did one thing - Ted Washington, Steve Neal, guys like that.

They never did anything but play one position for a long time... well Ted was only here a year, but throughout his career or throughout the time he was here, he did one thing [and] he did it pretty well. Great. Other guys, the Mike Vrabels of the world, the Rodney Harrisons, guys like that, Troy Brown, those guys did a lot of things. They did them pretty well too. A football team is comprised of a lot of parts, certainly a lot of moving parts. You need a lot of different things through the course of a season, through the course of a game. Some guys provide one thing, other guys provide others things. In the end you just have to comprise your team so you can put the best group together that you can. That's the only way I can explain it.

**Q: In the learning process for players like Haynesworth and [Chad] Ochocinco and whoever else you bring in, do you have one specific role that you want them to learn now or do you just kind of throw it all at them now and see what they come up with in a few weeks?**

**BB:** I think it varies from player to player. With every single player on the team, we have certain goals for them and we have certain responsibilities. We tell him, 'Look, this is what you're responsible for and this is what we want you to learn.' Maybe we tell him what the rotations are going to be or how many reps they're going to get doing whatever it is that's scheduled for them and those kinds of things. So each player has his own set of priorities and his own, I would say, guidelines or expectations for him as far as what he's going to do or how he's going to do it or what things we want him to learn or what he needs to work extra on or that type of thing.

Every player has that, doesn't matter whether they're new or old, rookies or 20-year veterans. We try to prioritize things for every player so that when they start the season, they know the things that we feel like are most important and they improve on or show us in the early part of it. Then we reevaluate that as we go at the start of the season, at the bye week. At the end of the season we kind of recalibrate that going into the offseason. It's a continuous process and it's constantly being revised.

**Q: Are yards after catch more of a function of scheming and getting a player in space or is it partly his uncanny ability to run to**

### daylight and find that open space?

**BB:** You're always trying to get players into open spaces. That's just, fundamentally, that's what offense is. Whether it's the running game or passing game, you're trying to create space in the defense and get the ball to somebody in that area. Making yards in that situation, I think, is much more a function of the player who has the ball. There are a lot of different ways to gain yardage, whether that's speed, quickness, power, some combination of all those things. Guys that gain yards, you usually see the same players. The yards-after-catch guys are usually the yards-after-catch guys. If that's the skill that that player has, then he's usually able to produce there on a consistent basis. If some players, some receivers, are good at getting open and catching the ball and making positive yards in the passing game but they aren't great run-after-catch guys then they probably aren't going to be great run-after-catch guys a year from now, two years from now or five years from now.

It doesn't mean they aren't good receivers. A lot of times they're better receivers then the guy that can run with the ball because you've got to get open and catch it first, but once you get a player that combines all those skills together, then you're really... A guy catches a ball, he takes a five-yard play and turns it into 30 [yards] or 40 [yards], and that's tough for a defense. When you're playing defense, you want to try and keep things in front of you, keep things contained and those guys that can take those kinds of plays and break out of them and break into big plays are tough. Forte is a great example. In the Lions game, there's a minute to go in the half, they're on their own 10-yard line, threw a screen pass. I'm sure they weren't expecting to score. I'm sure they were just expecting to get a first down and it was 90 yards for a touchdown. Those are the kinds of plays that break a defense in half when you can't tackle. Hester, Knox, they're very dangerous with the ball in their hand. Cutler, that guy outruns most defensive backs. You see backs get the angle on him, [but] they can't get him; he's too fast.

**Q: The Ravens throw a good amount of screen passes and you guys have been very good against the screen. Can you talk about the challenge about defending that play?**

**BB:** Screens are complimentary plays to the passing game. They're designed to take the edge off the pass rush, so it depends on what defense you're in and what type of screen they run. The principle of the play is to separate the defense - to have some guys rushing the passer, and have other guys in coverage, and throw the ball in that in between area with some blockers ahead of them. Whatever your system is you have to have a way to deal with that. It's very challenging with backs like [Ray] Rice and [Willis] McGahee, [Mark] Clayton and guys like that. They get them the ball in space with a couple blockers ahead of them and you could be looking at a lot of yardage.

Those are always dangerous plays and plays that you've got to work hard on to both recognize and play correctly within the context of the defense because they're really true team plays, everybody's involved in those it's not just one guy that can stop the screen. You've got to have a coordinated defense against that. They do a good job and it will definitely be a challenge.

**Q: Is there a moment that stands out when you first saw a defensive package, like the one you guys have used the last couple weeks with the five linebackers and six defensive backs, standing guys up at the line?**

**BB:** I think we used it a couple times with the Giants. In fact, we did one game with the Giants was all the linebackers got on the kickoff team and it was all eight of them, expect for the safeties. They were the kickoff team. It was a pretty good team – Harry [Carson], Lawrence [Taylor], Pepper [Johnson], all those guys, Carl Banks, Andy Headon. Some of those guys were on it anyway. I think we did a little bit of that with the Giants. We had a lot of two defensive linemen, with Lawrence and Carl outside and Pepper and Harry or

Andy Headon were the inside guys. Then I think we got to a couple times where we just had one defensive lineman and we were in an odd front. There was a couple situations, where if I remember correctly, we didn't have any lineman on the field.

**Q:** Do you remember why you decided to do it?

**BB:** Not that the defensive lineman - I'm not saying they can't run - but it gives you a little more speed and more athleticism. And all those linebackers are potential rushers and potential droppers. I always remember my first year when I came in the league, Coach [Ted] Marchibroda would take like our second secondary with the quarterback and he would have me call coverages and we'd break the huddle and the secondary would rotate to the coverage, whatever it was and the quarterback would see the rotation and as soon as he saw it he would call it out, 'Cover Four'.

As soon as Burt Jones would take one or two steps out of his drop it would be Cover Four or Three C, and try to get it out as quickly as he could based on what the strength of the formation was, but there was only seven guys and the other four guys never dropped, so now you can play the same coverages with blitzers and different combinations, so it's seven guys of the 11, but it's not always the same seven and that's made it difficult for quarterbacks. And compared to back then when you almost never saw that happen, now that's pretty commonplace with the 3-4 defense and the two defensive linemen that a lot of teams use, most 3-4 teams use. It puts nine guys in coverage, sometimes 10.

There're potentially 11 guys that the quarterback has to read. You start thinking about, well the coverage drops off so you can drop the ball off the underneath zones and all that, but that's not always true because those guys that you think are rushing aren't always rushing and sometimes they drop off with those backs, too. It's tough on a quarterback.

**Q:** Is that something that's decided for the play?

**BB:** Yeah, there's some kind of a system. There is some type of a system. Since they can all sort of do the same thing it's easy enough for two guys to switch responsibilities. I'm covering and you're rushing and alright, you rush and I'll cover. And that happens sometimes at the line of scrimmage.

**Q:** Is it a balance? You obviously want to be clear on your responsibilities?

**BB:** Right, exactly. When we're confused it's no good. We don't want that. We want to know what we're doing and be able to change up and give them some different looks. But when it becomes confusing to us and there're too many options, we can do one of 19 things and there's 10 third-down plays in the game. We really don't want to be there. A lot of times those guys can tell, you can't tell from the sideline or you can't tell from film, but when you get out there on the field, they can tell who's going to block them. And Lawrence Taylor was really good at that.

He knew who was going to block him and who was assigned to him. And a lot of times he would take the coverage from somebody else and also to draw the block because he knew, like I said, a tackle was going to come and get him. He would start across. He would draw the tackle to him. He would take coverage on the back and that would allow somebody else to get a matchup or hit a gap somewhere else. Again, a lot of times, some of those adjustments take place on the field and a good experienced player can do that. Junior [Seau] does a good job at that. For example, a lot times when he's out there he can pick things up like that, and sometimes change it right on the spot almost because he can see what's happening.

## Q: What is the danger of blitzing a team like the Saints?

**BB:** Anytime you bring more people to the line of scrimmage you have fewer people behind them. The downside is if those people there, close to the line of scrimmage, are blitzing don't stop the play before it gets into where you have fewer people then you've got fewer people, more space to defend and that could potentially lead to bigger plays. As far as hitting people, defensively, you have 11 players and they've got 10, depending on how much of a runner [the quarterback] is, but let's say he's a passer or hand off guy then they've got 10 then you decide what you want to do with your 11 guys, so anytime you commit two to one then you're nine on nine somewhere else and that thins that out. Anytime you double team a guy, whether you hit him or two guys cover him or you commit coverage - three on two or four on three or two on one - whatever those numbers are - then that levels the field somewhere else, so you can only do that in so many spots. Anytime offensively one of your offensive players takes out two of their defensive players that gives you advantages somewhere else, which is no different than defensively anytime you can make two people account for one defensive player then that thins it out somewhere else.

That's kind of what all those matchups are about. Hopefully if you put two guys on somebody that will take care of it, it doesn't always, but hopefully it would. If you double team a rusher or double team a receiver, however you want to do it, you would like to think those two guys would be able to handle that one and then you have to deal with everybody else. It basically just comes down to numbers. You have so many options and you can do it a lot of different ways but in the end when you run out of people, you run out of people, you can't double everybody. It's like all those defensive linemen talk about how they're getting double teamed on every play, how many double teams can there be?

## Q: [On communicating on defense with all of the Saints' personnel groupings]

**BB:** It's definitely a process and you know you don't have a lot of time to talk about it. When they sub guys on and off the field, you try to identify what group they have out there. How many tight ends? How many backs? How many receivers? And then that information is usually relayed into the defense separately from the call because a lot of that times that happens at the same time the calls going on, so one coach might be giving the defensive call the play that we're going to run and then the other coach is giving a personnel signal to somebody else. So it's not a long string of things to the same guy. But within those groups it depends on who the players are. Last week, it depended on [Ben] Hartsock and [Dustin] Keller at tight end.

There was a difference between Leon Washington and Thomas Jones as running backs; things like that where you have players that have different skills. It's sort of the same, but it really isn't the same. That adds to it as well and then when you have a team that runs guys on and off field at the same position. You run two receivers off, you run two receivers on - well, you start to see those two receivers come on and you don't know if that's going to be four wide receivers. If it's going to be a two-for-two sub, if it's going to be two receivers for a tight end and now you have three receivers on there, so it delays the process. Really every second is precious on that because by the time the ball is spotted, and the offense makes their substitutions, and starts to make their play calls and all that you're usually between 30-35 seconds.

Just by the time they get off the pile and all that and now they're coming out of the huddle - you don't have a lot of time. And a lot of your calls are predicated on the personnel that's in the game. If you call a certain defense and you think a certain group's going to be out and it's a different group, then that can be confusing to the players. Sometimes you end up making mistakes, blowing a timeout or something like that and that's an issue, too. And the Saints really try to stress you on that, probably as much as any team I can remember.

**Q:** Is it important to relay that information to an experienced player, one that can think on his feet?

**BB:** That's always the case. That's part of football. There are always things that happen out there that are not by the book. They're not exactly the way it was drawn up or diagramed or presented - there's loose plays, scramble plays, guys line up where they're not supposed to, or they give you a new look you're not prepared for and you have to make some kind of adjustment for it. Or they run a play you haven't seen before and here's your read, but it's a little bit different. Some guys can handle that better than others, but you always need to handle that. That comes up in every game.

**Q: What do the guys have to do up front to handle the Jets blitzes?**

**BB:** Well, I think the biggest thing you have to do when you play the Jets is you just have to have everybody offensively on the same page. It's not about one guy, it's about six or seven guys seeing a picture and seeing it the exact same way. If somebody sees it differently, then you're going have a breakdown and that's where they do a good job. They give you looks and then things happen. They do things before the snap and then things happen after the snap and then you have to, as a team, identify the quarterback, the receivers, the protection, the offensive line, the backs [and] the tight ends. They very rarely put you in a situation where your linemen just have to block their linemen.

You have other guys involved, so your backs and your tight ends all have to be coordinated on that and your quarterback and receivers and running backs - whoever the hot guys are if there is one - then have to be coordinated on that, too, so that the guy you don't block, that you throw the ball to somebody before he can get there. That has to be part of the passing game. It just requires a lot of coordination on the offensive side of the ball as a total unit. It's not about one guy. It's individual matchups, too. Don't get me wrong, you still have to block them.

Just because I know who to block doesn't mean that guy gets blocked. But that's a big part of the problem is just making sure you have all the players that we're responsible for that we actually get that done. And then the guys that we're not responsible for - the quarterback and the receivers - have to handle that as in part of the passing game, however that's designed. That's the challenge. And they do a good job of it. They put a lot of pressure on you to execute that as a total offensive unit. In addition, you still have to block. You have to block [Bryan] Thomas. You have to block [Calvin] Pace. You've got to block [Shaun] Ellis. You've got to block those guys - [David] Harris, all the rest of them, [Bart] Scott, so that's a problem, too.

## Q: How do you decide how much you're going to blitz against an elite quarterback like Peyton Manning?

**BB:** I think, when you take a good look at what your personnel is, what their personnel is and then you look at situations, you consider blitzing as one of your options. You weigh that against the other options. Sometimes you feel like that's a good option compared to what else is available, sometimes you don't. We don't have any set formula for it and I couldn't even tell you at this point. I haven't studied them enough this year to even know the answer to that question, but it's something we'll look at like we always do every week - How much man? How much zone? How much combination? How much pressure? How much six-man pressure? How much five-man pressure and what you want to do it out of, what looks or what personnel groups?

That's kind of how we formulate the defensive game plan every week, so that's a process that Monday, Tuesday, even Wednesday - it's a two or three day process of formulating all that. Then you get into the game and then you have to decide, as far as calling that, you go in with a plan - OK, here are the situations we want to call these blitzes in or these coverages in - whatever it is. You many stick with that or you may get into the game and say we thought this was going to be good in this situation, but I don't think it is because here's what they're doing. Then you get into the adjustments and counter adjustments.

## Q: Can you talk about what an effective tight end could do for an offense?

**BB:** I think, generally speaking, the tight end could be the hardest position to match up on for a defense because it's hard to put a linebacker on the real good receiving tight ends, like some of the guys we've seen: [Tony] Gonzalez, guys down the road - [Jeremy] Shockey, Dallas Clark. [With] guys like that, the linebackers just can't cover - or

I should say it's hard for them to cover - and the defensive backs who have the speed to cover them, they're outweighed by 20, 30, 40 pounds [and] maybe give up two, three, four inches in height and length. So that's an issue.

It's really hard to find a guy that's the same size as a Tony Gonzalez, or the same size as a Dallas Clark or Jeremy Shockey, players like that that can cover them. You're either finding a smaller guy that can run with him or a bigger guy that can be physical with them, but probably can't run or doesn't have their kind of quickness. So it's a tough matchup, whereas the receivers and corners are much more matched, physically, for the most part. Every once in a while, you see those big, 6-4, 225-pound receivers that are hard to match up against. But for the most part those physical matchups are more in line than with a good receiving tight end. That's the challenge of those guys. They're really receivers in a tight end's body. Those are tough match-ups.

**Q: I was wondering, from an X's and O's standpoint, what's the best thing that a real productive third receiver can give you? Does it prevent Randy Moss from getting double teamed?**

**BB:** I think when you put a player on the field, you're kind of looking to see what match-up that will bring from your opponent. The question always comes: Do you feel like putting this player on the field? It gives you an advantage over the player they're going to put on the field. Or is the player their putting on the field better than the player you're putting on the field? Or what you're going to get out of it. Talk about - say Wes [Welker], as a slot receiver, as a third receiver - if that's what you're talking about there's not too many teams that match-up better against him as he would match-up against them.

So there are a lot of advantages to doing that from a match-up standpoint. Of course, the more receivers you have on the field the fewer guys you have on the edges, the fewer blocking combinations you have and things like that. From a scheme standpoint, those are the drawbacks to it. You have more options in the passing game, less options at protection, less options in the running game, which is OK [but] you just have to decide what you want to do, which match-ups you'd rather have. So it's part personnel, part scheme.

## Q: [On receivers matching up with cornerbacks]

**BB:** The advantages of it are that you get the match-up you want. You want this player covering that player, you got it. The disadvantage is, where do the other 10 guys go? Normally, that's not an issue because we just line up where we line up. But OK, now you're going to match-up to so and so. So where do I go? And alright, I take somebody else, but what if he's not in the game? What if we're playing zone? What if this happens? What is that happens? What if this combination of guys is in the game? What if that combination of guys is in the game, then who do we match up to? What if the guy that we're matching up to is out of the game, then who do you match-up to and who do I match-up to? There's a lot of moving parts there.

It's real easy to say we'll just take him, but it's not that easy. I mean, if you just want to play One Coverage, but nobody does that. You've got zones, you've got man's, you've got combination man/zone's, you've got blitzes, you've got zone-blitzes. So it's easy to match-up and it's easy for that player, the hard part is what does everybody else do, and we all have to wait and see where you go before we can all figure out where we go. A lot of times, the corners like that. Ty [Law] was like it. It seems like every other week he would come in my office and say, 'Hey, let me match up on so and so.'

That's great Ty, and we would love to have you on whoever that guy is, but everybody else has to get lined up, too. And they put him in the slot, they line him up at X, and then they line him up at Z, and then they have three receivers, and then they have four receivers and they move him around, too. It's not like they are just going to put him out there and say, 'Match up and do whatever you want with the guy'. It's like Randy. If you want to match-up with Randy, go ahead, but where is he going to be? He's been at X. He's been at Z. He's been in the slot. At times, he's motioned out of the backfield. Sometimes he's in there with another receiver, sometimes he's in there with two other receivers.

If you want to do that, you can do it, teams have done it. I'm not saying that, but there're some moving parts to it. Those are the pluses, those are the minuses; you just got to decide what you want to do. You can do whatever you want, but there's some upside, but there's also a little bit of downside.

### Q: What problems does the no-huddle pose?

**BB:** I think the biggest challenge is communication. They are used to running plays quickly, getting to the line, calling them and signaling them and not coming back to the huddle, doing it from extended formations, getting lined up and going. And defensively we're kind of used to doing it in an end of the half type of situation. But on an every-down basis it stresses your communication a little bit and recognition – making sure that you see the offense, see where they are located because they will move them around.

They don't just stay in the same formation all the time, which usually in the end of the half you see a lot more of that; you see more of the same formations because fighting time they don't want to take time to switch people around. Recognition [and] communication are two of the big things and then you can't let the pace of the game and the communication challenges take away from actually playing: the technique, reads, and doing your job, you can't let all that other stuff distract you. You get so caught up on that and the ball's snapped and you don't do anything.

### Q: What are the challenges of defending the Wildcat offense?

**BB:** I don't know about ... I guess what I would say is that if you have a running quarterback, offensively, you essentially have one more gap to attack the defensive with, or the defense has one more gap to defend. When you have a quarterback handing off to a running back - however many blockers you have - let's say you have seven blockers in front of him, a tight end, six linemen and a running back, then, defensively, you can pretty easily get into an eight-man front that accounts for every gap and still have defenders for the perimeter receivers.

Once that quarterback becomes a runner, you really have another gap to defend now. Those seven blockers and eight gaps now really become nine gaps and now you really only have eight defenders.

So that puts a stress somewhere on your defense, just like the Single-Wing offenses, just like the college Veer and Wishbone offenses, to some degree the Wing-T and to some degree, I guess, the Wildcat. The principles are all the same: that having another ball carrier, the defense has to defend another gap and you have to decide how you want to do that defensively. Instead of the quarterback handing off, now you have a guy that can actually attack the defense and run the ball, which most quarterbacks aren't a threat to do that. That changes some of your run defense principles. To me, that's the foundation of a running quarterback, whether you do it in the Single Wing, or do it in the option game, it all really comes down to defensively having enough people to defend all the areas they can create.

# 8
## STRATEGY & SITUATIONS

**Q:** Has it now become a part of situational football to decide whether or not to kick the ball off for a touchback or try one of those pop-up kickoffs to the goal line? Would your decision on the final kickoff to pop it up have been different if the touchback brought it out to the 20-yard line like in years past?

**BB:** Yeah, it might be. I don't know, I don't really think of it in those terms but I understand your question Mike [Reiss]. I can't sit here and say "Well what would we have done last night if the touchback was at the 20, at the 22, at the 18, at the 17," you know? There's some breaking point in there, wherever that is, but I think what ended up happening on that play [is] we kicked off and [Patrick] Chung and [Nate] Ebner made the tackle I think around the 16-yard line, but then with the penalty [against] Jonathan Jones it put the ball around the eight. And so the difference between the ball being on the eight and the 25 on that last field would've been pretty significant. I think at that point last night we kind of had the mentality of "Our kickoff team - it's their job to do go down there and get them." We're going to make them earn however many yards they get. We're going to make them earn them. We're not going to give them a quarter or 25 percent of the field. We're going to make them earn every yard that they get the ball out to. They're going to have to block, and run, and break a tackle, or whatever, to gain those yards, and the players - they made great plays.

[Matthew] Slater made a great play that helped free up Ebner, Ebner made a great play coming off of the block, Chung sliced in there and made the tackle and Jonathan Jones was the first man down. They had to hold him to block him so that he didn't get him sooner. All of those guys were a part of it but would it have been different if the rule had been different? I mean at some point it probably would've been. I can't tell you exactly where that is.

**Q:** Is the safety/ linebacker hybrid position like Deone Bucannon something that's new, or something that's old but has come back?

**BB:** I think that you are definitely seeing a strong trend in the league towards corners that play safety or corner-type athletes that play safety, bigger safeties that play linebacker. Both of those are trends. We've always put a lot of premium on the passing game even going back to when we had Eugene Wilson, who played corner at Illinois, and started for us at corner for a couple weeks and then we moved him to free safety, but that was an advantage when teams went to the multiple receivers.

Then we already had that third corner on the field and we could go nickel or we could leave our regular defense out there, or leave our corner on the third receiver, what we call penny defense, but things like that. That was really, I'd say, pretty successful for us. Devin [McCourty's] given us some of that, so has [Patrick] Chung. Devin's a corner but not that Chung is a corner, but he has corner qualities, he's had some corner-type responsibilities, particularly in the slot, even going back to when Wes [Welker] was here, and he would cover Wes pretty competitively in practice sessions and things like that.

I'd say that has always been something that's, if you have a player that can do that, somewhat appealing. The other problem is if you get mismatched with the receiver against a safety who's not a very good coverage player, then that can blow up in a hurry. Rodney [Harrison] was a guy that you mentioned that was a very good coverage safety even though he was a big physical, and he played the run as well as anybody. He could also cover the run and that's very unusual and that made him very special. You could literally matchup on anybody, receivers, tight ends, blitz him, play him on goal line. He could do it all. He was tremendous. I'd say, yeah, as the offenses have gotten more spread out, as the offenses have put more skill players on the field, as the tight ends have become more athletic and less of the conventional kind of power-blocking type guys, those matchups keep getting tougher and tougher.

I'd say there's definitely a movement towards safeties that can play corner or have some corner-like qualities to them and that extends to the linebacker level as well. You see less of the big run stopping Ted Johnson, Brandon Spikes type players. It's just harder when the offense spreads you out and then they go fast and you can't substitute and you're stuck with whoever you have out there, out there. That creates some problems out there, too. The colleges are seeing the same thing and they probably have to deal with it more than we do because there are so many fast-tempo offenses, so they are in the same boat so they are playing a lot of what we call dime defense, or little nickel, or whatever it is, but where they put a lot of fast guys on the field.

Ends are playing tackle, safeties are playing linebacker, and corners are playing safety. It's just kind of getting a little bit smaller in a lot of areas. I don't know if that's different., There are some differences but going back to Wilson and Harrison, and those guys from 02-03-04, back in there, there's a lot of similarities to the Chung-Harrison, Chung-McCourty, corner/safety type that had more coverage ability than some other guys that you would see out there.

**Q: How do you balance the decision to react to the adjustments that Manning makes at the line of scrimmage versus staying in your defense and reacting as the play is developing?**

**BB:** That's a great question and that's really the basis of trying to come up with a game plan and figure out how you want to play a team like that. You don't want to put yourself in bad situations. At the same time you don't want to make it too much of a game where there are a lot of multiples – 'if they do this we do that,' 'if they do that we do this' – that just can go on forever. At some point you've got to line up and play what you're going to play. Look, just because they know you're in something isn't always the worst thing in the world. All good teams have tendencies.

All good players have tendencies. That's not a bad thing. It's a good thing. It means you're doing something well. At some point it's going to come down to you have to play well. You have to do what you do well better than what they try to do against it. I think there are elements of all those things in a game. You certainly don't want to make it easy for them, but you can outsmart yourself sometimes by trying to play too much of a mind game. Manning's a great quarterback. He's a hard guy to fool. He has seen it all.

**Q: On the catch on the sideline by James White in the third quarter, how do you decide when it's a good idea to rush to the line to pressure them to either challenge or not challenge?**

**BB:** I think we've kind of talked about that a little bit through the years of the whole process and the challenges and so forth, and to me there are certain plays that are probably going to get challenged pretty much regardless just based on the importance of the play, what happened on the play and kind of how important the play is to the game at that particular point in time. At times we've run up to the line and run a quick play and then it's second-and-10, and that's not really the answer.

And a lot of times if they're going to challenge a play, they're going to challenge it anyways if it's an important enough play. In that case, first of all, I think Bill [O'Brien] would have challenged both those plays regardless. They were both very close plays and when we saw them up on the screen I think our feeling was that they were close enough that they looked like they were catches. I don't know how you felt looking at the play, as soon as you saw it you knew was going to be overturned. If that's the way you saw it, maybe the right thing to do would have been to hurry up and run a play, but if you don't feel that way about the play then I don't know why you would want to rush up there and do it. Even after looking at the play, both of them are really, really close. If you know how it's going to turn out then it's always easy to make the decision. If you don't know how it's going to turn out then you just go on what you see, but just running up there and snapping the ball and running a bad play, I don't know if that's the answer.

**Q:** Those were both close. I was 0-2 myself on which way both of those were going.

**BB:** I think you look up there and see, 'OK I don't think we have this,' then yeah, it's probably worth the gamble – not the gamble – but it's probably worth it to go up there and snap it quickly and hope they don't challenge it if you think you probably aren't going to win the challenge. That would absolutely be the right thing to do if that's the way you feel. Let them challenge it. Let them waste the timeout. If you feel like you're OK with the play, I don't necessarily think it's the right strategy.

I think in particular the White play it goes back to the whole issue of the angle of the camera and was his heel actually on the white or was his toe on the ground and his heel above the white, how close it was. And I think I just would say what I've said many times before that I think because of the plays on the sideline, on the goal line and on the end line that the league ought to have cameras there. I don't think we should be worried about how much it's going to cost. If we need to raise money, we should raise money and get those set so that on those kinds of plays we have an absolute down-the-line angle of the play and not I would say the angles that I saw shown up on the screen, which none of them were down the line.

They were all coming from either behind or from the field or from kind of the sideline. I think that leads to the … If 100 people saw that play, it might be 55-45, I don't know. There is some that we can all look at and say, 'Yeah it's this,' or, 'Yeah it's that,' but those ones that are just kind of a really close call and a toss-up, it's one thing when it's very close, it's another thing when you don't have a really good angle to see it and then therefore you can't make a good decision. I would still like to see a sideline camera on that so that we get the call right, whatever it is.

Whether it was in bounds or out of bounds, let's just get an angle on those plays. If they happen out in the middle of the field, we all understand that, that's the way it goes. Whatever angle you see, you see. But on the sideline, to not have a down-the-line angle on plays like that or on a goal-line play or on an end-line play, scoring plays, I think we should have those in place.

**Q: In regards to the finish Thursday night between Green Bay and Detroit, I was wondering if there is any kind of strategy to the Hail Mary pass or do you just kind of throw it up?**

**BB:** I think it's not an overly strategic play. You want to get the ball into the end zone and you want to get people around it. However you orchestrate that, I mean you don't want to throw it short and you don't want to throw it out. It's got to come down in the area of a guy to go up and get it or if he can't get it, you can't outjump the team and go out and get the ball, you have players hopefully in the end zone so that if it's tipped they have a chance to catch it before it hits the ground.

You don't really want to catch it in the field of play, although we've seen a couple of those I'd say luck out. The guy catches it on the two and falls in because there doesn't happen to be anyone near him, but we've also seen a few of those where a guy gets tipped, the ball gets tipped and the guy gets tackled on the one or two-yard line. Well, whether it's on the one or if it's incomplete it doesn't really matter at that point. Trying to get the ball to somebody that has a chance to go up and get it and fight for it and then having other people there to be able to, if you will, rebound the ball if it comes up.

Defensively, it's sort of the reverse of that. You've got to have somebody go up and you don't want to get outjumped for the ball, then you never really get a shot at it, but at the same time you want to be able to box out or keep the other players who don't go up and jump for it from coming down with the rebound.

There are a lot of other components to the whole getting the ball off, throwing it, protection, the rush and so forth. There are other things that play into that as well. It's hard to throw the ball – I mean how far did he throw it, 70 yards? I mean it's hard to throw the ball 70 yards. You can't just stand back there and there are not too many guys that can drop back and throw it, so there's another component to have enough time, be able to create some momentum, be able to get the ball that high. I wouldn't say it's just, I'm not trying to brush off like it's some simple thing. I think there's really a lot of things that go into that, doing it and also defending it, but as far as the actual where the ball comes down, we want a big guy to try and go up and get it and you want as many other people as you can have there to try to get it if it's a live ball. At the same time you've got to be able to get it all off so if you send everybody down there then you've just got to be able to protect with five people. Maybe you can; maybe you can't. That's another element of the play.

**Q: What is your philosophy at the end of a half when deciding between kicking a long field goal and having Tom throw it downfield in the end zone?**

**BB:** My thought process is always really the same – try to do what's best for the team based on the situation, whatever the conditions are and so forth. Believe it or not, I always try to make the best decision for the team. If I thought that the best decision was to kick a field goal, I'd kick a field goal. If I thought it was to go for it, I'd go for it. I'm not saying they're all right. Probably a lot of them are wrong, but I try to do what I think is best. So whatever all the factors are that go into that, then that's what we do.

**Q:** I think you've said before though that the decision at halftime is different than the decision at the end of the game. Is that right?

**BB:** I don't know about that. It's definitely a lot different than it is in the first quarter. I mean, you miss a long field goal in the first quarter and they've got the ball at midfield. If you miss a field goal at the end of the half then the half is over. But if you get it blocked or we've seen in some other big games where somebody puts somebody back there and now you're trying to cover a long field goal with a bunch of guards and tackles out there. I don't think that's a great play. If you think you can make it, that's one thing. If you can't get it there, now you've given the ball to probably one of their better players.

You've got a bunch of offensive linemen trying to cover against that. I don't personally think that's very smart to do if you know you're not going to be able to get it there or if you've got like a one percent chance of getting it there. I don't think that would be a good decision. Now if it's the last play of the game, it's your only chance, it doesn't make any difference if they run it back or not at that point. But if that's a factor in the play, then that's part of the whole decision making process, too. I'd say it's one thing to miss it; it's another thing to get it run back. It's another thing to get it blocked. It's a combination of all those things. Somehow you put it together and try to do what you think is best.

**Q:** On plays like that, I think of Arizona in 2004 when you guys threw to the end zone and Deion Branch got injured on the run back on the final play of the half.

**BB:** I mean look, you can't take out insurance on players, so you've got to go out there and play the game. I don't know who's going to get hurt, when they're going to get hurt, what play they're going to get hurt on or what's going to happen in the game. I don't know how anybody ... Once you can figure that out then you need to get out of your business, I need to get out of my business and we can all do a lot better doing something else once we know the answers to those questions.

**Q:** I'm just talking about the relative upside of those plays.

**BB:** Yeah, I think when you call a play I don't think you're thinking about that like, "Am I going to call this play because I think this guy might get hurt?" I don't know how you could coach a game like that. I couldn't coach it like that. I don't know.

**Q:** Roosevelt Colvin said on Twitter last night that you taught your players that specific rule and practiced that situation. Is teaching players the rules an ongoing practice throughout the season, and do you have to teach all new players the rules because it seems a lot of players across the league are unfamiliar with the NFL rulebook?

**BB:** I think it's a really good question, but it would entail probably a pretty lengthy answer. There are so many different levels that that question encompasses. Let's start with rookies coming into the league. The first thing we do is teach them the rules in the National Football League and in particular make them aware of the changes between the college rules and the pro rules, which there are a significant number. And we don't really assume because we have no way of knowing how educated or uneducated they are on the rules, if they even are the same between the two – between college and professional football.

So, it starts there. The NFL comes in and they go through all the rules changes with the team and the coaching staff, they meet with the coaching staff in the spring, which is a very informative meeting, and then they meet with the team in training camp and go through the rules changes and it's usually done during the time when the officials come to work the few days of training camp that they do for each team. So, that's also good. It creates a good dialogue between the officials, the players and the coaches, and gives coaches and players an opportunity to ask questions.

Sometimes the dialogue goes back and forth – how's this being coached, how's this being officiated and so forth. All of that is done with the intention of trying to get everybody on the same page. Each of our position coaches devotes a significant amount of time in the spring and then also in training camp, particularly in individual, one-on-one-type drills where a lot of times there are only two or three guys on the screen instead of all 22 so you can really get a good, close-up look at a lot of rules like that – the holding and illegal contact and offensive pass interference, defensive pass interference – all those kinds of things. So that's covered very much on an individual basis, specifically to that position. Obviously, the offensive guard doesn't have to know everything about pass interference and vice versa, but it's important for them to know the things in their position and how the game is being officiated.

And then those things are also pointed out in various other team or individual settings as they become pertinent over the course of the year, whether it be a particular play or particular opponent or that type of thing. And then I talk to the team on a regular basis on situational plays, which involve officiating, timing, utilization of timeouts and so forth and so on, so that's probably on a regular basis from training camp all the way through the end of the season – call it once a week or something like that – somewhere in that vicinity. Sometimes it's more than that, but always trying to keep our team aware of situations, and a lot of times we change the situation a little bit just to extend the conversation about a play.

So this is what happened, but if something else or if they hadn't had timeouts or if the ball was here, or the ball was there, just try to understand and comprehend totally what we're doing from a team standpoint or an individual situation. The whole sideline, ball security, whistle, all those kind of ball possession plays, those are very important for everybody to understand and we stress those a lot. Any time the ball is loose, like it was in last night's game, try to make sure everybody understands what they can do, what they can't do.

And of course once you get into the kicking game, you can multiply everything that happens on offense and defense exponentially because you not only have the possession plays, but then you have all the plays that happen when the ball is kicked, and those rules sometimes are, well they are different than plays of possession like a runner or a receiver or a returner who's carrying the ball. There is the whole handling of the ball and the kick and did it cross the line of scrimmage and so forth and so on. It's a lot for the officials to understand, it's a lot for the coaches to understand, and it's a lot for the players to understand.

But in the end we try to look at the rule book as a useful tool, something that can benefit us if we know what we have to work with, how to make the best of a situation based on the way the rules are written and try to maximize our opportunities there. But that being said, there is still a lot happening in a short amount of time. It's challenging for all of us – players, coaches and officials. I don't know if that really answers your question. We could probably talk about that one for weeks.

**Q:** The noise at Arrowhead could be a factor. How, if at all, does that affect what Tom Brady can do at the line in terms of making checks? Does it reduce the number that he can make and only make certain checks?

**BB:** I think you have to be careful. I'd say in every away game there are going to be times, certain situations that it would be really hard to do that. Other times, I'm not saying it's easy, but it's doable. But there are plenty of times when it would be really hard, when the crowd really gets going or you're backed up on your own one or you're going in for a touchdown and in the red area and it's just – so, I think you have to be aware of those situations, be aware of game situations. Josh [McDaniels] is a very experienced play caller and coordinator.

He can hear it, he can feel it and I don't think it's the type of call [where] we could run one of two or three plays depending on the look and the crowd is in that kind of frenzy, I don't think that's really when you want to make that call. Obviously, third down is a challenging down in Kansas City with their defense and the multiple looks they give you on the front and pressure. So, to identify those, that's – but third down is challenging on the road everywhere. It might be a little louder there, probably is, but it's all, I don't want to say the same, but pretty much you're dealing with the same thing in every away game in that situation.

**Q: Before James Develin's touchdown run, it looked like Shane Vereen may have been in the end zone. How do you balance waiting for a replay and moving quickly to the next play to keep the defense off-balance?**

**BB:** I don't think you can wait to challenge the play. I think as the play caller, if you're – [Offensive Coordinator] Josh [McDaniels] in this case – calling the plays, you have to call the play. You can't wait and 'Is there going to be a replay? What's going to [happen]?' You can't operate like that. You have to say, 'OK, the person up in the press box that relays that information says, 'OK, the ball is spotted, it's inside the one or it's on the one-and-a-half or wherever the ball is or it's first-and-goal if we've gotten a first down or it's third-and-one if we haven't gotten a first down, whatever it is.' Then you have to make your call.

You can't wait. Now, while that's all going on, we have somebody else who would be seeing if there is a replay and then they would tell me or I would say, 'OK, Josh we're going to challenge the play.' That type of thing. We're a little bit independent on that. As the play caller, you can't be – you have to see the situation, see what the down-and-distance is or what the field position is, is it inside the 20? Is it inside the 10? Because maybe you have a breaking point on your calls there possibly. Then you want to know what their personnel is. So if you're changing personnel, you want to know what's in the game. Is nickel in or did they stay regular?

Or did they come in with dime or whatever it is. As soon as you get that information, then you make your call. You can't have five people talking at once. You get the information from the press box as quickly as we can see it. The ball is on the two, it's second down, here comes nickel. Then, alright, you make your call. Or sometimes they hold their subs until you make your subs. Here comes goal line, whatever it is. As soon as you make your call, you say, 'OK, give me whatever it is – give me three receivers.' Three receivers start on there and then as the call is being made, the person in the press box says, 'Here comes nickel. Or here comes dime. Or they're staying regular.' Then he'll finish making his call because that might affect what he's calling. It might not, but it might. That's kind of how – meanwhile the whole replay thing is separate from that.

**Q: You're big on situational football. Is this something you would do in training camp, like all of a sudden in the middle of practice you would say, 'Team A or Team B is doing something completely different, now we have to switch' and you pull that on the coaches or players?**

**BB:** I think in training camp you're really trying to build a foundation of what you do. Definitely we have situation practices in training camp. We'll create a situation - it's 15 seconds to go, we have the ball at midfield and we need a field goal, we have no timeouts or we have a timeout or we're defending that situation or whatever it is. That may incorporate if it's a field goal, then that incorporates the kicking situation into it as well.

Yeah, we definitely practice those. I think the preparing for the game is more of a weekly thing and a lot of times as a coach there's kind of two ways you can attack it. One, you can go out to practice, we run 30 plays on defense. I know the play, I know the defense, I want to see how the defense handles a certain play so I run a play action pass against a certain coverage and I want to see whether we can cover it. That's one way of doing it. The other way of doing it is you draw up the play, I call the coverage, whatever happens happens and let's see how it goes.

We don't know what's coming and you can't really prepare the player for it, if you know what I mean. That's more realistic in the game but you don't quite get sometimes the exact matchup that you really want to coach. Like you tell players, 'Okay, look when they do this, here's how we're going to do it. You're going to cover him, you're going to cover him and you're going to do that.' Then you run it and see whether you have it or not. You make sure going out to practice that you've covered that. Okay, 'You understand this situation, this happens, this happens, you do that, okay.' Then you run it.

But if you kind of randomly hit those, then you don't necessarily get that part of it, you just have to, you call a play if they blitz, you pick up the blitz. If they play a three man rush, then you run the play against a three man rush and get the spacing that you need on it. I think there's a place for both. Do we change it around? Yeah. We throw things against the offense and the defense that they're not expecting because the coaches and players don't know what plays are being called. I control that or somebody else controls it so the coaches don't know.

Then there are other times when the coaches absolutely know what it is so they can make sure that the players are able to handle that situation against whatever it is we happen to be doing. Same thing in the kicking game, we create those situations in the kicking game too. There's 10 seconds to go in the game, we're up by three, punt the ball out of bounds, we're not going to give the returner a chance to handle the ball. Or we're down by seven, there's 30 seconds to go in the game, they're punting, here's our punt rush. Now are the gunners in tight? Is one of them in tight? Are they split? Who knows? How do we run that rush against, we're not sure what look it's going to be. Sometimes we know but other times you really don't know you just have to - we make the players figure it out as it happens. It may or may not work out that way in the game but it's a good process for them to go through.

**Q: A lot of teams script the first 10 or 15 plays on offense. Is that something you guys do?**

**BB:** I think that's kind of a West Coast thing. Coach [Mike] Holmgren and a lot of his disciples really popularized that. I've never been in that system, but from what I know about it, that's kind of a pretty disciplined script: play one, play two, play three. I think the thing that you have to take into consideration is the situations. Do you want to call the same play on first-and-15 that you want to call on second-and-one?

Do you want to call the same play on third-and-six that you want to call on second-and-four? If you follow the script then, 'Ok, here's the fourth play.' But would you really want to call that play in that situation or would you rather call your second-and-short play in second-and-short and your third-and-long play in third-and-long? It's a couple different philosophies on that. There's merit to both of them. I've don't it both ways. At times, we've said, 'Ok, this is what we want to do sequentially.' Other times we've said, 'The first time it's second-and-long, this is what we're going to call. The first time it's second-and-short, this is what we're going to call.' It's not the same play. I think there is a place for both. It's really kind of a philosophy of either how you want to start the game or how you want to start a particular game with your sequence of call.

Again, that's usually an end of the week decision - Thursday, Friday, Saturday. You've practiced everything. Here's how it looks. Here's what our comfort level is of calling the plays with our players and our team and then you make the decision of, 'Ok, this is what it's going to be.' But again, the same thing; last year against Baltimore we started off the game and recovered a fumble and we got the ball at the 15-yard line. So what play do you want to call there? The first play of your script or your 15-yard line play or your first play after a turnover? You've just kind of got to decide how you want to handle those situations because it isn't always that clean how it comes up.

**Q:** When your team gets a safety, as they have the past two weeks, how do you look at that from the standpoint of how quickly it can change the flow and opportunity to build on that momentum during the game?

**BB:** Sure, yeah it gives you a chance to kind of go on a run which is hard to do in football. But that's how you do it, is scoring on defense or creating really good field positon. Like for example on kickoff coverage and then if you can get a stop and get the ball back, and then you have good field positon or a turnover. You need something like that. You need a turnover, you need a safety, or you need a good field positon play and three-and-out to have that kind of field positon to be able to string a couple of scores together like that.

It's a great opportunity defensively, well as a team, but set up by that defensive score to try to go on a run and go from behind to ahead or go from ahead to two or three scores ahead, that kind of thing. Unfortunately we haven't had the kind of returns off of the two safeties the last two weeks that would really enhance that. Getting the ball back is good. If we could've turned those returns into a little more production that would've helped us. But yeah, it's a great opportunity, sure.

**Q:** Are there examples that come to mind from the past where you've been able to get a safety and turn that into a nice run that sort of catapults the team?

**BB:** Well, I think when you look statistically, to me I would kind of put that into the bonus points category. You go into a game and you think 'Alright, well how many points are we going to score offensively? How many points are they going to score offensively?' And that's, you know, kind of the way the game normally flows. When you get points from a defensive score, points from a special team's score, whether it be a blocked kick, or a safety, or a defensive return, something like that - I mean you can't count on those points. You can't go into a game and think 'Alright, we're going to get seven points on a defensive score.'

Over the course of the year that maybe happens two or three times a year, whatever it is. I mean you know one team might have a bunch of them like Alabama has this year but that's unusual. Just the normal team, the normal stats on it, you get two or three of those a year so you can't really count on those, so when you get those in a game then that's pretty significant. I think the overall statistical advantage to scoring a non-offensive touchdown is pretty heavily -

that team is going to win more games. You put turnovers in there, you recover a fumble on the one-yard line - that's not a defensive score - but if that ends up being a score you kind of have a similar result. So those turnovers - that's why the turnovers are so important because they aren't always point-plays but they usually result in points, especially if you get them in good field position then you're already in the scoring zone. But a safety is part of that. Yeah, it's definitely part of that conversation because even though its only two points it is possession so it's a little bit of an added benefit.

# Two Point Conversions

**Q:** The Steelers have been outspoken about being advocates of going for the two-point conversion after touchdowns and have done it a few times this season. Do teams typically have specific play packages set up for those two-point conversions and as a defense does it require you to do more prep work this week against an opponent like that?

**BB:** It'll definitely require some extra preparation. And again, they've had a lot of success with doing that. I think they did more of it last year but we know they kind of like to do it. They've done it so we've got to be ready for it I'd say more so than an average game. This game there's more of an element of that. I think you've seen a little bit of a shift in the two-point play, so it's a really good question Bob [Socci]. Overall I think there are generally two philosophies on the two-point play. One philosophy would be to run a red area play that you would run with that field position anyways just as if it was fourth-and-goal on the two [yard line], if you will.

The other philosophy was to run a play that the defense had never seen before; unusual formations, some type of play, you know, the play that they couldn't possibly be working on because only – and I'd say the Steelers are a team that used to like to do that especially under Coach [Bill] Cowher. They were very successful in doing that in some of their critical situations; put Hines Ward somewhere or run a reverse and throw off of it or things like that. And there wasn't any downside to doing that. I think the issue now is, you know, with that play being a defensive play as well, so an interception or a fumble or something, if the defense got the ball they'd be able to score on that play, so I think we've seen a little bit less league-wide of kind of the once-a-season type of play in that situation. You see it occasionally but for the most part it looks like the philosophy has gone more towards a red area play. Something that we're good at, something that we've repped a lot that we've seen with multiple looks and we have a lot of confidence in, and the teams are taking more of that type of philosophy towards it. In the past on a two-point play we're always kind of having in mind, and especially to alert the defensive players, there's a good chance you're going to see something you've never seen here before, whatever it is, and either personnel group or formation or a type of play that this team has never run that we can't work on. We have no idea if they're drawing it up themselves. But I'd say that that's become less prevalent in the last couple of years. At least it seems like it has to me. Definitely extra preparation for that situation this week.

**Q: What's your approach to two-point conversions? In Sunday's game, the score was 17-12 and you chose to kick the extra point. Was there any thought to going for two there? Was there any thought to going for two before overtime?**

**BB:** Yeah I mean I think to me the two-point conversion really doesn't come into play until later in the game. The two-point try in the first quarter, there is so much football left to play that again, I would not say never, but I think it would be a very small percentage of the time that it would really be a factor. For me the factor would come at the end of the game when you have limited possessions left and then how you want to look at those opportunities – the opportunities of two versus one – how many more possessions are left in the game. But in the end ultimately it comes down to how confident you are about the play in that situation.

If I was 90 percent confident about the play, maybe we would do it in the first quarter. If you feel that good about it, why not do it. The success rate on that is – I don't know what it is – but it's basically a 50-50 proposition. It's in that ballpark. But yeah, we considered it. We talked about it. In the end I think there was enough time left that it looks good if you get that point and then if you didn't the way the game played out you needed that point to tie the game. There are some calls that could go either way. I would say those are the ones that kind of could. At the end of the game, that was another one. We had two timeouts so even if we hadn't made it we still would have had a chance to get the ball back with timeouts and a deep kick and all that and only needing a field goal.

By kicking the extra point we felt like we ensured overtime assuming that we could stop them, which puts the pressure back on them again. They've got to either get a first down or we get the ball back with timeouts and a chance to score, which could have happened if we didn't have the interference penalty on third down. If that play, if there is no penalty there, we have the ball back with two timeouts with good field position, then that puts us in the driver's seat in that situation. But yeah I think you could make an argument for a two-point conversion there.

**Q:** In both situations?

**BB:** I think you could look at the Cleveland-Denver game was a good example of Cleveland went for two, didn't make it, next play 80-yard touchdown, and now that point ends up being – because there are now a couple of extra scores that maybe you don't think about are going to happen there in the middle of the fourth quarter or whatever it was – now all of a sudden that point looks a lot differently than it did without those extra scores. You get a quick score after that and now that kind of changes things. You've just kind of got to be careful about ... The more scores there are, the longer the game goes, the more that point can hurt you. With less time, fewer possessions, you need the point to either tie the game or to get into position to get the score tied and there aren't many opportunities left so maybe you take advantage of that and do it. But again if there is enough time left then there is a cost to doing that.

**Q:** Would you not look at the two-point conversion chart until a certain point in the game?

**BB:** Yeah, I would say I don't think it really comes into play until a certain point in the game. Like I said I think if you went into the game and felt like OK we feel like 90 percent about our two-point play here and use it the first time you score, it probably wouldn't make any difference if you score first or they score first. If you feel good about the play, might as well run it, unless you wanted to save it for the situation that you're talking about. Yeah, to me it's an end-of-the game chart. It's not a first-quarter chart.

**Q:** Will you bring in multiple two-point plays for that type of situation or are those plays similar to what you would run in short-yardage situations?

**BB:** It would depend on ... I mean first of all, fundamentally you have a basic philosophy in that situation, whatever it happens to be, which I think that's changed a little bit with the new rule, making it a potentially defensive play as well. I would say in the past there were a lot of teams that would run a gadget play or a play you've never seen before in that situation – some razzle-dazzle kind of play – and if they hit it they hit it and if they didn't then they didn't.

But now you do something you've never done before and you end up turning the ball over or it gets stripped or whatever, it could cost you on the other end, so I think you see a little bit less of that or I've seen a little bit less of it. But I'd say that's water under the bridge. So you have your basic philosophy but then whatever information you have on that particular opponent that week, how they play two-point plays depending on how many of them you've seen, probably not too many, but maybe you have a history on it or just in general how they would play in that two-to-three-to-four-yard line range – whatever you have on tape, whatever evidence you have, then you would probably set up your game plan based on that. If that's what a team calls on third-and-goal at the three or third-and-goal at the two, it's probably what they're going to call in that two-point situation. It's probably going to come from that type of menu.

# Red Zone

**Q:** The end-of-game situations, such as when to use timeouts, have become so intricate over the years. How have you developed over the years a sort of feel or way of managing those intricacies when each situation is not identical?

**BB:** Well, yeah Tom [Curran], it's a really good question and a very hard one to answer. There are so many factors in football that it's really hard to find two situations that are the same. Even in some situations that are similar there's usually something in there, the conditions on the field, or the game, or the wind, or something else that adds another variable in there besides just point-differential and time and timeouts. But I would say even with the three timeouts involved, which could be three, two, one, zero, so there's another four possibilities there and the field position and, again, the score spread, the differential in points. There's really a lot of moving parts there, a lot of factors.

So, with all of that being said we had the general guidelines that we followed. But like just for example on a simple thing like two-point conversion chart, you can't necessarily get everybody to agree with that and you're talking about we can tell what the score is, like how many points you're behind by or ahead by, about just whether to go for two or not. Forget about everything else and we can't even all agree on that in certain situations. When you put it all together, again, we have our guidelines and there's certainly a feel, if you will, for certain things. There are certain teams that based on how good or maybe how not good they are in certain situations that would incline you to do one thing more than another, versus that same situation against another team with the strengths and weaknesses matched up a little bit differently.

I've always felt like going for it on fourth-down had a lot more to do with how confident I was in the play that we were calling as opposed to really anything else. If we felt like we had a good play then you're inclined to go for it in the first quarter, in the fourth quarter, whatever the score was. Not to be reckless about it but if the situation came up and you felt like you had a good play then that was a situation we wanted to do it in. If we didn't feel good about it then [we're] just not as inclined to do it. Then again, there are definitely some strategical situations that trump all of that, but just sort of as an example that's one of the things that can go into it.

I think it's an ever-changing thing. I don't know that this week's the same as last week or if last week is the same before that. They're all different. Again, we have our guidelines that we try to follow. I always try to alert the coaches as to what I'm going to do so that they don't get surprised or get caught off-guard. We've seen some of those situations before between the quarterback and the offensive coordinator and the head coach. Maybe not everybody understood exactly what they're trying to do. We try to definitely avoid that at all costs. Even if it doesn't work or we don't do it right at least we all know what we're trying to do and there's not a miscommunication there, but that's not the easiest thing in the world either because those situations can change in a hurry.

It can go from third-and-10 to fourth-and-one in a matter of seconds and now you're in a whole different ballgame, especially if the quarterback or the offensive coordinator isn't expecting to go for it and then all of a sudden is, that kind of thing. A lot of it is just basic communication and making sure that I think the players understand what we're trying to do in certain situations regardless of what the play is that's called. Just to understand what the situation entails, what are the most important points of an individual situation.

It's interesting how after all of these years and we've been together as a staff, a lot of us for a long time, double-digit years in some cases and so forth, and still every week there are new situations that somebody will bring up, or will come up in another game, or something that we'll talk about and kind of review our strategy and just say "Well, this is normally what we would do here, but you know, the way that situation came up – that's not really quite what we want.

We want something just a little bit different than that," whether that's a play or so forth. I thought it was certainly interesting but not unexpected the way that the Cardinals used the timeouts; trying to conserve the time when we had the ball and willing to deal with fewer timeouts when they had the ball at the end of the game. And I've done that before.

I'd say that's not the normal way to do it but I don't think there's anything wrong with doing that. You have three timeouts, you use them; whenever you use them, you use them. It's just a question of strategically when you want to call them. I think there's a lot of different ways to do it and I'm not sure there's a right or wrong way on a lot of these things. Again, I'd say the most important thing is making sure that you just have it right. That everybody understands what they're doing, what the strategy is so that you have a chance to execute it. Again, in all honesty it's not the easiest thing to do. It sounds easy now but when those situations come up in a game and they change quickly it's a lot harder to do than what it is an hour after the game when you really can sit there and think about it.

**Q:** It's just my observation that you could try and sit there and conserve a timeout but then you run the risk of having maybe the wrong guys out there or some miscommunication amongst the defense.

**BB:** Right, well and you know, giving you another point on this – some of those same things really you're just talking first half and second half because I don't think – well in my opinion – there's no question that the timeouts are a lot more valuable at the end of the game than they are at the end of the first half. I'm not saying they aren't valuable at halftime but if you use a timeout in the first quarter or the second quarter to get a play right or a substitution, whatever it is, even though you don't want to use it – nobody wants to waste timeouts – but sometimes things happen and how much is that timeout really worth in the first half? There are definitely times when you wish that you had them but they're nowhere near as valuable as they are at the end of the game and you never want to waste them.

I'm not saying that. But using them in the first half is one thing and will those timeouts ever really come into play at the end of the first half?

On a percentage basis it's not that high. They're always going to come into play at the end of the game. It's just a question of which team is going to use them. I think there's a whole different priority and importance to those at the end of the game. Like for example, the one that we used at the end of the game to try and help us on defense – had the game gone a little differently we might've wanted that timeout. We might've needed it on offense but you've got to use them when you think it's the most important and when it will help you. Again, those situations at the end of the game – the same situation at the end of the game and the same situation at the end of the half are actually two different situations.

## Q: What changes for a defense inside the twenty-yard line?

**BB:** Less field. Offensively everybody's closer to the line so the safeties are linebackers; linebackers are in a lot of cases borderline defensive lineman. Everything's just compressed. So, there are a lot of things you have to handle differently. Routes are different, coverages are different.

**Q:** Do the physical matchups become underscored when there is less field like that in the red zone?

**BB:** They could; they could, yeah. It depends, again, on the matchup but generally you see more size in that area because there's less space so speed is less of a factor. It's always a factor but less of a factor. There's only so far you can run. Technique is important, coordination offensively or defensively is important, the proper spacing, the proper leverage, using the space that you have and of course everything happens so much quicker down there because there's less space and less time so throws and catches have to be good, a lot of tight coverage, a lot of catches away from the body into a short space. Defensively you're fighting for every inch, every yard. It's critical. Two yards at midfield is one thing. Two yards on the five-yard line is 50 percent of the length; 50 percent of the field. So, it's all heightened, it's all a little bit more urgent and there are definitely some personnel and scheme factors that - there's a transition period in there but once you get down there low like inside the 10-yard line or inside the five-yard line you're talking about real tight space.

**Q:** The first drive in the red zone, you guys threw three times. Was that scheme related or was that because you thought that was the best way you could get in? Then on the final drive, you threw to the end zone and I was guessing it was just as advantageous to throw from a deeper spot on the field to give those guys time to uncover.

**BB:** I'd say generally speaking, you're better off throwing closer to the goal line than farther away from it, to a point. Once you get inside the five yard line, then I'm not sure that that's true. But I'd rather throw from the 10 than the 15, just keep going on like that. I thought we had a mixture of plays in the red area. The first drive, we hit the quick out to Julian [Edelman] down there on their sideline and we were second-and-four, which isn't a bad place to be and ended up not being able to finish it. Then I think on the other series, we ran the ball on second down – first down threw it, second down we ran it, got it to third-and-two and they pressured us and we weren't able to get a good execution on the passing game. They were trying to disguise their coverages. They pressured us some down there, they showed some pressure and pulled out of it, which are things they've done in the past. It's kind of what they do, it wasn't anything we hadn't seen before but they did a good job of it. We probably need to collectively, from our plays to our execution, just obviously need to be a little bit sharper down there.

**Q:** What needs to be working defensively to have success once the offense gets inside the red zone?

**BB:** I'd say really pretty much everything. You're playing in close quarters and so every yard, every inch really, is important. The plays happen very quickly, you don't see a lot of slow-hitting, delayed-type plays. You see runs that attack the line of scrimmage quickly, passes that could be very quick, like slants or fades or quick combination routes with receivers, seams down the middle or whatever it happens to be, but plays that really hit fast so you have to get to your spots, your areas, your man. You have to recognize things quickly and react quickly down there.

So does the offense - it's just a game now in a much smaller space than what it is when you have the ball out there at midfield, for both sides. I think those are some of the key points. Obviously you have to tackle well because every couple yards down there is percentage-wise a lot closer to scoring than it is out in the field. Fighting for the yards when you're tackling, knowing where your help is, knowing where the goal line is, where the end line is, where the sideline is, trying to use your leverage and make throws tough and defend what you have to defend and use the sideline or your defensive personnel help, I think all those things are a big part of the conversation.

### Q: The defense has less space to defend in the red zone, but are there advantages for the offense in the red zone?

BB: You don't have as far to go. You only need a few yards and then you hit pay dirt. It's not like you have to go out and execute 10, 12, 14, 16 plays and drive 80 or 90 yards. You're already down there, you just have to make usually one good play. One good play from the eight can score or three pretty good plays from the eight could score. But if you make one really good one, you're close enough where you can strike so that's the good thing. But, of course it's tighter down there. The defenders don't have anywhere to go. There are more of them closer to the line of scrimmage. It's easier for them to blitz, easier for them to disguise, less space to cover on all the above. It's tighter quarters, it all happens quicker. Defensively you have to make that adjustment as well. All the plays happen faster, a lot of times the running plays hit quicker, they're designed to hit into the hole quicker. The passes hit quicker, there's less of the normal rhythm and timing that you see out on the field because of the space involved. Those are adjustments the defense has to make too, from a timing standpoint. It's less area on paper but the actual in-game execution of it is quicker and different. There are a lot of scramble plays down in the red area, quarterbacks see tight coverage, no space to throw, they pull the ball down, like what happened to us in the Baltimore game, run out of the pocket, not letting him scramble in as the sixth receiver or get out of the pocket and the receiver is uncovered in the end zone in space. You see a lot of touchdowns scored like that in the red area. That's part of the red area attack, red area defense. It's just inherent in that field position. Those are other important components of it.

## Q: Where have you seen that the offense has problems in the red zone and how are the challenges different down there?

**BB:** For every offense, you just have less space in the throwing game. The holes are smaller. The defenders sit on the routes tighter because they don't have to get run off and in the running game you are dealing with more people. [If] the ball's at midfield, you have safeties and corners that are playing deep enough that really don't affect the running game, until you gain eight or 10 yards. They are just not close enough to really be a part of it because of their coverage responsibilities.

That's different in the red area because, again, those players don't get run off and they don't have to carry their receivers very deep because they can't go very deep. They are able to show up quicker in the running game and a lot of times - like most defenses do - the secondary key for the run first and then they get back on their man. And again that's a little harder to do out on the field because of plays like flea flickers and hard play-action passes, where the receivers can run by them. Down there, offensively, you're dealing with more guys in the running game and tighter fits in the passing game. So if the defense does a reasonably good job offensively you need a good throw, a good catch and a good route to really stick it in there in a tight hole. And those holes are a lot tighter than they are out in the field, generally speaking; unless there's some kind of major mistake, or a receiver runs a great route and gets a lot of separation on the defender down there. But that's harder to do.

Good throw, good catches, good routes, good timing, that's really what you need in the passing game down there. And then in the running game, you have to take care of more guys, whether that's to run them back, run through them, breaking a tackle, putting his head down for another yard or two. Or [you have to] come up with some type of a scheme play that either eliminates those guys from fitting into the run game, or bringing receivers in to block them and having somebody less dangerous - like the corner - be the unblocked guy as opposed to a safety. I mean, those are your options.

**Q:** You have been good in that area in the past. Do you think there is something lacking there right now where you guys can do certain things better than good red zone teams typically do?

BB: Absolutely and that's something that we've spent extra time working on in the last few weeks, including over the Bye Week and we'll keep working on it. We're not doing as well in that area of the field as we'd like to do, as we feel like we can do and we need to do a better job of it. There's no other way to put it and those are important points - the difference between three and seven - those are important points both ways and we have to coach it better, we have to play it better. We've got to play our best football in that area of the field because there's a lot at stake and there are a lot of things we need to do better. It's not any one thing, it's a lot of different plays and we're in different coverages and the offense runs different plays. It's not just one thing, but it's certainly as a composite on the whole we need to do it at a higher level.

For more books by Alex Kirby, go to AlexKirbyFootball.com

Made in the USA
San Bernardino, CA
12 December 2017